Reinventing Government in the Information Age

Can information technology help 'reinvent' government? It can, but only if it is correctly managed. This book provides a new model for management of 'information age reform', based on a review of international experience. It offers practical guidance, analytical insights and detailed case studies. It will therefore be of value to practitioners, students, educators and researchers in both public administration and information systems.

The book begins with a review of government reinvention and the contribution of information and information technology to that reinvention. The rapid spread of information age reform is charted. Ineffective approaches to reform used by many public managers are described, and contrasted with the effective, integrated approach used by a small minority. A model is developed to explain why information age reform initiatives succeed or fail. From this, a set of practical techniques for successful information age reform is identified, based on international best practice.

These management insights are supplemented by more than a dozen in-depth case studies, drawn from the US, the UK, mainland Europe and developing countries. The studies cover all aspects of reform: efficiency, decentralisation, resource and performance management, 'marketisation', accountability and democratisation. An educators' guide is provided for those wishing to use the cases as the basis for individual or group training.

Richard Heeks is a Senior Lecturer in Information Systems at the University of Manchester, UK, in the Institute for Development Policy and Management, a postgraduate centre for public sector managers from developing and transitional economies. His PhD, on IT policy, is published as *India's Software Industry* (Sage Publications, 1996). He has provided consultancy inputs to public sector organisations world-wide.

Routledge Research in Information Technology and Society

Reinventing Government in the Information Age

International practice in IT-enabled public sector reform

Edited by Richard Heeks

London and New York

First published 1999
by Routledge
11 New Fetter Lane, London EC4P 4EE

Simultaneously published in the USA and Canada
by Routledge
29 West 35th Street, New York, NY 10001

Routledge is an imprint of the Taylor & Francis Group

Typeset in Times by RefineCatch Limited, Bungay, Suffolk
Printed and bound in Great Britain by
TJ International Ltd, Padstow, Cornwall

British Library Cataloguing in Publication Data
A catalogue record for this book is available from the British Library

Library of Congress Cataloging in Publication Data
Reinventing government in the information age / edited by Richard
  Heeks.
      p. cm.
    Includes bibliographical references and index.
    1. Public administration – Data processing.   2. Administrative
agencies – Data processing – Case studies.   3. Information
technology – Political aspects.   I. Heeks, Richard.
JF1525.A8R46   1999
352.3′57′0285 – dc21   98–45760
                              CIP

ISBN 0–415–19037–1

Contents

PART 4
NATIONAL PLANNING FOR INFORMATION AGE REFORM

Figures

Tables and boxes

Tables

Boxes

Notes on contributors

Kim Viborg Andersen (andersen@cbs.dk) is an Associate Professor at Copenhagen Business School, holding a PhD from the University of Copenhagen, Denmark. He has been a visiting scholar at the University of California at Irvine (1991–2 and 1993) and at the University of Tokyo (1996–7). His research concentrates on the implementation, use and effects of information systems in the public sector. He has published extensively in international journals and books. His homepage is located at http://www.cbs.dk/~andersen.

Joan A. Ballantine (afinjba@wbs.warwick.ac.uk) is a Lecturer in Accounting and Finance at Warwick Business School, University of Warwick, UK. She has a degree in Accounting and a Masters in Data Processing. After graduating, she joined a computing services company as a financial systems consultant. She subsequently worked at Queen's University, Belfast, as a lecturer in Accounting and Finance with computer applications. Her present research interests focus on performance management, information systems evaluation and cost management systems.

Peter Benjamin (peter@wn.apc.org) is a Lecturer at the Graduate School of Public and Development Management, University of the Witwatersrand, South Africa. Originally from England, he has a bachelors degree in Physics from Oxford and a Masters in IT from De Montfort University. He moved to South Africa during the elections of 1994 and is involved with a range of community computing projects, including a secondment to the Universal Service Agency.

Subhash Bhatnagar (subhash@iimahd.iimahd.ernet.in) is CMC Professor of Information Technology at the Indian Institute of Management, Ahmedabad, where he was formerly Dean. He has worked in 40 countries, including time as a visiting professor in Tanzania and the US. He has published 70 research papers and six books in the field of IS and IT. He is the founder chairman and newsletter editor of IFIP working group 9.4, dealing with the social implications of IT in developing countries. He is a fellow of the Computer Society of India.

Stewart Bishop (osbishop@uwichill.edu.bb) is a Senior Lecturer in Information Systems and Mathematics at the University of the West Indies, Barbados. Currently he is researching the application of IT for socio-economic development in Caribbean countries, especially in the public sector. An active member of IFIP working group 9.4, he has participated in a number of international IT conferences. He is President of the Information Society of Barbados.

Douglas M. Brown (dmbrown@mail.lmi.org) serves as a consultant to US Federal agency executives and managers. In the past 12 years his work has included electricity deregulation, environmental management, military base closures and privatisation of facilities and services; he has developed data systems and performance measures to support all these efforts. As a former Army officer he served several years in Europe. He received his doctorate, with a specialisation in policy analysis, from the American University in Washington, DC.

Piers Cain (pcain@irmt.btinternet.com) is Director for Research and Development of the International Records Management Trust (IRMT) based in London, UK. He has worked in the archives and records field since the early 1980s. He has extensive operational experience in a wide range of organisations including business, international financial institutions and local government. IRMT is a non-profit institution working to develop new approaches to the problems of managing public sector records in developing countries.

Nigel Cunningham (ncunningham@caht.n-i.nhs.uk) is a Senior Information and Computer Services Manager with a UK National Health Service Acute Trust. He has degrees from Queen's University Belfast and the University of Lancaster. He was formerly a university lecturer and management consultant. His present research interests focus on systems thinking, change and strategy within public healthcare organisations, and he is also undertaking part-time doctoral research in this area.

Anne Davies (a.davies@queens-belfast.ac.uk) is Assistant Director (External Relations) in Queen's School of Management at Queen's University Belfast, UK. Her research interests are in: organisational factors surrounding the implementation of information systems in the public sector; the outsourcing of information systems; and information strategy formulation. Recent projects have included information use in the acute hospital sector, information needs of general practitioners, and the contribution of information to organisational learning in an energy company.

Richard Heeks (richard.heeks@man.ac.uk) is a Senior Lecturer in Information Systems at the University of Manchester, UK, in the Institute for Development Policy and Management: a postgraduate centre for public sector managers from developing and transitional economies. He has a

PhD in IT industry development, which led to the publication of *India's Software Industry* (Sage Publications, 1996). He has provided consultancy inputs to public sector organisations world-wide and currently directs a Masters programme in 'Public Sector Management and Information Systems'. His homepage is located at http://www.man.ac.uk/idpm.

Nancy J. Johnson (nancyj@msus1.msus.edu) is an Assistant Professor of Management Information Systems at Metropolitan State University in Minneapolis, Minnesota, US. She was awarded a Fulbright Grant in 1992, and worked in banking and information systems for over 20 years prior to her academic career.

Chipo Kanjo (ckanjo@unima.wn.apc.org) is a Lecturer in Computer Science at the University of Malawi, Chancellor College. She is also an Adjunct Faculty Member at Malawi Institute of Management. She has conducted research and undertaken consultancy assignments in both information systems and geographical information systems within Malawi.

Andrew Korac-Kakabadse (a.p.kakabadse@cranfield.ac.uk) is Professor of International Management Development and Head of the Human Resources Group at Cranfield School of Management, UK. He is also Vice-Chairman of the International Academy of Management; Visiting Professor at Curtin University, Perth, Australia; Visiting Professor at Hangzhou University, China; and a Fellow of the British Psychological Society. He has published over 110 articles, 12 monographs and 18 books.

Nada Korac-Kakabadse (n.korac-kakabadse@cranfield.ac.uk) is a Senior Research Fellow at Cranfield School of Management, UK. She has worked in Scandinavia, the Middle East and North Africa, as well as for the Canadian Federal Government. Her current areas of interest focus on information technology and organisational dynamics, diversity management, performance improvement in public sector organisations, and excellence in the politics of decision making. She has co-authored two books, contributed eight chapters to international volumes, and has published 20 scholarly and reviewed articles.

Peter Mtema (pmtema@unima.wn.apc.org) is a Lecturer in Computer Science at the University of Malawi, Chancellor College. He has conducted research and undertaken consultancy assignments in the field of information systems within Malawi, notably with public sector organisations including the Police Reform Commission. He has also been responsible for the development of information systems for Chancellor College.

David Mundy (david.mundy@man.ac.uk) is a Lecturer in Information Systems at the University of Manchester, UK, in the Institute for Development Policy and Management. He has considerable experience of working with IT, and has conducted IT research and undertaken IT consultancy assignments in a number of countries.

Agneta Ranerup (agneta@informatics.gu.se) is a Lecturer in the Department of Informatics at the University of Göteborg in Sweden. She received her PhD in informatics from the University of Göteborg in 1996. Her main research interest is democratic aspects of information systems development in the public sector.

Angel Salazar (mbzajs@mail1.mcc.ac.uk) works from the UK as an international consultant in institutional development and health services management for developing countries. He has a PhD in health informatics from Policy Research in Engineering, Science and Technology at the University of Manchester, UK. His professional and academic interests are health sector dynamics, innovations in health services management, management development and information systems strategies, and biomedical and clinical engineering.

Laurence Wolfe (larry.wolfe@gsa.gov) is the Director of Information Technology at the US General Services Administration. He is responsible for planning, directing and coordinating the development and execution of government-wide information technology policies, programmes and functions.

Introduction

The focus and content of this book

Richard Heeks

In 1992, David Osborne and Ted Gaebler's book *Reinventing Government* was published. It provided a new terminology of change in the public sector and an optimistic message about the positive potential of change. At the same time, however, it recognised that reinvention has a historical context: current change initiatives are part of a reform agenda that has been around since at least the 1970s.

'Reinventing government', therefore, is mainly a different way of presenting reform. The goals and components of reform remain much the same as they have for the last three decades. Thus, the key new focus of this book is not so much the *what* of reform, but the *how*. Although addressing the general area of change in the public sector, it has a number of differences to Osborne and Gaebler's work:

- *It focuses on the information age*. There is a significant and surprising gap in Osborne and Gaebler's analysis: they make virtually no mention of information technology (IT), despite the fact that governments spend US$ billions on IT every year and despite the fact that IT forms a part of many public sector reform initiatives. This gap is the focus of the present book. It does not aim for the broad sweep of the earlier work but looks at IT and information systems (IS), which are of increasing importance in this 'information age'. Reinventing government in the information age therefore means addressing a long-standing reform agenda with a greater emphasis on information and on the use of information technology.
- *It takes an international perspective*. Osborne and Gaebler criticise previous government texts for having too narrow a focus, dominated by Washington. Yet they also have too narrow a focus, dominated by the United States. In this book, the perspective is a global one, drawing on cases and experience from Europe, Africa, Asia, Australasia, Latin America and the Caribbean as well as from North America. There is a deliberate attempt to understand context and to understand that what works well in one country or situation will not necessarily work well in another.
- *It is rooted in pervasive reality*. The analysis and cases do not present relentlessly upbeat and potentially impractical messages that change is

happening successfully everywhere or that IT is government's saviour. Instead, they draw out some of the real issues that emerge during processes of change in the public sector. These issues include problems and failures, suggesting that many governments and public organisations are ill-prepared for information age reform.

In taking this approach, the book intends to address three main audiences:

- *practitioners*: those who are managing and/or implementing information age reform within the public sector;
- *students and educators*: those who are studying and teaching public sector management and/or information systems;
- *researchers*: those who are researching public sector management and/or information systems.

It addresses these audiences by providing:

- analysis of what it means to 'reinvent government in the information age';
- a new model that explains success and failure of information age reform;
- practical guidance on how to improve information age reform initiatives;
- international case studies that analyse aspects of information age reform and provide recommendations on best practice.

The book is divided into five main Parts, 1–5. Part 1 provides an overview, model and guidance on information age reform, while Parts 2 to 5 present the case studies. Each Part and chapter will now be described in more detail.

PART 1: INFORMATION AGE REFORM

Chapter 1, by Richard Heeks, briefly argues the synonymity between government reinvention and public sector reform. It reviews the background to, and typical contents of, reform initiatives. In particular it analyses 'information age reform': what reform means in the developing information age. This leads to a summary of the potential contribution of information systems and of information technology to the process of reform in government.

Chapter 2, by Richard Heeks and Anne Davies, describes the way in which information age reform is spreading throughout governments world-wide. Progress has been patchy and initiatives have tended to be technology-dominated. Indeed, four approaches to information age reform can be identified, summarised as: ignore, isolate, idolise and integrate. Only the last delivers full reform benefits. However, many barriers exist to information age reform and, more particularly, to diffusion of the 'integrate' approach.

Chapter 3, by Richard Heeks and Subhash Bhatnagar, identifies the key factors that contribute to success and failure of information age reform. From these, the 'ITPOSMO model' is developed – of gaps between reform conceptions and organisational realities – that helps explain success and failure. Evidence suggests that failure predominates, and the chapter provides three archetypes of failure when public sector realities mismatch reform conceptions based on: models inspired by rationality, models inspired by the private sector and models inspired by different country contexts.

Chapter 4, by Richard Heeks, looks at practical implications of the ITPOSMO model, and the need to close gaps between reform conceptions and organisational realities if information age reform is to succeed. It provides examples of best practice in closing gaps related to finance, skills and stakeholder objectives. It also describes ways in which some dimensions of organisational change can be frozen in order to increase the likelihood of reform success.

CASE STUDIES: PARTS 2–5

Some of the cases presented in Parts 2–5 are drawn from a conference on 'Public Sector Management in the Next Century' held by the Institute for Development Policy and Management at the University of Manchester, UK. Others were commissioned. They do not represent a comprehensive survey of information age reform; that would require thousands of cases. Instead, they were selected because they are globally representative of public sector reforms in terms of both countries and reform initiatives.

They were also selected because they are illustrative of the main themes of the book:

- Information age reform means an increasing role for information technology and information systems in public sector change.
- Success and failure of information age reform depend crucially on the conception–reality gap: the gap that exists between the conception of reform initiatives and the reality of public sector organisations into which they are introduced.

All cases support these themes, showing that they can be applied to many different countries, segments of the public sector and reform initiatives.

The section headings below indicate one classification method for the case study chapters. However, there are others, and Tables A and B are provided to assist readers who wish to select particular cases. All the cases present some generalised conclusions, but Table A indicates the regional location of the main evidence provided. Table B indicates the main component of reform, if any, addressed by the chapter. A listing in brackets indicates that the chapter covers a topic, but not as its primary focus.

Table A Regional basis of chapter evidence

Region	Chapter
Europe	8, 14, 16
North America	5, 11
Industrialised countries generally	10, 13, 15, 17
Africa	6, 9, 13
Latin America and Caribbean	7, 12
Asia	(15), (17)

Table B Reform initiative focus of chapter

Reform initiative	Chapter
Increased efficiency	5, 6, (16)
Decentralisation	7, (8)
Increased accountability/democratisation	(5), 8, 9, 10, 11
Improved resource management	5, 6, (7), (13), (16), (17)
Marketisation	(12), (14), 16
Generic reform	11, 12, 13, 14, 15, 17

Part 2: Management information systems

Information age reform involves reinvention of internal processes of government. Part 2 presents case studies of internal management information systems (MIS) in the public sector. (MIS are information systems that support the work of managers by making an input to the process of managerial decision making.)

Chapter 5, by Douglas Brown, evaluates the approach used by a US public agency in developing an MIS to support improved performance management. The agency ran into difficulties with this MIS. This was a result partly of the development approach used, and partly of the difficulties of measuring performance outcomes in government. Alternative development and measurement approaches are therefore identified.

Chapter 6, by Piers Cain, evaluates the automation of personnel records in three African governments, aimed at improving human resource management. The new systems did not make a significant contribution to reform initiatives for identifiable reasons. The chapter therefore recommends a new approach to information systems and records, focused on the context of reform.

Chapter 7, by Angel Salazar, evaluates the introduction of an MIS to support decentralisation of public health management in Ecuador. The outcome was only marginal use of the MIS because rational and centralised implementation conceptions did not match healthcare realities. Recommendations for a more realistic approach are made. The chapter also describes the value of applying interpretive and grounded theory approaches as evaluative tools.

Part 3: Extra-organisational information systems

Information age reform involves reinvention of external processes of government. Part 3 presents case studies of extra-organisational information systems in the public sector. (These are information systems that link government with organisations or groups outside government; typically with citizens.)

Chapter 8, by Agneta Ranerup, evaluates Internet-enabled applications in Sweden that aimed to democratise local government by improving citizen–government links. A series of contradictions emerge from the evaluation, and recommendations are therefore made about ways to address these.

Chapter 9, by Peter Benjamin, evaluates both the experience of and the potential for using IT for democratisation and community development in South Africa. The record of such initiatives to date has been mixed. Technical approaches have failed to address community information needs or issues of sustainability. Conversely, more systemic, needs-oriented approaches have produced some notable successes. Guidelines for IT-enabled democratisation are therefore proposed.

Chapter 10, by Andrew and Nada Korac-Kakabadse, describes models of electronic democracy and evaluates the contribution IT can make to democratisation. Democratic principles may remain intact but democratic processes must be reinvented if electronic democracy is to fulfil its potential. Some approaches to reinvention are suggested.

Part 4: National planning for information age reform

Information age reform imposes requirements for strategic planning across whole governments and across whole nations. Part 4 presents case studies of national-level strategic planning initiatives that are being, or need to be, undertaken by information age governments.

Chapter 11, by Laurence Wolfe, evaluates the impact of new US legislation on accountability for government IT projects. The evaluation is informed by survey results and an in-depth case study of a troubled information system. Based on a chronology of accountability phases in government, the chapter recommends management and accountability practices to increase opportunities for project success.

Chapter 12, by Stewart Bishop, evaluates the development of a government IT strategy for Barbados. The strategy was based on an imported model but gaps exist between this model's conceptions and Barbadian realities on issues such as skills availability, business practices, culture and use of information. A modified approach to strategy formulation will therefore be required.

Chapter 13, by David Mundy, Chipo Kanjo and Peter Mtema, evaluates training needs imposed by information age reform in the public sector, based on evidence from industrialised and developing countries, including a study in Malawi. A shortfall is identified between these IS-oriented training needs and current IT-oriented training provision. A radical overhaul of training is therefore proposed.

Part 5: Organisational planning for information age reform

Information age reform imposes requirements for strategic planning at the highest level of public sector organisations. Part 5 presents case studies of organisation-wide strategic planning initiatives that are being, or need to be, undertaken by information age organisations in the public sector.

Chapter 14, by Joan Ballantine and Nigel Cunningham, evaluates the relevance of strategic information systems planning (SISP) to public sector organisations undergoing reform. Most SISP frameworks derive from the private sector and conceive organisations as rational and machine-like. This does not match the complex, political realities of the public sector as exemplified by the UK healthcare sector. Strategic approaches based on soft systems methods are recommended as more appropriate.

Chapter 15, by Kim Viborg Andersen, evaluates the experience and potential of business process reengineering (BPR) in information age reform. BPR can be of significant value to government reinvention but it also originates from a private sector-inspired technical and rational school of thought. As a result, some underlying conceptions of BPR do not match public sector realities. A modified approach to reengineering is therefore recommended, which includes a special awareness of these realities.

Chapter 16, also by Joan Ballantine and Nigel Cunningham, evaluates a number of performance measurement frameworks. It then describes the application of one such framework to reform processes in a British public healthcare organisation. The framework, plus related processes of iterative understanding and discussion, has proven useful in highlighting gaps between performance information needs and current information provision.

Chapter 17, by Nancy Johnson, evaluates the human resource management problems that arise from information age reform in government. Increasing demands for information systems skills and staff are met with a continuing supply deficit and inequality with the private sector. This chapter therefore identifies and describes a series of creative techniques for public sector recruitment and retention of IS staff.

Part 1

Information age reform

1 Reinventing government in the information age

Richard Heeks

Abstract: 'Government reinvention' is largely a new terminology and repackaging of longer-term processes of public sector reform. Such processes have been particularly prevalent since the 1970s when three factors described in this chapter began to combine: a sense of crisis in the public sector, a renewed ideology that provided a response to crisis and, at times, political will and power to enact those responses. Typically those responses did and do consist of five main components: increased efficiency, decentralisation, increased accountability, improved resource management, and marketisation. After reviewing development of ideas about the information age, the chapter concludes that 'reinventing government in the information age' means delivering these ongoing reform components with a more overt role for information and with greater use of information technology. The role of information systems and information technology in reform is then analysed, with real-world examples provided around each of the main components of reform.

REINVENTING GOVERNMENT

In the late 1980s and early 1990s, a new terminology emerged in the public sector. Commentators spoke of revitalising or reengineering the public sector or – most notably – of 'reinventing government' (Osborne and Gaebler 1992). However, whilst the terminology and the examples were new, most of the concepts and processes were not since they drew on the longer tradition of public sector reform: 'Reinvention is only the latest initiative in the enduring cycle of reform' (Ingraham 1996: 454). To understand what is meant by 'reinventing government' we must therefore first understand what is meant by public sector reform.

Public sector reform is, if generally defined, change within public sector organisations that seeks to improve their performance. As such, public sector reform can be seen as an ongoing process since the inception of institutions that we now label 'public sector'. American presidents, for example, have been launching comprehensive programmes to reform government since at least the start of the twentieth century (Arnold 1995).

However, public sector reform is typically defined more narrowly. It is often associated with the ideology of the 'New Right' towards the public sector; an ideology that grew up especially from the 1970s and which sought particular types of change in the way the public sector was run.

The roots of government reinvention can therefore be traced back to a number of historical causes, three of which are overarching (and interlinked).

Crisis in the public sector

If all had been well in the public sector, no consistent trend, let alone ideology, of change in the public sector might have emerged. However, a perception of problems with the public sector, even of crisis in some countries, emerged during the 1970s. The perceived problems were focused on:

- *Inputs* In a number of countries, the public sector was seen to require unsustainably large and/or unsustainably increasing public expenditure.
- *Processes* There was concern about examples of waste, delay, mismanagement and corruption within the public sector, all of which contributed to inefficiency in the conversion of public expenditure into public services. In particular, public servants were seen as sometimes making decisions divorced from the interests of the public they supposedly served. That they were able to do so was seen as a twin failure: first, of centralisation, which made decision makers too remote from the locus of decision information and action; second, of unaccountability, which made decision makers too remote from those outside the organisation who were affected by their decisions.
- *Outputs* Finally, there was a perceived problem with outputs. Concerns were widespread in a number of countries that the public sector was not delivering what it should, from adequate defence and policing through support for agriculture and industry to education, housing, health, social welfare and a hundred other responsibilities. This, in turn, undermined the wider social outcomes of public sector activity.

The sense of difficulties came to cover both *what* the public sector was doing (the public sector's role) and also *how* it was doing it (public sector organisation and management).

A renewed ideology

If there had been no ideological peg on which to hang many of these concerns about the public sector, reform measures would have been less clearly identified and probably less strongly promoted. Such a peg emerged slowly after the Second World War and with gathering pace from the 1970s in the form of 'neo-liberalism'; otherwise known as the 'New Right'. This represented a resurgence of the ideas of liberalism that can be traced back to John Locke and Adam Smith in, respectively, the seventeenth and eighteenth centuries. It provides a substantial theoretical framework that can be used to justify a set of public sector reforms.

In its crudest form – 'market good, government bad' – neo-liberal thinking emphasises what it sees as the economic efficiency of markets, of the forces of competition and of individual decisions. It also emphasises what it sees as the inefficiency of governments and of the forces of collective, planned intervention. Three particulars flow from this viewpoint:

- that, wherever possible, there should be a 'rolling back of the state'; in other words, the replacement of the state with privately owned institutions;
- that the main justification for the continued existence of the state is its role in helping markets to function more efficiently;
- that, where state institutions remain, they should wherever possible be opened up to true (or, at worst, quasi-) market forces of competition, making the (bad) public sector as similar as possible to the (good) private sector.

The New Right therefore had something to say not just about the role of the public sector, but also about the way in which it might be organised and managed. It proposed comprehensive reform that can be read not merely as reform 'of government' but as reform 'against government' (Arnold 1995: 412).

Political will and power

A sense of crisis and an ideology of reform are necessary, but not sufficient conditions for reform. There must also be a third element: that of the political will and power to enact reform. A number of components of any nation's political economy can be identified that influence this:

- *the populace at large*, which has often borne the brunt of public sector crisis, has typically longed for reform, has sometimes pressurised government into a rhetoric of reform (e.g. 'reinventing government'), but has had only limited political capacity to have those reforms enacted;
- *politicians and public servants*, who may be powerful but have often been

divided, with conflict between those supporting and those resisting reform;

- *local and global capital*, which has sometimes been divided but has more generally sought reform in the belief that this will reduce business costs and increase transaction speed;
- *international organisations*, which have been a powerful driving force behind reform for the majority of the world's nations. These agencies have had the political and economic muscle to drive reform because countries, struggling with both international trade and domestic spending deficits, have had to request external sources of financial assistance. In return for that assistance, the domestic governments must commit to a reform programme. The late 1990s financial crisis is but the latest round in this continuing process.

The political economy of every country is different. However, one stereotypical outcome of these various forces has been a process of reform that is driven largely from outside the public sector, whilst being overtly or covertly resisted by at least some portion of public servants.

Components of reform/reinvention

The political roots of reform

Where public sector crisis prompted the call 'Something *should* be done', neo-liberal ideology provided the response 'Something *can* be done' and, in some situations, political driving forces demanded that 'Something *will* be done'.

This is not, of course, to argue that concerns about changing the public sector are the sole preserve of the New Right. Commentators and politicians from all shades of the political spectrum have constantly sought change of one kind or another, and have increasingly coopted reform or reinvention on to their own agendas. For example, there are now many examples in which the political left has welcomed and even driven aspects of change such as decentralisation or increased accountability.

There is equally a current approach that sees reform as a 'third' or 'middle way'. When the ideology of the New Right met the traditions of public administration, the result was the development of 'new public management', of which 'reinventing government' is but a recent fraction (Blundell and Murdock 1997). New public management has been portrayed as a kind of merger or compromise between public administration and neo-liberal ideology. Similarly, reinventing government is represented by Osborne and Gaebler (1992) as a non-partisan issue. From this perspective, there is a new, objective, optimal blueprint for government that transcends political debate.

In reality, these new reform initiatives are not so clearly balanced. They are fundamentally a set of changes that sings more from the New Right hymn sheet than from that of the left, as a look at Osborne and Gaebler's ten-point mantra of principles for reinvention of government indicates:

- steering rather than rowing;
- empowering rather than serving;
- injecting competition into service delivery;
- transforming rule-driven organisations;
- funding outcomes, not inputs;
- meeting the needs of the customer, not the bureaucracy;
- earning rather than spending;
- prevention rather than cure;
- from hierarchy to participation and teamwork;
- leveraging change through the market.

It is important to recognise that the roots of current reform/reinvention agendas lie in neo-liberalism, and that this remains a powerful driver of reform, even when those reforms are remodelled and delivered by parties traditionally seen to be of the centre or left.

Reform/reinvention agendas

What constitutes the reform/reinvention agenda? There is no agreed menu of elements but typical components include those listed below. As can be seen, these components overlap and real reform initiatives may contain more than one component:

- *Increased efficiency*: improving the input : output ratio within the public sector. The rationale of such reforms is to address the large size of public sector expenditure and/or the inefficiency of many of its processes.
- *Decentralisation*: the transfer of decision making to lower, more localised levels of the public sector. The rationale of such reforms is to reduce the costs of centralised decision making, and to create more flexible and responsive decision making.
- *Increased accountability*: making public sector staff more accountable for their decisions and actions. The rationale of such reforms is to increase the pressure on staff to perform well, to make them more responsive to recipient groups, and to reduce inefficient or corrupt practices. One particular form of this is *democratisation*, meaning the increased involvement of citizens in public sector decisions and actions; this often includes components of decentralisation and marketisation.
- *Improved resource management*: increasing the effective use of human, financial and other resources. The rationale of such reforms is clear from their definition. It often includes a refocusing of the way the performance of these resources is planned, measured and managed.
- *Marketisation*: increasing the use of market forces to cover relationships

within the public sector, relationships between citizens ('consumers') and the public sector, and relationships and boundaries between public and private sector. The rationale of such reforms is that market relations will drive costs down and increase efficiency and/or effectiveness of service delivery. It is obviously this component that most clearly shows its New Right roots.

There has been much criticism of the components listed: of what they seek to achieve in theory, and of what they do and do not achieve in practice. In this book, we are not going to participate in that particular debate because that is not our purpose. These components will be taken as a given; as initiatives that are being almost universally undertaken or imposed. For the majority of public servants, the issue is not the rights and wrongs of reform, but how best to implement reform initiatives in which they find themselves involved.

REINVENTING GOVERNMENT IN THE INFORMATION AGE

The roots of ideas about a new 'information age' – treated here as largely synonymous with emergence of an 'information economy', 'information society' or 'post-industrial society' – are invariably traced back to the work of writers such as Daniel Bell, Fritz Machlup, Yuji Masuda and Alvin Toffler (e.g. Bell 1974; Machlup 1962; Masuda 1983; Toffler 1980). Through analysis of extant trends, they described a vision of a new world paradigm that was already coming into existence and that would increasingly develop. General features of this new paradigm include a domination of services over other economic sectors, niche instead of mass markets, and the emergence of a 'post-bureaucratic' form of organisation.

The early, and optimistic, writings about the information age have been much criticised. Critics argue:

- that things have not changed as much as predicted. Peasant farmers in developing countries – who, with their families, form a major proportion of the world's population – continue to live and work much as they have ever done. They have yet to appreciate the pleasures of surfing the Net or teleworking. Even in the high citadels of the new world, shifts in working patterns and social life may be tangible and important, but they are not yet revolutionary. A modified criticism is therefore that change has been, and will be, a very uneven process that creates inequalities;
- that, when things do change, there will be problems as well as benefits. The information age may be marked by higher living standards but also by unemployment, insecurity, electronic surveillance and alienation;
- that the technology focus of information age writing distracts us from the human, social and political factors which explain – and therefore

ultimately determine – what happens in our world. To understand the impact of computers within organisations, for example, you would be better advised to learn about the 'wetware' between people's ears than about hardware and software.

There is a great deal of validity in these criticisms and they inform the writing within this book. However, what they do not deny is that – albeit slowly and unevenly, for better or worse – there are identifiable information age trends. Thus, while the concept of an information age retains a large measure of hyperbole, it does serve to highlight important trends that are shaping the world in which we live.

Box 1.1 Defining IT and IS

Information technology (IT) can be defined as computing and telecommunications technologies that provide automatic means of handling information. IT is therefore taken here to represent equipment: both the tangible hardware and the intangible software. A computer linked to other computers on a local area network represents one example of IT.

Information systems (IS) can be defined as systems of human and technical components that accept, store, process, output and transmit information. They may be based on any combination of human endeavours, paper-based methods and IT. A financial information system of staff and computers that gathers data and processes it into reports used for managerial decision making represents one example of an IS.

Thus:
- IT on its own does not do anything useful; in order to do anything, it must become part of an information system;
- information systems do not necessarily involve computers and telecommunications equipment;
- even when they do, information systems are much more than just IT because they involve people and their actions.

Some general features of the information age were outlined above but there are two specific and related trends of particular relevance to this discussion:

- the increasing importance of information, including the increasing visibility and value of information systems (see Box 1.1);
- the increasing use of information technology (see also Box 1.1).

What does this mean for reinventing government?

In overall terms, reinventing government is a continuation of existing new public management reforms, but reinventing government in the information age should mean two things that are different:

- first, a much greater (i.e. more overt) role for information and information systems in the processes of change;
- second, a much greater (i.e. more widely employed) role for information technology in the processes of change.

Examples of each are certainly not hard to find, as described below.

Examples of information systems-supported reform

Government has been, and still remains, the single largest collector, user, holder and producer of information. Information is a central resource for all staff levels and for all activities: 'In pursuing the democratic/political processes, in managing resources, executing functions, measuring performance and in service delivery, information is the basic ingredient' (Isaac-Henry 1997: 132). The work of government is thus very information-intensive, and four main types of formal information are identifiable:

- *Information to support internal management* This includes information about staff for personnel management, and information about budgets and accounts for financial management. Like the other three types of information, it can be used for everything from day-to-day operational implementation up to long-term policy analysis and planning.
- *Information to support public administration and regulation* This includes information that records the details of the main 'entities' in any country: people, business enterprises, buildings, land, imports/exports, etc. It is used for a variety of purposes such as legal, judicial and fiscal.
- *Information to support public services* This information differs according to the particular public service. Examples include education (e.g. school staff records), health (e.g. patient records), transport (e.g. passenger movement information) and public utilities (e.g. customer billing information).
- *Information made publicly available* This includes (POST 1998):
  — information government wishes to disseminate such as press releases, consultation papers, details of policies, laws and regulations, and details of benefits and entitlements;
  — information government collects that it may make available such as demographic or economic statistics;
  — information government is required to supply such as performance indicators, audited accounts, internal policy documents and correspondence, and responses to requests from citizens or journalists or politicians.

   Given this information-intensity, changes in information systems must be an essential part of all reform initiatives. If information runs through everything that government does, then changing anything in government must mean changing information, which must mean changing information systems. Parts 2–5 provide many examples, but others will be used here for illustration:

- *Increased efficiency* In the US, the Social Security Administration re-engineered a series of work processes and internal information systems in order to increase the efficiency of its client services (Laudon and Laudon 1998).
- *Decentralisation* In the UK, a fundamental redesign of information systems and relocation of information and information responsibilities was required in order to support the devolution of budgets from local government to individual publicly funded schools (Levacic 1992).
- *Increased accountability* In India, new information flows from government to people in Rajasthan and new forms of information presentation were used to increase the accountability of rural public works managers (*The Hindu* 1997).
- *Improved resource management* In the US, the Housing Revitalization Support Office of the US Army created a new information model to improve decision making about the management of Army housing (Forgionne 1998).
- *Marketisation* In Mexico, the introduction of business management practices and the creation of autonomous units within a public sector enterprise was accompanied by major strategic planning for new information indicators and systems (Avgerou 1996).

Examples of information technology-supported reform

In theory, everything that IT can do could be done by some other means. In practice, its ability to increase the speed and/or reduce the cost of information tasks mean it can do things that would not otherwise be contemplated. IT therefore does bring change and has three basic change potentials within reform:

- *Supplant*: automate existing human-executed processes which involve accepting, storing, processing, outputting or transmitting information. For example, the automation of existing clerical functions.
- *Support*: assist existing human-executed processes. For example, assisting existing processes of government decision making, communication, and decision implementation. (This can also be seen as a potential to *empower* if IT assists the activity of citizens outside government.)
- *Innovate*: create new IT-executed processes or support new human-executed processes. For example, creating new methods of public service delivery.

IT can bring five main benefits to the reform process. In practice, these are not neatly differentiated but they can be summarised as:

- *Cheaper*: producing the same outputs at lower total cost.
- *More*: producing more outputs at the same total cost.
- *Quicker*: producing the same outputs at the same total cost in less time.
- *Better*: producing the same outputs at the same total cost in the same time, but to a higher quality standard.
- *For the first time*: producing new outputs.

The first three represent efficiency gains for the public sector; the last two represent effectiveness gains. Of course, these are the direct and objective benefits. IT can bring many others such as better staff motivation, greater political control, or an improved public image for the organisation.

IT is therefore seen to have a great potential to contribute to reform (Traunmuller and Lenk 1996). Examples related to the main identified components of reform are given below, drawn from subsequent sections of this book and from other sources.

Increased efficiency

IT's role in increasing efficiency has just been described, mainly relating to its 'supplant' role:

- In the US, the Lawrence Livermore National Laboratory developed a World Wide Web-based system to reduce the cost and increase the speed of parts procurement (Gebauer and Schad 1998).
- In Ghana, the Controller and Accountant General's Department introduced and linked up more than 150 computers in order to reduce data gathering and communication costs and therefore to increase the efficiency of the government's personnel management function (Chapter 6).

Decentralisation

IT can provide support for more efficient and more effective decision making at decentralised locations and create new information flows that incorporate those locations:

- In Ireland, the Department of Social Welfare created more than a dozen computerised applications in order to support the decentralisation of responsibilities from Dublin to outlying offices (Cooney and O'Flaherty 1996).
- In Ecuador, the World Bank funded new computers and modification of existing software to promote the decentralisation of health planning and management (Chapter 7).

Increased accountability

IT can create new accountability information and can deliver accountability information to new recipients, providing for more efficient or effective accountability:

- In the US, 'collusion detection software' was developed and applied to root out impropriety in bids and contract awards for supply of public school milk (Anthes 1993).
- In Sweden, the World Wide Web and other Internet-enabled applications were used to increase the democratisation of local government in Göteborg (Chapter 8).

Improved resource management

IT can create new performance information and deliver it to decision makers, providing more effective managerial control over government resources:

- In Malaysia, government development authorities collaborated to develop a computerised system to facilitate land resource management (Raman and Yap 1996).
- In the US, a computerised management information system was created to help improve the management of facilities in a regulatory agency (Chapter 5).

Marketisation

IT can supply the new information necessary for the establishment of market relations, and can also form the conduit for delivery of new forms of public service:

- 'In Spain and Portugal, smart cards are issued to people to claim unemployment benefit at kiosks, and to check on job vacancies and training opportunities' (Gosling 1997: 69).
- In the UK, computerised systems were introduced throughout public healthcare in order to cope with the creation of an 'internal market' that divided healthcare purchasers from healthcare providers (Chapter 16).

SUMMARY AND CONCLUSIONS

Government reinvention may be a relatively recent phrase, but it is regarded here as merely the latest manifestation of a longer-term process of reform. The central components of reform have been in place for roughly three decades, and the focus here is not on those components but on the manner in which they are being delivered.

Information age reform is seen as a relatively new activity that recognises a significant – at times even central – role for information systems and information technology. Information systems change has always been an essential part of all organisational change in government (though this may not have been well recognised at times). But what is palpably new in information age reform is the presence of information technology.

Few see IT in government reform as problem-free. Even those who are positive about IT see ongoing challenges that include (NAPA 1997):

- *access and help*: ensuring that government use of IT does not create information haves and have-nots; ensuring that trained specialists are on hand to provide support for users of IT-based systems and services;
- *finding the right information*: ensuring that information can easily be found by users of IT-based systems, and that data elements have common definitions;
- *archiving and preserving*: ensuring that government IT-based information is archived rather than lost; ensuring that it can be retrieved by future generations using new technologies;
- *security and privacy*: ensuring that sensitive information held on government computers is accurate and secure from malicious or accidental access and alteration.

Nevertheless, for the optimist, these challenges are just that – challenges rather than insuperable obstacles – and 'IT is identified as the key to the reinvention and indeed to the reinvigoration of public administration' (Bellamy and Taylor 1994: 3). The next task – undertaken in Chapter 2 – is to analyse the different ways in which governments attempt to turn this IT key in the reinvention lock.

REFERENCES

Anthes, G.H. (1993) 'Stat tool weeds out bid-rigging companies', *Computerworld* 27, 27: 58.
Arnold, P.E. (1995) 'Reform's changing role', *Public Administration Review* 55, 5: 407–417.
Avgerou, C. (1996) 'Transferability of information technology and organisational practices', in M. Odedra-Straub (ed.) *Global Information Technology and Socio-economic Development*, Nashua, NH: Ivy League Publishing.
Bell, D. (1974) *The Coming of Post-industrial Society*, New York: Basic Books.
Bellamy, C. and Taylor, J.A. (1994) 'Exploiting IT in public administration: towards the information polity?', *Public Administration* 72, Spring: 1–12.
Blundell, B. and Murdock, A. (1997) *Managing in the Public Sector*, Oxford: Butterworth-Heinemann.

Cooney, M.J. and O'Flaherty, B. (1996) 'Structural change via information technology in the Irish civil service', in M. Odedra-Straub (ed.) *Global Information Technology and Socio-economic Development*, Nashua, NH: Ivy League Publishing.

Forgionne, G. (1998) *HRSOS: A Decision Support System to Facilitate the Privatization of Military Housing*, draft paper, Baltimore, MD: Information Systems Department, University of Maryland.

Gebauer, J. and Schad, H. (1998) *Building an Internet-based Workflow System*, Working Paper 98-WP-1030, Berkeley, CA: Fisher Center for Management and IT, University of California.

Gosling, P. (1997) *Government in the Digital Age*, London: Bowerdean.

The Hindu (New Delhi, India) (1997) 'Making a song and dance of it', 12 May: 4.

Ingraham, P.W. (1996) 'Reinventing the American federal government: reform redux or real change?', *Public Administration* 74, Autumn: 454–475.

Isaac-Henry, K. (1997) 'Management of information technology in the public sector', in K. Isaac-Henry, C. Painter and C. Barnes (eds) *Management in the Public Sector*, London: International Thomson Business Press.

Laudon, K.C. and Laudon, J.P. (1998) *Management Information Systems*, 5th edn, Upper Saddle River, NJ: Prentice-Hall.

Levacic, R. (1992) 'Local management of schools', in C. Pollitt and S. Harrison (eds) *Handbook of Public Services Management*, Oxford: Blackwell.

Machlup, F. (1962) *The Production and Distribution of Knowledge in the United States*, Princeton, NJ: Princeton University Press.

Masuda, Y. (1983) *The Information Society as Post-industrial Society*, Bethesda, MD: World Future Society.

NAPA (1997) *Information Technology: Overview and Table of Contents*, Washington, DC: National Academy of Public Administration.
http://www.alliance.napawash.org/alliance/index.html

Osborne, D. and Gaebler, T. (1992) *Reinventing Government: How the Entrepreneurial Spirit is Transforming the Public Sector*, Reading, MA: Addison-Wesley.

POST (1998) *Electronic Government: Information Technology and the Citizen*, London: Parliamentary Office of Science and Technology.
http://www.parliament.uk/post/egov.htm

Raman, K.S. and Yap, C.S. (1996) 'From a resource rich country to an information rich country', *Information Technology for Development* 7, 3: 109–131.

Toffler, A. (1980) *The Third Wave*, New York: Morrow.

Traunmuller, R. and Lenk, K. (1996) 'New public management and enabling technologies', in N. Terashima and E. Altman (eds) *Advanced IT Tools*, London: Chapman & Hall.

2 Different approaches to information age reform

Richard Heeks and Anne Davies

Abstract: Reform in general and information age reform more specifically are spreading world-wide, with perhaps US$500 billion being spent on public sector information systems every year. Many governments and inter-governmental organisations have now embarked on ambitious plans for information age reform. The chapter describes three approaches to such reform – 'isolate', 'idolise' and 'integrate' – plus the pre-information age approach of 'ignore'. It also describes different outcome strategies, including 'automation' and 'informatisation'. It is argued that those methods – such as the integrated approach and informatisation strategy – which bring greatest reform benefits are also those which are least found in the public sector. Analysis within the chapter of a set of drivers and barriers helps to explain why this happens.

THE SPREAD OF INFORMATION AGE REFORM

Chapter 1 provided evidence that information age reform exists, but is there evidence that it is spreading?

If we first consider reform in general, then there is no doubt about its spread: whatever their guise or terminology, public sector reform initiatives have been on the increase. They have spread to all corners of the globe (Bekke *et al.* 1996): to Europe (Hesse 1993; Kickert 1998), to North America (Kettl 1996; Osborne and Gaebler 1992), to Australasia (Boston *et al.* 1996; Davis 1996), and to developing countries (Adamolekun *et al.* 1997; Commonwealth Secretariat 1996). Within individual countries, they have increasingly set the agenda for public sector managers.

As noted in Chapter 1, this spread of reform generally has been going on for many years, but what about the spread more specifically of 'information age reform'? The most tangible evidence of this comes from the increasing use of information technology (IT) within government.

The origins of information technology in government are often traced back to Herman Hollerith, who worked for the US Census Bureau in the 1880s. He developed a tabulating machine based on punched cards which was first used for the 1890 national census, and subsequently for tabulating military payroll. The company Hollerith founded to produce his machines is today's IBM: the largest IT firm in the world.

Just as IBM has grown huge from small roots, so too has government use of IT. There are no reliable figures, but one can guesstimate that up to US$500 billion per year is being spent world-wide on IT-based information systems in the public sector. Some fairly random examples include annual spending of:

- more than US$27 billion by the US government (ICA 1998);
- more than US$6.5 billion by UK central and local government, divided into roughly 20 per cent capital expenditure on new projects and 80 per cent recurrent expenditure on existing projects (Kable 1998; McNevin 1994);
- just under US$5 billion by the Canadian government (Dorris 1997);
- around US$670 million by the Norwegian central government (Gahre 1996);
- around US$400 million by the New Zealand government (Commonwealth Secretariat 1995);
- around US$100 million by the Malaysian government (Bhatnagar 1997);
- around US$65 million by the Irish civil service (Embleton 1996);
- around US$50 million by the Philippines central government (NITC 1997).

Stated figures are, to put it politely, approximations. Other sources, for example, cite US government spending of US$40 billion in the mid-1990s on hardware alone (Talero and Gaudette 1995); and UK spending of nearly £6 million (US$10 billion) (Beck 1998). Method of calculation also varies considerably. The UK figure, for instance, is divided roughly equally between equipment and people/services. The Irish figure, on the other hand, excludes staff costs.

No one knows for certain, but it seems likely that the vast majority of this expenditure takes place in pursuit of one of the five reform objectives listed in Chapter 1. As explained in greater detail below, public sector organisations undertaking their initial computerisations will typically see IT as a means of increasing efficiency; automating the human effort within existing manual procedures and thereby attempting to cut staff costs. It is here (in 'supplant' mode) that the majority of IT has so far been implemented in the public sector (O'Higgins 1998; POST 1998). At the other end of the spectrum, a number of countries have been investing in 'electronic government' projects, with a particular emphasis on using IT to improve the delivery of public services, combining the aims of increasing efficiency and becoming more customer-responsive.

Information age reform is also very much on government's agenda because of the perceived failure or limited success of many past reform initiatives. The managerial world is now suffused with a constant supply of 'six steps to instant success and happiness' and of 'silver bullets' and 'killer apps' that promise to deliver quick and simple results from complex and difficult reality. Like the alchemists of old, public managers now seek the philosopher's stone that will transform base government into golden government. IT is being pushed forward as a prime candidate, as the quote at the end of Chapter 1 made clear.

In dynamic terms, the IT base available to support the reinvention of government is increasing every year. In many governments, increasing hopes about IT's contribution to reform translate into increasing IT investment rates. Recent (though pre-Asian crisis) real average increases in annual government IT expenditure include 8 per cent in the US, 23 per cent in Malaysia and 61 per cent in Singapore (Bhatnagar 1997; Federal Sources 1998).

The relationship between IT and government reinvention is increasing not only in terms of investment, but also in terms of visibility, with a number of high-profile initiatives having been launched during the 1990s. These have spread on a policy wave from early epicentres: notably the US but also Singapore (Karlsson 1996). They include:

- *Australia* Initiatives to make use of IT in government reinvention were launched in 1996 as an 'IT blueprint' for the public sector. By 1998 the portfolio of initiatives included Fedlink, which will create a whole government intranet, and the Commonwealth Information Centre, which will provide a single point of access to government information (OGIT 1998).
- *Canada* Canada's 'blueprint for renewing government services using information technology' was approved in 1994. It includes provision for single-window delivery of government services and implementation of a government-wide computing and information infrastructure (McLellan *et al.* 1996).
- *European Union* The Interchange of Data between Administrations (IDA) programme, initiated in 1995 and entering its second phase in 1998, uses computer networks to enable exchange of public sector information between European governments (IDA 1998).
- *G7 group of industrial nations* The Government On-Line (GOL) project, initiated in 1995, supports IT-based transaction processing, mail and service delivery by G7 governments (CCTA 1995).
- *India* The Leadership and Excellence in Andhra Pradesh in the twenty-first century (LEAP21) initiative, launched in 1997, aims to use IT as a significant lever to the creation of better government in Andhra Pradesh state (Naidu 1997).

- *Japan* The Administrative Informatisation Promoting Plan was first proposed in 1993. It provides a strong link between reform of government and use of information technology, including measures to improve the quality of public services through one-stop service centres and online service delivery (Kajiwara 1996).
- *Netherlands* The 'Back to the Future' white paper was adopted in 1995 with an emphasis on information management. The aims of this policy included greater transparency of, and greater access to, government information for Dutch citizens. Information technology has been seen as one tool for implementing the policy (Haarmann 1996).
- *Philippines* The government's National Information Technology Plan (NITP 2000) was approved in 1994. It is a comprehensive strategy for competitiveness and empowerment that includes plans for extensive computerisation of government operations in order to 'improve government's capacity and efficiency across the board' (NITC 1997). (In 1997, the plan was renamed IT21 and target dates altered from the explicit 'year 2000' to the rather fuzzier 'turn of the 21st century'.)
- *Singapore* The IT2000 Intelligent Island masterplan, first formulated in 1991, aims to make use of IT pervasive throughout the whole of Singapore society. It includes a significant component of reengineering public services through use of IT (NCB 1997).
- *South Africa* The Government Information Project (GIP), initiated in 1995, uses IT and process reengineering as tools to improve the strategic use of information in government (PRC 1998).
- *South Korea*. The snappily titled Implementation Plan for Governmental Administration Informatization Promotion, originating in a 1987 information systems project, strives to increase the efficiency and quality of government services through use of IT (Yoong-Gil 1996).
- *United Kingdom* The Information Society Initiative (ISI) of 1996 aims to harness the benefits of IT for the whole UK economy. It includes a public sector-specific component – government.direct – which is trying to increase the electronic delivery of government services (CITU 1996). More recently, the incoming Labour government set a target of 25 per cent of government services to be delivered electronically by 2002 (COI 1998).
- *United States* The National Performance Review (NPR) of 1993 and subsequent Access America plan of 1997 aim to create better, cheaper government with a substantial role for IT in that process (see Chapter 11).
- *World Bank/developing countries* The Information for Development (InfoDev) programme was designed in 1995 to harness the 'information revolution' for Third World development. It includes the aim of using IT more widely in government reform programmes (Talero and Gaudette 1995).

Within these initiatives, IT has often been much more strongly identified as a part of information age reform than have information and updated information systems:

- 'The primary objective is to investigate the scope for a significant increase in the use of on-line technology to transform government so that, by the turn of the century, most administrative business is conducted electronically' (CCTA 1995: 1).
- 'The initiative focuses . . . on using Information Technology as a strategic tool for improving the quality of life for the people of Andhra Pradesh' (Naidu 1997: 1).
- 'The vision of IT2000 is based on the far-reaching use of IT . . . to see how IT can be pervasively applied to improve business performance and the quality of life' (NCB 1997: 2).
- '[government.direct] will be founded on the new possibilities offered by information technology, and it will learn from the way that these are starting to be harnessed by other governments and the private sector' (CITU 1996: 2).

However, it would be a mistake to regard this IT-dominated model as the only approach to information age reform. As the next section describes, there are others.

DIFFERENT APPROACHES TO REFORM

The approach to reform in the public sector has changed over time as regards IT and information. In large part, these changes relate to the changing nature of senior public officials (both politicians and managers), who have tended to set the implementation agenda for reform. We can categorise four different approaches to reform that appear over time in a 'four-eyes' model:

- *Ignore* Public officials are ignorant about IT and information systems (IS). They therefore do not include consideration of either in their plans for reform. IT expenditure is minimal and any IT managers accidentally appointed in the public sector have a pretty thin time.
- *Isolate* Public officials remain computer-illiterate and lack an understanding of information's role. They nevertheless are aware of IT and its potential. Investment in IT is therefore included in reform plans but is seen as the responsibility of 'IT experts'. It is mainly associated with automation and some (often spurious and concocted) idea that efficiency gains will result. For other reform agendas, it is added as an afterthought ('Oh yes, and we should have some computers') and is not linked in any systematic way to the process of reform. This, none the less, represents the first step on the path of information age reform. IT managers get the

budgets they always wanted and a certain amount of freedom from management oversight.

- *Idolise* Public officials have become semi-literate. They use computers and are over-aware of IT's potential. They believe that IT can transform the business of government (or at least transform their own career prospects if they are seen to initiate a high-profile IT project). They are dimly aware that information ('Or was it knowledge?') is something important. The public sector becomes awash with IT-driven reform projects which place technology at the heart of the change process. IT managers get huge budgets, immense workloads and the boss always looking over their shoulder and claiming any credit; sometimes they regret those IT-awareness sessions they ran for senior staff.
- *Integrate* Public officials have become information-literate. They recognise information as a key organisational resource that is central to all government functions (see Box 2.1). IT is relegated to a secondary role: it is seen as a valuable means to achieve certain reform ends, not as an end

---

Box 2.1 Information as a resource: implications for government

- *Managing government information*: government information in all forms (e.g. print, voice, electronic or image) is a strategic resource and will be effectively managed throughout its lifecycle.
- *Data administration*: all government information will be subject to data administration to ensure common definitions, integrity and consistency of data.
- *Sharing and re-using information*: information will be captured once, as close to the source as possible, then shared and re-used by authorised users.
- *Exchanging information*: once captured, government information should be stored and exchanged electronically to avoid transcribing and re-entering it manually.
- *Protecting information*: the security, integrity and privacy of government information will be ensured by integrating information technology security measures with physical, personnel screening, and other security measures.
- *Retaining information*: government information will be retained only while there exists a business need, a legislative or policy requirement, or when it has historical or archival importance.
- *Stewardship*: specific organisational units will be accountable for managing designated classes of government information to ensure its integrity, quality and relevance, and to restrict its accessibility to authorised users only.

(Adapted from Treasury Board Secretariat 1994)

in itself. The reengineering of information systems and the introduction of IT are now fully integrated into the process of organisational change, driven by reform objectives. The IT manager is surpassed, sacked, demoted or reskilled and his or her role is taken over by an Information or Information Systems manager (or CIO – chief information officer – for those agencies going the whole private sector hog).

Some obvious caveats follow:

- The brief approach summaries above represent considerable simplification. Any boundaries between approaches will, for instance, blur into some messy continuum in practice.
- Between and within countries, even within governments and individual organisations, there are immense differences, with 'ignore' found in the next office to 'integrate'.
- This should not be read as a four-stage progression. Individual chronologies will be uneven and may involve movement between any two approaches. Bhatnagar (1997), for instance, analyses the situation in India and sees that country as still struggling to move away from the 'ignore' stage. If anything, it seems likely to move directly to 'idolise', as exemplified by the LEAP21 initiative. On the other hand, Bellamy and Taylor (1994) characterise the UK's main problem as being that of moving from a pervasive 'isolate' approach to 'integrate'.

Despite the caveats, however, the 'four-eyes' model is a useful characterisation in evaluating the dynamics of information age reform in government.

Evaluating the different approaches

As indicated above, the ignore approach does not constitute information age reform, and therefore is not the focus of this book. However, this approach is still to be found in many public sector organisations. There is no definitive proof but it seems a fairly safe bet to say that the majority of public servants world-wide have yet to use a computer. Pay a visit to a regional government office in the world's most populous countries, like China and India, if you don't believe it. Then look at the computers in the offices of senior officials in Western governments and ask: 'Managerial tool or executive paperweight?' In many cases, the latter. It is worth remembering this, and thereby staying in touch with reality, as one contemplates notions of 'wired government', 'online democracy' and, indeed, 'information age reform'.

Senior officials with computers as executive paperweights are equally likely to adopt the isolate approach. As already noted, any contribution of IT to reform here is largely fortuitous. The cases in Chapters 6 and 7 are both examples of this approach. In the former, new databases were intended to improve efficiency and personnel management. In practice, this was just 'lip service':

- Contracts for database creation were hived off to external consultancy firms.
- The databases were only implemented after completion of the downsizing initiative with which they were supposedly linked.
- The IT therefore made no contribution to this reform initiative.

The fact that both chapter examples come from developing countries should not allow industrialised country governments to preen themselves. They behave no better. In the UK, for example:

> information agendas are usually perceived to lie in the technologists' domain, and this seems to be a product of the 'two-cultures' thinking which still afflicts public life in the UK. . . . the management of information systems in government has tended to remain the province of IT directorates, the responsibility in the civil service of 'operational' management at senior and middle management grades rather than of top management and ministers.
>
> (Bellamy and Taylor 1994: 7)

Despite the frequent emphasis on efficiency and automation within this approach, the benefits seem limited. The Turkish government, for example, broadly followed the isolate approach during the 1980s and early 1990s. Investigation of more than US$500 million-worth of expenditure on IT concluded: 'Despite various attempts to coordinate investment, improve procurement practices and develop complementary human resources, computerization does not appear to have resulted in any measurable increase in public sector productivity' (World Bank 1993: 21).

It may even result in reform failure. The Canadian government abandoned a computerisation project for reform of its federal payroll system in the mid-1990s at a cost of around US$30 million (McLellan 1996). The failure arose because computerisation was undertaken as an isolated initiative, separated from other necessary reforms to payroll rules and systems.

Does the idolise approach fare any better? Not much. Many electronic government schemes are still in their infancy, but government has a long history of failure to deliver reform objectives via technology-driven projects (Bhatnagar 1997; Davies 1997; Kraemer *et al.* 1981). Chapters 8, 9 and 10 all warn of the dangers of an IT-driven approach to reform. Chapter 9, for example, cites two problem cases from South Africa:

- the introduction of an intranet into Johannesburg Metropolitan Council's one-stop property information centre. A year later, the system was little used because its introduction had been technology-focused, ignoring the skills, information needs and communication preferences of relevant stakeholders;
- the introduction of touch-screen kiosks into rural communities in South

Africa's North-West Province. This project was focused mainly on the imagery and 'gee-whizzery' of kiosk technology. It failed to consider community information needs and was soon scrapped, having contributed nothing to broader decentralisation or democratisation agendas.

Likewise in the UK, the much-cited failure of the London Ambulance Service's new despatching system has been put down, in part, to an overemphasis on the technology and an underemphasis on the skills and information requirements of the paramedic users (Health Committee 1995). This, in turn, has been partly blamed on pressure for rapid, tangible action from politicians, the public and the media (Isaac-Henry 1997). In Australia, too, problems with the Automated Job Search kiosk system in the mid-1990s arose because public servants took their eyes off the 'information ball' and 'became dominated by technology-driven processes and considerations' (Milner 1997: 24).

Even where technology-centred projects initially appear to succeed in delivering reform objectives, Bhatnagar (1997) warns that they may not be sustainable or replicable since they so often depend on a single 'idolising' figurehead. When that senior official transfers to a new post, the project often collapses; when other organisations try to copy the original, the project often fails. In both situations, the cause is the lack of the original IT-focused champion.

If the key to effective information age reform does not lie in the idolise approach, what, finally, of the integrate approach?

As seen in Chapter 1, government is an information-intensive business and reform of government is an information-intensive process. The integrate approach therefore places information in the driving seat, relegating technology to an important but enabling role. In very simple terms, we can see four main steps in initiation of this approach:

1   acceptance by key stakeholders of the need for reform;
2   identification and communication of an agenda for reform;
3   identification of the new and/or reengineered information systems requirements of this reform agenda;
4   identification of the role, if any, that information technology has to play in meeting these requirements.

Such is the shift in emphasis within this approach – towards information and away from technology – that IT is no longer seen as essential to information age reform. A reengineered information system is essential but, as already noted, IT is just a means to an end. If that end can be achieved more efficiently or effectively without computers, then so be it. In practice, IT is almost always present but it is integrated with and subservient to information systems change which is itself subservient to the reform agenda. By contrast, the idolise approach would start by asking 'What kind of changes can IT bring about?' and then use these to create the reform agenda.

The integrate approach will often mean taking a more strategic approach to reform since the integration of reform objectives, information and technology requires organisation-wide, top-level management activity. Taking this approach clearly offers considerable potential for information age reform. Box 2.1, for example, described implications of a strategy that treats information as a key resource to support government. In theory, such a strategy would bring improved efficiency and effectiveness through its re-use and exchange of information.

In practice, too, the integrate approach can bring reform rewards. Chapter 9 presents two South African public information systems that worked because the 'IT tail' was not allowed to wag the 'reform dog'. Chapter 15 describes a few successful examples in which IT has been used to support a wider process of information systems reengineering. Similarly, Chapter 16 describes one British public healthcare organisation that is adopting an information-driven approach to change.

In Denmark, the Work Injury Office took an integrated approach to the introduction of computerised document management systems, using them as one part of a broader drive to reengineer workflow (Hertzum 1995). The result was an increase in both organisational efficiency and output quality. By contrast, the country's Emergency Management Agency took an isolated approach. The computer systems act merely as an archiving system which is little used and which brings few, if any, benefits.

Yet examples of the integrate approach remain few and far between in the public sector. Some public sectors have yet to embrace information age reform at all (Bhatnagar 1997); others are dominated by technology-focused approaches (Isaac-Henry 1997; Lenk 1990). In either situation, the integrate approach is largely absent. Why should this be? The next section provides some answers.

BARRIERS TO AN INTEGRATED APPROACH

In simple terms, the previous section concluded that integration was the approach most likely to produce information age reform benefits, yet it was also the least common. There are a number of reasons for this, investigated below:

- barriers that restrict progress from the ignore approach;
- drivers that encourage continuance of the idolise approach;
- barriers that restrict diffusion of the integrate approach.

Barriers to progress from the ignore approach

In many public sector organisations, serious barriers still exist to any type of information age reform, as described below. These organisations therefore currently remain stuck with the ignore approach.

Skills and knowledge

Senior public officials – both managers and politicians – often lack IT skills and even IT awareness (Isaac-Henry 1997; POST 1998). They are therefore reluctant to support, or even to discuss, reforms that involve information technology. Where skills of computerised information systems analysis, design, construction, operation and maintenance are absent, or cannot be recruited and retained by the public sector, this too will encourage a continuing ignore approach.

Finance

IT costs money, and money is often in rather short supply in the public sector. Providing desktop computing, software and support in government costs around US$10,000 per employee per year for total cost of ownership (McDonough 1997). It is therefore no surprise that, for example, senior managers cite financial barriers as far and away the most serious constraint to IT diffusion in UK local government (SOCITM 1997). Similarly, in a survey of European government department heads, over 80 per cent cited lack of finance as the main impediment to progress in electronic government initiatives (*Electronic Government International* 1998).

Risk

Like all reform initiatives, those involving IT require political support and personal motivation from key stakeholders in order to proceed. Yet IT is often seen as risky in a public sector that typically has risk-aversion as one of its cultural mainstays (Assirati 1998). In this situation, stakeholders will not be motivated to support or to contribute to IT projects.

Suspicion

The public sector has had more than its fair share of IT project failures (see Chapter 3), and of reports questioning the value of benefits, if any, produced by IT-based reforms. In this situation, public sector managers may rationally choose to ignore IT, as they perceive a lack of clear evidence about its positive impact. Thus, in the public sector, 'a common concern was that in a large number of cases IT systems did not deliver the anticipated benefits.' (Isaac-Henry 1997: 141). Indeed, benefits have often proven very hard to measure in IT projects.

There is also continuing evidence of:

> a fear among . . . employees that the introduction of computers will lead to a loss of jobs. Along with the added stress from being asked to master the technology, this fear is a significant force hindering the move towards improved public service delivery.
>
> (Wirszycz 1997: 12)

Infrastructure

In many countries, an infrastructure of electricity, telecommunications and local supplies of IT goods, spares and consumables is taken for granted. Yet, for hundreds of thousands of public sector managers world-wide such infrastructure is patchy, unreliable or even non-existent. Some comparisons will illustrate:

- Industrialised countries produced over 7,500 kilowatt-hours of electricity per person in 1994 while least developed countries produced less than 75 (UNDP 1997).
- High-income nations had more than 50 main telephone lines per 100 inhabitants in 1995 while low-income nations had less than two (Mansell and Wehn 1998).
- Industrialised countries had over 220 Internet users per 10,000 population in 1994 while developing countries had 1.5 (UNDP 1997).
- Singapore spent US$1,500 per head on electronic data processing equipment in 1995 while India spent less than US$1 (Mansell and Wehn 1998).

In the latter countries cited, an ignore approach is often forced on government, whatever the aspirations of its staff.

Drivers supporting the idolise approach

Where government organisations are able to move beyond the ignore approach, there may be a number of drivers that reinforce continuing technology-focused reform, especially the idolise approach.

The image of IT as reform solution

Alongside negative reports about IT, there is a rather louder fanfare of success stories. These promote an image of IT as a solution to reform problems. IT vendors are in the vanguard of this promotion since, like all firms, they must keep selling their products or services in order to survive. They provide a constant backdrop of IT-oriented pressure on government managers with their clear messages from all sales and marketing output that (a) IT can solve government's problems, and that (b) this year's IT can solve government's problems better than last year's.

But it is not just the IT firms that have a vested interest in promoting this image. To their number we can add:

- all the IT consultants whose jobs depend on IT;
- all the training companies that survive through IT training;
- all the journalists and other workers who produce IT magazines, news-papers and Web sites;
- all the staff within government IT departments whose jobs depend on IT.

And, lest we forget:

- all the academics who work in computer science, information systems or management departments who find it easier to sell their teaching, their research grant applications, and their books if, instead of a realistic image of IT, they present an upbeat one, such as:

  Computerization of the public service is expected to improve state capacity by making up for deficiencies in bureaucratic analyses, cur-tailing drag and red tape, promoting unbiased treatment in the bureaucracy's dealings with the public, ensuring accountability, injecting speed into operations, generating necessary and accurate data, and curtailing corruption through proper record keeping.

  (Tettey 1997: 2)

Thanks to this image-making, IT therefore becomes an icon for modern management, turning use of IT within reform into an end in itself rather than a means of improving public service.

Pressure from other external institutions

'Average' public opinion about IT has shifted over the past couple of decades in most countries. Once, the view was mainly negative, seeing computers as something to be avoided because of associations with job losses. Now, the view – at least as expressed via the mainstream media – is mainly positive, seeing computers as something to be embraced because of associations with modernity, efficiency and new job opportunities. This pressurises government organisations to place IT centre stage within their reform programmes as a public signal of improvement and progress.

For providers of political and financial support, such as politicians, central government and other funding agencies, IT represents a very tangible sign of money spent and of changes being made. Politicians find it much easier to be photographed by the media standing next to a new set of computers than next to a new performance appraisal scheme. This, too, pressurises government organisations to have a central focus on IT within the reform process.

As an example, state welfare agencies in the US have been more successful in obtaining federal funds if they use a management information system (MIS) for tracking clients. Independent evaluation of these MIS rated them 'relatively useless', but for the organisations, 'The presence of a computer system enhanced their image as an effective administrative unit' (Burns 1984: 190).

Finally, examples were given above of the many IT-oriented reform initiatives deriving – with funding attached – from national and international agencies. These encourage, or sometimes force, public sector organisations to play along with the IT game.

Continuous novelty and unfamiliarity of IT innovations

'Information technology is so dynamic and fast changing, that it is in an almost constant state of revolution' (Isaac-Henry 1997: 131). The revolutions can often seem like those of a deranged merry-go-round of innovation. Those public managers who step aboard must ride ever faster and faster just to keep up, spending more and more of their time focused on IT and IT change. For them, a choice between thick clients and thin clients now means network architecture, not spending priorities on education and nutrition. They are drawn deeper into a continuous stream of innovation that is both novel and unfamiliar. Even if the current set of IT fails to bring the desired reform benefits, there is the constant seductive promise that the ideal technical solution is just about to emerge over the horizon. IT therefore demands ever more of their limited attention capacity.

'Me too' attitudes

Through word of mouth, visits and the mass media, public managers are becoming increasingly aware of staff in similar organisations at home and abroad who are using IT in reform initiatives. Senior staff in particular often translate this awareness into a desire that they or their organisations should also be using IT for reform. By so doing, they gain membership of a powerful club: 'those who have control over the workings of a particular technology accumulate power and inevitably form a kind of conspiracy against those who have no access to the specialised knowledge made available by the technology' (Postman 1992: 9). The lure of imitation and club membership reinforces an IT focus for reform.

Other enabling trends

IT-focused approaches to reform are enabled by technological and other trends. IT is getting cheaper, more powerful and easier to use. Coupled with rising IT awareness, exposure and skills, the barriers to its use come down. It becomes ever more conceivable that information technology should be used as part of the reform process: even more so as the costs of employing human alternatives to IT tend to rise over time. Thus, perhaps ironically, government IT budgets often rise as overall budgets are squeezed in the search for cost savings.

Other barriers restricting the integrate approach

All the factors listed above act as barriers to diffusion of an integrated approach. Other barriers can also be identified that contribute to this restriction, as described below.

Technical barriers

The inertia of existing information systems – manual or computerised – restricts an organisation's freedom to reengineer those systems. This therefore restricts the scope for information systems reengineering to be entirely driven by reform objectives. Where existing systems are computerised, they can represent an 'electronic concrete' that renders reform outcomes practically impossible, as was the case with decentralisation of managerial control in some UK social services departments in local government:

> Probably the most serious problem facing social services in these changes is the inadequacy of their information systems. Most social services departments rely for much of their financial and management information on mainframe systems run by and for the local authority's central departments. These systems are not geared up to organizations with a large number of decentralized units making their own resource management decisions. . . . There is a minimum investment requirement of about £100–£200 million [*c*.US$150–300 million] over three years or so to bring social services information systems up to some minimum standard of what is required to effectively manage devolved care systems . . . Many politicians are unwilling to make the investment required.
>
> (Warner 1992: 191–192)

As already noted, most IT investments in government have related (and, in many places, continue to relate) to efficiency reforms. Such investments tend to reinforce existing vertical and horizontal boundaries within government. Computerisation has therefore been making it harder, not easier, to achieve more information-driven, boundary-crossing reforms such as decentralisation or improved delivery of public services. This has been the case in US welfare services, where prior state-level computerisations made inter-state tracking of welfare recipients more difficult rather than easier

(Ragan 1997).

Skills and knowledge barriers

There is a dearth of information-related skills and knowledge within the public sector, with a meeting of 90 US government IS managers noting 'limited understanding and appreciation for the value of information for program planning, monitoring and evaluation on the part of executives and policy makers' (CTG 1998: 1). The US General Accounting Office (1994) has also complained that federal agencies have not kept pace with evolving management practices and skills necessary to define and manage critical information needs. In the UK, there has been a pervasive lack of top-level interest in information and information systems (O'Higgins 1998).

This all seems most ironic given the public sector's information-rich history:

- Two thousand years ago, 'The Roman empire undertook regular censuses of the populations under their control' (Eele 1994: 110).
- In centuries past, Chinese applicants for government were locked in a room until they had written down all the information they knew, since this was seen to be the key asset of government employees.
- The science of statistics was developed in Britain in the seventeenth century to help 'with the use of demographic and economic data to support policy making, especially to support an efficient taxation system' (Eele 1994: 100).
- In Victorian Britain, the Benthamite-model civil service saw the information of surveys, statistics and reports as its very lifeblood (Roszak 1988).

Perhaps the public sector became so obsessed by other resources during the twentieth century – money and people and institutions and, more recently, technology – that it just plain forgot about information. Now, like a heavy sleeper, the government body is proving hard to awaken to the centrality and importance of information.

In part, this is a problem of perceptions. Information is intangible, so managers have difficulty seeing it as an integral reform resource with costs, values and management planning needs. By contrast, technology is very tangible and this has led both managers and IT staff to hold on to their 'automation mind-set' (Hastings 1996: 148).

All of this has had a knock-on into debate, publications and training about information age reform. Most of these remain IT-dominated. For example, there may have been a recent growth in articles putting information first and technology second in public sector magazines and journals. Nevertheless, the 'Wow! Computers made this department a winner!' approach still predominates (followed some way behind by 'Gee! Computer screw-ups made this department a loser!').

Data barriers

The lack of skills and knowledge noted above has a further knock-on: into the quality of data within the public sector. Such problems are sometimes temporary. When New Zealand's Education Department introduced a new centralised payroll IS, thousands of teachers were incorrectly paid on the first pay day and up to a quarter of some schools' staff were still wrongly paid two months later. But one further month later, payments went out correctly (Myers 1996).

However, problems often run deeper. Russia's government statistics are chronically inaccurate because of double counting, over- and under-reporting, data mishandling, a massive black market and de-motivated state officials who work within an environment of widespread bribery (Chepaitis 1996). Sampling of US Federal Bureau of Investigation criminal records found more than half to be 'inaccurate, ambiguous, or incomplete' (Laudon and Laudon 1998: 648). In part, both of these problems also derive from the fact that many state officials value informal information more highly than formal information (Lucey 1997; Pietarinen 1996).

Such situations easily create a self-reinforcing feedback loop: government staff do not value formal information, so data quality remains poor; because data quality is poor, government staff do not value formal information. They therefore find it hard to place information as a key factor in the reform process.

Structural and cultural barriers

If information technology is to be integrated into the reform process, IT structures and staff must be integrated into the mainstream activities of public sector organisations (PSOs). Yet this is not the case in many PSOs, which adhere to the 'ITernal triangle' model described in Figure 2.1 (Knight and Silk 1990). More generally, we can describe this three-way gap as follows:

- *Top managers* They do not adequately understand IT or information in government. They will not initiate an integrated approach, and will resist suggested integration they fear they cannot understand or control. Once semi-literate about IT, they may have a computer age vision of government, but they do not have an information age vision.
- *IT staff* They do not understand government's business or managers' information needs and they are only really interested in the technology. They will not readily support or easily contribute to reform-/ information-led approaches. Instead, they will prefer to be left alone to plan and support technology-led approaches.
- *Mainstream staff* They have little strategic understanding of information but can be divided into:

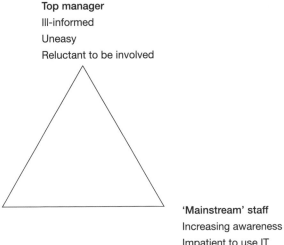

Top manager
Ill-informed
Uneasy
Reluctant to be involved

IT professional
Data processing outlook
Defending IT unit
Lacks a strategic view

'Mainstream' staff
Increasing awareness
Impatient to use IT
Piecemeal adoption of
personal computers

Figure 2.1 The 'ITernal triangle' of gaps between different staff

— computer illiterates who feel threatened by IT, its jargon and its association with change and the unknown. They will resist any type of information age reform because of their fears;

— computer literates who want to pursue their own agenda without seeing the need for coordination of IT activities or for 'interference' from IT staff and others. They do not wish to sublimate their efforts into a wider reform agenda and are therefore likely to undermine any organisational integrated approach to information age reform.

This three-way gap is partly a gap of objectives, of knowledge and of culture, with each group talking a different 'language', holding different worldviews and/or interests, and not trusting the others. However, the gap also relates to organisational structures. For example, a centralised IT unit will remain independent with little involvement in mainstream reform unless it is explicitly staffed and structured to create that involvement. Similarly, where there is hierarchical and structural separation of senior policy makers and planners from mainstream administrators and implementers, barriers will be hard to cross.

ALTERNATIVE REFORM MODELS

The 'four-eyes' model presented above focuses mainly on the way that managers approach information and IT within the reform process. However, there are other managerial issues around reform that can be used as the basis for quasi-chronological models. Table 2.1, for example, focuses on the intended outcome of information age reform.

Let us take the example of a government's Bureau of Statistics:

- In the *Automation* phase, it undertakes its first computerisation. Once collected from the field, statistical survey data is typed by clerical staff on to a computer instead of being held on paper. Tabulations are now performed by the computer and not by hand.
- In the *Optimisation* phase, the survey forms and data entry screens are simplified, and networked computers are placed in regional offices. This enables direct entry of data by field staff instead of central entry by a pool of clerical staff at headquarters.
- In the *Reengineering* phase, survey questions are redesigned to provide the information that is actually required by the Bureau and its clients. In the past, by comparison, data had been gathered regardless of whether or not it was required. The computer systems of the separate sectoral analysis departments are also redesigned and linked. This means that all data sets are available across the whole organisation and that there is little duplication of information between departments. A new central analysis department is created to analyse cross-sectoral trends.
- In the *Transformation* phase, the Bureau is renamed the Statistical Services Agency. It has outsourced much of its data gathering and has set up a commercial unit that provides income-generating statistical services for foreign and domestic private firms. These services include an annually-updated CD-ROM of national data sets; access to certain national data sets via the Internet; and an online analysis service for the provision of customised trend analysis and reporting.

A closely related model has been that which sees a progression within public sector reform from strategies of automation to strategies of 'informatisation' (and, in some cases, subsequently to strategies of transformation). Informatisation can be seen as a strategy of public sector reengineering enabled by the new information flows that IT permits and supports.

These new flows include (Bellamy and Taylor 1994, 1998: 47):

- 'the integration of data from a number of sources, thus enabling the memory of organizations to be vastly magnified'. For example, a 'whole person' approach to citizens or clients, and 'one-stop shops' to bring together multiple government services;
- 'the significant enhancement of organizational intelligence, by enabling new ways of integrating or matching data that will yield much more information about its external environment . . . and internal processes'. For example, relocation of the 'intelligence' of client services to the point

Table 2.1 Phases of management strategies for information age reform outcomes

	Phase 1	Phase 2	Phase 3	Phase 4
Reform objective	Automation	Optimisation	Reengineering	Transformation
Change sought	Changing the technology from manual to IT via automation	Changing applications by rationalising data structures and work processes	Changing the organisation by redesigning data structures and work processes	Changing the organisation by completely transforming data structures and work processes
Typical IS management issue	Getting the information systems to work and stay working	Controlling the information systems costs and staff	Coordinating information systems across the whole organisation	Harnessing information systems to meet the needs of organisational customers
IT's role	Supplant	Support	Innovate	Innovate
In lay terms	Efficiency: doing the same things in the same ways but faster or cheaper	Incremental effectiveness: doing the same things in somewhat better ways	Radical effectiveness: doing the same things in radically better ways	Transformation: doing new things

of public contact: the front desk, not the back office, with a greater ability to take rule-based decisions at that contact point;

- 'greater flexibility in arranging who may access and exploit information resources, and how information-dependent processes are undertaken'. For example, 'prosumption' in which the consumer is also the producer of information, as in electronic self-assessment for tax and social security, that can produce greater efficiency and accuracy;
- 'new kinds of interactive communications within and between organizations'. For example, greater flow of information across public agency boundaries, say to the citizenry, who then come to have a greater input to a more responsive and accountable public sector.

There is no simple relationship between the models described in this section and the 'four-eyes' approaches described above. Automation could occur as part of any information age reform approach. The three other phases/informatisation could be seen as elements of an integrated approach, but might also form part of an idolise approach. Certainly some of the writings about informatisation cross the line to extol IT-driven rather than IT-enabled change. None the less, we can draw some similar generic conclusions about these quasi-chronological models.

Just as the integrate approach offers greater information age reform benefits to government so, too, do the post-automation strategies described here. If successful, automation delivers just efficiency gains and, perhaps, some improvement in resource management. This can be seen as part of an older, more 'traditional' approach to information age reform.

If successful, post-automation strategies, such as informatisation, deliver the whole range of reform objectives. These strategies and objectives can be seen as part of truly *new* public management, being intimately intertwined because of the new information flows that underpin reforms such as marketisation (Bellamy and Taylor 1998).

Just as development of the integrate approach remains constrained by barriers of technology, skills, knowledge, structures and culture, so, too, does development of the post-automation strategies described here. Indeed, seeing these strategies as part of information age reform helps identify additional barriers, such as those which follow.

Political barriers

Information is a component of organisational power. If information age reform means new information flows, it also means new arrangements of organisational power. Informatisation in particular makes explicit the reform requirement of sharing information with others. Yet no one likes to share information (or, hence, power) with others: 'collaboration and cooperation across agencies and programs raise issues of turf' (NAPA 1997: 3). Some therefore argue that 'the information-based organisation is largely a fantasy'

(Davenport *et al.* 1992: 53). The greater the importance of information to the organisation, the more constricted the information flows: 'When information is the primary unit of organizational currency, we should not expect its owners to give it away' (ibid.: 54).

Structural/cultural barriers

In addition to such barriers described above *within* public organisations, they also exist *between* organisations, with government still largely consisting of 'vertical, functional lines rather than a focus on objectives or delivering services to customers' (O'Higgins 1998). American government IS managers have therefore 'voiced substantial concern about the general lack of incentives, policy coordination and practical mechanisms for intra- and inter-agency information sharing' (CTG 1998: 1). Because of these structural barriers, but also related cultural and political barriers like those just described, governments find it hard to create cross-cutting information flows to support reform. In the UK, for example, the MINIS initiative sought to develop a centralised, cross-department information system but 'in practice, departments asserted their independence by producing their own information systems' (Blundell and Murdock 1997: 48). Such problems may well increase as a result of reform initiatives that decentralise and marketise, thereby fragmenting government (Muid 1994; Willcocks 1994). We are then faced with the paradox that public sector reform may simultaneously increase the requirement for, but decrease the possibility of, informatised strategies.

Other barriers

An international survey of governments indicated that 'By far the biggest barrier to information sharing is privacy and security' (ICA 1997: 4), with that barrier being represented most in the form of citizen concerns about the data that government holds on them. Financial and technological barriers to informatisation were ranked next. There are also legal and policy barriers, since many laws and policies never foresaw cross-functional or inter-organisational information flows: 'A complete overhaul of the regulatory and policy framework is necessary and new legislation has to be enabled to make that happen.' (McLellan 1996).

Because of such barriers, the real-world incidence of post-automation reform strategies is severely limited, as was the case with the integrate approach.

SUMMARY AND CONCLUSIONS

Information age reform is spreading rapidly world-wide but there are many different approaches to reform, as summarised in Table 2.2. Similarly, there

Table 2.2 Summary of approaches to information age reform

Approach	Role of IT in reform	Role of IS in reform	Delivery of reform objectives	Prevalence
Ignore	None	Unrecognised	Weak	Widespread, but declining
Isolate	Peripheral	Unrecognised	Weak	Widespread, perhaps static
Idolise	Primary role	Limited recognition	Weak	Relatively limited, perhaps growing
Integrate	Enabler	Central role recognised	Strong	Limited, growth constrained

are changes over time in the intended outcome of information age reform, from a strategy of automation and efficiency gains to one of reengineering and effectiveness gains.

Yet there remain substantial barriers (a) for governments to enter the information age reform era; and (b) to move on within that era to approaches that will deliver reform objectives and deliver more innovative reform objectives.

There is no magic recipe for overcoming these barriers but education and training must surely form a substantial part of the package. Yet most current MPA (Masters in Public Administration) and related training programmes can be described as 'isolate going on idolise' in their approach. There is little attempt to build the hybrid managers – spanning managerial, IT and IS skills – that information age government requires (see also Chapter 13). These skill sets remain unintegrated within current training and partly ignored. Potential employees and in-service trainees on most programmes may gain computing skills, but they do not gain information or information systems knowledge and skills. Any view of IT beyond the hands-on is, typically, simplistically positive.

Not only does this hamper integrated approaches today, it also hints at a dangerously self-reinforcing spiral. If the present generation of public managers cannot value or manage information, that sets the 'information-blind' agenda for current training and debate, thus ensuring that the next generation, too, will be unable to value or manage information.

Barriers will also need to be addressed through the adoption of more strategic approaches by public managers; strategic approaches that drive technology needs from information needs, and information needs from reform objectives. Strategic information systems planning of this type is very much in vogue in the private sector, though the application of such techniques in practice and in the public sector remains questionable (see Chapter 14). Perhaps more realistic is a 'core–periphery' approach that balances strategic and tactical, central and local needs (Heeks 1999).

In addition, overcoming the barriers described above will require cultural and structural changes in government to ensure that technology is the servant of reform. Such changes are never quick and so the move to an integrated approach can only be seen as a long-term process. In the interim, information age reform initiatives are likely to remain dominated by isolate, idolise and automation approaches. Not only do these undershoot in their delivery of potential reform objectives, they also have a habit of failing. Chapter 3 investigates why.

There is a final sting in the tail. Initiatives guided by the integrate approach and the post-automation strategies described above may bring greater reform benefits to government. However, such initiatives are also failing. Placing reform and information systems at the core may therefore be good potentially, but it is not a panacea for success. Again, Chapter 3 investigates why.

REFERENCES

Adamolekun, L., de Lusignan, G. and Atomate, A. (1997) *Civil Service Reform in Francophone Africa*, Technical Paper no. 357, Washington, DC: World Bank.

Assirati, B. (1998) 'Private finance, public accountability – the lessons', paper presented at 'Government Computing 98' conference, 17–18 June, London.

Beck, S. (1998) 'Digital government', *Government Computing* 12, 6: 28.

Bekke, A.G.M., Perry, J.L. and Toonen, T.A.J. (1996) *Civil Service Systems in Comparative Perspective*, Bloomington, IN: Indiana University Press.

Bellamy, C. and Taylor, J.A. (1994) 'Exploiting IT in public administration: towards the information polity?', *Public Administration* 72, Spring: 1–12.

Bellamy, C. and Taylor, J.A. (1998) *Governing in the Information Age*, Buckingham: Open University Press.

Bhatnagar, S.C. (1997) 'Information technology-enabled public sector reforms: myth or reality?', paper presented at conference on 'Public Sector Management in the Next Century', 29 June–2 July, University of Manchester, Manchester.

Blundell, B. and Murdock, A. (1997) *Managing in the Public Sector*, Oxford: Butterworth-Heinemann.

Boston, J., Martin, J., Pallot, J. and Walsh, P. (1996) *Public Management: The New Zealand Model*, Melbourne: Oxford University Press.

Burns, A. (1984) 'Information technology – for better or worse?', in A. Burns (ed.) *New Information Technology*, Chichester, W. Sussex: Ellis Horwood.

CCTA (1995) *G7 Government On-line Project Executive Summary*, London: Central Computer and Telecommunications Agency.
http://www.open.gov.uk/govoline/execsum.htm

Chepaitis, E.V. (1996) 'The problem of data quality in a developing economy: Russia in the 1990s', in P.C. Palvia, S.C. Palvia and E.M. Roche (eds) *Global Information Technology and Systems Management*, Nashua, NH: Ivy League Publishing.

CITU (1996) *government.direct: A Prospectus for the Electronic Delivery of Government Services*, London: Central IT Unit, Office of Public Service.
http://www.open.gov.uk/gdirect/greenpaper/index.htm

COI (1998) *Our Information Age: The Government's Vision*, London: Central Office of Information.
http://www.number-10.gov.uk/public/info/releases/publications/infoagefeat.html

Commonwealth Secretariat (1995) *A Profile of the Public Service in New Zealand*, London: Commonwealth Secretariat.

Commonwealth Secretariat (1996) *Current Good Practices and New Developments in Public Service Management*, London: Commonwealth Secretariat.

CTG (1998) *Using Information in Government: A Program Framework*, Albany, NY: Center for Technology in Government, University at Albany.
http://www.ctg.albany.edu/projects/usinginfo/framewrk.html

Davenport, T.H., Eccles, R.G. and Prusak, L. (1992) 'Information politics', *Sloan Management Review* 34, 1: 53–65.

Davies, C.A. (1997) 'The information infrastructure approach for developing countries', paper presented at conference on 'Public Sector Management in the Next Century', 29 June–2 July, University of Manchester, Manchester.

Davis, G. (ed.) (1996) *New Ideas, Better Government*, St Leonards, Australia: Allen & Unwin.

Dorris, M.A. (1997) 'Canada's benefit-driven procurement system', *ICA Newsletter* 39: 7–9.
http://www.ica.ogit.gov.au/Publications

Eele, G. (1994) 'The changing role of government statistical agencies', *IDS Bulletin* 25, 2: 110–116.

Electronic Government International (1998) 'Limited electronic government in Europe', May: 3.

Embleton, E. (1996) 'Ireland', paper presented at conference on 'Electronic Government in the Information Society', 6–10 October, Budapest, Hungary.

Federal Sources (1998) *FY98 Revenue Projections*, Washington, DC: Federal Sources, Inc.
http://www.fedsources.com/fy98rev.htm

Gahre, A.P. (1996) 'Norway', paper presented at conference on 'Electronic Government in the Information Society', 6–10 October, Budapest, Hungary.

General Accounting Office (1994) *Improving Mission Performance Through Strategic Information Management and Technology*, Washington, DC: General Accounting Office.

Haarmann, W. (1996) 'Netherlands', paper presented at conference on 'Electronic Government in the Information Society', 6–10 October, Budapest, Hungary.

Hastings, C. (1996) *The New Organization*, London: McGraw-Hill.

Health Committee (1995) *London's Ambulance Service*, Report HC20, London: Her Majesty's Stationery Office.

Heeks, R.B. (1999) *Centralised vs. Decentralised Management of Public Information Systems: A Core-Periphery Solution*, ISPSM Working Paper no. 7, Manchester: IDPM, University of Manchester.
http://www.man.ac.uk/idpm/idpm_dp.htm

Hertzum, M. (1995) 'Computer support for document management in the Danish central government', *Information Infrastructure and Policy* 4, 2: 107–129.

Hesse, J.J. (ed.) (1993) *Administrative Transformation in Central and Eastern Europe*, Oxford: Blackwell.

ICA (1997) *ICA Information Sharing Within and Between Governments Study Group Report*, Washington, DC: International Council for Information Technology in Government Administration.

ICA (1998) *Procurement Study Group Report*, Washington, DC: International Council for Information Technology in Government Administration.

IDA (1998) *Preparing for the European Information Society*, Brussels: IDA Programme, European Commission.
http://www.ispo.cec.be/ida/text/english/ovrvuk.htm

Isaac-Henry, K. (1997) 'Management of information technology in the public sector', in K. Isaac-Henry, C. Painter and C. Barnes (eds) *Management in the Public Sector*, London: International Thomson Business Press.

Kable (1998) *Kable Local Government IS Market Profile to 2000*, London: Kable.

Kajiwara, M. (1996) 'Japan', paper presented at conference on 'Electronic Government in the Information Society', 6–10 October, Budapest, Hungary.

Karlsson, M. (1996) 'Surfing the wave of national IT initiatives', *Information Infrastructure and Policy* 5, 3: 191–204.

Kettl, D.F. (ed.) (1996) *Civil Service Reform: Building a Government that Works*, Washington, DC: Brookings Institution Press.

Kickert, W.J.M. (ed.) (1998) *Public Management and Administrative Reform in Western Europe*, Cheltenham, Glos.: Edward Elgar.

Knight, A.V. and Silk, D.J. (1990) *Managing Information*, London: McGraw-Hill.

Kraemer, K.L., Dutton, W.H. and Northrop, A. (1981) *The Management of Information Systems*, New York: Columbia University Press.

Laudon, K.C. and Laudon, J.P. (1998) *Management Information Systems*, 5th edn, Upper Saddle River, NJ: Prentice-Hall.

Lenk, K. (1990) 'How adequate are informatization strategies?', in P. Frissen and I. Snellen (eds) *Informatization Strategies in Public Administration*, Amsterdam: Elsevier.

Lucey, T. (1997) *Management Information Systems*, 8th edn, London: Letts Educational.

McDonough, F.A. (1997) 'From the chair', *ICA Newsletter* 37: 1–2.
http://www.ica.ogit.gov.au/Publications

McLellan, P.M. (1996) 'Electronic commerce: serving the business community', paper presented at conference on 'Electronic Government in the Information Society', 6–10 October, Budapest, Hungary.

McLellan, P.M., Riddle, J. and Ober, H. (1996) 'Canada', paper presented at conference on 'Electronic Government in the Information Society', 6–10 October, Budapest, Hungary.

McNevin, A. (1994) 'Hardware budgets cut as civil service revises IT expenditure', *Computing*, 28 July: 8.

Mansell, R. and Wehn, U. (eds) (1998) *Knowledge Societies: Information Technology for Sustainable Development*, Oxford: Oxford University Press.

Milner, E. (1997) 'Uncertain growth after Labor's pains', *Government Computing* 11, 10: 24–25.

Muid, C. (1994) 'Information systems and new public management: a view from the centre', *Public Administration* 72, Spring: 113–125.

Myers, M. (1996) 'The Wellington Education Board: converting to a new payroll system', in S. Alter (ed.) *Information Systems: A Management Perspective*, Menlo Park, CA: Benjamin/Cummings.

Naidu, N.C. (1997) 'IT strategy group in Andhra Pradesh', personal communication with author.

NAPA (1997) *Information Technology: Overview and Table of Contents*, Washington, DC: National Academy of Public Administration.
http://www.alliance.napawash.org/alliance/index.html

NCB (1997) *IT2000: A Vision of an Intelligent Island*, Singapore: National Computer Board.
http://www.ncb.gov.sg/ncb/vision.asp

NITC (1997) *IT21 Philippines*, Manila, Philippines: National Information Technology Council.
http://www.neda.gov.ph/

OGIT (1998) *Government OnLine*, Canberra: Office of Government Information Technology.
http://www.ogit.gov.au/gol/gol.html

O'Higgins, M. (1998) 'Information, performance and better government', paper presented at 'Government Computing 98' conference, 17–18 June, London.

Osborne, D. and Gaebler, T. (1992) *Reinventing Government: How the Entrepreneurial Spirit is Transforming the Public Sector*, Reading, MA: Addison-Wesley.

Pietarinen, I. (1996) 'Electronic government', paper presented at conference on 'Electronic Government in the Information Society', 6–10 October, Budapest, Hungary.

POST (1998) *Electronic Government: Information Technology and the Citizen*, London: Parliamentary Office of Science and Technology.
http://www.parliament.uk/post/egov.htm

Postman, N. (1992) *Technopoly*, New York: Vintage Books.

PRC (1998) *Developing a Culture of Good Governance*, Pretoria: Presidential Review Commission.

Ragan, M. (1997) 'Welfare reform in America', paper presented at conference on 'Integrated Service Delivery: Changing the Role of Government', 26–30 October, Sydney, Australia.

Roszak, T. (1988) *The Cult of Information*, London: Paladin.

SOCITM (1997) *IT Trends in Local Government 1997/98*, London: Society of Information Technology Management.

Talero, E. and Gaudette, P. (1995) 'Harnessing information for development', *Information Technology for Development* 6, 3/4: 145–188.

Tettey, W.J. (1997) *Informatics Training in Ghana and the Quest for a Computocracy*, Ontario: Queen's University, mimeo.

Treasury Board Secretariat (1994) *Working Together for Better Public Services*, Ottawa: Treasury Board Secretariat, Government of Canada.

UNDP (1997) *Human Development Report 1997*, New York: United Nations Development Programme.

Warner, N. (1992) 'Changes in resource management in the social services', in C. Pollitt and S. Harrison (eds) *Handbook of Public Services Management*, Oxford: Blackwell.

Willcocks, L. (1994) 'Managing information systems in UK public administration: issues and prospects', *Public Administration* 72, Spring: 13–32.

Wirszycz, R. (1997) 'Smashing the glass hurdles of human fear', *Government Computing* 11, 10: 12.

World Bank (1993) *Turkey: Informatics and Economic Modernization*, Washington, DC: World Bank.

Yoong-Gil, R. (1996) 'Korea', paper presented at conference on 'Electronic Government in the Information Society', 6–10 October, Budapest, Hungary.

3 Understanding success and failure in information age reform

Richard Heeks and
Subhash Bhatnagar

Abstract: In this chapter, a model is developed of information systems within information age reform, based on case examples of reform success and failure. It is argued that failure is far more prevalent than success, and that the root causes of both must be investigated. From analysis of both theoretical and real-world examples, these root causes are seen to lie in 'conception–reality gaps': gaps that exist between the way in which reform is conceived and the public sector realities into which it is introduced. These ideas are simplified into the ITPOSMO model that focuses on seven key dimensions of conception–reality gap. Three archetypal situations are identified and discussed in which conception–reality gaps arise, each of which can form the basis for information age reform failure. The archetypes relate to reforms conceived around models based on organisational rationality, private sector functioning and different country contexts. They point to some general conclusions about better information age reform.

DEVELOPING A MODEL OF INFORMATION SYSTEMS AND REFORM

Whether recognised by stakeholders or not, it is information systems that are central to the process of information age reform. In Chapter 1, we provided a definition of information systems. We now need to develop a more comprehensive model of information systems within the reform process and will do so from cases of success and failure in information age reform.

These cases highlight critical success or critical failure factors (CSFs and CFFs) which can be categorised under a number of headings.

Information factors

- CSF/CFF: Australia's Department of Employment, Education and Youth Training rolled out a flagship application of information technology (IT) in the early 1990s: a kiosk-based service containing job vacancy information for use by job seekers, intended to improve the delivery of employment services. The project began to fail because of information content problems with both the quantity and quality of vacancy information. The result was a steady decline in system use. A concerted effort was made to improve content and match job seekers' information needs. This led to a revival of the system so that, by 1996, six million searches per month were contributing to 180,000 employee placements (Milner 1997). (Political and policy changes have subsequently led to renewed problems, but that's another story.)

Technical factors

- CSF: the Queensland Department of Lands, in Australia, was responsible for registration of land title transfers and was faced with an ever-increasing workload in the early 1990s. The success of its decision to increase efficiency by automating the process was due in part to its choice of the right combination of hardware and software. The relational database at the heart of the system, in particular, has been flexible enough to cope with workload growth, fast enough in its operation to significantly speed work processes, and user-friendly enough to avert operational resistance (Power 1996, cited in Laudon and Laudon 1998).
- CFF: the UK's 'Coordination of Computerisation in the Criminal Justice System' initiative seeks to enable information flows between criminal justice agencies, including the courts, prisons, police and probation service. The initiative ran into difficulties because, in part, of incompatibilities between the IT systems of the different agencies (Bellamy and Taylor 1998).

People factors

- CSF: the Ships Support Agency, an agency within the UK's Ministry of Defence, 'spent only £1,500 [*c*.US$2,400] developing an online system that was originally estimated at over £100,000 [*c*.US$160,000]' (*Government Computing* 1998a: 23). The system was a hypertext manual giving details of business procedures within this recently marketised agency. Development of the manual was intended to be outsourced and custom-built at great cost: £15,000 [*c*.US$24,000] to be spent on supplier identification alone. However, thanks to the presence of skilled and motivated in-house staff, a much cheaper option was identified, using in-house customisation of an existing software package.

- CFF: California Environmental Protection Agency staff were not properly trained to use a new database that was meant to improve tracking of hazardous waste shipments. They therefore:

  accidentally inserted hundreds of thousands of duplicate identification numbers ... The resulting output was so unreliable that it became difficult, if not impossible, to find out when toxic waste was being transported and dumped, or to prosecute the perpetrators of hazardous-waste violations.

  (James 1997: 7)

Management factors

- CSF: decentralisation was enabled in the Irish Department of Social Welfare through the introduction of new computerised information systems. The development of these systems was successfully managed in a 'core–periphery' manner: retaining sufficient drive from the centre to overcome pre-existing obstacles, but according sufficient weight to users' views and devolving sufficient resources to the local level to ensure that new obstacles rarely arose (Cooney and O'Flaherty 1996).
- CFF:

  Management ignorance was rampant in Texas recently, when state agencies rushed to upgrade their computers systems without understanding the risks involved. The state has ended up paying $1 billion a year, without its managers knowing whether the money was being spent wisely or well. One system – a statewide computer for tracking deadbeat parents – is more than four years late and is costing three times more than the originally budgeted $25 million. The situation became so bad that a Senate committee voted last April to move responsibility for child-support payments to a completely different government agency.

  (James 1997: 4)

Process factors

- CSF: in Nicaragua, reform of the national public health system was planned. This included a new information system that would feed health information collected at community level up via the regions to national level. Additional processes were included which fed back health information to the communities from which it was gathered. Communities therefore used this information to discuss their health needs, and so saw the value of information. This, in turn, significantly increased data quality and coverage, ensuring that the new system had a viable base of health data (Horejs 1996).

- CFF: the UK's Bristol Royal Infirmary, a public hospital, was part of a reform process that included the benchmarking of performance. As a result, information came to light in the 1980s that death rates in its paediatric cardiac surgery unit were well above national averages. Yet remedial measures were not taken for nearly ten years because there was no set of effective processes in place to feed that information into public decision making and action (O'Higgins 1998).

Cultural factors

- CSF: Thailand's Ministry of the Interior has been involved in a series of population registration projects since the early 1980s. These use computerised information systems to issue a personal identification number to all citizens and retain details on a 'central population database'. The system was introduced in a top-down manner, and operates according to centralised and bureaucratic principles that provide the government with considerable powers of 'bureaucratic surveillance' over Thai citizens. The system is rated a 'tremendous success' by users and won a Smithsonian Computerworld Award. Its success is due particularly to a supportive organisational culture that runs throughout the Ministry. The culture is one of centralisation, bureaucratic role fulfilment and a lack of concern for the privacy rights of individual citizens (Ramasoota 1998).
- CFF: as part of its transition to a market economy, Mongolia instituted a series of wide-ranging reforms in its public sector. These included the introduction of decentralisation – supported by a plan for a decentralised information system – in its public health sector. The new computerised system that emerged is not particularly decentralised, and usage of the system remains very limited at local levels. To a large extent, this is because the organisational culture of public health in Mongolia is still strongly rooted in the top-down, centralised Soviet model that sees no place for local initiative (Braa 1996).

Structural factors

- CSF: Kent County Council, a local government unit in the UK, wanted to devolve management responsibilities as part of its desire to improve service delivery. New information systems were an essential part of this reform. At first, reforms were stymied by the traditional, centralised IT structures within the organisation. However, the IT function was then restructured, broadening its remit to cover information systems and devolving many responsibilities and staff to individual departments. As a result, the reform programme was able to proceed (Moreton and Chester 1997).
- CFF: the Finance Division of Kenya's Ministry of Agriculture was supported by a technical assistance project that introduced microcomputers

in an effort to improve the management of financial resources. There was little improvement in the monitoring of expenditure because of a three-way structural division between central finance officers who held the monitoring information but had no powers of enforcement, senior finance officials who had the power to enforce expenditure warnings but had no information or incentive to do so, and district officers who actually spent the money (Brodman 1987).

Strategic factors

- CSF: Portugal's Infocid project has been able to provide a very wide range of government information to citizens as an integrated package via electronic channels. It covers health, education, military service, elections, employment and training, social security, tax, legal matters, housing, economic activity, consumer protection, environmental issues, culture and tourism. It has been able to do this by adopting a strategic approach that cuts across traditional intra-governmental divisions and which used outsourcing to overcome resource constraints (Vidigal 1997).
- CFF: in the 1980s Sacramento, a city in Northern California, took a top-level decision to devolve computing decisions to individual departments. The result after a few years was a patchwork of incompatible applications, no city-wide information or computing infrastructure, and wide inequalities in the extent of computerisation. All this presented serious barriers to further progress of information age reform (King and Kraemer 1991). (The authors contrast the situation in Charlotte, Virginia, where a strategic decision had been made to retain central, city-wide control over information systems.)

Political factors

- CSF: Indianapolis/Marion County in the US has been a leader in providing local government information and services via the Web, with a goal of becoming one of the first truly electronic city halls. In large part, this process has been driven by the political support and championing of reinvention via IT from the Indianapolis Mayor, Stephen Goldsmith (Poulos 1998).
- CFF: India's Income Tax Department decided to computerise part of the tax system in order to produce better statistical information on the country's revenue base, thus permitting improved management of revenue. However, the project ran into difficulties due to political antagonisms between various groups, notably between regional tax commissioners and the central tax board and between management and unions (Singh 1990).

Environmental factors

- CSF: social security reform in Sweden has been supported by changing environmental factors. In the 1960s and early 1970s, reform aimed to centralise and control the social security system. This was supported by the dominant host–terminal computing architecture of the time, by a national ideology of 'big government' and by social distrust of local politics amongst the Swedish people. In the late 1970s and 1980s, reform reversed and aimed to decentralise social security. In the changing environment, this was supported by emergent microcomputing technology, by a new ideology of 'small government' and by a new desire among citizens for more active local government (Ingelstam and Palmlund 1991).
- CFF: a generic example is the millennium bug. Here an environmental factor – the date – threatens to be the cause of a number of public sector information system failures.

On the basis of these factors and their structural relations, we can draw up an 'onion ring' model of information systems within the reform process, as shown in Figure 3.1. From this model, we see that information age reform is a comprehensive process that can involve change in a wide variety of factors. The relationship between the extent of change and reform success is discussed in more detail below.

Figure 3.1 can also be seen to summarise some of the problems of the isolate and idolise approaches described in Chapter 2:

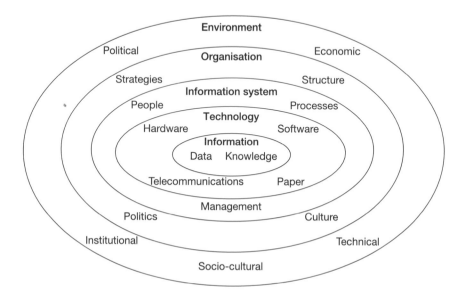

Figure 3.1 Information systems and information age reform model

- they fail to place information and information systems at the heart of change, but instead marginalise them, replacing them with technology alone in the idolise case;
- they fail to recognise the contextual factors that form an important and integral part of information age reform.

Indeed, the integrated approach to reform approximates to driving reform from the outer rings of the model inwards, whereas the idolise approach approximates more to trying to drive reform from the inside of the model (or at least from its second ring) outwards.

In addition, we can draw a few conclusions about information systems (IS) that expand upon points noted earlier in Box 1.1:

- Information systems are social systems; that is to say, information systems are rooted in a context of people and of social structures and are themselves made up partly of people and social structures.
- Information lies at the heart of all information systems.
- All information systems operate within a reform context that has two main components. The first is the *organisation* within which the IS is located. This has an organisational culture, a political dimension, a set of overt or covert management strategies relating to reform, and both formal and informal organisational structures. The second is a wider *environment* outside the organisation. Within this wider environment there are other institutions; there are new technologies being developed; there is the state of the economy and markets; there are political pressures which are likely to be particularly significant in reform; and there are a variety of cultures and other social systems. All of these factors have a bearing on the information system as well as on the broader process of reform. Sometimes the influence is too weak to detect, but in other cases the influence may be strong, as in the integrated approach.
- Information system means information technology *plus* information *plus* people *plus* processes *plus* management. For an IS to be successful in supporting reform, it must succeed in all these areas. Some systems succeed technically but fail in other ways: not providing the right information; not being usable by the people involved; not involving work processes that produce the right organisational outputs; etc. Reform initiatives where the technology works but other IS components do not are reminiscent of the old medical joke: 'The surgical operation was a success, but unfortunately the patient died.' This summarises the outcome of many idolising reform initiatives like those described in Chapter 2. Indeed, it is sadly appropriate, given the deaths that occurred during the failed implementation of the London Ambulance Service information system, as emergency victims awaited the much-delayed arrival of paramedics.

UNDERSTANDING SUCCESS AND FAILURE: CONCEPTION–REALITY GAPS

Chapters 1 and 2 presented examples of both successful and unsuccessful information age reform. We have likewise seen just above that reform may end in failure as well as success. Even the integrated approach, though it may promise greater reform benefits, also seems to have its failures. In general, failure of information age reform seems more common than success.

What is failure?

The last statement must be qualified by explaining that failures can be divided into two camps:

- *total failures*: in which proposed reform is never implemented or in which reform is implemented but soon abandoned. In 1994, for example, California's Department of Motor Vehicles abandoned a seven-year, US$44 million reform project to improve efficiency and effectiveness by replacing its 1965-vintage mainframe systems. No workable system was ever produced from this project and no reform objectives were achieved (King 1994);
- *partial failures*: in which reform is implemented but has something wrong with it. In the Indian Income Tax Department case mentioned above, for example, only parts of the information system and only a sub-set of intended process reforms became operational and even these were resisted by staff. There was therefore only limited achievement of reform objectives (Singh 1990).

We can be more specific on the point of 'something wrong with it', and can categorise two aspects of failure:

- *goals unattained*: expected outcomes that someone wanted to happen but which did not happen. In cases of total failure, no reform objectives are attained. In cases of partial failure, objectives relating to the unimplemented or non-operational components of reform are not attained;
- *undesirable outcomes*: unexpected outcomes that someone did not want to happen but which did happen. In the Californian case, there was the undesirable outcome that money, time and reputation were all lost. In the Indian case, there was unexpected and fierce staff resistance.

In explaining both of these aspects, the word 'someone' was used. This alerts us to the fact that failure can be a subjective phenomenon. For example, we can ask questions such as 'Whose goals were not attained?' or 'For whom were the outcomes undesirable?'. It is quite likely in cases of information age reform failure to find different groups experiencing failure in different ways. We may also find some groups who see a reform initiative as a failure alongside other groups who see it as a success.

The extent of failure

Having defined failure, we can look for some sense of its prevalence. This is not readily found because failures tend to be swept under the carpet, whilst successes (real or imagined) tend to be shouted from the rooftops. The same handful of rose-tinted 'good news' reform stories do the rounds continuously. There is surely global legislation that all books on IT and the public sector (this one included) must mention Singapore, where everything the government touches turns to silicon. Yet most published cases on Singapore come across like a government-sponsored press release. Critical appraisals of information age reform – in Singapore or anywhere else – are few and far between.

We are also faced with the problem that few, if any, comprehensive reviews of information age reform exist, least of all those which understand that failure has subjective components. We are therefore left to rely on the independent assessments of public sector information systems that are occasionally undertaken. These suggest that failure is widespread:

- Research on information systems in the UK public sector estimates that 20 per cent of all IT expenditure is wasted, while a further 30–40 per cent leads to no net benefits accruing (Willcocks 1994).
- A survey of all African public sector IT projects funded by the World Bank concluded: 'in the majority of cases, several factors have constrained organisations from effectively using the technology and the information it provides, or have proved to be constraints on the sustainability of IT' (Moussa and Schware 1992: 1750).
- Even the biggest spender of all, the US government, has problems: 'Despite spending more than $200 billion on information management and systems in the last 12 years, the government has too little evidence of meaningful returns' (General Accounting Office 1994).

A number of the cases presented in this book, particularly in Parts 2 and 3, would also be classified as total or, more typically, partial failures of information age reform. To these we can add a few more, on a rising scale:

- the Canadian government's attempt to reform its payroll system, as reported in Chapter 2. This was abandoned at a cost of *c*.US$30 million (McLellan 1996);
- California's Department of Social Services, which began reform of its child support payments system in 1992 through an automation project. The project – 'the largest and most expensive state-run, single-unit

information system in our nation's history' – was terminated late in 1997 with 1,400 outstanding problems (Newcombe 1998: 1). Expenditure had reached US$100 million at that point and final costs could be up to US$345 million. (America-wide, reform of child support systems through automation has cost around US$2.7 billion and produced the following dismal equations: pre-automation case collection rate in 1990 = 20 per cent; post-automation case collection rate in 1998 = 20 per cent);

- the UK public health service's Resource Management Initiative, which attempted to improve the monitoring and control of hospital resources: 'information technology and systems were introduced in virtually every hospital in Britain but it appears few of them were successful by any criteria'. The total cost was 'Hundreds of millions of pounds' (Westrup 1998: 9);

- the US Internal Revenue Service, which takes the current prize, albeit mainly defined in terms of revenue forgone: 'Despite an annual computing budget of $8 billion, the IRS has managed a string of project failures that have cost taxpayers $50 billion a year – roughly as much as the yearly net profit of the entire computer industry' (James 1997: 1).

Of course, failure is not a problem restricted to the public sector. Surveys in the US private sector, for example, indicate that 'the success rate for software projects is only 27%' (James 1997: 1) while others estimate failure rates of 'at least 80 per cent and often higher' (Korac-Boisvert and Kouzmin 1995: 134). It's just that the private sector has been better than government at keeping these failures quiet thanks to:

- fear of shareholders, who take a dimmer and more vociferous view of wasted expenditure than citizens;
- better-paid public relations staff;
- a habit of keeping nosy academics, eager for case studies, at arm's length;
- no public audit and oversight agencies breathing down their necks, stuffed with politicians and staff eager to score points by highlighting the shortcomings of others.

Why do success and failure happen?

There is a yawning gap between the positive potential of information age reform and the largely negative reality. Huge sums of money are being invested but a large proportion of this is going to waste on unimplemented or ineffective reform.

Clearly, something needs to be done about this but, before moving to that in Chapter 4, we must first understand why these failures occur and why, less frequently, there are successes. There are almost as many explanations as there are reform initiatives. What follows must therefore be seen as just one approach, albeit one that runs throughout all the cases presented in this book. It is based on the work of Heeks (1998a).

Conception–reality gaps

We know that the assumptions made by those involved in information systems-related change contribute significantly to success or failure (Bostrom and Heinen 1977; Hirschheim and Klein 1989). More specifically, we can say that the conceptual models held by key stakeholders or implicit within reengineered information systems are important. They are important because the gap that exists between these conceptions and public sector realities will determine success or failure. A couple of generic examples will illustrate.

First, imagine a reform initiative focused around the introduction of a decision support system (DSS). Such DSS-based initiatives are typically conceived according to a model of organisational rationality. This model assumes:

- that decisions are made in order to produce outcomes that best meet formally stated organisational objectives;
- that outcomes are produced on the basis of what is the optimal solution according to logical criteria.

This DSS-based reform therefore incorporates rational assumptions:

- about the objectivity of information that is present in the system;
- about the formality of processes and management involved;
- about the skills and role of people;
- about the presence of organisational strategies;
- about the rationality of organisational culture;
- about the absence of organisational politics, etc.

Where such assumptions match the reality of the public sector organisation, the DSS-based reform is likely to be introduced successfully. However, where the assumptions do not hold – in other words, when there is a gap between the initiative's conception and organisational reality – the reform is not likely to be introduced successfully. The smaller the gap, the greater the chance of success. Conversely, the larger the gap, the greater the risk of failure.

Second, imagine a reform based on the introduction of word processing. This makes a few assumptions about skills, about technical infrastructure and about cultural values related to technology and to documentation. However, these assumptions are far fewer than for the DSS-based reform. The chances that there will be a gap between these assumptions and organisational reality are therefore smaller. As we find in practice, word processing-based reform therefore succeeds in far more situations than initiatives requiring the introduction of decision support systems.

Two further points emerge from this analysis:

- *No gap means no change* The logical extension of the arguments above is that an initiative involving no gap between conception and reality will be 100 per cent successful. But no gap means that nothing changes in the organisation. If they are to create any change, all information age reform initiatives must therefore involve some kind of conception–reality gap. They all therefore run some risk of failure, that risk being proportionate to the size of the gap.
- *Gaps, risks and benefits* Larger conception–reality gaps may bring greater risks of failure, but they may also bring greater organisational benefits. As discussed further in Chapter 15, major reengineering that introduces new information systems, work processes and structures can be perilous for a public sector organisation. However, if successful, it can dramatically improve organisational efficiency and effectiveness. Public officials may therefore find themselves in a dilemma, torn between one reform project that is revolutionary, high benefit and high risk and another that is incremental, limited benefit and low risk. Given that the former is likely to be more 'high profile', officials – especially politicians – will often be tempted by it, regardless of the risks.

The dimensions of the conception–reality gap

The DSS and word processing examples provide general illustration, not specific evidence, so let us now move on to real examples of information age reform. Matches and mismatches between conception and reality were implicit within many of the success and failure cases cited at the start of the chapter. These matches and mismatches are made explicit for each of the international cases analysed in Parts 2 to 5. Two of those cases will be summarised here.

Chapter 7 describes the introduction of an information system to support decentralisation of public health management in Ecuador. This reform initiative was a failure because a significant gap existed between the conception of the information system and the realities of the context into which it was introduced. Gap dimensions included:

- *a structural dimension*: the information system design assumed a centralised management structure. There was a major gap between this conception and the decentralised realities of Ecuador's district health centres;
- *a process dimension*: the IS design assumed a rational and objective approach to implementation processes. There was a major gap between this conception and the reality of a very politicised implementation process.

By contrast, Chapter 9 describes a successful intranet-based system introduced by Johannesburg Metropolitan Council in South Africa. This reform initiative succeeded because it was conceived in a way that matched Council realities. Matched dimensions included:

- *an information dimension*: the new system provided just the kind of information that Council users wanted, creating little gap between conceived and actual information needs;
- *a technology dimension*: the system relied mainly on existing technology within the Council, creating little gap between conceived and actual technology;
- *a people dimension*: consisting of two parts. First, system developers had the necessary skills to produce the system. Second, developers had the necessary motivation to produce the system. Overall, there was therefore little gap between conceived and actual 'people factors';
- *a resource dimension*: the system was set up cheaply and incrementally, without particular time pressures, creating little gap between conceived and actual resource requirements.

These ideas can equally be applied to the strategies and techniques of information age reform. Chapter 16, for example, describes the use of a framework for analysing performance information needs: the Results and Determinants Framework. The framework is flexible and imposes few preconceptions. Relatively few conception–reality gaps can therefore exist, and the framework can be successfully applied in a wide variety of organisational contexts.

Having presented the general idea of conception–reality gaps, we can be more specific about them. These gaps could be assessed on each and every one of the elements listed in Figure 3.1, from information out to environmental factors. In practice, analysis of cases like those just described suggests that we can whittle this down to focus on gaps in:

- Information;
- Technology;
- Processes;
- People: **O**bjectives, values and motivations;
- People: **S**taffing and skills;
- **M**anagement and structures.

Most of the other factors listed in Figure 3.1 are incorporated within those listed here. Strategies are derived from the objectives of organisational members. Politics and culture can also be understood through the people factors and through an understanding of informal processes and structures. Environmental factors are either constants that do not change significantly during the reform process or they are the driver from which other gaps are manifest.

We do need to add two other resources, essential to organisational change and obvious from the cases, but not made explicit within the diagram. These will be included as:

- **O**ther resources: money and time.

In all, then, seven dimensions of conception–reality gap are presented here, summarised by the ITPOSMO acronym.

CONCEPTION–REALITY GAP ARCHETYPES

Conception–reality gaps can arise in any situation, but we shall highlight three archetypes that make information age reform failure more likely.

Rationality–reality gaps

The ideas behind rational models of organisations arise from a particular social and historical context which, among other things, believes that:

- science has an underpinning of logic and objectivity which gives it great validity;
- such 'scientific values' can be applied outside pure science to human systems, such as management and organisations;
- some desirable outcomes result from applying these values.

As already described in the DSS example, rational models assume that logic and objectivity underlie the workings of organisations.

Alternative behavioural and political models of organisations have subsequently been developed. They assume that factors such as self-interest, personal objectives and subjectivity underlie the workings of organisations, with processes of conflict, bargaining and compromise. These models are also more comfortable with the idea of informal information flows (see Box 3.1).

Despite the development of these behavioural and political models, many reform initiatives are still based on models of organisational rationality. This seems to be particularly true of information age initiatives, including a number of those described in this book. In part this may occur because of the continuing emphasis on IT within information age reform; an emphasis that is particularly apparent in the idolise approach. Technology is conceived by the average public sector stakeholder as an objective and rational entity, not as something that incorporates particular cultural and political values. Reform initiatives associated with that technology are therefore themselves likely to be conceived according to an objective and rational model.

Where an organisation conforms to the rational model, initiatives based on

Box 3.1   Formal and informal information flows

One consequence of the dominance of rationality in information age reform is that formal information is seen as much more important than informal information. In reality, however, this is not so.

Detailed studies show again and again that the real decision making processes of organisations – both formal *and* informal – rely extensively on informal information (Daft and Lengel 1986; Hastings 1996; Heckscher 1994). Research in UK public service organisations by Davies (1997), for example, demonstrates the importance of personal contacts, 'invisible colleges' and face-to-face meetings both in the normal operation of these organisations and during processes of reform.

Informal information is valued because, compared with formal information, it often:
- provides more background and explanatory detail;
- enables a fuller evaluation of the consequences of decision alternatives;
- is more timely;
- is easier to interrogate for further details;
- better serves personal objectives and interests.

Hence government's fascination with lobbying, backroom meetings, and focus groups, all of which produce informal information that feeds into decision making.

A gap thus often exists between the formal information conceptions of reform initiatives and the informal information realities of the public sector. This may serve to undermine either the reform initiatives or the vital role of informal information.

As knowledge management rises to the top of the management fad agenda, an equivalent gap is likely to emerge between the explicit knowledge-based conceptions of some reform initiatives and the tacit knowledge-based realities of much public sector activity (see, for example, *Government Computing* 1998b).

that model are likely to succeed. The problem is that such rationality is more often an ideal that does not exist in reality. In reality, many organisations seem to adhere more closely to behavioural and political models.

This gap – between the rational conceptions of reform initiatives and the behavioural/political realities of organisations – is likely to be greater in the public sector than in the private sector.

For example, in the private sector, there tends to be greater insecurity about jobs, units and even whole organisations. One element of self-interest – of preserving one's own job – therefore tends to be a more overt part of decision making, and this generally overlaps with the interests of organisational efficiency and effectiveness. Similarly, there tends to be a single, clear organisational objective (profit or market share or survival) guiding behaviour. Related to this, a focus on personal performance and a personal sense of the need to create added value within the organisation are often strong.

In the public sector, on the other hand:

- formal organisational objectives often relate to the objectives of a group (the public) which is not directly represented within the organisation, and these objectives are often less than clear. In such cases, it is less likely that personal objectives can be aligned with formal organisational objectives;
- loyalties may be greater to one's professional peer group than to one's organisation;
- there are a greater number of internal and external stakeholders, creating greater conflicts of interest;
- political conflict and compromise over resource allocation have come to be seen as activities inherent to the public sector and its power culture;
- job insecurities may be fewer;
- personal performance measurement and a sense of value added are often poorly developed.

Therefore, in the public sector, a strongly emphasised façade of organisational rationality often covers a seething mass of very different political realities.

The sum result is frequent and significant gaps between rational conceptions and political realities in information age reforms. The outcome – as observed – is frequent failure of such reforms. The US agency example described in Chapter 5 is a case in point. In this case a rationally conceived reform came unstuck because it mismatched reality on a number of the ITPOSMO dimensions. For instance, the presence and usage of formal information was less than anticipated; and staff motivations were driven as much by self-interest and 'internal politics' as by conceived models of formal organisational objectives.

Traditional strategic information systems planning is also flawed as an information age reform technique, as described in Chapter 14. It relies on a rational conception of organisational business objectives that are known, unitary and unproblematic. This is hardly ever the case in real public sector organisations. As a result, this technique fails far more often than it succeeds.

Information technology as a variable

Computer applications themselves differ in the extent to which they derive from approaches of organisational rationality or organisational reality. A continuum of application types can therefore be drawn up, as shown in Figure 3.2.

Figure 3.2 Continuum of computer applications

Rationality-imposing applications are developed from an organisationally rational perspective. They are information systems that incorporate a significant set of rational structures, processes and even culture and strategies for their operation. These rationalities could cover most of the rings in Figure 3.1.

Figure 3.3 provides an example of what might be required, although not all rationality-imposing applications will be the same. The shaded areas represent the rationality requirements of the decision support system described earlier. They must either be present in the organisation as a precondition for successful implementation of this application, or they must be imposed. Successful introduction of rationality-imposing applications may strongly support the reform process. The DSS, for instance, might well support

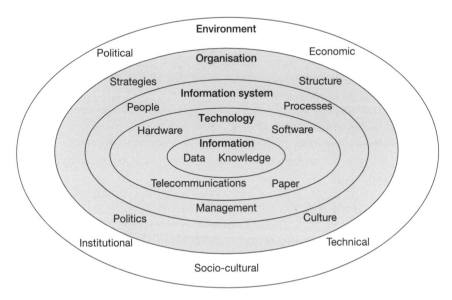

Figure 3.3 The rationalities required by a typical rationality-imposing application

more organisationally effective decision making. In many situations, though, the introduction will not succeed because of the large gap between the application's required rationalities and current organisational realities.

Reality-supporting applications are not developed from a strongly organisationally rational perspective. They are often information technologies more than information systems. In other words, they incorporate few 'hard' rationalities, covering only one or two rings in Figure 3.1 at most. Figure 3.4 provides an example drawn from the earlier example of word processing.

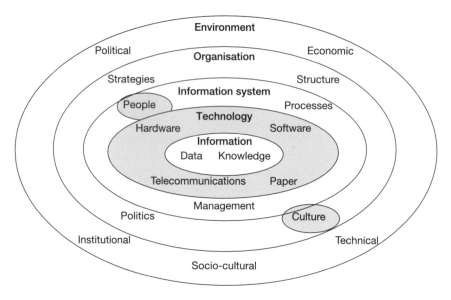

Figure 3.4 The rationalities required by a typical reality-supporting application

By comparison with rationality-imposing applications, reality-supporting applications require fewer rationalities to be met as pre-conditions or to be imposed. They can therefore work successfully in a wider variety of organisational environments. Reality-supporting applications like word processing may lead to relatively limited reform benefits, but will succeed in far more situations than the introduction of rationality-imposing applications.

Private–public gaps

A central theme of reform – particularly as inspired by the New Right – is that government could improve if only it would knuckle down and start behaving more like the private sector. Such ideas may be based on flawed understanding of the private sector:

> Those arguing for the introduction into the public sector of better – private sector – management practice often fail to address the mixed

record of private sector organizations on both IT and non-IT issues, and often fail to point to the considerable long-standing debate on how far private sector management practice needs to be improved.

(Willcocks 1994: 16)

The ideas may also be based on flawed understanding of the public sector: 'Government is not a business. Forcing government managers into private sector thinking usually causes more problems than it solves' (Goddard and Riback 1998; see also Osborne and Gaebler 1992: 20–22).

We have already alluded to certain differences that exist between the public and private sectors: the greater prevalence and possibly even greater legitimacy of 'politicking' in the public sector, and a greater dissonance between personal and organisational objectives. We can specifically relate this and other factors to information-related differences between the sectors (adapted and expanded from Pollitt and Harrison 1992; see also Bretschneider 1990).

Different objectives

Public sector objectives are typically broader than those of the private sector, encompassing social and political and economic factors rather than having a more narrow financial focus. As a result, the public sector works with a broader range of information than the private sector. Policy making, for example, is a thoroughly political process and requires qualitative, often informal, information about the political strengths and opinions of various individuals and groups. Public sector organisations (PSOs) therefore have to work with a broader range of institutions than private sector organisations.

Different accountability

Private sector organisations are accountable to their shareholders and, perhaps, to their customers and employees. Public sector organisations have a broader set of political and legal accountabilities. This means that information will flow between the PSO and other institutions such as the legislature, the public, the judiciary and other government ministries. There is an obligation to keep records of information for legal and other reporting purposes. Consequently, 'legal norms and political requirements make themselves felt during the building processes of IT systems and influence the systems from the outset.' (Willcocks 1994: 18). The environment of accountabilities is also unstable. Working within the framework of constant changes in legislation, policy initiatives, political parties and questions from politicians can create one-off and/or short-term information needs to which considerable resources have to be devoted.

Lack of competition

Public sector organisations rarely find themselves in direct competition with other organisations. They therefore have less need and desire for 'strategic information' than the private sector. This includes both short- and long-term information about competitors, customers and prices. Where PSOs do compete, it is with other PSOs for resources. This competition tends to take place in the political arena where qualitative, informal information is used. The lack of competition also creates a tolerance for two things which, though present, tend to be suppressed more in the private sector. First, as noted above, the promotion of personal rather than organisational objectives. This (yet again) requires information that is qualitative and informal. Second, an aversion to risk and to innovation. This aversion requires information on past practice, particularly on past decisions, from which public actors tend not to diverge.

Lack of production and sales

The majority of public sector organisations are service sector organisations and produce little, if anything, that is sold. As such, they have no use for information that forms the bedrock of much private sector functioning, such as information on sales, marketing, production, accounts receivable and so forth. It is also more difficult for PSOs to identify clear organisational outputs, let alone outcomes. Information on outputs provides clear performance signals for the private sector and helps to guide many of the decisions and activities of private firms. Such guidance information is harder to produce in a PSO.

A view of the 'whole person'

Private sector organisations tend to understand their customers merely in terms of what those customers buy. By contrast, the public sector as a whole holds and uses information on virtually every aspect of people's lives: their location, health, education, finances, criminal record, children, business activities, etc.

Other

Public sector IS projects are often larger and more complex on average than those in the private sector. See Box 4.2 in the next chapter for further details.

Given all these differences, information systems or techniques developed for private sector use can easily be based on conceptions that do not match public sector realities. Information age reforms that rely on these systems or techniques will be more prone to failure. Examples appear later in the book:

- Chapter 14 notes the private sector roots of strategic information systems planning (SISP). SISP is based on conceptions of unitary organisational objectives, apolitical decision making and the presence of skilled support for implementation that do not apply in many public sector organisations. This conception–reality mismatch makes SISP risky and/or impractical in the public sector.
- Chapter 15 notes the private sector roots of business process reengineering (BPR) and its rational basis. It then analyses the problems created in trying to transfer BPR to a public sector where many organisations have a reality of informal groupings, power games and self-interested behaviours.
- Chapter 16 argues for the transferability of particular performance measurement techniques from private to public sector, on the grounds of their flexibility and few preconceptions. Even here, though, a number of limitations are noted in the applicability in one sector of techniques developed in the other.

Such problems – and the attendant likelihood of failure – are likely to increase if/as the private-sector oriented reform agenda of the New Right takes hold.

Country context gaps

Information systems or techniques developed in the context of a particular country will incorporate common assumptions of that context. This can cause problems in the transfer of information age reforms between industrialised countries. For example, a patient information system was developed in the US to support improved health resource management. When similar reforms based around this IS were introduced in the UK, they ran into difficulties. British nurses found it hard to use the new information system because of the US-inspired assumptions it made about the planning and costing of patient care (Westrup 1998).

Even greater can be the problems of transfer from an industrialised to a developing country (DC). Such countries stereotypically differ in many ways, including those identified in the ITPOSMO model (adapted from Bhatnagar 1990):

- *Information*: formal, quantitative information stored outside the human mind is valued less in developing countries. Thus, for example, industrialised country assumptions about the perceived value of a computerised information system may not match DC realities.
- *Technology*: the technological infrastructure (telecommunications, networks, electricity, etc.) is more limited and/or older in DCs, as illustrated in Chapter 2. Thus, for example, industrialised country assumptions about availability of Internet connections to support inter-agency information flows may not match DC realities.

- *Processes*: public sector work processes are more contingent in developing countries because of the more politicised and inconstant environment. Thus, for example, industrialised country assumptions about the viability of automating an overt, stable set of processes may not match DC realities.
- *Objectives and values*: developing countries are reportedly more likely to have cultures that value kin loyalty, authority, holism, secrecy and risk aversion (Haque 1996; Ojo 1992; van Ryckeghem 1996). Thus, for example, industrialised country assumptions about the value of a leading-edge IS that will help public managers share information may not match DC realities.
- *Staffing and skills*: developing countries have a more limited local skills base in a wide range of skills. This includes IS/IT skills of systems analysis and design, implementation skills and operation-related skills including computer literacy and familiarity with the Western languages that dominate computing. It also includes a set of broader reform skills covering the planning, implementation and management of reform initiatives. Thus, for example, industrialised country assumptions about the presence of skills necessary to assess the feasibility of kiosk-based service delivery may not match DC realities.
- *Management and structures*: developing country organisations are more hierarchical and more centralised. Thus, for example, industrialised country assumptions about the acceptability of reforms that disperse information and power may not match DC realities.
- *Other resources*: developing countries have less money. In addition, the cost of IT is higher than in industrialised countries whereas the cost of labour is less. Thus, for example, industrialised country assumptions about the financial benefits of efficiency reforms which replace clerical staff with an automated system may not match DC realities.

Of course, these are stereotypes, and many cases can be found in which they are reversed. Nor is the Third World some computer-free wasteland. Countries like Iran, India and Morocco introduced computers into public service in the mid-1950s and have expanded their use of IT continuously ever since. Developing countries are producers as well as users of IT, exporting some US$3 billion-worth of software in 1998, from locations as diverse as Chile, Barbados, Egypt, South Africa, India and China (Heeks 1998b). Vast gulfs also exist within industrialised countries: compare Beverly Hills with South Central in Los Angeles for instance.

None the less, there is a major problem with the 'If it works for us, it'll work for you' mentality being peddled round the Third World by IT multinationals, international consultants and aid donor agencies. Transferring ideas from one context to another can save waste by stopping the recipient from 'reinventing the wheel'. But – to continue the analogy – this approach fails when the recipient needs a motorcycle wheel and is instead offered one from an American train.

Chapter 12 provides the salient example of an IT strategy prepared for Barbados by British consultants. The strategy was of questionable worth because it incorporated Western conceptions of electronic government, cultural values and the business environment that did not match Barbadian realities. The IS difficulties reported in Chapter 6 are also, to some degree, the result of trying to impose Western-conceived systems in an African environment.

SUMMARY AND CONCLUSIONS

Information age reform succeeds or fails – it is argued here – dependent on the degree of mismatch between the conceptions of that reform and the realities into which it is introduced. We can assess that mismatch along seven main dimensions, described above in the ITPOSMO model. Given that failure is naturally of more concern than success, and given that information age reform fails more often than it succeeds, three archetypal conception–reality failures were presented which may occur:

- when reforms, systems and techniques derived from rational models of organisation meet a political reality;
- when reforms, systems and techniques derived from the private sector are transferred to the public sector;
- when reforms, systems and techniques derived from one country are transferred to another country.

Having provided an explanation for failure within information age reform, the obvious question is: 'OK, so what do we do about it?' A few general points will be made here.

With reference to the first archetype, information age reforms based on the realities of public sector organisations, rather than on some theoretical model of rationality, seem more likely to bring success. Public managers would do better to open their eyes and ears to their immediate surroundings rather than burying their noses in MBA textbooks in seeking guidance on reform. Similarly, reforms based around reality-supporting applications will succeed more often than those based around rationality-imposing applications.

With reference to the other archetypes, the public sector has been criticised in the past for the costly, often unsuccessful, development of unique IT applications. It has been advised to make greater use of off-the-shelf packaged solutions. Yet this pendulum swing clearly must not go too far. One general message from the archetypes is that whole governments, public sector organisations and even individual public servants must learn to recognise, express and have satisfied their unique requirements. 'Customised' must therefore take precedence over 'ready made'. Adaptive and participatory approaches must therefore take precedence over mechanistic and control-oriented approaches. In many cases, this will require both national and public sector-specific IS development capacities to be strengthened.

Overall, the role – even the nomenclature – of public sector IT professionals must also be scrutinised. The analysis of Chapter 2 suggested that, instead of IT professionals, there was a greater need for staff who are IS professionals, or even hybrids who combine IS and IT skills with an understanding of public sector management. From this chapter, too, we see that a focus on technology is too narrow and that information age reform must be seen as a multidimensional process of change.

Professionals must therefore see themselves more as change agents (Markus and Benjamin 1996). They may become facilitators by increasing the capacity of others to change, or they may become advocates who take responsibility for implementing change along the identified dimensions. In either case, their technology skills will be complemented by those of change management and of communication, negotiation and advocacy. To support this, there must be a change of organisational structures and management processes away from the old 'central IT unit' model.

These responses to the question posed above are fairly general. However, the question can also be answered in much more detailed and specific ways. This forms the focus of Chapter 4.

REFERENCES

Bellamy, C. and Taylor, J.A. (1998) *Governing in the Information Age*, Buckingham: Open University Press.

Bhatnagar, S.C. (1990) 'Computers in developing countries', in S.C. Bhatnagar and N. Bjorn-Andersen (eds) *Information Technology in Developing Countries*, Amsterdam: Elsevier Science.

Bostrom, R. and Heinen, S. (1977) 'MIS problems and failures: a socio-technical perspective', *MIS Quarterly* 1, 3: 17–32.

Braa, J. (1996) 'Decentralisation, primary health care and information technology in developing countries: case studies from Mongolia and South Africa', in M. Odedra-Straub (ed.) *Global Information Technology and Socio-economic Development*, Nashua, NH: Ivy League Publishing.

Bretschneider, S. (1990) 'Management information systems in public and private organizations: an empirical test', *Public Administration Review* 50, September/October: 536–545.

Brodman, J.Z. (1987) 'Key management factors in determining the impact of micro-computers on decision-making in the governments of developing countries', in S.R. Ruth and C.K. Mann (eds) *Microcomputers in Public Policy: Applications for Developing Countries*, Boulder, CO: Westview Press.

Cooney, M.J. and O'Flaherty, B. (1996) 'Structural change via information technology in the Irish civil service', in M. Odedra-Straub (ed.) *Global Information*

Technology and Socio-economic Development, Nashua, NH: Ivy League Publishing.

Daft, R.L. and Lengel, R.H. (1986) 'Organizational information requirements, media richness and structural design', *Management Science* 32, 5: 554–571.

Davies, C.A. (1997) 'The information infrastructure approach for developing countries', paper presented at conference on 'Public Sector Management in the Next Century', 29 June–2 July, University of Manchester, Manchester.

General Accounting Office (1994) *Improving Mission Performance Through Strategic Information Management and Technology*, Washington, DC: General Accounting Office.

Goddard, T.D. and Riback, C. (1998) 'The eight traits of highly successful public officials', *The Hill* 6 May.

Government Computing (1998a) 'Manual work', 12, 4: 23.

Government Computing (1998b) 'Knowledge management in the public sector', special supplement, 12, 7.

Haque, M.S. (1996) 'The contextless nature of public administration in Third World countries', *International Review of Administrative Sciences* 62, 3: 315–329.

Hastings, C. (1996) *The New Organization*, London: McGraw-Hill.

Heckscher, C. (1994) 'Defining the post-bureaucratic type', in C. Heckscher and A. Donnellon (eds) *The Post-bureaucratic Organization*, Thousand Oaks, CA: Sage.

Heeks, R.B. (1998a) *Management Information and Management Information Systems*, London: School of Oriental and African Studies, University of London.

Heeks, R.B. (1998b) 'Flying software: is the information society heading South?', *Insights*, 25: 3.

Hirschheim, R. and Klein, H.K. (1989) 'Four paradigms of information systems development', *Communications of the ACM* 32, 10: 1199–1215.

Horejs, I. (1996) 'IT in rural development planning: the case of Nicaragua', in E. Roche and M. Blaine (eds) *Information Technology, Development and Policy*, Aldershot, Hants: Avebury.

Ingelstam, L. and Palmlund, I. (1991) 'Computers and people in the welfare state: information technology and social security in Sweden', *Informatization and the Public Sector* 1, 1: 5–20.

James, G. (1997) 'IT fiascoes . . . and how to avoid them', *Datamation* November. http://www.datamation.com/PlugIn/issues/1997/november/11disas.html

King, J.L. and Kraemer, K.L. (1991) 'Patterns of success in municipal information systems: lessons from US experience', *Informatization and the Public Sector* 1, 1: 21–39.

King, R.T. (1994) 'California's DMV computer overhaul ends up as costly ride to junk heap', *Wall Street Journal* 17 April: B5.

Korac-Boisvert, N. and Kouzmin, A. (1995) 'Transcending soft-core IT disasters in public sector organizations', *Information Infrastructure and Policy* 4, 2: 131–161.

Laudon, K.C. and Laudon, J.P. (1998) *Management Information Systems*, 5th edn, Upper Saddle River, NJ: Prentice-Hall.

McLellan, P.M. (1996) 'Electronic commerce: serving the business community', paper presented at conference on 'Electronic Government in the Information Society', 6–10 October, Budapest, Hungary.

Markus, M.L. and Benjamin, R.I. (1996) 'Change agentry – the next frontier', *MIS Quarterly* 20, 4: 385–407.

Milner, E. (1997) 'Uncertain growth after Labor's pains', *Government Computing* 11, 10: 24–25.

Moreton, R. and Chester, M. (1997) *Transforming the Business: The IT Contribution*, London: McGraw-Hill.

Moussa, A. and Schware, R. (1992) 'Informatics in Africa: lessons from World Bank experience', *World Development* 20, 12: 1737–1752.

Newcombe, T. (1998) 'Big project woes halt child support system', *Government Technology* February.

http://www.govtech.net/gtmag/1998/feb/

O'Higgins, M. (1998) 'Information, performance and better government', paper presented at 'Government Computing 98' conference, 17–18 June, London.

Ojo, S.O. (1992) 'Socio-cultural and organisational issues in IT applications in Nigeria', in S.C. Bhatnagar and M. Odedra (eds) *Social Implications of Computers in Developing Countries*, New Delhi: Tata McGraw-Hill.

Osborne, D. and Gaebler, T. (1992) *Reinventing Government: How the Entrepreneurial Spirit is Transforming the Public Sector*, Reading, MA: Addison-Wesley.

Pollitt, C. and Harrison, S. (1992) 'Introduction', in C. Pollitt and S. Harrison (eds) *Handbook of Public Services Management*, Oxford: Blackwell.

Poulos, C. (1998) 'IndyGov.org paves the road to an electronic city hall', *Government Technology* May.

http://www.govtech.net/gtmag/1998/may/

Power, K. (1996) 'Australian agency breaks new ground', *International Software Magazine* February.

Ramasoota, P. (1998) 'Information technology and bureaucratic surveillance: a case study of the Population Information Network (PIN) in Thailand', *Information Technology for Development* 8, 1: 51–64.

Singh, A. (1990) 'Computerisation of the Indian Income Tax Department', *Information Technology for Development* 5, 3: 235–251.

van Ryckeghem, D. (1996) 'Computers and culture: cases from Kenya', in E.M. Roche and M.J. Blaine (eds) *Information Technology, Development and Policy*, Aldershot, Hants.: Avebury.

Vidigal, L. (1997) 'A single window for citizenship in Portugal', *Electronic Government International* 2, 16: 5–6.

Westrup, C. (1998) 'What's in information technology', paper presented at conference on 'Implementation and Evaluation of Information Systems in Developing Countries', 18–20 February, Bangkok, Thailand.

Willcocks, L. (1994) 'Managing information systems in UK public administration: issues and prospects', *Public Administration* 72, Spring: 13–32.

ACKNOWLEDGEMENTS

The Public Policy and Management programme of the School of Oriental and African Studies, University of London, and the University of Manchester are acknowledged for the support they have provided during the development of ideas expounded in this chapter.

4 Better information age reform

Reducing the risk of information systems failure

Richard Heeks

Abstract: This chapter looks at practical implications of the ITPOSMO model of conception–reality gaps developed in Chapter 3. If large conception–reality gaps promote reform failure, then techniques to close those gaps should increase the success of information age reform initiatives. This chapter therefore focuses on various 'gap-closing' techniques drawn from international best practice in government. In particular, it describes ways to address finance gaps, including outsourcing; ways to address skills gaps, including use of consultants; and ways to address gaps of stakeholder objectives and motivations, including reward and punishment, communication, participation, consensus formation, prototyping and end-user development. It also describes ways in which reform success rates may be improved by freezing or part-freezing some of the ITPOSMO dimensions. The chapter concludes, however, with a reminder that the applicability of such techniques will be constrained by factors such as organisational context and managers' personal room for manoeuvre. As such, there is no panacea for information age reform.

BACKGROUND

From previous chapters, we have seen that failure is common in information age reform. Chapter 3 offered a model suggesting that failure is more likely to occur when there is a large gap between current realities and the conceptions inherent within any proposed reform initiative. The present chapter picks up this issue and analyses its practical implications for those who are trying to introduce information age reform.

We have seen that new information systems (IS) are central to government reinvention in the information age. This suggests that if the risks of IS failure can be reduced, the chances of success in reinventing government will be increased. This chapter therefore focuses mainly on conception–reality gaps relating to reform information systems rather than those relating to broader aspects of reform. It describes a variety of different techniques for closing the conception–reality gap and therefore reducing the risk of IS and reform failure.

These are all brand new techniques that will guarantee a perfect information system every time. Ah, if only this were true, but alas it is not. Such statements are fit for the bright, clean world of washing powder adverts, not the murky, messy world of information systems and public sector reform.

In practice, readers may already be familiar with some or all of the techniques described, and public sector managers are regularly admonished for their failure to follow such techniques. In many cases, their failure to do so may be put down to ignorance and lack of training. In other cases, though, managers are well aware of what they are supposed to do. Their failure arises not from ignorance but from the gap between the assumed rationality of the techniques and the practical realities in which managers find themselves working. Thus information systems and their related reforms continue to fail in spite of the presence of such techniques.

All this should act as a warning that the contents of this chapter may be of value to certain public organisations in certain contexts, but may not all be applicable and cannot guarantee perfect results.

The conception–reality gap

There is no straightforward method for analysing the gap between current reality and the conceptions assumed within a proposed new information system. One approach – arising from Checkland's Soft Systems Methodology (Checkland 1981; see also Chapter 14) – is to undertake (a) analysis of current reality and (b) design of the new information system. In the case of both analysis and design, the seven ITPOSMO dimensions of change outlined in Chapter 3 can be incorporated: information; technology; processes; objectives, values and motivations; staffing and skills; management and structures; and other (financial/time) resources. Design can be used to expose inherent conceptions, so comparing reality and the design proposal along these dimensions will give an idea of the extent of change gaps (see Figure 4.1).

There are no hard and fast rules that say 'this gap is OK' or 'this gap is too large'. Any assessment of gaps – and, hence, of project risk – must therefore be subjective and based on opinion and experience. If this subjectivity is accepted, then rating scales can be used. For example, stakeholders can be asked to rate each of the seven ITPOSMO dimensions from 0 for 'no change between current reality and design proposal' to 10 for 'complete and radical change'. Such analyses can be built into the process of reform project management as part of regular project review.

Soft systems methods often advocate recognition of gaps as potential

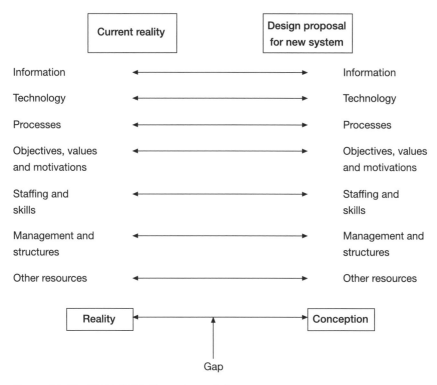

Figure 4.1 The ITPOSMO dimensions of change

changes, which can then be discussed in participative fora to identify those which are desirable and feasible. Where gaps are identified as both desirable and feasible changes by participative groups, it may well be that they will be successfully implemented.

In tandem, however, it will be valuable to make use of techniques which either (a) prevent large gaps arising in the first place, or (b) reduce those gaps once they have been identified. In the latter case, there are two main ways in which a gap between reality and proposal can be reduced:

- change the proposal to make it closer to reality; for example, by making the design simpler and thereby reducing financial costs;
- change current reality to make it closer to the proposal; for example, by seeking support from a central government fund and thereby increasing the supply of available finance.

A sample of techniques to accomplish gap prevention or gap reduction is presented in more detail below. This is not a comprehensive review of all dimensions, but an indication of some ways in which public sector organisations (PSOs) currently try to improve the success rate of information age reform initiatives.

One point, though, should be repeated from Chapter 3. As noted there, systems that require a greater reality–proposal gap – i.e. a greater degree of change – may bring greater organisational benefits (although there is no necessary link between size of change and size of benefits). In some cases, therefore, a trade-off is being made: reducing the size of the reality–proposal gap may increase the chance of system success but also reduce the organisational benefits of that system. Certain public officials might balk at this and be inclined to adopt a 'high risk, high gain' strategy instead.

ADDRESSING THE FINANCE GAP

If it is to be sustainable, the lifetime costs of the reform information system must be less than or equal to the financial resources available. If this is initially not so, there are two ways to address the finance gap.

Changing financial realities

Changing the reality of the finance available is not easy. More internal finance can be turned to information systems if senior managers can be persuaded, but such sources tend to be relatively constrained. So, too, does the practice of selling public information in order to raise funds: this often runs into a minefield of both privacy and legal issues. A longer-term approach focuses information systems development on revenue maximisation. In Massachusetts state government, for example, investments were made in a new state-wide billing and accounts receivable system (Harris 1997). Among other things, this stopped the government paying someone who owed it money. In all, US$10–20 million extra receivables were generated *every* year as a result. It is hoped this will release additional funds for investment in information age reform projects.

External finance from central government or international agency initiatives is hard to control and sometimes comes and goes in cycles of 'feast and famine' that make it difficult to plan sustainable information systems. Nevertheless, centralised funds to support electronic government initiatives exist in an increasing number of countries and regions, as described in Chapter 2.

Where regulations allow, some public sector organisations are turning to private sector sources of finance. Some PSOs, for example, can take out loans from private finance institutions, which can be used to fund information systems. In other cases, private companies develop, own and operate the PSO's new information system and are paid an annual fee over an agreed period for this service only if the service meets agreed criteria. This, for instance, has been one component of California's Performance-based Procurement and of the UK's Private Finance Initiative, which had nearly

£3 billion (about US$5 billion) of reform projects under consideration in 1998 (POST 1998). Such arrangements tend to work particularly well if the new IS provides clear cost savings that can be funnelled into payments or – less typically for the public sector – if it provides some income generation. Such arrangements, of course, only work if the private sector is willing and able to bear the financial risks of public sector information technology (IT) projects.

Finance can also be raised from the private sector by charging business users of electronic government services. The Information Network of Kansas is an example. It is a Web site run by the Kansas state government that includes a facility for electronic filing of government forms. Private businesses pay an annual subscription for this service, providing a cross-subsidy for the citizen information that is also carried on the site (Mechling and Sweeney 1997).

Changing financial designs

Overall, changing reality by increasing the finance available is harder than changing the proposed design by 'cutting your coat according to your cloth'; that is, by reducing the costs of the new information system until they meet available resources. This would typically involve scaling down the ambitions of the new information system by, for example, postponing the achievement of some objectives. However, there are alternatives.

Government's bargaining power and scale economies are often used to drive down costs by purchasing for groups of public sector organisations. The US General Services Administration and the UK's CCTA/Government Centre for Information Systems both make use of this approach, essentially providing public agencies with a shopping list of discounted items via central framework agreements. Such agreements typically cover hardware items, although the range is increasing. In smaller countries, such as Cyprus, Israel and Portugal, government-wide software licenses (including training and support) have been negotiated with leading vendors. In the UK, Denmark and some other countries, agreements are being extended into the provision of IT services.

The old cost reduction model – often disliked by PSOs – was compulsory centralised control of all or many IT purchases. This still exists to some extent in countries such as Australia, Hungary, Malta and South Korea, where up to 80 per cent of government IT purchases are made via the central body (ICA 1998). However, it has now been widely replaced by an 'opt in' model that means PSOs use these channels only if they wish.

A related mechanism is the 'one for all' contract, where a contract negotiated by one public agency or ministry is used by other public sector organisations, rather than starting from scratch with a vendor. Not only does this save on administrative costs, it also helps close time gaps by speeding the process of procurement. Cyprus, Israel, Norway and the United States are all active users of these contracts, while the Australian government has made them mandatory (ICA 1998).

Inter-agency collaborations can go further than sharing contracts. Neighbours, from the level of countries down to the smallest units of local government, can work together and save money on infrastructural projects, on bulk purchase of consumables, on shared data centres, on common information systems, etc. Major finance savings have been achieved from just such a collaboration between Los Angeles City, Los Angeles County and geographically associated public agencies for transport and education (Hanson 1998).

Costs can be reduced in more innovative ways by acting in concert with the private sector. For example, in Texas, the state government collaborated with a private sector utility company to convert the latter's digitised address database into the basis for a geographic information system (GIS). Both government and company shared the resulting data and both saved costs in creation of their GIS base (McGarigle 1998). Costs were also saved on this project through the collaboration of various public agencies, all of whom made use of the GIS, thus reaping scale economies for government.

Vendors may occasionally donate equipment to the public sector if close personal relationships are involved or if there is a payoff from good publicity or goodwill generated. In Taiwan, IT firms have covered the costs of five public access sites located in government buildings, each with several dozen computers (McDonough 1997). Vendors may also agree to develop an information system at low cost as a 'loss leader' if it is a leading-edge application that can then be sold to other public sector sites.

Finally, use of project management techniques may help avoid project overruns and other wasteful uses of resources, thus reducing unnecessary expenditure. At the very least, using such techniques is likely to result in more accurate analysis of system development costs. Because of this, the Singapore government targeted the development of pervasive IS project management capability as part of its government-wide reform strategy (Cheong and Koh 1991). Other governments have developed their own generic approaches to project management. The UK's CCTA, for example, developed the PRINCE (Projects In Controlled Environments) and subsequently PRINCE 2 methodologies to encourage best practice in the public sector.

Outsourcing

Outsourcing is the use of an external organisation to provide a service that might otherwise be provided in-house. As such, outsourcing can cover a wide variety of information systems activities, including:

- analysis and design, e.g. feasibility study or process redesign;
- construction, e.g. procurement advice or programming;
- implementation, e.g. training or data conversion;
- operation, e.g. running the computer system or providing maintenance.

It can also include ownership of the IT facilities used to run public sector information systems.

One of the main intentions behind IS outsourcing by public sector organisations is to cut costs and thereby achieve more within existing financial constraints. In other words, it may be an attempt to close the gap between the current reality of finance and the proposed requirement for finance. For example, one UK local authority outsourced its data centre, telecommunications and office systems support services during the 1990s, achieving cost savings of between 17 and 22 per cent (Willcocks *et al.* 1997).

Outsourcing may also provide access to skills and ideas that are not available in-house and so help to fill skill or time gaps. Other perceived benefits of outsourcing include:

- the provision of a higher quality of service;
- greater certainty about costs;
- greater flexibility, especially of labour since it is easier to 'hire and fire' external staff;
- greater ability to focus management on the core business of the public sector.

Of course, if these benefits are to be realised, one precondition must be the presence of sub-contractors who are willing and able to take on outsourcing contracts. As described in Chapter 12, this is not always the case.

Even if outsourcing can proceed, benefits do not come automatically: the relationship with the sub-contractor must be well planned and well managed. Yet, sometimes, outsourcing proceeds without sufficient in-house project management and contracting skills to coordinate and continuously monitor the outsourcing process. Even if these skills are present, evidence of cost savings compared to use of in-house staff is not always found. The costs of managing the relationship are often higher than expected and there can be other problems:

- a clash of work cultures and understanding between the public sector client and the private sector sub-contractor;
- a loss of control over the service being provided, with the sub-contractor starting to dictate to a dependent client;
- a loss of core information system competencies to the sub-contractor.

In Canada, there have been concerns that outsourcing and related initiatives such as privatisation present 'a potential challenge to common services delivery and the critical masses that can help build efficient common IM[information management]/IT infrastructure' (McLellan *et al.* 1996: 4). Similarly, Barbados's experience with outsourcing – described in Chapter 12 – has been less than positive.

However, whilst the rhetoric and dogma of outsourcing may be receding slightly from their high-water mark in some governments, overall outsourcing seems set to increase. In the UK, for example, central government had out-sourced over £1.09 billion-worth (about US$1.8 billion) of IT activities up to 1994, including a transfer of 24,000 staff to the private sector (McNevin 1994). Yet, in that same year, a single ten-year outsourcing contract – from the Inland Revenue to computer services firm EDS – was valued at £1 billion (about US$1.65 billion) (POST 1998). A survey in 1997 therefore found that over 80 per cent of IT directors in central government had outsourced at least some of their IT services, with outsourcing growing by 11 per cent per year (Martin 1997). An average 41 per cent of the IT budget was committed to outsourcing (twice the private sector average), with systems support and systems development the two main outsourced services.

Other countries are also increasing outsourcing:

> Australia is examining the viability of outsourcing all of its mainframe, network and desktop facilities. . . . Israel is implementing a policy to outsource almost all the IT services in the government. . . . The United States government has a policy to outsource all but the very largest computer facilities.
>
> (ICA 1998: 8)

Rationality requires that outsourcing should only proceed if the following three conditions are satisfied:

- outsourcing total costs are lower than the in-house option;
- outsourcing total costs are lower than hiring new staff or training existing ones to cover any missing skills;
- there are no problems associated with information systems confidentiality.

In practice, the growth of outsourcing has often been more in tune with behavioural/political explanations. Managers are found who outsource because they:

- have been naïve in their assumptions about the benefits that will ensue;
- believe association with such an initiative will be good for their careers;
- wish to 'clip the wings' of the in-house IT unit;
- stand to gain financially thanks to the covert generosity of the sub-contractor.

Public sector outsourcing has also grown because of legislative requirements in some countries, such as the UK during the early 1990s (which helps explain the 41 per cent figure above).

Whatever the rationale behind outsourcing, a sub-contractor must be chosen following the outsourcing decision. Sub-contractors are typically selected on criteria such as:

- cost;
- reputation;
- past experience and past client satisfaction ratings;
- level of service quality provided;
- informal relationship with PSO staff;
- lack of alternative options.

However, the key to a good outsourcing experience and to closure of finance and skills gaps, beyond all other factors, is a good working relationship between in-house clients and the sub-contractor. Contracts are important, but a good working relationship will overcome a bad contract far more often than a good contract will overcome a bad working relationship. Team-building and trust-forming activities between client and contractor – from social events to outdoor management activities – are therefore as important as a sharp in-house lawyer.

Such activities may not themselves be sufficient to close gaps between sub-contractor staff conceptions and public sector realities. The UK government has recognised this and the problems that contractors have understanding government's business. It therefore devised the Adapt98 project (Pollett 1998). Under Adapt98, contractors provide a staff team free of charge for up to 12 months. This team's sole objective is to shadow the work of public servants and get to understand public sector realities. Their hope is to be awarded outsourcing contracts at the end of the year.

This is but one example of a more general trend towards partnership rather than distance in outsourcing, although this is a delicate path to tread to ensure that competition and openness are maintained. There is a similar trend towards negotiation of longer-term outsourcing contracts. The French government, for example, found three-year contracts simply too short to create any kind of viable partnership arrangement between client and sub-contractor.

Gaps can also be closed if an in-house team is allowed to bid for contracts. Indeed, part of the logic for some public sector outsourcing initiatives has been to act as a stick to encourage restructuring of internal IT services. With the threat of outsourcing looming, IT staff at the UK's Contributions Agency radically overhauled their structures, management methods and working practices (Yazel 1993). As a result, they beat off competition from IT industry sub-contractors in order to win a £12 million (US$20 million) systems operation contract.

However, this threat must be carefully managed. In-house staff continue to fear job losses when outsourcing is mooted. Long-term statistics from the US show that 94 per cent of affected government staff are placed in alternative government jobs or transfer to the contractor or retire (NCC 1993).

Nevertheless, some governments – as in the UK – have put 'no redundancy' agreements alongside outsourcing initiatives and 'transfer of undertakings' legislation that ensures maintenance of public sector pay and conditions for staff transferring to the contractor. Such moves help ensure that outsourcing successfully closes finance and skills gaps.

ADDRESSING THE SKILLS GAP

The development of any new information system is likely to require new skills, thus creating a gap between the skills staff currently hold and those they need. In fact, as described in more detail in Chapter 13, gaps may exist in three domains: knowledge, skills and attitudes.

Examples of training aimed at closing the skills and knowledge gaps are fairly straightforward, covering mainly project management, change management, IS and IT issues. More sophisticated training would aim to develop the hybrid manager skills and knowledge described in earlier chapters.

Training to change attitudes is less widely used, more varied and harder to implement successfully. Examples might include:

- *case study analyses* of information systems failure and/or best practice; these might persuade stakeholders of the dangers of ignoring basic systems development practice, or of the importance of understanding the organisational and human context of information systems;
- *role-play exercises* to highlight the gap between users and IT staff; these might convince staff of the need to improve communications and build consensus;
- *group-forming activities* for key stakeholders; these might build a sense of unity to assist the formation of consensus on major reform issues;
- *demonstrations* of functioning information systems to highlight system benefits; these might persuade users to become involved in systems development when they would otherwise be reluctant.

However, closure of any of these gaps through training will be greatly undermined if those trained leave the organisation. IT staff turnover rates from the public sector are generally seen as high because it is felt that pay and conditions cannot compete with those of the private sector. This is not always so. Turnover of insourced government IT staff in the US is estimated to be around 10 per cent per annum (Barth 1998). This is much the same as that for the private sector and, in some cases, is actually lower. For example, private sector turnover rates for IT staff in Europe rose from 8 per cent in 1997 to 19 per cent in 1998 (Lambeth 1998).

However, in other situations, staff turnover can rise to haemorrhage levels. US state government IT turnover is much higher than that of federal or local government (Barth 1998). In Canada, many staff left during the successive budget cuts of the late 1980s and 1990s because 'Many government workers in the IM/IT field see a better opportunity outside government' (McLellan 1996: 6). Two Kenyan ministries trained 62 staff to Masters level in IT over a seven-year period (Peterson 1990): at the end of the period, only two of the 62 were still with their original ministry.

The result of this level of skills losses is a substantial skills gap in the public sector, leading to information system delays and failures. Contextual factors clearly have a role to play in sustaining this problem. Nevertheless, there is a wide range of actions that can be taken by government to address recruitment and retention, many of which are discussed in Chapter 17.

Use of consultants

Public sector organisations frequently use external consultants to close the gap between available and required skills. The hiring of consultants is a form of temporary outsourcing, mainly associated with particular stages of the systems development lifecycle: analysis, design, technology acquisition, training and evaluation.

Consulting may be temporary and is now seen as the 'poor cousin' of outsourcing, but it is still big business. In the UK, central government is the second largest consumer of IT consulting services behind banking, spending around £200 million (US$330 million) in 1996 – nearly 8 per cent of total IT budget (*Computing* 1997).

Potential benefits of consultants

The potential benefits of using consultants include their provision of:

- *missing skills* A gap can arise either because in-house staff lack necessary skills or because they have the skills but are busy on other assignments. Consultants can therefore fill skill and/or time gaps;
- *new ideas and experience* Consultants may have past experience of similar situations that in-house staff lack. They may therefore fill a knowledge gap. This can allow them to introduce, for example, design proposals that others had not thought of;
- *an external viewpoint* Where insiders may not be able 'to see the wood for the trees', an external consultant may perceive the root causes of problems or the possibility for a new approach. Consultants may also be able to rise above the internal politics of the organisation and propose, say, tough or unpopular options that an insider never could. (This, however, may fail more often than it succeeds as an outcome);
- *access to external funds* Some external funders insist on the presence of a consultant as a prerequisite for release of funds for system development and technology acquisition, thus closing finance gaps;

- *staff motivation* In-house staff may feel that issues are being taken seriously if an outsider has been brought in to listen and take action;
- *a convenient scapegoat* If the outcome of systems development is failure, organisational staff find it much easier to blame the consultant than themselves.

Potential disadvantages of consultants

The potential disadvantages of using consultants include:

- *financial cost* The difference between the cost of in-house staff and the cost of external consultants may not be as great as it first appears if overheads and productivity are taken into account. Nevertheless, consultancy almost always costs a great deal of money, as noted in the UK example cited above, and may therefore increase the finance gap;
- *lack of objectivity* The first rule of consultancy is: 'find out who is in charge, find out what they want, then do it or recommend it in your report'. Consultants may therefore fail to rise above internal politics, but merely align themselves with one stakeholder group's objectives. A possible example of this is provided by the Barbados case study analysed in Chapter 12, when the consultants' report closely matched the interests of the country's IT Minister. Consultants may also have links with particular suppliers or have a familiarity with one type of information system solution, leading their recommendations or actions to have an in-built bias;
- *failure to understand organisational realities* Consultants frequently work on short-term assignments. During this time it is difficult for them to understand the realities of the organisation that are critical to systems development: not just hard information and technical realities but also the soft political and cultural realities. Many consultants do not even look for soft realities because their role is frequently defined – normally implicitly – as being 'the voice of rationality'. Those who do search for soft realities may find staff unwilling to confide in them. Short timescales lead consultants to recommend or try to develop their 'standard solution' regardless of its applicability: sometimes a solution picked up from private sector practice applied to the public sector. Their solution may therefore diverge so far from current realities that it is rejected as patently unworkable or, worse, may lead to an implemented system which fails wholly or partially. Chapter 12's case study may also be seen to exemplify some of these problems;
- *lack of sustainability* Consultancy can fail sustainability in two ways. Some consultancies are one-off and fail to provide the long-term support a project needs. Others may be continuous and create a dependency on the consultants who obtain 'revolving door' contracts. A government agency in Kenya, for instance, was continuing to rely on consultants to

sustain its information system seven years after the first contract for the system was issued (Odedra 1992). In the UK, too, there has been a rise in the number of contractors taken on for short-term assignments with attendant dangers of 'a self-perpetuating trend in staffing, where reduction in permanent staff leads to more contractors coming in, leading to a dilution of skills in the permanent work force, which in turn requires more contractors, and so on' (Martin 1997: 9). In either case, the failure is that of not transferring skills and ownership to in-house staff. Systems introduced in this way in some countries have been abandoned immediately the consultants leave or once the first problem arises;

- *demotivation of staff* Consultants are not superhuman and almost every-thing they do could be done by in-house staff already or with some injection of training and/or confidence. Thus staff are often demotivated when they see highly paid outsiders coming in to do something that could have be done in-house. Worse, public sector workers see consultants hired who are all bluff and bluster, but cannot do the job: these consultants either rely on in-house staff or propose unworkable systems. As one Montana state staffer complains: 'We waste a lot of money on them, and we end up still developing much of the systems in-house after the fact' (Wojciehowski 1998).

Selecting and managing consultants

There is frequently no room for manoeuvre in the selection of consultants. They may be chosen by external institutions or by one or two senior managers. If there is some latitude, then two things need to be chosen:

THE CONSULTING ORGANISATION

These can be categorised into three main types:

- *Large consulting organisations*: may be able to draw on a wide range of staff, but sometimes assign whoever happens to be available; they may have strong technical backup but often cost most.
- *Small consulting organisations*: provide a smaller range of skills but may give greater choice over who is sent; they are often a compromise between the other two options on cost and backup grounds.
- *Individual consultants*: provide only a very limited range of skills but provide certainty about who will be sent; they can normally provide little backup but often cost least.

In the selection of the organisation, then, there may often be trade-offs between closing the skills gap and closing the finance gap.

THE CONSULTANTS

These are more important than the organisation. If there is room for manoeuvre over selection, then typical criteria include:

- *relevant experience*: of similar problems or systems in other PSOs, or of different systems in the same PSO. References from previous clients can be checked to find out about objectivity, awareness of human and organisational factors, and transfer of skills;
- *specific skills*: the particular skills required for the consultancy project;
- *general skills*: such as listening, communicating, enthusiasm, willingness to share expertise and work alongside in-house counterparts;
- *availability*: to meet any necessary timetable;
- *cost*: generally ranked low down the criteria list since cheap is by no means best for consulting to the public sector (though equally there is no cast-iron proportionality between cost and quality in the consulting game);
- *approach to problem and understanding of requirements*: judged by talking to potential consultants or getting them to state how they will undertake their work. This can also be a point at which to attempt to identify and reject biased, technology-oriented and dependency-creating consultants;
- *personal contact*: usually between someone in the PSO and the consultant;
- *ignorance of other candidates*: and lack of capacity to identify them.

As with the consulting organisation, selection of individuals may involve juggling and trade-offs between a number of the conception–reality gaps, including those relating to skills, time, finance and even objectives. As with outsourcing, effective management of the consulting relationship will be a key to ensuring that gaps are closed as much as possible.

ADDRESSING THE GAP OF STAKEHOLDER OBJECTIVES AND MOTIVATIONS

Stakeholder objectives and motivations can be manipulated in a variety of ways. In this section, the techniques described can be seen as representing a continuum of involvement, from the relatively arm's-length approach of reward and punishment, through the median approach of passive participation, to the intense involvement of end-user development.

Changing stakeholder self-interest: reward and punishment

Self-interest may come from some immutable drive for survival within the human psyche, but the way it manifests itself changes all the time. An example can be given from the Indian public sector. In the 1970s, 'computer' was something of a dirty word, associated with job losses. Most senior public servants and politicians therefore did not feel it was in their self-interest to become champions for information technology, and they adopted the ignore approach. When Rajiv Gandhi and his 'computer boys' came to power in 1984, they set high store by the new technology. The self-interest of senior figures then flip-flopped to the idolise approach, and they began falling over themselves to come up with the most ambitious plans for computer system implementation.

Stakeholder self-interest can therefore be manipulated by external factors, to align it more with other stakeholders' or organisational interests. Put another way, stakeholder motivations can be altered to make them support, or at least not resist, the introduction of a particular reform-enabling information system. Any gap of objectives, values and motivations can therefore be reduced.

One common way in which this manipulation takes place is through the use of financial rewards for primary users. This has often been in the guise of a 'computing skills payment': a one-off award or a regrading in recognition of the additional skills or responsibilities that go with use of information technology. In some cases, this has been little more than a bribe to persuade users to stop complaining about a new system or to withdraw a threat of employee action.

Other examples of the 'carrot' approach include:

- explicit messages of support for the system from senior managers or politicians, possibly suggesting that staff career progress will benefit from accepting the system;
- offering training courses for stakeholders, perhaps in a desirable location;
- improving the stakeholders' working environment;
- providing stakeholders with new job titles or other non-financial rewards;
- involving stakeholders more in the process of systems development (see below).

In India's public sector railway system, a major programme was introduced to reform travel reservations through computerisation (Heeks 1998). There was potential for considerable resistance to this change from front-line clerical staff involved. However, the danger was averted, partly thanks to encouraging statements made by senior public servants and politicians. In large measure, however, the rewards provided were those of a changed working environment. Reservation offices were provided with good lighting and air conditioning. Clerks were encouraged to think of themselves as skilled computer operators, even to the extent of being issued with white coats of the type that laboratory technicians wear. All this was a great improvement from the Dickensian setting of the pre-computer reservation offices. As a result, the reform was implemented with few problems.

The 'stick' approach has also been used to modify perceived self-interest. For example, staff may be threatened with worse job content, with stagnating pay or careers, with transfer, or even with retrenchment if they continue to resist the new system. Finally, the 'removal of stick' approach can be used. In such cases, there may be some threat (real or invented) such as job losses or deskilling or loss of personal power that the information system is felt to pose to stakeholders. If those managing the development process then remove this threat, it may cause stakeholders to feel their interests are being served by the new system.

Communication and expectation management

This can be a one-way process of telling those involved what will be happening. This helps to reduce stakeholder uncertainty and ensure there are not too many surprises. It also ensures that expectations about satisfaction of, or conflict with, self-interest do not become overblown. It provides stakeholders with a sense that they are involved and that their interests are not completely divorced from system objectives.

Communication and expectation management has two main elements:

- selling the benefits of the new system to stakeholders; in particular, communicating the personal benefits that will emerge;
- discussing the negative aspects of the new system directly and denying them if untrue or admitting them if true; honesty about negative outcomes is widely advocated as a technique, though many managers find it hard to accept and employ.

When New York State's Department of Agriculture and Markets embarked on automation of its dog licensing service, frequent communication with stakeholders throughout system development was seen as vital to success. A clear, concise newsletter was sent out to all stakeholders during development, supplemented by phone calls and meetings that kept key individuals further informed (Dawes *et al.* 1997). The result was a successfully implemented system that increased efficiency.

Participation

A gap can arise between reality and proposal if the reform proposal represents the interests of only one stakeholder, or one stakeholder group, within the organisation. This can occur particularly around the three-way division between senior managers, mainstream staff and IT staff described in Chapter 2. More generally, it will occur if some of the key stakeholders are not represented in the systems development process.

The likelihood of such gaps arising can be reduced, then, if all the stakeholder groups participate in systems development. Participation is widely cited as a critical success factor in the development process.

When putting together the project team to oversee systems development, a check can be made to see if all stakeholder groups are represented. At least four roles will normally be present if a participative approach is used, based on the 'ITernal triangle' illustrated in Chapter 2:

- senior managers with the power to allocate resources and have decisions implemented (their particular case is discussed further in Box 4.1);
- IT staff who can provide the necessary technical input;
- mainstream managers within whose work sections the new information system will be introduced, and who will use the system's output;
- primary users who will actually operate the new information system.

In addition, larger projects may involve other specialist staff such as finance and human resource specialists. There will also be a need for collaboratory participation across institutional boundaries for cross-government and intersectoral information systems.

Other roles that may be addressed are those of key opinion leaders, who can be involved early. In particular, those opinion leaders who might resist the changes may be targeted. Nothing kills off resistance better than getting those likely to resist to participate in and 'own' the systems development process.

A more radical participative approach would include client groups outside the organisation since they are likely to be affected by information systems change and, hence, are likely to have been identified as stakeholders. This is an approach that has been implemented in some Nigerian public hospitals, where development teams consist not just of technical specialists and hospital staff, but also representatives of the local community that the hospital is intended to serve (Korpela *et al.* 1998).

As a way of encouraging participation, some governments have developed best practice guides or standard methodologies that incorporate participation. Thus the UK CCTA's PRINCE 2 method, mentioned above, includes procedures for involving management, users and other stakeholders in the IS development process.

The larger the project team, though, the greater the cost in staff time and the longer it takes to communicate and to make decisions. There are therefore pressures to keep the team small, and so exclude some stakeholders. In this case, then, a participative approach will at least involve two-way communication with non-team stakeholders and getting their feedback about current reality and about new design proposals.

Active participation and consensus

Allowing stakeholder groups to be heard does not necessarily mean that they are listened to, and some approaches may just pay lip-service to *participation*. This 'passive participation' may still be of value. It can make stakeholders feel that they are involved, and therefore help them view the new system more positively. However, reducing reality–proposal gaps is more likely if the intention is that participation should be an active process.

Box 4.1 Senior management support

The support of senior managers is identified by studies as a critical success factor in systems development perhaps more than any other factor. For example, Bellevue in Washington State 'began its information systems operations with top-management commitment' (King and Kraemer 1991: 32). Conversely, the nearby city of Seattle never got this commitment. The result: 'Although it started on the path of information systems 15 years later, by the mid-1980s, Bellevue led Seattle in many information systems areas, including online integrated financial management, geographic information systems and office automation' (ibid.).

Similarly, the computerisation of tax information systems in Indonesia's Ministry of Finance was able to proceed smoothly and reduce some taxation irregularities because of the support of senior civil servants in the Ministry. Conversely, in the Planning Division of Kenya's Ministry of Agriculture, a computerised statistical analysis system remained unused by a majority of officers due to a lack of senior management commitment (Brodman 1987).

In cases where senior staff become positively involved, their support:

- brings access to organisational resources, including political 'clout';
- signals the importance of the project to other stakeholders;
- may suppress some types of user resistance.

Where there is a lack of commitment, this arises from two particular gaps, as described below.

A gap of objectives

Where senior staff do not feel their interests are being served by the proposed reform information system, they will not support it.

This gap can be addressed by ensuring that senior staff participate in the system development process, and that their interests are considered in setting system objectives. Given that senior management support is such a key factor, it may sometimes be relevant to let system objectives be almost entirely determined by senior staff. Of course, the danger here is of ignoring other stakeholders and thereby running the risk of system failure.

A gap of knowledge or skills or attitudes

Where senior staff do not understand IT or the role of information systems and where they lack systems development or project management skills and confidence, they may try to suppress new information systems. They do this partly because they feel unable to control the systems development process, and because they fear that exposing their ignorance will undermine their authority. Senior manager (and politician) ignorance about IT appears greater in the public than in the private sector.

This gap is mainly addressed through training and presentations, though special allowances may need to be made for senior staff. For example:

- they may be trained first, before all other staff, to give them a head start;
- they may be sent to some prestigious training institution commensurate with their perceived importance;
- they may be trained one-to-one, to avoid having to expose their ignorance to other staff members.

In the Ugandan government, this approach was adopted during reform of the legal system. Senior judges were the first to be trained about IT via one-to-one coaching in their offices from staff based in the country's leading management training institute (Muhenda 1998). The result was a development of competence and confidence that led to senior-level support for a roll-out of IT skills and applications throughout the country's legal institutions.

Attitudes can be addressed using the attitude training techniques described previously. Producing an information system (or even just a demonstration) that meets some senior management need – even a minor one – can also help to change attitudes. The only danger here is the risk of system failure: of overselling the benefits of a new system and then under-delivering. This can kill off support for IT-enabled

---

Box 4.1 continued

reform for years. Use of prototyping (see below) can help avert this and can also address objectives and knowledge gaps.

Even simpler can be a demonstration of systems already in use of which senior managers and politicians are unaware. Both Massachusetts and California state governments in the US run one-day 'IT Expos' (Harris 1997). These are aimed at the public in part, but also at closing knowledge and attitude gaps amongst politicians, legislature staff and government managers.

Senior staff are also particularly susceptible to presentations that pander to their vanity and insecurity, of the 'Your peers in sister organisations have got wonderful new information systems, don't you think you should have one too' variety.

Unfortunately, the message of such presentations and of management training may be wrongly to over-emphasise the technology and under-emphasise information and contextual factors in reform. The result may be a job half-done that is worse than not being done at all. Senior managers may be converted into the semi-literate idolisers described in Chapter 2, who feel technology will solve all problems. They rush head-long into information age reform, but using the wrong approach and in ever-changing directions blown by the winds of technology fads and fashions.

A recent survey of the UK public sector indicated:

> many projects are still being run by technicians, and although things have improved over the years and users are engaged to some extent, the issue of truly empowering the users is still real for many public sector projects. . . . not doing this may result in the fact that 66% of the respondents state that the requirements are ill-defined.
>
> (Martin 1997: 11)

One way of managing this and making participation active is to allocate particular tasks to particular stakeholders, as described in the section below on user involvement. However, this still allows gaps to emerge between one group's proposals and other groups' realities. Closing these gaps may require the use of active participation techniques to build *consensus*.

In essence, this requires the different stakeholder groups to develop an agreed view of reality and/or problems and/or objectives and/or design choices. For example, all stakeholder personal objectives could be combined and compromised in order to create a single set of agreed reform objectives. Such consensus involves perceived self-interest being made to converge with perceived group (or even organisational) interests.

Creating consensus within a participative project team depends partly on how that team is managed. The team leader can demand a single consensus output from all team activities, or can allow one or two stakeholder groups to dominate, in which case there will be no consensus.

Consensus can be created using relatively formal techniques, which are sometimes known as 'joint application development' techniques when applied to information systems development. These bring different stakeholder groups together for a structured meeting with a facilitator. Meeting participants and outputs are agreed beforehand. Where plenary meetings are difficult, the facilitator may become more of a negotiator and mediator, going round to stakeholders one by one trying to narrow down differences.

Technology may have a role here in facilitating the journey to consensus. For example, a group decision support system (GDSS) was used by a broad group of stakeholders, including legislators and administrators, associated with the newly created Hungarian Parliament (Vari *et al.* 1992). Within a two-day period, the GDSS enabled the group to brainstorm and then produce consensus priorities on a full set of information systems and services needs for the Parliament.

Consensus can also be created indirectly. For example, a group of stakeholders can be set a task, such as to create a diagram of the information system, or produce a single, final version of some rating table for subjective cost/benefit analysis. The group is focused on the particular output required. In practice, though, the output may be much less important than the process of working together, of mutual learning through sharing knowledge and values and perspectives, and of reaching some kind of agreement.

Training also has a role to play. It can help in group-forming and in trying to reduce the 'distance' between stakeholder positions. Finally, consensus can be achieved by locating multiple stakeholder roles within the same individual, the ultimate expression of which is end-user development (see below).

Prototyping

Prototyping is a form of active participation. It is the use of a working model of the final system, which users can see, comment on and have revised before the final version is produced. With the advent of customisable application packages, fourth-generation programming languages and the like it has become relatively quick and easy to create a prototype system.

One possible prototyping methodology is described in Chapter 5. At its core is presentation of the prototype to stakeholders by being either demonstrated to them or used by them. Their reactions can be recorded about system elements they would like kept, removed, altered and added.

Reactions and suggestions can be probed further by individual and group discussion during prototyping or after. Prototyping – like other participative techniques – therefore demands developers who listen to, and empathise with, other stakeholders.

Next, revisions to the prototype are planned and implemented, and the process of presentation and stakeholder reaction can be re-run. Iterations around this cycle may continue several times until stakeholders are satisfied. The scope of this cycle may need to be widened if issues raised during prototyping indicate, say, that the initial focus of reform or the initial project feasibility assessment were misguided.

The main benefit of prototyping is that, being faced with an actual system, stakeholders can express requirements or objectives that they would otherwise find hard to state. Such requirements may be quite general (e.g. about the overall objectives sought from the reform process) or may be quite specific (e.g. a comment on the nature of the system interface). The presence of a system helps focus stakeholders' attention, imagine what they need from the system and point out what they do not like.

In turn, this means that:

- the final system is more likely to match stakeholder objectives;
- stakeholders are more realistic in what they expect from the final system;
- the final system *may* be produced more quickly;
- major problems are spotted earlier, and can therefore be addressed at lower cost.

Conception–reality gaps of objectives and values but also of finance and possibly time may therefore be tackled.

Such benefits were found when prototyping was used in the development of an executive information system for senior health managers in a UK public hospital. This not only led to improvements in the system, but also to greater levels of interest and commitment from the managers (Afferson *et al.* 1995). Prototyping also created interest and commitment when the New York State Office for the Aging developed a new information system to support coordinated delivery of client services: 'The prototyping method produced positive results. . . . early demonstrations of the system created an enthusiastic response among local governments and generated positive interest in the system among the user community' (Dawes *et al.* 1997: 69).

Like any technique, prototyping can have its drawbacks. Time pressures may force premature acceptance of the prototyped system as a final system before all requirements have been fully analysed, before non-technical components of the system have been designed, or before the system has been properly tested and documented. Prototyping may encourage corners to be cut, yet it does not substitute for techniques to create consensus or for good communications between IT staff and users.

Nevertheless, prototyping is increasingly used in systems development and is often seen as a critical success factor in the development process. Systems development methodologies that incorporate prototyping have been around for many years. For example, prototyping has been successfully incorporated into Dynamic Systems Development Method. This provides a standard, non-proprietary approach to IS development that combines both rapid and joint application development methods (Stapleton 1997).

Such combinations of prototyping and active participation can be particularly effective. The Royal Netherlands Air Force, for example, used both techniques through a management game involving the simulation of the entire organisational information system for a planned air base. Not only did this create a shared vision for change among participants, it also facilitated discussion of key issues and created a sense of unity between those involved. As a result, this has been recommended as a standard approach to public sector change (Quanjel and Wenzler 1998).

User involvement and end-user development

IT staff and senior managers can easily fall into the 'idolise trap' and develop a belief that the formal objectivity of technology represents the best path for organisational reform. Senior managers and external sponsors can easily develop a belief that formal and objective models of the organisation represent best practice that should be aimed for. All these groups may therefore attempt to impose technology-/rationality-driven designs on the reform process.

Of all the stakeholders, the users are those who tend to be most rooted in current system realities and who best understand when technology-/rationality-driven models will be inappropriate. Giving users a bigger say in systems development can therefore help guard against information age reform failure.

In the Canadian Ministry of Public Works and Government Services, for instance, a new information system was required to replace the antiquated procurement system. The Ministry's IS department proposed a costly, complex, mainframe-based solution. However, end users countered with a client/server solution that was nearly 90 per cent cheaper, involving outsourcing and management by end users rather than the IS staff. The latter was chosen, the system was developed in just over one year, and it now handles around 100,000 requisitions per year (Caldwell 1996, cited in Laudon and Laudon 1998).

A number of techniques for involving users in the systems development process have been described above. Another technique is the allocation of certain systems development responsibilities to users. Typical examples include:

- making one of the users responsible for managing the whole project;
- getting a user or user group to undertake the analysis of current reality;
- getting a user group to recommend which of various design options should be adopted;
- making users responsible for process design while IT staff work on technical design;
- getting a user to write the system documentation;
- having the training designed and delivered to users by users;
- requiring a formal user acceptance test of the new system.

In the development of a new management information system to support reform of material requirements planning, the US Air Force Logistics Command involved users throughout the IS development lifecycle (Tripp 1991). Users were made responsible for current system analysis, requirements specification, review and acceptance of detail design, preparation of test data, setting of acceptance criteria and user acceptance. They were also involved with the testing and data conversion processes. Coupled with formal project management procedures, this helped to ensure a good fit between user needs and system outcomes.

The ultimate expression of this process of giving responsibilities to users is *end-user development*, which vests all – or almost all – systems development roles in a single person. This will close the reality–proposal gaps of information needs and of objectives, values and motivations. It can significantly reduce the money and time resource requirement, and end users are most unlikely to create unmanageable levels of change for themselves on the other ITPOSMO dimensions. As such, end-user development should greatly increase the chance of producing a successful system.

There can be drawbacks. Allowing insufficiently skilled users to develop systems can lead to poor-quality analysis, design, construction and implementation. Either user training or some type of 'core–periphery' responsibility-sharing compromise between users and the IT unit is appropriate in order to provide the knowledge and skills support that users need (Heeks 1999). Even where this is provided, it must be recognised that end-user development is only appropriate for certain types of information system but that, if adequately supported, it represents a significant improvement on other systems development methods by inherently managing the degree of change.

CHANGING THE DESIGN

Information age reform initiatives that attempt radical transformation of government are unlikely to succeed because they require too much change along too many of the ITPOSMO model dimensions. These and other reform initiatives are more likely to succeed if they reduce the size or scope or complexity of the information age reform project proposal, thus bringing it closer to existing reality. This adheres to a polite variant of the old systems development adage, *KISS: Keep It Small and Simple.* This is of especial relevance to the public sector, as Box 4.2 describes.

Any dimension of the design proposal can be altered to make it smaller or simpler and thus closer to reality. For example, the technical complexity of the proposal could be reduced. This sometimes happens when customisation of an existing software package – rather than creation from scratch of custom-built software – is chosen as the design option, creating smaller time, skills and money gaps. This was the case in the example already given in Chapter 3 of the UK Ships Support Agency.

Box 4.2 Large and complex IS projects in the public sector

The need to keep projects small and simple is a particular problem for the public sector because:

- the average public sector project is usually larger and more complex than the average private sector project, interacting with a larger number of different stakeholders.
- public sector organisations tend to see their problems as complex and unique, thus requiring tailor-made, high-risk, state-of-the-art solutions even when alternative, off-the-shelf, cheap, tried and tested systems are available;
- perhaps for reasons of prestige, governments tend to favour large, complex, often-untested, high-technology projects supported by relatively generous funding.

Such projects often run into considerable difficulties because:

- they have a large number of stakeholders whose different objectives, values and motivations must be accommodated, potentially increasing this gap dimension:
  - they often involve a large number of organisations whose different cultures and structures must be accommodated;
  - they require a large allocation of resources, thus drawing in even more stakeholders, like bees to the honeypot. This results in more politicking and longer delays in decision making;
  - the size of their likely impact attracts inputs from politicians and policy makers who would not interfere with smaller projects;
- they are far removed from the users' level, increasing the dangers of non-participation and non-acceptance of the system due to gaps between system conceptions and user realities;

Box 4.2 continued

- their size demands new organisational structures and processes that are hard to implement, increasing the gaps on both these dimensions;
- they often require the installation of a sophisticated new data and technology infrastructure, increasing the gaps on the information and technology dimensions;
- there is less experience and there are fewer models of best practice to guide them.

Put more generally, then, such projects are problematic because they require more change along more dimensions of change than smaller projects. Large public sector IT projects are therefore failures more often than not (Korac-Boisvert and Kouzmin 1995). Yet, in many situations, 'There are more flexible alternatives available, technologies which involve more incremental changes, having shorter lead time, smaller unit size, lower capital intensity and infrastructure requirements, and which can be developed in a more decentralized way' (Collingridge and Margetts 1994: 70).

(Adapted from Jain and Raghuram 1992 and Willcocks 1994)

This design alteration could go as far as making the new proposed design exactly match current reality along one particular dimension, by 'freezing' that dimension. Going further, the proposal could match reality along several of the ITPOSMO dimensions. Going yet further, an attempt could be made to freeze *all* the change dimensions except one. Examples of all three of these approaches are discussed below.

Freezing one dimension: doing without or postponing computers

Many negative impacts, problems and limitations have been associated with the introduction of computers to support reform in public sector organisations. Does this mean that we should reject computerisation or try to prevent it wherever possible? This is unrealistic. IT should be seen as one weapon in the armoury of reform, but there are clearly occasions on which that weapon does not need to be unsheathed.

Understanding when to use IT is first a question of understanding what IT can do. Principally, it can address problems pertaining to:

- the speed or precision or consistency of information processing and transmission;
- the capacity for information storage and retrieval;
- the format of output.

However, there is a much larger category of problems that relate to information systems but which do not necessarily require a computer for their reform. Examples include:

- poor data quality;
- irrelevant or incomplete information being provided to managers;
- poor structuring of data records;
- improvements required in informal information systems;
- non-use of information provided;
- inefficient or ineffective processes;
- conflicting objectives for the information system;
- inadequate skills for information analysis or interpretation or use;
- sub-optimal management structures to control the information system.

Where such problems exist:

> computers will not clean up a mess that exists already. They will simply process that mess faster. If the existing procedures are muddled, if there is incomplete data, if the personnel information does not match the payroll information, a computerised system will not untangle the confusion.
>
> (Cain 1996: 163)

The cases presented in Chapters 5 and 6 both provide examples. The State of Vermont also ran into just such problems, leading its Commissioner of Personnel to comment:

> In retrospect, I'm not convinced that the approach of changing software to automate existing procedures is advisable. From my perspective, the Department of Personnel should have perhaps done a more thorough job of seriously questioning procedures that could very well be inefficient or ineffective.
>
> (Cats-Baril and Thompson 1995: 562)

IT is no substitute for poor management or poor governance, and broad/deep IS problems must either be addressed without computerisation at all, or must be addressed first before computerisation can be of any wider value to the reform process. As reviewers of the Vermont case concluded: 'first reengineer, then automate' (ibid.: 565).

Introducing IT can help lever solutions to some non-IT-related problems, such as inefficient processes or poor staff motivation. Nevertheless, the presence of IT in reform projects needs to be challenged more than it is and/or delayed until other problems are sorted. Allowing the 'no computer' option, or the 'no computers yet' option, to be considered presents the opportunity to freeze change along the technology dimension. This can make reform more manageable and more successful.

Freezing several dimensions: supporting tacit knowledge and informal information systems

Informal information systems can be damaging to the organisation, and there are arguments for stamping them out. Some public sector organisations – even some whole governments – are riven with a culture of informality and rumour, and require a healthy injection of formal IS to encourage some rationality in decision making.

On the other hand, as noted in Box 3.1, informal information systems play an essential role in public sector organisations, and one that may become increasingly valued with growing recognition of tacit knowledge (TK) as an organisational resource. Too often, though, there is a pretence during reform initiatives that such resources and systems do not exist. At best, new information systems may fortuitously work round them. At worst, tacit knowledge and informal IS may be impaired or driven out. These outcomes can be counter-productive for individual stakeholders, for the organisation as a whole and, hence, for reform of the public sector.

However, this does not have to be the case. A first step is the recognition of tacit knowledge and informal information systems in the analysis of current reality. This requires that their existence be brought out into the open and their potential for improving effectiveness clearly legitimised. Stakeholders may then feel able to discuss their use of TK and informal IS in decision making.

Going one stage further, TK and informal information systems can be supported by systems development. Where this is done, it will often create a manageable degree of change by supporting current reality. This can mean that several potential dimensions of change – such as objectives and values, staffing, management and structures – are frozen and do *not* change.

Ways in which this can be done include:

- *Making use of reality-supporting information technology* Technologies such as office automation and electronic mail are described as 'reality-supporting' because they can incorporate informal information and assist the sharing of tacit knowledge. They can also enhance informal information systems by, for instance, improving the processing of informal information, increasing the speed at which it was transmitted, or filtering it to remove 'noise'.
- *Building up informal relationships* Increasing the opportunities for transmission of tacit knowledge and informal information can be done in a number of ways. For example, computer networks can help build up larger or new informal social groupings. Such 'social networking' can also be developed without the use of IT through meetings, mentoring,

one-to-one coaching, social events, and sports activities. Simply creating a non-work space within the organisation, such as a coffee room, can also help achieve this.

- *Encouraging end-user development* As already discussed, users tend to be more 'in touch' with organisational reality than other stakeholders, or at least are less prone to trying to impose organisational rationality on their situations. End-user development is therefore more likely to incorporate tacit knowledge and informal information than other development methods.

When Scottish Enterprise, a government agency based in Glasgow, wanted to create a 'workplace of the future' for its staff, it made a deliberate attempt to harness the organisation's human knowledge resources by supporting informal information systems. Initiatives included cross-functional work teams, an open office layout to encourage communication, informal wire-free workspaces to encourage face-to-face discussions, an onsite staff café, and the introduction of a comprehensive internal email service (Mackay and Maxwell 1997).

Freezing all dimensions except one: 'simple' automation

Some public sector organisations attempt to freeze all change dimensions of reform except the technology dimension by simply automating their existing manual system. They retain the same staff, same information, same processes, same management structures and so on. The only change is that some paper-based information is put on screen, with screen layout exactly duplicating paper forms. Organisations new to information age reform sometimes try to follow this strategy.

In the midst of the developing information age, it is easy to forget how challenging this strategy of just changing the technology can be. Yet for many organisations the apparently simple processes of installing and running information technology are a major hurdle. Why? Because one dimension cannot be completely isolated. The same would be true of trying to individually change any ITPOSMO dimension. They cannot be completely dissociated and so changes in any one dimension will require at least some change in other dimensions.

Changing the technology, for example, requires:

- new skills to use it;
- new finances to pay for it;
- new attitudes towards information to sustain it;
- new infrastructure in order to run it.

This means that many years may pass before the technology can be regarded as institutionalised.

As noted in Chapter 2, there is a general assumption that organisations move on from automation to informatisation once new technology becomes institutionalised. Yet this may be difficult if organisations find themselves constantly trying to adapt to new technologies. In practice, these technologies may never become fully institutionalised. Technology upgrades and innovations may take up almost all of the organisation's 'change capacity', leaving hardly any for changes along other dimensions.

For example, some organisations which were struggling to institutionalise their minicomputers in the 1970s spent the 1980s getting used to microcomputers and the 1990s trying to cope with local area networks, the Internet and the World Wide Web. As they reel from the shock of wave after wave of new technologies, they never find the capacity to deal with far more important areas such as information and information systems. They may only find this capacity by ignoring the constant pressures of technological change; something that – as seen in Chapter 2 – is very difficult to achieve.

'Simple' automation may be even more problematic if, as noted above, it tries to automate an existing manual system that functions poorly or not at all. For instance, automation of the admissions system at a publicly owned university in Uganda created considerable change because it ignored and overrode the reality of informal information systems that were operating alongside a poorly performing formal manual system (Avgerou and Mulira 1996). What, at first sight, appears to be a simple reform therefore ended in complex difficulties. Not only was this a failure to reengineer before automating, it was also a failure of analysis since this took formal descriptions of existing systems at face value and failed to uncover informal information systems and motivations.

Incrementalism

Where a major set of changes is planned as part of a reform initiative, breaking these down and introducing them only slowly and in an incremental manner will help to reduce the extent of any given change. This, in turn, will increase the likelihood of successful system introduction. Within an individual system development project, incrementalism could mean changing only a few ITPOSMO dimensions at a time. Alternatively, it can mean selecting a slow and incremental method of system installation.

An instance of this being put in practice comes from the US 1996 IT Management Reform Act. This both highlights and encourages 'modular contracting', which divides large IT projects into a set of relatively separate modules as part of an incremental strategy: 'Recognized . . . as a cutting edge approach, modular contracting has the potential to greatly improve the chances of success in large Federal information technology development programs' (Wolfe 1997: 7).

Incremental installation has been used in Austria with its online tax system, FinanzOnline. This was first rolled out to a pilot group of selected tax consultants for a six-month evaluation period. Roll-out then continued first to all tax consultants, then to companies, then to ordinary taxpayers. The dangers of major failure were thereby significantly reduced (Dittrich 1997). Piloting has also been central in the UK's strategic approach to electronic service delivery (CITU 1996).

CONCLUSION: THE APPLICABILITY OF THESE TECHNIQUES

Many of the techniques described above make some assumptions of rationality. At the very least, they assume that systems development is a process that can be managed and controlled to some extent to allow these techniques to be used. More importantly, the techniques also have an associated set of pre-conditions, such as certain organisational structures and cultures that need to be present. These assumed requirements are *not* always present, and therefore these techniques are *not* applicable in all circumstances.

Participative techniques, for example, require an organisational culture that can accept the idea of users, such as clerical staff, being involved in a decision making process. Yet such a culture is not typically found in public sector organisations. The idea of participation by external client groups – farmers for a Ministry of Agriculture system or welfare claimants for a social security system – will have even more difficulty being accepted.

In practical terms, the organisation must have sufficient time and money to invest since participative approaches tend to take longer and require more effort than autocratic approaches. Yet PSOs are often beset with time and financial constraints.

Participation finally requires that other stakeholders are willing and able to participate. Political antagonisms, lack of skills and confidence, previous poor experiences of participation, a failure to see the relevance of the new system and pressures of other work may thus block participative methods such as consensus-building and prototyping (see Chapter 5 for an example). As a result, many public sector organisations remain rooted in more traditional, costly, time-consuming, failure-prone methods (Korac-Boisvert and Kouzmin 1995).

To take another example, it is harder for the selection and management of consultants to produce positive results if there are no in-house skills to cover tasks such as:

- definition of project scope and objectives;
- definition of consultant responsibilities;
- learning of consultancy skills.

Finally, reducing technical complexity or even freezing the technology dimension may not be possible. This is unlikely to be accepted in situations where external or top-down diktat has decreed that a large, state-of-the-art system is required in a high-profile project. Nor is this likely to work if senior organisational staff are being induced by suppliers to purchase unnecessarily costly and large-scale technology.

These gap-closing techniques are therefore likely to help the reform process, but they cannot always be applied. The techniques are fairly well-known, but the continuing high failure rate of public sector information systems is a reminder that there is no panacea for information age reform. All will depend on the room for manoeuvre that stakeholders have. Managers interested in applying these techniques are therefore advised to first check room for manoeuvre by asking questions such as:

- *Personal objectives* What do I personally want from this information age reform project?
- *Personal qualities* To what extent do I have the skills and confidence to intervene in the process of reform?
- *Direct control* What money, time and human resources that could be brought to bear on the reform project do I have direct control over?
- *Indirect control* To what extent do I have influence over other stakeholders? Could I influence them to change their objectives, to provide more resources, to choose a different consultant or supplier, etc.?
- *Overall* To what extent can I introduce new techniques into the reform project?

If the techniques described cannot be applied, or if they are being applied unsuccessfully, and the reality–proposal gap is still felt to be sizeable, then there are two courses of action for the organisation:

- abandon the project;
- proceed, knowing that there is a high risk of failure.

The first option will be the less costly outcome for the organisation in many situations. However, it is less likely to occur because it is politically and psychologically far more difficult to stop than to continue.

If the information system does proceed and then fails, this should not be written off as a completely negative experience. Failure provides powerful opportunities for organisational learning, though whether these are recognised and taken up is another matter. Failure may also leave a residue that is built upon. For example, fear or ignorance of new technology may be reduced. Unused computers sitting in the corner of the office may prick a public servant's conscience or interest, drive them to try to make use of information technology and, possibly, improve their information systems. Thus, even if unsuccessful, the introduction of new information technology and systems is still a way of changing current reality.

Individual stakeholders faced with a reform initiative that seems doomed to failure also have two choices:

- focus on personal objectives;
- abandon the organisation.

Although it can be disheartening to work on a project that is going to fail, such an experience can be beneficial to individuals involved. They can gain in terms of money, prestige, experience, on-the-job skills, training, access to new technology, networking with potential future employers, and so on. Where such gains seem unlikely to emerge, staff may well choose to decamp to 'greener pastures'.

REFERENCES

Afferson, M., Muhleman, A., Price, D. and Rushworth, T. (1995) 'Determining management information requirements within a health sector application', *Information Infrastructure and Policy* 4, 1: 67–86.

Avgerou, C. and Mulira, N. (1996) 'A study of a university admission system in Uganda', in E.M. Roche and M.J. Blaine (eds) *Information Technology, Development and Policy*, Aldershot, Hants: Avebury.

Barth, S. (1998) 'Re: IT staffing stats', *Govpub@listserv.nodak.edu* list, 9 July.

Brodman, J.Z. (1987) 'Key management factors in determining the impact of micro-computers on decision-making in the governments of developing countries', in S.R. Ruth and C.K. Mann (eds) *Microcomputers in Public Policy: Applications for Developing Countries*, Boulder, CO: Westview Press.

Cain, P. (1996) 'Making the transition to the electronic age', *Information Technology for Development*, 7, 4: 159–167.

Caldwell, B. (1996) 'User revolt pays off in Canada', *Information Week* 18 November.

Cats-Baril, W. and Thompson, R. (1995) 'Managing information projects in the public sector', *Public Administration Review* 55, 6: 559–566.

Checkland, P.B. (1981) *Systems Thinking, Systems Practice*, Chichester, W. Sussex: John Wiley.

Cheong, L.K. and Koh, G.L. (1991) *Information Technology in the Civil Service: Singapore*, Singapore: National Computer Board.

CITU (1996) *government.direct: A Prospectus for the Electronic Delivery of Government Services*, London: Central IT Unit, Office of Public Service. http://www.open.gov.uk/gdirect/greenpaper/index.htm

Collingridge, D. and Margetts, H. (1994) 'Can government information systems be inflexible technology? The Operational Strategy revisited', *Public Administration* 72, Spring: 55–72.

Computing (1997) 'Consultancies thrive despite dip in IT work', 27 March: 17.

Dawes, S., Pardo, T.A., Green, D.E., Connelly, D.R. and DiCaterino, A. (1997) *Tying a Sensible Knot: A Practical Guide to State–Local Information Systems*, Albany, NY: Center for Technology in Government, University at Albany, SUNY.

Dittrich, A. (1997) 'FinanzOnline', *ICA Newsletter* 39: 6. http://www.ica.ogit.gov.au/Publications

Hanson, W. (1998) 'CIOs think regionally, act in concert', *Government Technology* February.
http://www.govtech.net/gtmag/1998/feb/

Harris, B. (1997) *How to Finance 'Service to the Citizen' Projects*, Sacramento, CA: Government Technology.

Heeks, R.B. (1999) *Centralised vs. Decentralised Management of Public Information Systems: A Core-Periphery Solution*, ISPSM Working Paper no. 7, Manchester: IDPM, University of Manchester.
http://www.man.ac.uk/idpm/idpm_dp.htm

Heeks, R.B. (1998) *Management Information and Management Information Systems*, London: School of Oriental and African Studies, University of London.

ICA (1998) *Procurement Study Group Report*, Washington, DC: International Council for Information Technology in Government Administration.

Jain, R. and Raghuram, G. (1992) 'Implementation of the Operations Information System: the case of Indian Railways', in S.C. Bhatnagar and M. Odedra (eds) *Social Implications of Computers in Developing Countries*, New Delhi: Tata McGraw-Hill.

King, J.L. and Kraemer, K.L. (1991) 'Patterns of success in municipal information systems: lessons from US experience', *Informatization and the Public Sector* 1, 1: 21–39.

Korac-Boisvert, N. and Kouzmin, A. (1995) 'Transcending soft-core IT disasters in public sector organizations', *Information Infrastructure and Policy* 4, 2: 131–161.

Korpela, M., Soriyan, H.A., Olufokunbi, K.C. and Mursu, A. (1998) 'Blueprint for an African systems development methodology: an action research project in the health sector', paper presented at conference on 'Implementation and Evaluation of Information Systems in Developing Countries', 18–20 February, Bangkok, Thailand.

Lambeth, J. (1998) 'Outsourcers go in for the skill as firms flounder', *Computing* 30 April: 16.

Laudon, K.C. and Laudon, J.P. (1998) *Management Information Systems*, 5th edn, Upper Saddle River, NJ: Prentice-Hall.

McDonough, F.A. (1997) 'What I learned in Taiwan', *ICA Newsletter* 39: 4–5.
http://www.ica.ogit.gov.au/Publications

McGarigle, B. (1998) 'COGs keep government wheels moving', *Government Technology* April.
http: //www.govtech.net/gtmag/1998/april/

Mackay, M. and Maxwell, G. (1997) 'Future shop', *People Management* 9 October: 44–47.

McLellan, P.M. (1996) 'Electronic commerce: serving the business community', paper presented at conference on 'Electronic Government in the Information Society', 6–10 October, Budapest, Hungary.

McLellan, P.M., Riddle, J., and Ober, H. (1996) 'Canada', paper presented at conference on 'Electronic Government in the Information Society', 6–10 October, Budapest, Hungary.

McNevin, A. (1994) 'Hardware budgets cut as civil service revises IT expenditure', *Computing*, 28 July: 8.

Martin, B. (ed.) (1997) *UK Government IT Survey 1997*, London: Price Waterhouse.

Mechling, J. and Sweeney, V. (1997) 'Finding and funding IT projects', *Government Technology* December.
http://www.govtech.net/gtmag/1997/dec/

Muhenda, M. (1998) Personal communication with author.

NCC (1993) *Outsourcing, Guidelines for IT Management* no. 179, Manchester: National Computing Centre.

Odedra, M. (1992) 'Is information technology really being transferred to the African countries?', in G. Cyranek and S.C. Bhatnagar (eds) *Technology Transfer for Development*, New Delhi: Tata McGraw-Hill.

Peterson, S.B. (1990) 'Microcomputer training for the Government of Kenya', *Information Technology for Development* 5, 4: 381–412.

Pollett, M. (1998) 'Suppliers: no money in government work', *Government Computing* 12, 4: 10–11.

POST (1998) *Electronic Government: Information Technology and the Citizen*, London: Parliamentary Office of Science and Technology.
http://www.parliament.uk/post/egov.htm

Quanjel, M. and Wenzler, I. (1998) 'A participative approach to organizational design: the case of the Royal Netherlands Air Force', paper presented at Association for Information Systems 1998 Americas conference, 14–16 August, Baltimore, Maryland.

Stapleton, J. (1997) *DSDM: Dynamic Systems Development Method*, Reading, MA: Addison-Wesley.

Tripp, R.S. (1991) 'Managing the political and cultural aspects of large-scale MIS projects: a case study of participative systems development', *Information Resources Management Journal* Fall: 2–13.

Vari, A., Rohrbaugh, J. and Baaklini, A.I. (1992) 'Group decision support systems for legislative deliberation: decision conferencing in the Hungarian Parliament', *Informatization and the Public Sector* 2, 1: 27–45.

Willcocks, L. (1994) 'Managing information systems in UK public administration: issues and prospects', *Public Administration* 72, Spring: 13–32.

Willcocks, L., Lacity, M.C. and Fitzgerald, G. (1997) 'IT outsourcing in Europe and the USA: assessment issues', in L.P. Willcocks, D. Feeny and G. Islei (eds) *Managing IT as a Strategic Resource*, London: McGraw-Hill.

Wojciehowski, P. (1998) 'Re: IT skills in government', *Govpub@listserv.nodak.edu* list, 2 July.

Wolfe, L. (1997) 'Modular contracting for major information technology systems', *ICA Newsletter* 38: 7–8.
http://www.ica.ogit.gov.au/Publications

Yazel, L. (1993) 'Agency reaps the benefits of change', *Computing* 5 May: 24.

Part 2

Management information systems

5 Information systems for improved performance management

Development approaches in US public agencies

Douglas M. Brown

Abstract: Ideally, government managers should develop outcome-oriented performance management systems but, generally, we have not learned how to separate programme outcomes from confounding factors. Therefore, US reform ('reinvention') efforts have primarily addressed only internal processes. Information systems that attempt to capture outcome measures – that are neither understood nor accepted – will not be completed or used. Information systems must for now be confined to answering the practical needs of internal processes, thereby helping agencies to be at least more efficient if not more effective.

But how should such systems be developed? Traditional 'structured' information systems design is a comprehensive approach, often measured in years. That approach flourishes in the US public sector where time and money are seldom serious constraints. Development cycles that consume two to three years guarantee the delivery of an obsolescent product because computer technology changes entirely during that period. Modern computer-using managers can easily generate alternative systems and will not accept such delays that result in operational failure of an information system. The alternative – described in this case study of a US public agency – is an evolutionary design process, emphasising rapid prototyping and subsequent integration of small-scale data sets.

BACKGROUND

The context of reform

The demand for governmental reforms

Beginning in the 1980s, American public opinion swung away from a half-century of experimenting with government as the first solution to all problems. President Reagan achieved a consensus that government was too big and spent too much. The fall of the Soviet empire allowed President Bush to initiate major cuts in defence spending. Social service agencies began to feel the pinch under President Clinton; despite a preference for increased social interventions, he is caught up by voter pressure to reduce federal spending and his own rhetoric urging his party to reject its tax-and-spend tradition. His administration is a vocal advocate for reinvention, possibly because making the agencies more efficient is the only way to increase constituent spending within a fixed budget. Thus, US government agencies have been dealing with the current reform ideology for almost 20 years.

Government Performance and Results Act

The Government Performance and Results Act (GPRA) of 1993 (US Public Law (PL) 103-62) required all federal agencies to develop (or modify) strategic plans to include specific goals and performance indicators and to report on their progress. The initial plans were required to be completed by September 1997, with implementation activities running through to the year 2000. As the primary duty of Vice-President Gore, the initiative received more publicity than most internal reorganisations and was taken seriously by many agencies.

A simple model of the public agency environment distinguishes between outcomes (or outputs) and the input activities to which government managers are more often accustomed. Figure 5.1 portrays observable system components and their interactions. Performance measurement quantifies the association between inputs and outcomes, as shown in Figure 5.2 using dashed lines and italics. Other links are important factors, but are not performance measures.

Osborne and Gaebler (1992) advocate a transition to outcome orientation, and this was taken up in the GPRA. However, in practice, most agencies have been unable to articulate their performance measures (GAO 1997; OMB 1997) or to distinguish between measures of outcome as opposed to output (NAPA 1994). Several agencies were able to accomplish the transition but even in some of these cases the output orientation remains: police agencies using successful prosecution rates rather than reduced crime rates is a clear example (NAPA 1994).

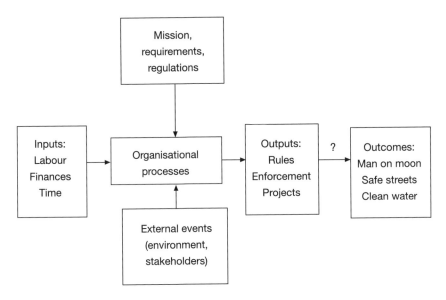

Figure 5.1 Public agency organisational environments

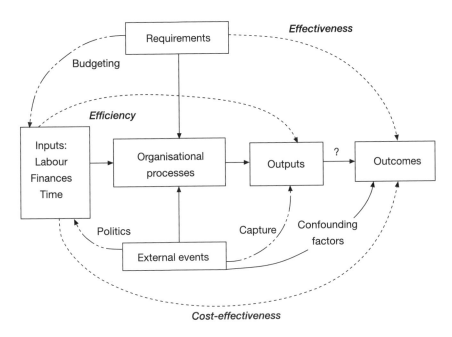

Figure 5.2 Public agency performance measures

Progress of reinvention

The formal reviews noted above concur that there are few reinvention success stories, at least by the standard of establishing and using outcome-oriented performance measures. However, cost-effectiveness is not the only focus of the GPRA. There is still considerable value in having agencies improve efficiency, i.e. their internal processes.

Some agencies have clearly process-oriented missions, so that the successful accomplishment of the process is sufficient of itself. An example is the Social Security Administration, which issues payments very well and has benefited greatly both from reinvention and automation. Among 'operating' agencies (those which execute their functions directly rather than through financial transfers or regulatory processes), the relationship between internal improvements and mission is less clear.

The National Aeronautics and Space Administration (NASA, the space agency) and the Federal Aviation Administration (FAA, the air travel safety agency) are often cited as models of efficient internal planning and administrative processes. Perhaps this is because these agencies have sharply focused missions with little political debate over desirable outcomes. None the less, even these two agencies received rather undistinguished reinvention implementation ratings from the National Academy of Public Administration (NAPA 1998), and the FAA remains embroiled in years of delay and huge costs incurred in a still-unfielded primary data system (see Chapter 11 for further details).

Operating agencies argue effectively that the outcomes of activities aimed at wide goals (such as eliminating poverty or cleaning up the environment) cannot be separated from other confounding factors. The corollary to such an argument is that when the outcomes of agency activities cannot be distinguished from random events, then public investments must be questionable.

The role of IT in reinvention to date

A national government necessarily deals with large-scale activities. Simply keeping national pension accounts in the US requires the maintenance of some 300 million records in various stages of completion. Agency budgets are measured in the billions of dollars, but are spent not more than a few thousand dollars at a time. To be affordable, such activities require automated systems.

None the less, information age reform in the US has not been problem-free. There are few good examples of the use of automated systems to assist in reinvention at the mission level. The Social Security Administration's success with data systems was launched long before the current vogue for reinvention. The FAA's failure in fielding a primary data system, noted above, is matched by similar experiences in the Veterans' Benefits Administration and the

Internal Revenue Service, among others. Nobody really knows how much has been spent on these systems, but Carl Sagan's astronomy estimator ('billions and billions') is a conservative figure.

Computerised information systems used within agencies to manage their own operations have had much better success. Such systems directly benefit agency managers and can be reduced to manageable proportions.

For example, the US Postal Service is improving the management of its utility bills, and automated processes are needed to overcome the problems of magnitude and data availability. This agency has over 35,000 facilities, with well over 100,000 accounts served by over 5,000 utility vendors, many of whom cannot bill electronically. One year's worth of electricity invoices from one single utility in one single state makes a stack of paper about 5 inches high. Manual analysis of such data is prohibitive and data entry is taking a lot of time, but all the data will consume less than a gigabyte, fitting easily on to a modern desktop computer. Even with just the data that it has collected to date (less than 25 per cent of the total), the agency has been able to perform cross-facility comparisons that immediately unearthed erroneous rate charges. Savings of several hundred thousand dollars at one facility were twenty times the cost of the data collection and automation effort.

Clearly, information systems are indispensable in public sector reform: the key is to find appropriate and feasible applications and, as discussed next, to develop them in an effective manner.

Information systems standards of practice

This case study addresses the institution of a management information system (MIS). Any such system must meet three tests:

- *Management*: the system can answer the types of questions that managers need to ask.
- *Information*: information must be produced; that is, data organised to provide added insight not available from the input alone.
- *System*: the product must integrate various data sets to provide a single information source for managers.

When developing such an MIS, there are a number of different models that can be applied. Here three are described that have proven useful in particular public sector contexts.

Structured development

The IBM Business Systems Planning methodology has served as the core for many other development methods (IBM 1978). The approach works well for understanding interactive uses of data and designing large-scale systems. Government organisations can afford the enormous effort and highly skilled people needed. The approach takes a long time; in the past this has never really been a problem for agencies concerned more with input than output.

Until the mid-1980s, information systems managers directed system development efforts because there were no personal computers to accomplish business-sized tasks. Today, any manager's desktop system can store, manipulate and communicate data by the megabyte. Users are no longer willing to wait three years or longer to get a system that meets today's needs.

One of the principal failings of this type of top-down model is that even the most sophisticated design will fail if the system has no data in it. The only source of data is the individuals at the levels where events actually happen. If a data system demands input from, but has no utility for, lower levels there will be little support or quality control. To be effective and self-sustaining, a data system must provide utility to everyone who must work with it; otherwise, the system must be so strongly emphasised by agency executives that the appropriate emphasis and resources are devoted to its maintenance.

Evolutionary development

The 'evolutionary' alternative integrates information held in discrete existing systems (Hussain and Hussain 1981). This approach, often associated with executive support systems, emphasises performance measures or 'critical success factors' (Forster and Rockart 1989). Where requirements can be specified, the needed data can be transferred from each of the existing systems and, if necessary, the existing data sets can be modified to accommodate one or two new standard elements. This approach avoids replacing working data systems with untried systems and accommodates internal concerns over the ownership of the systems and data. It also promotes the successive successful inclusion of data sets in order of priority (Sprague and Carlson 1982).

Evolution saves time and money but has drawbacks. Accepting whatever data sets are available creates a continuing maintenance problem. Adopting the 'best' of similar existing applications creates resistance to a system invented in a rival agency. Institutionalising an acceptable application using obsolete technology (e.g. a DOS-based program in a Windows environment) may result in scepticism. While not crippling faults, these issues complicate management of the system. Finally, evolutionary approaches are only possible where data is already being held on an existing information system.

Prototyping approach

An alternative is the 'prototyping' approach, now used at the Logistics Management Institute in almost all its public sector systems development work. It is based on two observations:

- any automated system is likely to be technologically outdated within three years of being designed;

- any automated system will be effective only to the extent that the lowest-level managers can use it, or believe that it will be used, to make decisions that affect them.

Prototyping is a refinement of the evolutionary approach, but it is output-oriented: rather than focusing on programming issues or the existing data content, prototyping asks what the customer wants to do with the information. Once that is established, it is much easier to determine what data is needed, where to find it, and how to absorb it or collect it as required. It shifts the focus of the system from the programmers' convenience to the users' requirements. This shift of power is not always received warmly by programmers, but the process does increase managerial buy-in: having seen (and defined) the prototype, managers want to have the working version available as soon as possible.

The prototyping system development process follows the general model indicated in traditional literature, scaled down to reflect immediate implementation of the most important data modules. Capabilities may be expanded once the basic data system has gained acceptance. The steps in the process are:

- *Gain the commitment* Top level managers must make adequate resources available and must make it clear that this system is going to be the one that will be used.
- *Review the business objectives and processes* Define with top managers what things are important and how they want to present them. One way of doing this is by 'mocking up' an executive briefing with notional data. In public sector reform terms, this is where appropriate outcome measures are defined.
- *Determine the data needed to support system displays* Once it is possible to specify how the displays must appear, defining the minimum set of data elements is fairly simple. However, the developer must pay attention to effective data gathering and use, with particular concern for future aggregation levels. (The term 'displays' is used to avoid confusion between computer system outputs (displays) and agency outputs, such as regulations or projects.)
- *Determine where the data is created and used* The display structure drives what the input data must be; on the other hand, the feasibility of gathering the data may limit the possible displays unless the organisation is willing to commit the resources to ensure that data can be gathered.
- *Design information systems and gain prototype approval* Use commercial software already adopted as an agency standard. This facilitates its acceptance at all levels as well as permitting wide user testing of the prototype.
- *Rapid implementation* Once the prototype is modified to meet initial comments, the system must be issued and must be placed into service

quickly and forcefully. The agency head must begin using it as a basis for demanding action from subordinate executives. Comparative embarrassment tends to be a highly effective prod for implementing a new system.

• *Modification and improvement* The agency proponent for the new system must be prepared to make changes quickly in response to field-identified issues. This is simplified by the use of standard software suites, but it must be accompanied by the capability to make the necessary changes. The prototype may become the primary system, or the prototype can be transferred quite easily to a more powerful data system.

The application of this approach in a US agency attempting to implement performance management is described in the following case study.

ANALYSIS

Case background

The case study in this chapter examines how one public agency attempted to use automated systems to help its executives refocus the agency on its mission. The agency was not successful and so is left anonymous. However, it should be understood that even the 'failures' were honest efforts by agency staff members to implement approved processes – processes that may no longer meet the standards of users with current technology.

General agency description

The agency is a bureau within a US Cabinet Department: that is, it is three layers deep. Above it, there is the Department and an intermediate agency. The organisational setting is shown in Figure 5.3. Within the agency are several programme offices, responsible for executing the agency's major mission areas, and a number of geographically oriented field offices which also report to the agency head. Each of the field offices has one major line organisation/centre that supervises the technical work programmes of the one or more facilities where the actual work of the agency gets done. Because the money is spent in the field, a great deal of political support comes to the field locations, which therefore have more power than would appear from the chart.

Perhaps one-quarter of the agency's employees are located in the national headquarters, where they do all the paperwork that presumably facilitates the mission execution by the rest of the organisation. There is no great confidence in the field offices that this is in fact the case, and those offices sometimes try to minimise the headquarters' opportunities to provide oversight.

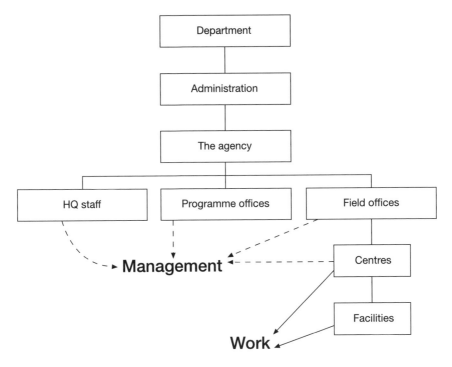

Figure 5.3 Organisation of the case study agency

Agency missions

This agency's charter requires it to enforce regulations and to enhance the commercial viability of the industries that it regulates. The nature of the problem being regulated and the effects of the regulated community's actions cannot practically be observed directly. They must therefore be assessed by indirect data gathering and by extrapolation from scientific models. Consequently, there is a strong scientific component to the agency's activities and it now considers itself a science agency rather than a regulatory or developmental one. The majority of its activities are directed at information gathering, despite its notional mission of enforcement. The information gathering requirements far exceed the capacity of the agency, which must depend on a wide range of university-affiliated research centres through grants or contracts.

Automated systems

The agency's scientific background provides its personnel with excellent skills in automated systems use, as well as excellent suites of computers. However, at the time that this case study begins (1996), the corporate information management office was newly created and newly staffed.

In keeping with the agency's science ethic, in 1994 it undertook a peer review of its activities. The large volume of information collected to support this science review provided agency managers for the first time with reports on activities, costs, deliverables (at least for the current year) and the major programmes that these activities purported to support. Recognising the potential value of this data set, the agency head directed that it be used as the basis for a 'corporate management information system'.

Agency technical staff members formed an MIS working group, but did not consider how data elements were to be used either for data manipulation or to address managerial data needs. The resulting 'database' consisted of a series of report pages; a system that this author calls a 'report-generator': data is entered in a given format, and printed out in the same format. It had no query capability without programming and, because data elements were not defined to be mutually exclusive, the system could not aggregate financial information accurately. The agency referred to this product as its MIS, but for the purposes of this chapter it will be referred to as the 'report-generator' to avoid confusion with the subsequent effort to develop a real MIS.

The working group members did have a good knowledge of computer technology: they instituted a client/server architecture and began to implement Internet-based access to the system (needed to bypass the problem of multiple computer platforms within the agency). However, there was no effort to require the use of the system or to collect any more data. Thus, by the end of 1996, the system still contained only the original 1994 data.

As a rule, financial management systems are among a public agency's most sophisticated. This agency had a Department-wide financial system which, however, only reported actual expenditures. The agency had supplemented that system with a more detailed financial tracking system to record also funding that had been budgeted and obligated (i.e. costs incurred but not disbursed). That system served the agency's field offices and financial staff well, but had little value to agency managers because expenditures could not be related to programmes or facilities.

Facilities consolidation study

Congress had been a good friend to the agency through the 1990s. While other agencies were labouring under budget freezes and real reductions, the agency was experiencing 10 per cent real annual growth in its operating budgets. The general support for the agency made it an excellent place for its Congressional sponsors to hide 'pork-barrel' projects (public works projects of dubious general utility, targeted to specific districts, creating jobs and accordingly good publicity for lawmakers in their home constituencies). In 1994, as usual, the agency was constructing several new facilities.

The 1994 national elections brought the first change in Congressional party control in 40 years. As it happened, most of the agency sponsors kept their seats, but they had lost their influence. In 1995, Congress required the agency to determine whether it would be cost-effective to consolidate or elim- inate some facilities from the inventory. However, the agency leadership (of the same party) treated the minority-party lawmakers as its sponsors, even though they had lost their committee chairmanships. The agency therefore ignored the requirement. By 1996, the change of control appeared to be durable; besides, Congress refused to confirm the Department's new Cabinet officer until a stack of overdue reports was submitted.

The project team assembled for the facility consolidation study was dir- ected to obtain its data from the report-generator which, however, failed abysmally in the task. It contained no current information; the information that it did have was structured as text and thus unable to support analysis; and the types of information that were included did not address management issues. During the study process, the available data was re-entered into a real database system but a great deal of additional information had to be col- lected. After the facility consolidation study was completed, the agency head directed that the new data set be used as the basis of a new MIS to replace the report-generator.

Case evolution

This section describes the agency's passage through the steps of a prototyp- ing approach to system development, as outlined earlier, in developing this new MIS.

Gain the commitment

The MIS design effort enjoyed top-level support from the beginning, but that support was soon undermined by bureaucratic challenges, particularly agency reorganisation. Top-level support was conveyed in several important ways:

- the agency head had insisted since 1994 that an MIS be used as the principal source of data for external briefings and activities, in order to present a consistent story from one meeting to the next;
- to maintain the perception of the 'MIS' (i.e. the report-generator) as the official repository of agency data, the data collection during the facility study was presented as an update of the prior data;
- the initial meeting for the MIS project (i.e. the development of a real MIS, building on the results of the facility consolidation study) was chaired by the agency head, who made it clear to all that she was solidly behind this requirement.

However, two reorganisation actions occurred at the very outset of the new

MIS project. In the first, the agency instituted a formal information management activity under the direction of a new administrative office reporting to the agency head; the MIS project was then assigned to this new information management office. Although this provided a focus for the development of a system, there was no real hand-off of the report-generator product. The group that had developed the report-generator had (through the facility consolidation project) accepted the need for major changes. Unaware of this epiphany, the new group saw the report-generator as the natural baseline for the new MIS because of its technological sophistication and its title as the 'agency MIS'. Additionally, having little experience with systems development on this scale, they required contracted support but relied on the incumbent report-generator contractors who had been unable to deliver the desired data system in the past.

In the second reorganisation, occurring shortly afterwards, the agency head was promoted and moved to another agency within the same department, taking along some key staff members. During entry briefings, the information management office staff could easily have disavowed the legacy report-generator system, but they chose to tell the new agency head that the system was functioning well. Meanwhile, numerous office directors stated that the report-generator was useless.

After a demonstration in which an 'upgraded' report-generator failed to run at all, the new agency head directed a halt to programming work on the MIS until the requirements definition was complete. But instead the information management staff refocused their efforts, and those of their contractors, to frantic programming to prove that their system did indeed work. Thereafter, information requirements developed from programme and field office interviews were constantly met with statements that the desired improvements were already included in the latest version of the report-generator.

Essentially, then, two parallel processes of MIS development were underway within the agency: one described in detail below that began with a fundamental review of agency objectives and processes, and one based on an attempt to resuscitate and incrementally adapt the report-generator.

Review the business objectives and processes

At the same time that the agency was undergoing its reorganisations, the entire Department (in response to the GPRA) was reviewing its mission statements and programme goals. While beneficial in the long run, potentially changing missions made it very difficult for the agency to commit to performance measures. Even without that, the definition of outcomes was very controversial: in resource regulation, the health of the resources is subject to a large number of factors other than the involvement of the agency. For instance, the much-discussed El Niño weather cycle in 1998 will certainly have an effect on resource stocks. Another challenge was to define the utility of basic research activities, inherently aimed at knowledge for which the value can only be assessed after it is acquired.

The decision was made to segment managerial information into two parts: mission and administration. Until specific goals for the mission programmes could be established, the agency would manage its mission funds generally, using relative priorities. The MIS definition process refocused to address primarily administrative issues.

The prototyping process started by developing a proposed executive briefing that offered data displays on some 50 indicators showing the general direction of the agency and its administrative functions. About half of the information could be obtained from the report-generator data set. Even this outdated information was useful in demonstrating prototype displays because the content and numbers were generally familiar to managers. Almost all of the remainder of the prototype was built with the data gathered during the facility consolidation study. In a very few cases, notional data had to be added in order to illustrate a specific function, such as earned-value tracking, for which the agency had no supporting data at all.

The executive briefing was developed, using agency standard software, in approximately one week. It served as a much more fruitful base for the subsequent interviews than simply asking senior managers for listings of the types of data that they needed.

Information requirements interviews were conducted in each programme and special staff office. The programme office responses were nearly unanimous, and the special staff offices shared a great number of the requirements. Clearly, above a certain level, programme management responsibilities do not vary greatly, regardless of programme content.

The Appendix to this chapter shows the pattern of the responses. Almost all programme managers expressed the most interest in budgetary information. In the interviews, there was no interest in the logistical data gathered during the facility consolidation study because these programme managers did not fund specific facilities. However, the agency head and her immediate staff had a strong demand for logistical data, as did the field directors interviewed informally before the project ended.

Managers seldom sought outcome measurement information. The interviewers tested each of the managers on this issue and all responded that there were far too many confounding factors. Key issues and accomplishments were instead shown on a 'hot sheet' of current visible issues, although there was a consensus that these hot items were urgent but not really important.

The executive briefing was used only after letting managers express their priority needs for information, which in most cases resulted in no significant response. Once shown the executive briefing, managers became much more involved and were able to generate several additional ideas. Several managers became indignant that the data they wanted could have been delivered by an MIS but for implementation failures.

Determine the data needed to support system displays

Prototyping renders the data definition process almost trivial. Once the executive briefing was adjusted to accommodate managers' ideas that had not been considered, the supporting data sets served as the application data requirements.

Determine where the data is created and used

The process model that the new MIS would support, which emerged as a result of the study, was one that followed the normal budgeting flow: the headquarters staff would make fund allocations that served as the constraint on field action. At the other end of the chain, field facilities would develop proposed project plans. Intermediate offices (regional offices and centres) would be responsible for allocating their shares of programme funds to the different projects based on their prioritisation schemes, whatever those might be. That allowed the field facilities to use the information on approved projects as the basis for their project management at the field level.

Resistance to this process model came from two directions. Some intermediate office managers correctly saw that allocation by the central programme offices reduced the power of the regional offices and centres, which had been black holes for money. However, other intermediate office managers did endorse the concept.

The other principal source of resistance was the agency's administrative office:

- the information management staff were (as described earlier) already involved in a frantic parallel effort to get the report-generator working. To them the MIS definition effort seemed to be an embarrassing interference;
- the budget staff saw this initiative as a bureaucratic war between the headquarters staff and the field offices, in which the budget office would do most of the work yet be left in a crossfire from both sides.

Without the cooperation of the administrative office (which was also the contract manager for the project), the MIS definition effort began to wither.

Design information systems and gain prototype approval

Again, with the data defined by the executive briefing and the use of commercial software, the development effort was trivial. The primary issue to be resolved was how to distribute the system. Given the small number of organisational units with access to the MIS, spread across several time zones, a simple client/server architecture could have been employed; a file-transfer architecture would have worked just as well. The tools for data management via the Internet in 1996 were not able to meet serious applications; by 1999 such an approach would be a strong contender. As a result of the resistance of the administrative office, the MIS recommendations were never approved (or considered, for that matter). As of a year later, the amended report-generator system was still not working properly either.

Rapid implementation

One of the programme offices had a manual process for developing an annual report. The office staff obtained project reports on paper from the field and bound them together, using a calculator to add up total programme numbers to use in a cover letter. After seeing the executive briefing, that programme office requested a tool to collect data from the field in a database. A stripped-down version of the executive briefing database, including a data entry module to preclude data entry errors, was provided within a few days. The entire system was compiled to a run-time version so that even those field units which did not yet have the agency standard system (not an uncommon occurrence in any US government agency) could run the program. The entire system was also carefully coordinated with the most recent version of the in-house report-generator effort to ensure that the data would be able to be imported directly to it once collected.

Despite the apparent win–win nature of this arrangement, it actually caused the death of both the sanctioned MIS effort and the in-house report-generator effort. Ostensibly concerned that a programme office system might be incompatible with the future MIS, but really worried that successful use of this small data system would replace the MIS effort entirely, the information management staff prevailed on the agency head to terminate the programme office's effort. However, through the discussions that ensued, the information management office was also directed to use a version of the stripped-down system as the basis for yet another planned agency-wide MIS. Whether and when that directive will be followed on its third issuance remains to be seen.

Modification and improvement

As related, the case study never reached the modification and improvement phase. For systems that are implemented, whether arrived at by a systematic approach or an evolutionary approach, a process of continuous improvement is essential.

CONCLUSIONS AND RECOMMENDATIONS

The role of management information systems in public sector reform

Information systems and reform in this case: a mixed bag

This case at first glance appears to be a refutation of information systems standard practices. Certainly it illustrates at least one example (and the case is not atypical) where a top-down big-system approach aimed at producing an unsinkable MIS resulted in no product whatever. The alternative approach, through evolution from successful prototypes and modules, might perhaps have resulted in a lifeboat by comparison, but it would have allowed agency executives to get where they wanted to go. And, as often happens in maritime disasters when the ship is not abandoned soon enough, the suction of the sinking MIS took the lifeboat down with it anyway.

The literature and theory allow for evolutionary and prototyping approaches, particularly where the goals or duration of the end product are unclear. Information systems professionals may resist because of the threat to their control, profit margins and possibly their jobs, in no particular order. Those human failures are not the fault of information systems theory (although the theory would be stronger for incorporating them).

This case study has successful aspects:

- *The stripped-down system* It worked. It was developed very quickly, met the users' needs and indeed may yet form the kernel of the new system (and eventually there must be one: it is unthinkable that a major government agency can simply continue forever with no management information system).
- *The MIS definition process* It demonstrated the ability of a prototype to define customer needs quickly with standard commercial database and presentation graphics software. That development process followed the standard IS procedures, as described above.

The failures in this case can be attributed to several causes, principally the determined opposition from the agency's information management staff, and the new agency head's reluctance to challenge them. The author must share some of the blame for being unable to convey the proper win–win vision to those staff members.

Considerations for the potential use of information systems

Public agencies are almost invariably very large. Although armies of bureaucrats worked numbers manually for thousands of years, effective management of modern agencies requires effective automated systems. Figure 5.2 showed a number of places where data comparisons are essential to effective management. At every point, the power of computerised information systems makes an enormous task feasible, as in the earlier US Postal Service example of managing energy consumption data.

In this case, the information systems environment itself was one of the aspects of the agency that needed the most reform. Some of these dysfunctionalities are worth bearing in mind whenever a public agency is involved with information systems:

- *Limited user capabilities* Field users are incorrectly assumed to be incompetent. The result is a desire for a totally foolproof system that tolerates no use of local judgement.
- *Slow procurement cycles* Government procurement rules favour large long-term contracts. Small wonder that the systems look the same.
- *Need for consensus* Because there is generally no 'bottom line', most government activities are based on consensus building and conflict avoidance. A product that is acceptable to everybody must be either impossibly complex or devoid of content. Small non-threatening prototypes can defeat this pathology.
- *Primary motivations* Where there is no measure of accomplishment, many government managers aim for an absence of criticism instead. This agency's staff persisted in a vain project, rather than admit a need for help, and chose to have no system rather than accept system imperfections.

Implementation of information systems for public sector reform: recommendations

There are a number of lessons to be learned from this case study (and much other work not discussed here). They pertain to system approaches in general, and public sector implementations in particular.

Information systems approaches

- Use prototypes! Although many information managers are schooled in the structured (top-down, big-system) approach, the evolutionary or prototyping approach can make them heroes much faster.
- Any system over 3–4 years old is obsolete. A contractor offering up a desktop application in 1999 using dBase-III (now out of business) would be rejected out of hand, yet that technology produced very useful results little more than five years ago. A problem identified five years ago has certainly changed in the interim – if it still exists at all.
- Small practical systems beat large unkept promises. A system – even with quirks – can be improved. Systems that are never delivered cannot be improved.
- A picture is worth a thousand words. Requirements definition documents

are often incomprehensible to most non-programming managers. When the customer is unhappy with the finished system, the developer feels betrayed because the customer 'reviewed and approved the specifications'. A picture that shows what the system would look like, followed quickly by a prototype that works like the real system, results in common expectations among managers and developers.

Implementing performance measurement systems in the public sector

In addition to the general comments about information system development, there are some special considerations when dealing with the public sector.

• The 'golden rule' of public administration: follow the money. Public agency work is political, and everybody has a title of some sort: whether they have any influence is another matter. The sure sign of influence is control over funding.
• There is no bottom line. Therefore, there is little to buffer public sector managers' agendas and self-promotion. The case study should have reinforced the idea of being wary of personal sensitivities.
• Time has no urgency. Few US agencies will really be able to implement outcome-based management, but most will engage in endless taskforce meetings. A system development process that depends on such a taskforce's guidance is doomed to non-delivery.
• If you cannot manage outcomes, at least manage inputs and processes. Today's technology puts affordable computing power on every desktop. Rather than wasting resources on unachievable measures of mission performance, reform advocates should begin by insisting that every agency at least manage its internal affairs efficiently, beginning with the technology and knowledge available right now.

Conception–reality gaps

The flow of events described in this case study indicates that there are some significant gaps between conceptions and realities in the information systems field. 'Dilbert' is a comic strip from the US that deals largely with the inability of computer professionals to operate in a social world. Dilbert's huge popularity indicates the degree to which the general public has been exposed to this gap.

Without revisiting the case study in detail, Table 5.1 may serve to illustrate some of the gaps between IS concepts and the everyday reality managers must face, especially but by no means exclusively in the public sector. It includes gaps relating to all but the technology and other resources dimensions of the ITPOSMO model described in Chapter 3.

This list is by no means exhaustive; other conclusions may be drawn from the case study. What is important is to cause information systems

Table 5.1 Case study gaps between information system conceptions and realities

Conception	Reality
Government agencies are hierarchical	The field offices of many agencies often have great political strength
The information system should facilitate each person contributing better to the organisation's mission	Many people have no incentive to start contributing
Detailed fact-gathering and process modelling will result in both process improvements and an effective IS design concept	Automating and improving a process that does not produce results will end up with a system that also does not produce results, only faster and more voluminously
A formal design process with maximum input will produce an accepted and useful system	Lengthy processes result in obsolescent systems; also, they favour those who view the project as a career plan to retirement age
Managers need more data to make better decisions	Managers already have too much data: what they need is useful information
Given the facts, managers will make the rational decisions that IS processes, and data in general, support	Political decisions are not rational. The purpose of public agencies (in democracies) is often to add subjective values and considerations to preclude the effects of too much rationality in society
Pressure from the top will make an IS effort take root	Minor functionaries can outlast political appointees
Agencies need and demand accurate information	If information is absent at the moment of need, somebody will make it up; nobody will find out or do anything about it
Agencies have large computer systems and therefore capable information design and management staff	Good information systems people in the 1990s rarely work for the half pay that public sector compensation packages represent

professionals and public administrators to understand that the job is not to build a system but to manage the agency. A computerised information system is an essential tool – but only a tool.

REFERENCES

Forster, N.S. and Rockart, J.F. (1989) *Critical Success Factors: An Annotated Bibliography*, Cambridge, MA: Massachusetts Institute of Technology.

GAO (1997) *GPRA: 1997 Governmentwide Implementation Will Be Uneven*, Washington, DC: General Accounting Office.

Hussain, D. and Hussain, K.M. (1981) *Information Processing Systems for Management*, Homewood, IL: Richard D. Irwin.

IBM (1978) *Business Systems Planning*, White Plains, NY: IBM.

NAPA (1994) *Toward Useful Performance Measurement*, Washington, DC: National Academy of Public Administration.

NAPA (1998) *Effective Implementation of the Government Performance and Results Act*, Washington, DC: National Academy of Public Administration.

OMB (1997) *The Government Performance and Results Act: Report to the President and Congress*, Washington, DC: Office of Management and Budget.

Osborne, D. and Gaebler, T. (1992) *Reinventing Government: How the Entrepreneurial Spirit is Transforming the Public Sector*, Reading, MA: Addison-Wesley.

Sprague, R.H. Jr and Carlson, E.D. (1982) *Building Effective Decision Support Systems*, Englewood Cliffs, NJ: Prentice-Hall.

APPENDIX: INFORMATION REQUIREMENTS

Information type	Number of offices citing[a]	Contained in MIS[b]
Mission information		
Scientific database	4	X
Trend tracking tools	2	X
Compliance rates	1	X
Plans and policies		
Administration mission, strategic plan, milestones (text)	7	A
Administration performance rating (undefined)	7	X
Agency mission, strategic plan, milestones (text)	7	A
Agency performance rating (undefined)	7	X
Programme performance rating (undefined)	7	X
Programme-level missions, plans and milestones (text)	7	X
Sub-milestone accomplishment status	7	X
Accomplishment of regulatory requirements	4	X
Agency overhead percentage	4	B
Programme overhead percentage	4	B
Projects affecting programme area	4	B
Agency operating plan	1	B
Status of Administration milestones	1	X
Status of agency milestones	1	B
Organisation		
Access to other programmes' milestone data and issues	6	X
Partnership or shared resource information	6	B
Primary research centres involved in projects	1	B
Directing (project execution)		
Accomplishments	7	X
Tasks and objectives	7	B
Projects by location	3	B
Staff costs per project	3	C
Staff time per project	3	B
Current status of projects	2	X
Overtime per project	2	X
Deliverable dates	1	X
Level of science performed	1	C
Project schedules	1	B
Science quality of projects	1	C
Budget		
Agency budget	7	B
Project budget and funding	7	B
Funding for projects addressing areas of concern	6	B
Funding sources	6	B
Funding for priority issues	4	B
Summaries of project expenditures	1	A
Staffing and training		
Personnel (headcounts by location, project, etc.)	7	B
Projections of staff allocations	5	X

Information type	Number of offices citing [a]	Contained in MIS [b]
Staff skills	3	C
Collateral duty contact persons	1	X
Staff availability (workload)	1	B
Training funds	1	A
Training status	1	X
Coordination (communication and outreach)		
Top-10 issue listings	7	X
Activity and budget proposal process/data	3	B
Group document processing tools	3	X
Outreach activities	3	X
Congressional inquiry history	2	X
Contract listings	2	C
Controlled (i.e. high-visibility) correspondence	2	X
Partnerships by location	2	A
Regional management issues	2	X
International activities and negotiations	1	B
Public access to agency activities (Internet)	1	X

Notes:
a   Number of offices citing: maximum is seven. Four are line programme offices, three are headquarters staff offices.
b   Contained in MIS:
    A = Data in original report-generator MIS (restructured to database form)
    B = Data in MIS restructured with project as record level
    C = Data in MIS if facility consolidation study database had been incorporated
    X = Data not in MIS (new data collection process required)

6 Automating personnel records for improved management of human resources

The experience of three African governments

Piers Cain

Abstract: The rapid developments in information technology are often seen by policy makers as an opportunity for developing countries to accelerate public sector reform for a relatively low level of investment. This chapter addresses this perception by describing the results of public sector information system evaluations in Ghana, Uganda and Zimbabwe. These information systems involved automation of personnel records, aimed at improving the management of human resources. However, this study demonstrates that the real costs of computerisation projects are high. The preconditions for such projects are often not in place, so that attempts are being made to layer computerised systems on top of collapsed paper-based information systems. Data quality remains poor because current realities provide little motivation for maintaining accurate data. In addition, a move from paper-based to electronic records creates significant audit and legal problems in providing documentary evidence in the prosecution of fraud and other cases. A conclusion is made about new approaches to information systems and records, focused on the context of reform.

BACKGROUND

The context of reform

Structural adjustment programmes

During the 1980s and 1990s most countries in sub-Saharan Africa experienced economic hardship and participated in structural adjustment

programmes (SAPs), often as part of conditionality for loans from international institutions such as the World Bank and International Monetary
Fund. The three countries examined in this evaluation study – Ghana,
Uganda and Zimbabwe[1] – have all implemented SAPs with varying degrees
of success since the 1980s.

The country programmes differed in detail, but were broadly similar in
objectives and strategies. Policy objectives included making the policy
environment more market-oriented, accelerating growth and expanding
employment. Strategies included prudent fiscal and monetary management
by boosting incentives to the private sector, reforming the regulatory framework and developing human resources through investments in education and
health. In addition, public sector reform was seen as a key strategy element.

Public sector reform: efficiency and human resource management

Two components of public sector reform strategies are particularly relevant
to the cases reported here: first, increased efficiency in the use of both money
and people; second, improved human resource management, which has long
been recognised as an important requirement for the public sector in sub-
Saharan Africa (World Bank 1989). Recommended improvements have
included staff testing, competitive entrance examinations, regular appraisals,
promotion on merit, selective improvement in the pay structure and accurate
personnel records.

In all three countries, these two components have been combined in efforts
to alter public sector pay. One main objective has been to reduce the total
wage bill in government, typically by substantial downsizing of the public
service. A second main objective has been to enable governments to pay
public servants a living wage by dividing the remaining total wage bill
between fewer staff. Poor pay is the primary factor in government's inability
to attract and retain sufficient numbers of capable staff. This in turn leads to
inefficiency. Moreover, inadequate salaries are recognised as a significant
cause of low-level corruption.

Between 1986 and 1996 Ghana cut its public service by about one-third.
During the first phase of the public sector reform programme, the government (on the insistence of the World Bank) agreed to cut the number of
public service posts by 15,000 a year for three years. In fact the number of
public servants has dropped from 143,260 in 1986 to around 80,000 in 1996
through a combination of cutting posts, privatisation and hiving off
functions to parastatals (Coopers and Lybrand 1993; Marshall 1996).

The number of employees on the government payroll in Uganda has been
cut by half, from 320,000 in 1991 to 148,000 in 1996 (Lagara 1996). The
purpose of downsizing was to reduce the cost of government and to increase
salaries of remaining public servants. This would improve efficiency by eliminating the necessity for them to 'moonlight' to earn enough money on which
to live.

In Zimbabwe the focus of the public sector reform programme during the first phase of structural adjustment was a reduction in personnel costs, which comprised about 30 per cent of the national budget. By contrast to Ghana and Uganda, in Zimbabwe most of the savings came from allowing wage increases to fall behind inflation rather than by cutting posts (World Bank 1996). Real wages fell 30–40 per cent and, as a result, in 1996 there were strikes for higher salaries in the public sector which were extensive and well supported.

Computerised personnel management information systems and reform

In all three countries the experience of public sector reform, and of downsizing in particular, has highlighted deficiencies in the personnel information available to managers in government. At the beginning of the public sector reform process, apart from ageing mainframe payroll systems, there were no computerised systems available to provide statistics on staff numbers. These legacy systems were not designed to support human resource planning and lacked both the necessary data fields and the functionality to support this work.

In Uganda and Ghana there was no reliable data on the size of the public service. Both countries experienced a serious 'ghost workers' problem which inflated the size of the payroll. It was unclear whether government retrenchment exercises were cutting real people or 'ghosts'. In short, these governments lacked the information needed to make informed decisions about who should be retrenched. This point was particularly important when reductions in the size of the public service were tied to disbursement of World Bank loans.

This perspective also informed the thinking of the 1989 Public Service Review Commission (PSRC) in Zimbabwe, where concerns over the efficiency and accountability of the public service drew attention to the absence of reliable personnel information. The PSRC believed that the public sector recruitment boom of the early 1980s had led to a significant number of senior posts being filled by relatively young people, thus blocking career opportunities for junior staff. It noted that information on staff, such as age by grade data (together with other grade-related data on turnover and vacancies) was essential for sound human resource planning to avoid the recurrence of similar situations (Government of Zimbabwe 1989). Yet such data was not available.

Because of these personnel information deficiencies, projects to implement automated personnel management information systems (MIS) have been a prominent feature of the information technology (IT) effort of many African public services in recent years. An example of such a project, from Ghana, is provided in Box 6.1.

In theory, a computerised personnel MIS offers significant advantages over conventional manual methods because of its speed, precision and flexibility.

Box 6.1 Ghana's integrated personnel and payroll database (IPPD)

The IPPD project was the largest and most complex IT project ever undertaken by the Government of Ghana. It combined information about staff salaries and personnel data to support the public service payroll function within the Controller and Accountant General's Department, and to support the central human resource management function within the Office of Head of Civil Service, Ghana Education Service and Audit Service.

IPPD is a relational database, using a package called SIGAGIP supplied by CGI Informatique in Paris. It uses a central minicomputer with 150 microcomputers and dumb terminals over an Ethernet network using the TCP/IP protocol. The system is located in Accra, the capital, and was planned to be accessible up to a maximum of two miles from the centre, though most terminals were initially within half a mile.

The original project objectives centred upon the need to provide more reliable and useful information on Item 1 of the national budget (personnel emoluments) and staffing. The objectives also included improving the efficiency, responsiveness and timeliness of personnel management; enabling the use of manual personnel records to be minimised; and allowing for a substantial rationalisation of personnel registries.

In 1993 there were changes of emphasis in the light of developing policy objectives and the experience of Ghana's Civil Service Reform Programme. There was greater stress on the importance of providing information for use in human resource management and to support an ambitious staff training and development programme. The objectives also placed greater emphasis on the need to allow a wider and much more geographically distributed clientele of end users.

Computerised systems may offer any, or all, of the following functions which can provide a valuable contribution to the reform process.

First, administrative actions, using the database to:

- produce listings of employees by age, length of service, job category, job grade, rate of pay, etc.;
- generate reports analysing distribution in such areas as relationships between age or service and job grade or pay;
- initiate and print internal memoranda and documents such as notification of pay increases or contracts of employment;

- produce external letters such as offers of employment;
- combine with electronic mailing facilities to transmit data and corre-spondence between terminals.

Second, decision support, using the database to:

- answer 'what if' and other *ad hoc* enquiries;
- carry out modelling and trend analysis;
- produce projections.

Some more advanced systems integrate three main areas of administration: people, payroll and pensions. An integrated database system allows payroll, pension and statutory sick-pay applications to use the data stored on the computerised personnel MIS. The advantages of swifter and cheaper human resource management arising from linking these areas is obvious.

As we shall see in the cases evaluated here, however, there is a major gap between theory and practice.

Evaluation method

Following a review of secondary sources, the evaluation of case studies reported here comprised interviews with key individuals involved in design-ing, developing and using personnel MIS; and a technical evaluation of the relationship between system capabilities and user requirements. Taken together, the information gathered through these approaches provided a basis to evaluate critically the degree to which the systems will be capable of underpinning effective human resource management.

A detailed list of questions was prepared for discussion with key indi-viduals involved in identifying user requirements for the personnel databases. The interviews were carried out principally in: the central institutions respon-sible for managing the personnel and payroll functions; the bureaux charged with providing central computing services; and with personnel officers in several key ministries and agencies such as health and education.

Filing systems and proposed or existing database structures at the central, ministry and district levels were examined for the validity of data entered in computerised systems and the nature of linkages between existing paper-based records and the database.

ANALYSIS OF CASE STUDY FINDINGS

IT project drivers and timetables under structural adjustment

In Ghana, Uganda and Zimbabwe, projects to create human resource data-bases were started with funding from international development agencies (referred to here as 'donors'). As already noted, the projects were closely connected with the implementation of broader adjustment and public sector reform programmes. The objectives of these programmes strongly influenced the direction, timing and pace of the computerisation projects. The process is outlined in Figure 6.1.

The broader programmes usually set specific targets for reducing the number of public servants, tied to a timetable for implementation. Yet, when the governments attempted to reduce staff numbers, they often discovered that they were unable to find the basic information needed to accomplish this task,

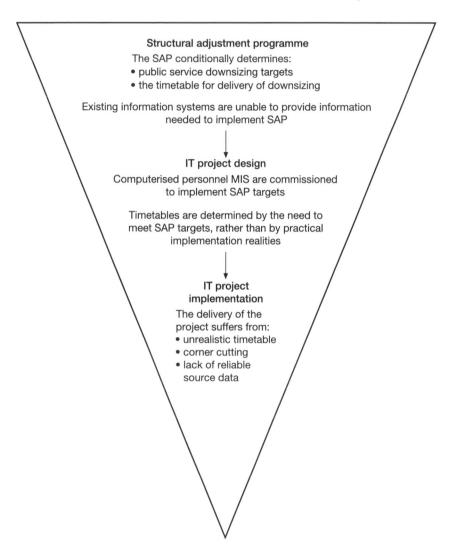

Structural adjustment programme
The SAP conditionally determines:
• public service downsizing targets
• the timetable for delivery of downsizing

Existing information systems are unable to provide information needed to implement SAP

IT project design
Computerised personnel MIS are commissioned to implement SAP targets

Timetables are determined by the need to meet SAP targets, rather than by practical implementation realities

IT project implementation
The delivery of the project suffers from:
• unrealistic timetable
• corner cutting
• lack of reliable source data

Figure 6.1 How structural adjustment programmes drive IT project implementation in Africa

such as accurate staff numbers or details of staff grades and location. Consequently, donors usually advised countries to create computerised personnel MIS to assist in achieving their reform objectives. The timetable for computerisation was framed by the timetable for downsizing.

The need to meet this latter timetable placed pressure on governments to implement the personnel automation projects very quickly. External consultancy firms bidding for the contracts to manage and implement these projects tended not to recommend realistic project timetables for fear of losing the business to a rival. Too often projects were designed with unrealistic timetables, leading to corner-cutting and the rejection of more time-consuming options that might have had a better long-term chance of success.

The SAP and public sector reform context, especially the downsizing of the public service, provided a rationale and a framework for computerisation in all three countries. Ironically, though, in each case the downsizing operation was completed *before* the databases became operational. In other words, although the high cost of creating the databases was justified by the downsizing exercise, in practice the databases did not contribute to the implementation of this public sector reform component. These were therefore cases of the 'isolate' approach to information age reform (see Chapter 2).

Poor data quality in personnel management information systems

Ghana's IPPD project was scheduled to take 18 months to complete. In retrospect this would appear to have been highly optimistic, given the technical obstacles and the prevailing culture of the Ghanaian public sector. The project timetable was extended several times, with IPPD finally going live in July 1995, 45 months after the project began. Delays were caused partly by software procurement problems but also by severe difficulties in capturing accurate data. The impact of the data inaccuracies were serious, resulting in large numbers of staff not receiving pay cheques for several months. In part this reflected delays in data being input into the system. Questions were asked in Parliament and the story attracted the attention of the press:

> Fifteen thousand staff of the Ghana Education Service (GES) have not been paid since the new data base pay system became operational last year. . . . While some of the affected staff did not provide the needed inputs at all, others failed to provide the required inputs to the appropriate quarters, hence the anomaly.
>
> (*Daily Graphic* 1996: 1)

The data for computerised personnel MIS tend to be drawn from several sources, including paper-based personnel files held in registries, nominal rolls, other databases, and surveys, including head counts. The issues involved in using these sources are discussed below.

Paper-based personnel files

The most significant finding of the study was the fundamental importance to the success of personnel systems of traditional paper personnel records. These systems need to capture information about staff members from the time they joined the public service until the present day. Inevitably, a large proportion of the staff will have joined many years before the introduction of any computerised system; therefore the only original source data to be found is in the form of paper records.

Ghana, Uganda and Zimbabwe are all former British colonies and their information systems are all based on the paper registry. The registry is an office responsible for the creation, control and maintenance in files of the active and semi-current records of an organisation. Each country had a very similar registry system, although levels of efficiency varied from country to country and ministry to ministry. A well-run registry depends heavily upon the management and leadership skills of the supervisor because of the large numbers of staff involved and the need for the meticulous application of filing rules and procedures to large volumes of documents.

Differences in how the registries are managed in each of these countries reflect the histories of their economic and political fortunes. The registry systems in Ghana and Uganda had largely collapsed. However, in both cases, UK Department for International Development-funded registry improvement projects had renovated selected registries. In all three countries, public servants complained that personnel files were incomplete (and sometimes non-existent) and that finding missing information was a significant cause of delay in dealing with personnel issues.

Automated personnel MIS ultimately rely heavily on personnel records stored in registries as the only authentic, reliable and legally valid source of most of the data required for the systems. Personnel systems must be complete if they are to be of use for making decisions about individuals. Their reliability as a data source for statistical analysis of employment patterns for the public service as a whole also depends upon their completeness. This means having access to information going back 30 years or more, which is the typical length of service of a career public servant. Where the paper records are incomplete or fragmented, it is very difficult to populate the database with meaningful data.

Paradoxically, despite the importance of personnel files as a source of personnel data, they are not a popular source of data with those responsible for designing and implementing computerised personnel MIS. In Ghana, personnel files were very quickly rejected as a source, and in Uganda it took several years before it was accepted that they were the only reliable source of much of the data needed for the new system. There are several reasons for this:

- Shortcomings in the manual systems (i.e. mainly the registries) are typically cited as a justification for creating the automated system and there is little confidence that the manual systems will provide the required data.

- The timetables for delivering database projects are too tight for a records management-based approach to be realistic, and in any case the resources required to restructure the paper records are not available.
- The personnel files at headquarters (e.g. the Office of Head of Civil Service) are often very incomplete and tend to be restricted to personnel recruited as established staff.
- Records tend not to be available for non-established staff or established staff initially recruited in non-established posts.
- Personnel files held in the line ministries may be more complete than those at headquarters, but they are located in different buildings from the computer into which data is being entered.
- Other data sources – such as nominal rolls compiled by each ministry, dumps of data from existing payroll databases and staff survey question-naire forms – appear at first to be more suitable and more convenient for data entry.

If these problems are to be overcome there is a need to develop a method-ology for obtaining reliable records sources.

Nominal rolls

In all three countries, line ministries are required to maintain nominal rolls: lists of staff employed in the ministry. Initially this may appear to be a useful source of the basic data needed for a personnel database such as name, age, position, etc. However, maintaining the nominal rolls is often regarded as a task of low priority and records are often out of date.

For example, in Uganda, a sample survey found that 6.5 per cent of those who still appeared on the staff list had left the ministry (retrenched, retired, deceased, etc.). Moreover 38.2 per cent of Ministry of Public Service officers at headquarters were being held against non-existent posts (Ministry of Public Service 1995). Because the nominal rolls are typically compiled from other records, if there is a discrepancy in the information, it is necessary to go back to other records to resolve the problem. In this sense, nominal rolls are 'second-hand' information. On their own, nominal rolls are not a sufficiently accurate source of information on which to base a new personnel MIS.

Databases

The advantage of using other databases as source data for personnel MIS is that data may be transferred automatically without re-keying. However, there are problems and limitations in this approach. First, the source database may be inaccurate. In both Uganda and Ghana there were serious problems of ghost workers on the payroll database. Only in Zimbabwe, where the central payroll database is widely regarded as being a very accurate source of data, could dumps of data from the payroll system reliably form an important source for a new personnel MIS. Second, the source data may not be structured in a way that is suitable for the new database. It may be cheaper to re-key the data, though this creates the opportunity for new inaccuracies. Third, unless the new personnel database is an upgrade of an older system, the source database will have been designed for an entirely different purpose, for example payroll. Thus it is likely there will be fields on the new personnel database that cannot be completed from other databases.

Surveys

Surveys to gather data about personnel have several advantages. The information is up to date; the survey team can decide what information should be collected; the survey forms can be designed to arrange the data collected for ease of data input; and the forms can be stored as inviolable records and backup.

There are also disadvantages. For example, in Ghana, surveys were used that relied heavily upon the integrity of those individuals completing the forms. The data collection survey forms were not checked against available establishment files held in the Personnel Registry of Office of Head of Civil Service or in line ministries. With the benefit of hindsight, the decision not to use personnel files for checking the date of birth and the date of appointment to the public service was a mistake. The former date determines date of retirement and the latter has a bearing on pensionable benefits. As the IPPD system was to be used to generate lists of staff about to retire, it was in the interest of individuals wishing to avoid retiring to enter false dates. At the time the survey was collected it was widely believed that the implementation of IPPD would lead to the abolition of establishment files, or at least to a major running down of the Office of Head of Civil Service Personnel Registry. The consequent notion that there would be no means of checking data submitted on the data entry forms may have further encouraged false entries.

The methodology and level of resourcing for the surveys is also important. In Ghana the resources were far short of what was required to cover the whole public service. On reflection, it would probably have been better to limit the focus to specific ministries to ensure a more complete resource and to audit the information against the available paper records.

Another problem with the survey approach is that unless the survey is carried out as a census – in other words, the data is gathered on the same day throughout the country (which requires a large, well-trained and well-organised team) – there is a large chance that discrepancies will occur. These may be caused by differences in the way the data is gathered in different locations or, if the data-gathering exercise is protracted, in staff being posted from one location to another and appearing in more than one set of statistics.

Finally, the survey data very rapidly becomes out-of-date. Unless the new personnel database is fully functioning and the data can be entered into it quickly, and unless there are efficient procedures for gathering changes to the data and entering those into the database, the problems can be serious.

CONCLUSIONS AND RECOMMENDATIONS

The role of personnel management information systems in public sector reform

The positive potential for computerised personnel MIS to contribute to public sector reform was noted above. With donor encouragement, African governments have therefore invested in computerisation projects. These projects absorb a relatively large proportion of the discretionary expenditure of the public service in the purchase of equipment, and rely heavily on expatriate consultants for project management and technical implementation. Typically they take a minimum of three to five years to implement from start to finish, which represents a substantial opportunity cost.

In practice, computerisation of the personnel function in Ghana, Uganda and Zimbabwe fell some way short of the theoretical potential. Like a number of related automation projects, there has been a relatively high failure rate *vis-à-vis* stated objectives. The reasons encompass a broad range of issues, many of them related to data quality, including: institutional issues, project design, protection of information, sustainability, sharing of information, data input, data output, and records management.

Poor data quality

Figure 6.2 illustrates the dilemma facing public sector managers in much of Africa when computerising personnel information. When the downsizing process begins, managers realise they are unable to obtain accurate information about staff numbers because the paper personnel information systems inherited from colonial times have broken down. The next step is often to decide to create a computerised database to deal with the problem.

Typically there is a lack of realism about the source data upon which the systems must be built. This reflects the pressures of macro-level reform objectives on the implementation of IT projects as well as a simple underestimation of the importance of reliable source data to the long-term success of automated human resource management systems.

The paper-based personnel records held in registries tend to be so disorganised and incomplete (and the time frame for completing the automation project so short) that the option of reorganising the personnel registries is usually rejected out of hand. Automation teams are then forced to resort to techniques for gathering *secondary sources* of information, such as surveys

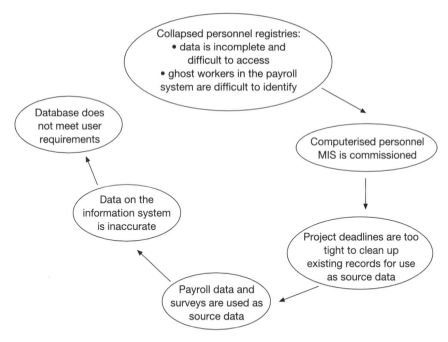

Figure 6.2 The source data trap

and head counts. Often there is no time to check the accuracy of the information against the available records. Yet the personnel files are the only authentic *primary sources* of the data needed for input into the automated system.
These record key events as they happened, such as promotions or gaps in
service, and they can be verified for authenticity. The result is that the data
entered in the new computerised database is often inaccurate or unreliable
in key areas.

Integrating the payroll and personnel functions on one database and a
system of personnel budgets, as has been done in Ghana, can do much to
reduce inaccurate data. This is because such budgets provide a financial
incentive for line managers to ensure database entries are kept accurate.

However, there is still a problem with verifying the accuracy of key information, such as dates of birth, dates of joining the service or breaks in
service, which are essential for calculating pension entitlements. The 'source
data trap' is sprung. The database cannot be used for the personnel management functions it was designed to fulfil because the data cannot be trusted.
Personnel management cannot function properly and the process has come
almost full circle.

In summary, then, automating a chaotic situation is likely to create yet
more chaos. Far from being in a position to take advantage of new technology, some developing countries therefore face formidable difficulties in

attempting to build upon unstable foundations. They are often moving rapidly towards an era of information age reform without adequate preparation. This has major consequences for the ability of these countries to implement public sector reform programmes.

Computerised personnel records and accountability

The problems of MIS data accuracy point to a further problem of computerisation: that computer records in general are not as reliable as paper systems. This relates to an additional public sector reform issue: that of accountability.

In many ways, this can be explained by the difference between a management information system and a record-keeping system. MIS contain timely, manipulable, non-redundant data. Record-keeping systems contain time-bound, inviolable, redundant data (AIIM 1989); they contain the institutional memory and, without them, public servants are not accountable to their political masters and subordinates are not accountable to their managers.

Yet these problems have rarely been articulated, and public managers have wrongly tended to assume that:

- appropriate and trustworthy source data was available for the computerised systems or that secondary data sources would meet the requirements;
- computerised systems had a records functionality already built into them;
- the necessary records management capacity existed to support these systems.

In reality, of course, these assumptions do not hold. Computerised databases tend to be inaccurate records unless there is a regular and rigorous audit by higher authorities, and computer-based data can easily become corrupted. Even when an uncorrupted backup exists, there are additional problems. First, the information is no longer a complete record of all transactions; there is only old data up to the time of backup. Second, unless it is possible to document precisely what data was entered into the system and what changes were made to existing data between the last backup and the discovery of data corruption, it will be impossible to recover the valid data.

Part of the solution is to use paper records as an integral component of the automated system. For example, there needs to be regular creation of hard copies with a printed time and date to provide a more reliable record. Second, hard-copy data input forms must be available to record what data, at what time, was input. Without this, the introduction of computerised personnel systems will undermine rather than support the accountability component of public sector reform.

Implementation of personnel management information systems for public sector reform: recommendations

The Appendix to this chapter provides details of a large number of problems encountered during the case studies and some potential solutions to those problems. Here, the focus will be solely on the issue of data quality since that proved to be a key problem. A summary of the approach is provided in Figure 6.3.

Part of the solution is to organise the paper-based records that do exist so that they can be used as source data for personnel databases. Without the source data which only records can supply, database projects will inevitably fail as tools for human resource management. Therefore, it is essential that far more attention and greater resources are devoted to this aspect of the automation project from the outset.

The scale of the problem is enormous. Governments need to recognise this as a priority issue and to build a capacity for large-scale records management projects, both to support automation and to maintain stable systems in the long term. Such projects will need to reorganise existing records where controls have been abandoned and to create sound record-keeping structures. To achieve the objective of providing source data for an entire public service within the time scale needed by the automation projects will require an intensive effort from the earliest possible stage of the automation project and the investment of significant resources.

Moreover, for one reason or another, some of the records needed for personnel management may not have been created, may have been lost or may have been destroyed. Countries such as Uganda, which have experienced a turbulent recent history, are unlikely to have public records which are as complete as those of countries that have enjoyed peace. Techniques will have to be created for efficiently filling in the information gaps and building a bridge between the traditional paper records and the automated personnel databases.

Potentially, information-gathering exercises such as surveys have an important role, but there needs to be a mechanism for verifying the information gathered against existing records and for making binding adjudication where necessary. The result should be a certified service record for every public servant, capturing all the data needed for the database and arranging it in a format to facilitate inputting to the personnel database.

There should be an incentive to encourage public servants to cooperate in this exercise and to search out any missing documents needed as evidence. An approach that might be worth exploring would be to link the gathering of data about staff personnel histories to job evaluation exercises.

The process of gathering the missing data should be a 'one-off' catching-up exercise. Once the new database is fully operational, there should be procedures to ensure security of the system and data backups; the paper-based personnel files should contain all the records needed for long-term use. The

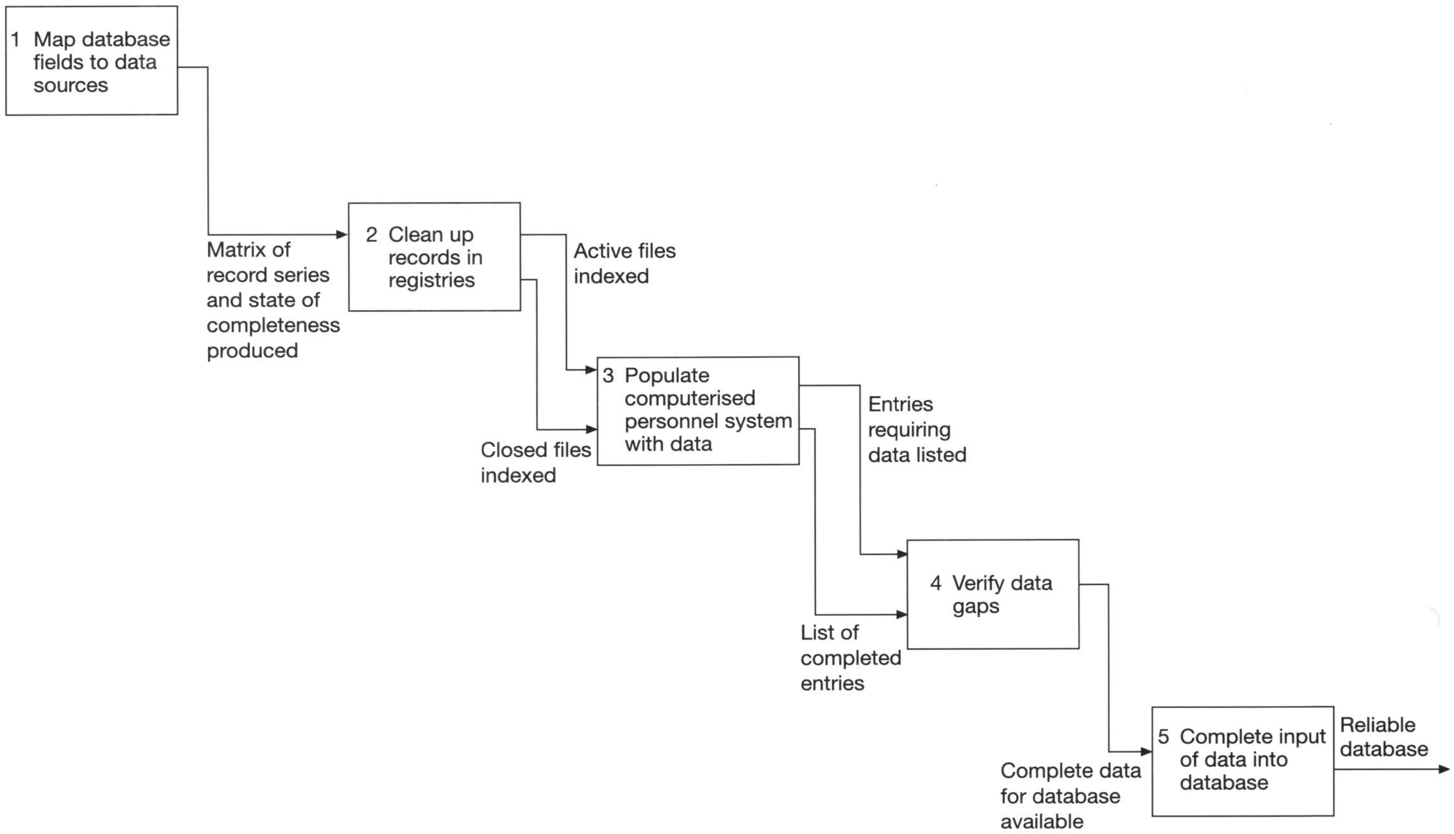
1 Map database fields to data sources
Matrix of record series and state of completeness produced
2 Clean up records in registries
Active files indexed
Closed files indexed
3 Populate computerised personnel system with data
Entries requiring data listed
List of completed entries
4 Verify data gaps
Complete data for database available
5 Complete input of data into database
Reliable database

Figure 6.3 Obtaining reliable data sources for a personnel MIS

data output will also need to be controlled by a records management system to provide an audit trail.

Finally, the study revealed the absence of guidelines and criteria for evaluating whether computerised personnel MIS are creating and maintaining authentic, reliable records. It demonstrates the need to develop a tool to verify that computerised systems generate records which meet requirements for accountability or are linked to paper-based systems where the records are legally verifiable.

Conception–reality gaps

Many public sector managers and consultants assume that the problem of inadequate information systems can be bypassed by the introduction of computers. This view is overly optimistic. Computerised information systems undoubtedly can be an important component in strategies of support for public sector reform, but they do not bypass the problems of the existing systems. The findings show that the need for reliable source data for automated personnel systems forces implementation teams to confront the problem of failing manual systems.

In terms of the information dimension of the ITPOSMO model (see Chapter 3), project designers often conceived the new information system in a way that was divorced from data realities. In particular, they underestimated the extent to which decades of inadequate investment in paper-based information systems had undermined the quality of source data for computerised personnel MIS. Attempts to layer computerised systems on top of collapsed paper-based information systems without making a substantial investment in refurbishing the paper system are likely to lead to under-performance or even failure of the computerised system in meeting its objectives.

There were other misconceptions revealed by the case study. For example, in terms of the motivation dimension, the design conceptions behind the Ghanaian IPPD data survey assumed objectivity and integrity in the completion of personnel data forms. The reality was one of subjectivity and self-interest that led to data inaccuracies.

In a nutshell, computerisation will improve the ability of an organisation to manipulate data, but it will not supply missing data. Project conceptions have tended to focus on only one part of the problem: improving the ability to manipulate personnel data; but in fact the real business need was also for a supply of accurate information for management purposes. Failure to find a convincing answer to the missing legacy data problem led managers to be disappointed by the limited utility of their personnel MIS as decision making tools for public sector reform.

NOTE

1   These three countries were chosen to illustrate different strategies adopted for implementing automated personnel information systems and different stages in the process of implementation. Ghana was chosen because it illustrates a strategy for a centralised, integrated payroll and personnel database. Uganda was selected because it illustrates a strategy for a decentralised personnel information system based on personal computers and because the Ugandan authorities were beginning to give attention to the relationship of paper-based personnel records to the computerised system. Zimbabwe was chosen because the Government of Zimbabwe was still exploring the available options and because there was a more developed capacity for computerisation than in the other two countries.

REFERENCES

AIIM (1989) *Information and Image Management: The State of the Industry*, London: Association for Information and Image Management.

Coopers & Lybrand (1993) *Civil Service Reform Programme Phase 3*, London: Coopers & Lybrand (authored in association with RIPA International Ltd).

Daily Graphic (Accra, Ghana) (1996) 'Accountant-General to the rescue', 17 January: 1.

Government of Zimbabwe (1989) *Report of the Public Service Review Commission of Zimbabwe*, Harare: Government of Zimbabwe.

Lagara, M. (1996) Personal interview with author in Uganda.

Marshall, H. (1996) Personal interview with author in Ghana.

Ministry of Public Service (1995) *Impact Evaluation Report on Feasibility Study of the Registry-based Computerised Personnel Information System at the Ministry of Trade and Industry*, Kampala, Uganda: Ministry of Public Service.

World Bank (1989) *Sub-Saharan Africa: From Crisis to Sustainable Growth. A Long-term Perspective Study*, Washington, DC: World Bank.

World Bank (1996) *Zimbabwe: Fiscal Management Review*, Report no. 15681-Zim, Washington, DC: World Bank.

ACKNOWLEDGEMENTS

The study reported here was funded by the UK Department for International Development ESCOR programme. It was undertaken by Piers Cain, Director of Research, International Records Management Trust, under the guidance of Dr Anne Thurston, Reader at the School of Library, Archive and Information Studies at University College London and Executive Director of the Trust. Jonathan Holley and David Crampin, having extensive experience in the management of personnel records and also experience of working in Africa, made valuable contributions to the approach taken. Case study drafts were circulated for comment to the relevant participating governments, and to Jonathan Holley, David Crampin, and Dr Shirin Madon of the London School of Economics.

APPENDIX: PROBLEMS ENCOUNTERED IN CASE STUDIES AND POTENTIAL SOLUTIONS

PROBLEM	SOLUTION
Institutional issues	
Lack of support from senior management	Develop strategies and interventions to foster management sponsorship of project
Central computing services tend to be reactive and defensive in the face of technological developments	Training for senior IT staff in developing and maintaining IT strategies
Project design issues	
Exaggerated expectations of ability of computerisation to solve all tasks	Provide training to sensitise users to capabilities of computers and limitations
Weak project and general management skills in central computing services	Change recruitment policy to include staff with management skills as well as technical skills
Unrealistic timetables	Recognise from the start that setting realistic timetables is key to a good final product
Expectation that computerisation will reduce need for personnel registries	Recognise that records will continue to provide essential legally verifiable information and that personnel registries should be strengthened
Expectation that computers will reduce delays in processing routine tasks such as promotions and retirements caused by gaps on the files	Recognise that any gains will be long-term and are not guaranteed
Timetable for data entry too short	Assign more time/resources to the task of data entry
Project extends beyond original objectives	Project management training
High-level priorities change, leading to distortion of IT project objectives	Conduct regular formal reviews of project objectives and make explicit any changes in direction; ensure that new objectives are properly resourced and included in a revised project plan
Protection of information	
Strategic systems vulnerable to natural or other disasters	Ensure that backup procedures are followed and disaster recovery programmes are in place; ensure that managers responsible for determining priorities understand importance of the issue – do not leave it in the hands of technicians
Networked system vulnerable to hackers and fraud	Improve system security and ensure accountants have easy access to audit trail
Lack of understanding of security issues	Sensitise managers and users to realities; educate database managers on best practice

PROBLEM	SOLUTION
Automation results in shift in 'balance of power' in favour of IT technicians	Recognise issue and take steps to protect strategic systems
Legal requirements for preservation of original documents not recognised	Review national legislation on admissibility of electronic evidence
No provision for long-term preservation of electronic records	Create dedicated unit in national archives

Sustainability issues

Insufficient number of staff qualified to undertake audit of application and general controls of computerised system to ensure security and accountability standards	Ensure pay levels of auditors are competitive with private sector
High staff turnover	Pay competitive rates; train larger numbers to allow for 'wastage'; use manual systems which show a much lower staff turnover
Unreliable power supply	Provide uninterruptible power supply or devise procedures for manual operation while power interrupted
Hardware maintenance is not included in project design	Ensure host government makes a commitment in departmental budget to finance system maintenance
Software maintenance is not included in project design	Ensure host government makes a commitment in departmental budget to finance system maintenance
Staff time is not allocated to data entry	Include data entry in departmental work schedules; sensitise managers at outset of project to long-term need for staff to be allocated to this task
Poor record keeping of computer operations	Ensure better supervision and include computer input and output records in records management schedule

Sharing of information: decentralisation requirements

Tension between central and local information needs	Ensure joint representation on committee determining system requirements and project objectives
Centre and districts require access to same personnel records	Agree which records will be held centrally and locally; copy key records; ensure shared access to personnel database data (initially in hard copy if necessary)
Need for centre and districts to share data	Standardise fields and codes
Difficulties with sharing personnel records of public service staff transferred to local authorities where government pension schemes are still funded centrally	Ensure secure long-term preservation of personnel records; provide copies (e.g. by microfilming) where feasible

APPENDIX: continued

PROBLEM	SOLUTION
Officials commissioning databases are reluctant to agree to and abide by common data standards	Education
Disparate data structures and codes prevent sharing of data between databases created for different purposes	Standardise fields and codes
Difficulties in providing districts with greater access to centrally held data	Organise distribution of data by disk; assign high priority to national infrastructure project to create trunk cabling; make network available to wide range of government users so cost is justified
Poor communications infrastructure in districts (no telephones, poor roads)	Select information systems that do not require state-of-the-art communications to operate successfully
Inadequate feedback systems compound poor communications with districts	Redesign procedures
Districts have poor capacity to manage their own records	Establish a training programme
Data input issues	
Appropriate source data has not been identified at the design stage	Incorporate identification and assessment of the quality of source data into every project plan
Data is of variable accuracy *within* a database (personnel data is often the least accurate)	Strengthen incentives to maintain up-to-date personnel information; identify best practice
Information does not arrive at centre to be processed, or arrives late	Strengthen incentives to maintain up-to-date personnel information
Personnel files are incomplete and disorganised	Introduce a records management programme
More information is held in ministry personnel files than in central establishment files	Decide what information should be held centrally and what in ministries
Large numbers of establishment files with only one or two sheets of paper in them	Decongest registry and build up files where necessary
Files are kept on individuals who were accepted for recruitment but had never taken up a post	Decongest registry
No files at centre are kept on non-established staff	Use ministry files for checking database entries, where these exist
Surveys used to capture data created before introduction of database fail to deliver accurate data	Use personnel records instead

PROBLEM	SOLUTION
Data output issues	
Computerised data does not provide contextual information needed to identify inaccurate data	Create links to paper records which are rich in contextual information
Large volume of paper output is clogging filing cabinets	Include paper output in records management schedule
Records management issues	
Users are reluctant to support the maintenance of manual systems	Introduce training to sensitise managers to the need to do so
No linkages between databases and personnel registries	Integrate design of database and manual systems (unique ID number to be used on both systems to identify staff records)
Data input forms are overflowing filing cabinets	Schedule the forms for transfer to records centre for storage and eventual controlled destruction
Manual systems are weakened by introduction of computerised system	Integrate design of database and manual systems
Large numbers of closed establishment files are still in current registry system	Decongest registry

7 Evaluating information systems for decentralisation

Health management reform in Ecuador

Angel Salazar

Abstract: This chapter presents an evaluation of information systems introduction to support public healthcare reform. Specifically, it investigates a national initiative – termed the Institutional Development Project – which aimed to implement information systems in the health districts of the Ministry of Public Health in Ecuador. The project had as a major objective the facilitation of radical decentralisation of management functions. The outcome of the project was mixed but a common feature was the marginal use of the information systems. A major explanation is the top-down, technical approach used in information systems implementation. This approach neglected organisational realities and led to problems including obstruction of decentralisation by key stakeholders and failure to support managerial work at district level. This case also describes the application of interpretive and grounded theory approaches as evaluative tools to help understand the implementation of information systems in public sector reform contexts. In addition, relevant recommendations are derived that can be applied to reform initiatives involving information systems.

BACKGROUND

The context of reform

Public sector reform initiatives in Ecuador have been on the management agenda since at least the 1960s. They really took off under the 1992–6 government, which initiated a formal reform programme focused on decentralisation: a key component of the reform/reinvention agenda (Osborne and Gaebler 1992: 250–279). As described below, the public health sector has been part of this reform process.

Health sector reform

In the early 1990s, public health expenditure by Ecuador's Ministry of Public Health (MoPH) accounted for about 1.6 per cent of gross domestic product, of which about 80 per cent went on hospital services (MoPH 1992). Yet hospital productivity was low, inefficiencies were widespread throughout the health system, and service quality was often poor. Thus, reform of the public hospital network and the health sector as a whole was seen as essential.

The overall strategy for reform was provided by the 'Basic Primary Care in Ecuador' (BPC) programme, which was initiated in 1992. This laid out an integrated, comprehensive primary healthcare model for the country, and gave particular emphasis to the construction of a series of local health provider units and to the decentralisation of healthcare management. The BPC programme was financed at a cost of just over US$100 million with the assistance of one of the world's main international development agencies (referred to here as IDA). The programme was organised as an autonomous unit, with its own operating and capital budget and with a staff and structure separated from, but still dependent on, the Ministry of Public Health's central administration.

Two programme components, initiated in the mid-1990s, are of importance here. The first is the National Emergency-Care Hospital Network (NECHN) project. Despite the primary healthcare aims of BPC, this invested US$10 million in the modernisation of three of the main referral hospitals in Ecuador via:

- rehabilitation of hospital buildings and equipment;
- implementation of computer-based management information systems;
- development of hospital services management.

The second programme component was the Institutional Development Project (IDP), which was intended to enable the decentralisation of planning and management in the primary healthcare system. The project was set up in 1995 because of perceived problems in the achievement of primary care goals. The BPC programme had successfully developed a primary care infrastructure in urban marginal and rural areas comprising 22 health centres, 166 sub-centres, 23 county hospitals and 4,000 medical staff. However, it had still failed to decentralise fully the planning and management of these local health provider units.

Intended decentralisation

Ecuador's public health system traditionally operated on a highly centralised model, in which plans were established by the central administration within the Ministry of Public Health. Management activities at the local level were limited to basic implementation and control actions guided by central diktat.

The BPC programme aimed to overturn this model and to promote decentralised planning and management. Decentralisation was intended to enable the MoPH as a whole to be more responsive to the community, and to orient healthcare actions towards primary care. According to the decentralised planning and management initiative, local units would be able to formulate health service plans and would have the necessary authority and resources to manage their implementation.

With this in mind, a new organisational structure was created with an intended new set of information flows, centred around a series of District Health Authorities (DHAs), as illustrated in Figure 7.1. The intention here was that the DHAs would form the financial and health performance focal points of the new health system, with finance allocated directly from the Ministry of Finance rather than via the MoPH. The districts would take a principal responsibility for gathering health, finance and other administrative information from the primary health sub-centres. This would be passed up to regional and national levels, but would also be used by administrators and health workers at district level for monitoring, evaluation and planning purposes.

However, by 1995 it was clear that decentralisation had not progressed as far as intended. Allocation of resources was still based on previous historical patterns, and local planning and budgeting processes were not associated with service production. Low participation of local service managers in planning and budgeting was still evident. Use of information technology (IT) was also low, with most administrative and clinical reporting still being done manually. It was in this context that the Institutional Development Project was proposed.

Institutional Development Project initiation

In 1995 a new set of senior central administration staff was appointed in the Ministry of Public Health. They decided to continue some existing projects and to initiate some new ones. One of the new projects added was the Institutional Development Project, driven by the need for further organisational change to truly decentralise planning and management. Its component initiatives included:

- development of staff holding managerial responsibility in local units;
- redefinition and decentralisation of management roles and responsibilities;
- development and implementation of decentralised information systems.

The implementation of information systems had the explicit intention of allowing local-level administrators and doctors to discuss information together in the planning and management of healthcare services.

Figure 7.2 illustrates the different actors involved in the IDP at both national and local levels. Despite the variety of actor groups, the formulation

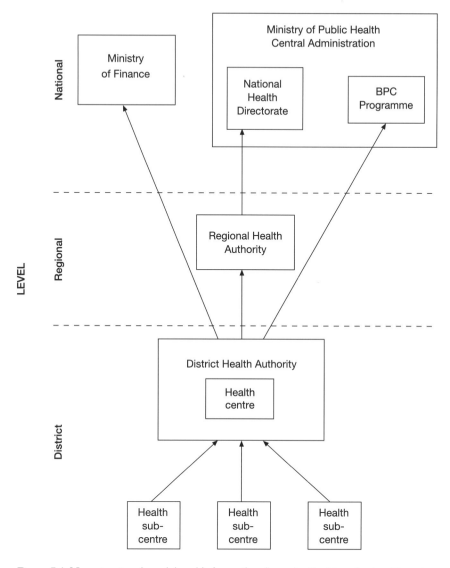

Figure 7.1 New structural model and information flows for the Ecuador health sector

of the IDP took place during a period of two weeks and involved only national-level players: mainly top executives from the MoPH and officers from the international development agency. The information systems (IS) component of the project was seen as an early priority, with development agency staff providing technical assistance on IS strategy formulation. A single consultant was appointed to identify the new decentralised management roles and to specify the management development requirements.

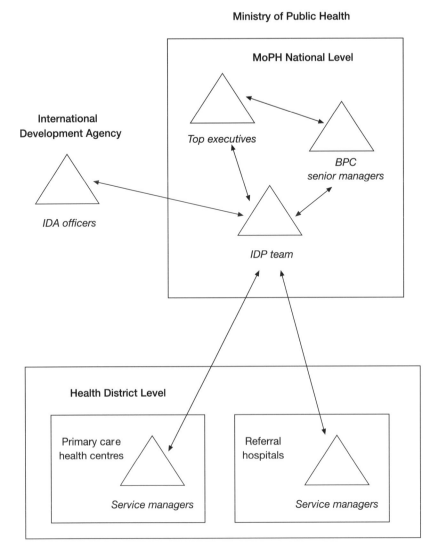

Figure 7.2 Actors and levels in the institutional development project

It was decided to incorporate the new project within the structure of the wider BPC programme. One rationale was that the IDP was due to initiate activities within the health districts being developed by the BPC programme. Also, this arrangement was intended to enable the project to have ready access to the required financial resources which were being managed by the BPC. Senior managers of the BPC programme were requested by the top executives to make the necessary arrangements for the allocation of those resources to the IDP. However, this meant that the IDP also had to sit alongside other reform projects. In particular, it ran in parallel with the new National Emergency-Care Hospital Network project, which top executives considered had greater national priority.

Once the project had been formulated, a top MoPH executive was designated project coordinator, with responsibility for creating a project team to implement the planned information systems. Consultants and software developers were then recruited to form the information systems team, with their recruitment based on components of the IS strategy devised by the top MoPH executives and their development agency advisers. In particular, the terms of reference explicitly stated that the responsibilities of each team member consisted of evaluating and modifying *existing* software applications, which had previously been identified and selected by top MoPH executives. These terms were incorporated into each member's contract.

The team's membership, responsibilities and working arrangements were therefore structured around a set of pre-existing applications, as illustrated in Figure 7.3, and consisted of:

- planning and resource allocation (PLANAN);
- costing and budgeting (SICCUS);
- local programming of activities (PLOPER, which had the same logic and data inputs as PLANAN);
- service production statistics and analysis (HEALTHWARE).

Some of these had previously been developed to support, for example, health promotion programmes such as child vaccination. However, the applications had been directed at, and only been implemented at, central and regional levels.

Evaluation method

The field study focused on three main sets of activities:

- *development and implementation of the information system*, e.g. studying how user needs were met, how the systems were created, and how staff were trained to use them;
- *management of the information system project*, e.g. studying how senior management or user support was gained and maintained;
- *ultimate adoption/non-adoption of the information system*, e.g. studying whether and how users used the system and its outputs.

In all cases, social aspects such as underlying stakeholder motivations and worldviews or political conflicts were seen as critical to understanding the situation. Qualitative techniques based around grounded research and interpretivist approaches (discussed in more detail in the conclusions and recommendations to this chapter) were therefore used. This required intensive

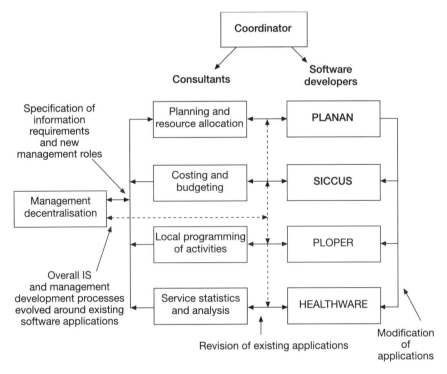

Figure 7.3 Working arrangement and core applications of the IDP

interaction with the various stakeholder groups, gathering data via semi-structured interviews, observation notes and analysis of meeting minutes and other documents.

The data gathered was used via a process of emergent discovery to create a structure of tentative categories and codes which, in turn, guided further data gathering, based around Strauss's (1987) coding schema. Integrative diagrams (see below) were also used to assist the field study. The data-driven categorisation ultimately delineated a set of socio-organisational and institutional elements that were key influences on the process of information systems development, implementation and adoption.

ANALYSIS OF THE INFORMATION SYSTEMS PROJECT

Initial activities

In August 1995, the IDP team began visiting prospective pilot sites. In addition to the BPC's primary care centres and their referral hospitals, the IDP team also visited four large metropolitan hospitals which belonged to the NECHN project. The devised IS strategy had considered the latter hospitals as prospective pilot sites for IDP, even though Basic Primary Care programme senior managers perceived the NECHN project as having competing development goals.

Concurrently, pairs of consultants and developers undertook evaluation and modification of the existing software applications. The working arrangement and emphasis on existing software applications stated in the IS strategy strongly shaped the priorities and activities of team members. The overall information systems and management development processes thus largely revolved around these existing applications. For instance, this affected the way new management roles and their associated information requirements were specified. The focus was on the national/regional arrangements embodied within the existing applications, with a consequent neglect of management needs at district level, despite the supposed intention of the whole project to drive forward the process of decentralisation.

Major project outcomes and causes

Figure 7.4 synthesises the major events, activities and outcomes of this information systems project. The main outcome described, after 15 months of effort, was only marginal use of the new information system. This outcome arose from (amongst other things):

- initial lack of support from BPC senior managers, who failed to allocate the required financial and material resources to the project, including recurrent budgets and computing equipment;
- lack of participation from service managers in the pilot sites.

Each of these will now be described in greater detail, based on evidence gathered during the evaluation study.

Lack of support from BPC senior managers

The initial coordinator for the IDP team was a top MoPH executive who was highly valued and had direct support from other top executives. The team relied upon him to solve project bottlenecks such as preparation and signing of contracts or allocation of recurrent budgets. However, empirical evidence suggests that the BPC senior managers associated the IS team with the perceived interests of the coordinator and his top executive colleagues; that is, with the implementation of the NECHN project. The NECHN project was in turn associated with a 'curative healthcare model', which was perceived by the senior managers to be in opposition to the 'preventative healthcare model' being promoted by the BPC programme. The following is an extract of the evidence that was collected during working meetings and through iterative interviews with the IDP team and BPC senior managers:

July	September	March	July	September
1 Initiation of the project 2 Planning of major set of activities by top executives 3 Pre-selection of existing software applications 4 Recruitment of implementation team and assignment of responsibilities	1 Visits to pilot sites: hospitals and health centres 2 Revision and modification of software applications 3 Administration of surveys by decentralisation consultant in health districts 4 Evidence on lack of support from BPC senior managers, i.e. bottlenecks in resource allocation to IDP	1 Change of coordinator 2 Implementation team shifts emphasis towards health areas 3 Increase of support from BPC senior managers, i.e. new offices, acquisition of additional computer equipment for IDP 4 IDP team starts to deploy computers and software applications 5 Evidence on lack of support from service managers in health districts	1 Most software applications are installed in several pilot sites 2 Software-based training in IDP offices 3 Testing of applications with participation of district managers, specifically statisticians and financial officers	1 Marginal use of information system in health districts: • non-routinisation of applications • emphasis on epidemiology and morbidity statistics • one-time costing estimate exercises • lack of integration of various types of data and printed reports
1995		1996		

Figure 7.4 Actual events and activity timetable of the IDP

Senior managers of the BPC project want *their* primary care model to work. In contrast, the priority of the coordinator is the top executives' objectives. The team has resistance from BPC senior managers. BPC senior managers create obstacles to avoid giving us resources. We have been able to obtain resources by the initiative of our team and the good personal relations we have with some MoPH top executives. BPC senior managers do not help us. *They* see *us* as enemies.

(IDP team member; emphasis added)

I would have liked most of the IDP team activities to have been oriented to the primary care level. If the IDP team had put emphasis on the fields relevant to the health districts *instead of hospitals*, the IS team would already have finished a long time ago.

(BPC senior manager; original emphasis)

The IDP project was never clearly defined and understood by BPC senior managers and MoPH top executives. The reason for this was the way the IDP project developed. There was confusion, loss of leadership, non-shared interests and contradiction and power-play. Direction was momentarily lost when healthcare reform was mentioned. There is a confusion of terms, methodology and vision. The major contradiction is that the BPC project is trying to implement a care model that has been declared by the World Health Organisation Alma-Ata as the strategy of Health-for-All in the year 2000. But what happened was that MoPH top executives give privileges to the National Emergency-Care Hospital Network, justifying it in that the current major cause of death in Ecuador is due to injuries and accidents. This produced a *division* between the reform project [NECHN as part of it] and the BPC project. From my point of view, a *hybrid* model has been generated. This model *does not* reflect the reality. To worsen the situation, the modernisation of hospitals is wanted. Regarding the information system strategy: to which model is it contributing? . . . Do we think in terms of community? The funding and support of initiatives should aim towards one single direction in order to develop a *coherent* healthcare model. Otherwise, two realities that are incompatible and in conflict are constructed.

(IDP team member; emphasis added)

The new top executives brought new ideas based on a deep and confused theoretical framework, that underestimated actions of basic [primary] healthcare, and with an expressed cult toward high technology for hospitals, with a limited vision over health–disease relationships. The BPC project was conducted with a clear and personal dominance of the top executives, with poor consideration of technical criteria. The BPC project was seen as a source of resources for the emergency [NECHN] project. . . . The process of institutional development had also serious problems in building a uniform and *compromised* team but *orphan* of political support, that should have concentrated its effort on the health districts to attempt a bottom-up organisational change, and based on the implementation of computing systems for decentralised management.

(BPC senior manager; emphasis added)

In February 1996, one of the IS team consultants was appointed as the new coordinator. This led to a change in attitude by the BPC senior managers and a change in emphasis for the project. However, as indicated in the quotes above, the legacy of the original project formulation and initial implementation also created confusion within the team between the original centralised and the new decentralised models.

Lack of interest and support from service managers in the health districts

Because of these legacies, there was a perceived mismatch between the management processes at district level and the software applications developed by the IDP team, leading to little demand for those applications. This was reflected in the attitude of the district managers towards the technology. For instance, one manager described the applications as 'inappropriate software solutions, which were predominantly oriented to resource costing and budgeting rather than supporting day-to-day management activities. I would have preferred to see the software applications being developed by the IDP team to be based on local realities and not on abstractions'.

Simultaneously, the performance and reward structure discouraged district managers from attending the information systems training courses organised at the central office. As one service manager put it: 'staff are not interested in receiving training. Courses are often available, but the staff usually do not attend. They are not evaluated by their skills or efficiency. They are paid the same salary if they perform better or worse. There is no incentive to improve services.'

Analysis

The marginal adoption of the information system was derived from the approach used in information system development and management training, and was influenced by the internal organisation and immediate context of health districts. In part, service managers, particularly medical professionals, did not feel compelled to adopt more novel costing and budgeting practices, hence limiting themselves to use of the medical-based software modules of the system. In addition, the use by the IDP team of a rational, top-down implementation approach, combined with the fact that service managers were not willing merely to assume the role of feeders of information, influenced the level of adoption of the system. The approach used by the IDP team was itself determined by the nature and context of the project formulation process.

System adoption therefore is determined strongly by the process – as well as the content – of IS project implementation and this, in turn, is strongly determined by the process of project formulation. This project went wrong in its initial two weeks, by using a top-down approach to formulation that was driven largely by top executive objectives. From that point onwards its fate was virtually sealed, despite mid-term attempts to reorient it.

Termination of the project and beyond

The IDP project cannot be considered a success if its original targets and realised outcomes are compared. Although project outcomes varied greatly from site to site, a common feature was the marginal level of adoption of the information systems. The IT infrastructure (computers and network hardware and cabling) was completed in some sites but utilisation of applications was, at best, partial and, at worst, non-existent. About the only positive outcome was the improved communication and learning experienced between the IDP team, BPC senior managers and district service managers.

In August 1996 a new government was elected and a new MoPH central administration group was appointed. The new top executives decided to terminate the IDP. The IDP team was dismantled in a gradual way. The top executives decided to wait for the normal termination of each member's contract, which occurred between September and December 1996.

At the time of writing, in 1998, the IDP is being reinitiated. With the new central administration appointed, the MoPH embarked on a broader evaluation of its development projects. This evaluation recommended, among other things, the rearrangement of the working layout of the IDP and the clarification of its project objectives. One of the most promising of these prospective changes has been the shift from a working arrangement based around software applications to one based around management development processes and specific decentralisation strategies.

CONCLUSIONS AND RECOMMENDATIONS

The evaluation methodology

This section analyses the socio-organisational perspective used to evaluate this case study's information system, and the approaches needed in order to put such a perspective into practice.

The socio-organisational perspective

A socio-organisational perspective was required in order to understand this public sector information system because a traditional, rational perspective would have been too limiting, as the following three examples will illustrate.

First, a traditional, rational perspective would have seen project formulation in a straightforward manner as an attempt to create the optimal project organisation in order to achieve overt project objectives. It would also assume that project structures and objectives control participants and lead them to rational reasoning and actions. In practice, however, the IDP team adopted a top-down and technology-led approach that was dissonant with the overt project objectives. A rational perspective cannot adequately explain this.

We need instead to adopt a socio-organisational perspective. This helps us to see project formulation as a complex interaction between social context and human actions which led the project team to reproduce the dominant social structure and culture of the Ministry in their actions.

Second, a rational perspective would regard the introduction of new IT-based information systems into the health districts as relatively unproblematic. Even a rationally political perspective might concur, expecting that the dominant position of the project coordinator (with support from other influential top executives) would be enough to persuade district managers to adopt the new systems. Yet this was clearly not the case in practice.

Again, we need to adopt a socio-organisational perspective. This helps us to see project implementation as a process involving stakeholders with differing subjective goals and perceptions. The district managers, for example, perceived the project as hindering their goals of decentralisation and as contributing to a maintenance of the existing organisational order. The project can be seen, then, as a clash of management sub-groups: between an IDP team that was reproducing a central command-type management style and a set of district managers who had committed themselves to the process of decentralisation since 1994.

Third, and related to the second example, a rational perspective assumes that all organisation members share common goals for the organisation and that they will collaborate to achieve these (Markus 1983). This would lead to an expectation of support for the project from the BPC senior managers, since there would be a presumed coalition of all central staff around all top-down institutional development initiatives. Even a rationally political perspective might expect the coordinator's power to force compliance. In practice, however, the BPC managers opposed the project and there was a struggle for power and resources between central Ministry groupings.

A socio-organisational perspective would expect such conflict between different stakeholder groups with their different perceptions and different interests. It would see the project as a clash of professional ideologies between the BPC senior managers on the one hand and the MoPH top executives on the other. The former perceived the latter as devaluing their primary healthcare ideology and as valuing instead a curative ideology based around high-technology hospital services. Although initially aligned with the top executives, the IDP team was subsequently, in some ways, caught in the middle, not knowing to which care model it was intended to contribute.

In order to put evaluation according to a socio-organisational perspective into practice, interpretive *and* grounded approaches were adopted. The use of these approaches in information systems evaluation has increasingly gained prominence. Several commentators have highlighted the applicability and enabling power of these approaches in promoting the generation of novel insights in the IS field (Boland 1985; Boland and Day 1989; Cavaye 1996; Galliers 1991; Myers 1994 and 1996; Orlikowski 1993; Orlikowski and Robey 1991; Walsham 1993 and 1995). One major reason is that researchers are increasingly acknowledging their utility in providing an insight into socio-organisational issues related to computer-based information systems. Consequently human interpretations and meanings are being taken into account in studying information systems.

The interpretivist approach to information systems

The interpretivist approach aims to understand information systems from the point of view of the participants who are directly involved, and it explicitly includes investigation of the context of those systems. The approach assumes that human participants are able to influence their immediate surroundings, including other people. Participants are also assumed to construct their own 'world' realities, which are based on their personal beliefs and experiences, and which are in turn externalised in the form of behaviour, attitudes and individual perceptions. The interpretive evaluator does not enter a social setting with a priori constructs. Instead, constructs are allowed to emerge whilst s/he is in the field learning about and trying to understand the information system.

The quality of interpretivist study is related to the evaluator's interpretation, which should be logically consistent, subjective and adequate. Logical consistency implies that the explanation of an IS-related event or behaviour must be compatible with the principles of logic. Subjectivity implies that the interpretation must reflect the meaning and understanding according to information system participants. Adequacy implies the interpretation must show evidence of grasping and explaining the underlying rationale behind IS-related actions and processes, however irrational they may initially appear.

By using an interpretivist approach, this study was able to investigate the process of IS implementation from the inside: from the perspectives of the different actors involved. It particularly generated empirical data and novel insights about the social aspects of IS implementation processes at diverse but interrelated organisational levels.

The grounded research approach to information systems

The work of Glaser and Strauss (1967), Strauss (1987) and Corbin and Strauss (1991) on grounded theory guided the design and instrumentation of evaluation used in this present case. Grounded research, according to Strauss (1987: 22–23) is:

a detailed grounding by systematically and intensively analysing data, often sentence by sentence, or phrase by phrase of the field note, interview, or other document; by constant comparison, data is extensively collected and coded . . . thus producing a well constructed theory. The focus of analysis is not merely on collecting or ordering a mass of data, but on organising many ideas which have emerged from the analysis of the data.

Grounded research therefore pushes the evaluator to generate theories grounded in the systematic analysis and interpretation of collected – mostly qualitative – empirical data, rather than generating data to fit the theory. The latter is the case of positivism, which seeks to test specific hypothesis formulated a priori. In contrast, grounded theory holds the assumption that the social world must be discovered using qualitative methods and an exploratory and interpretive orientation.

Following this approach, this evaluator entered the field without a priori hypotheses, but with a good background knowledge. As data was collected, it was coded and categorised. Initial analysis took place during data collection. Analysis itself suggested constructs and relationships (i.e. lack of support from BPC senior managers and lack of interest from service managers) which required further data collection. This, in turn, generated further constructs. Had a grounded approach not been followed, it is quite possible that key explanatory factors would have been missed.

Integrative diagrams

In order to achieve the integration of generated constructs, 'integrative diagrams' were thoroughly applied in this evaluation (Strauss 1987). Integrative diagrams can be defined here as pictorial devices which help to articulate distinct but interrelated explanatory elements. They were constructed in a highly iterative manner, guided by Strauss's coding schema. The practical value of integrative diagrams is their power to synthesise sets of complex relationships into relatively simple explanatory pictures. These diagrams also directly helped to integrate clusters of different analytical elements.

Figure 7.5, for example, integrates contextual and managerial dimensions that were found to affect the process of information systems implementation. This helped to develop an understanding of major causal factors and their relationship. In addition, by providing a clear structure of evaluation issues, these diagrams ensured that the evaluation itself remained well structured and clearly focused.

Summary of the information systems evaluation method

The analysis above has emphasised the importance of a socio-organisational perspective in the evaluation of information systems. Socio-organisational

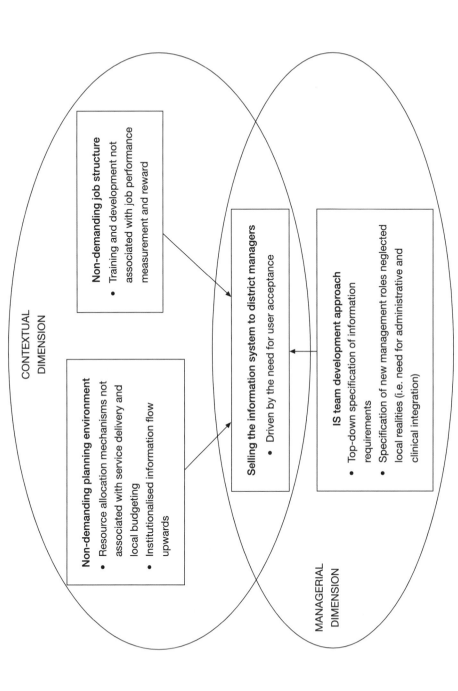

CONTEXTUAL DIMENSION

Non-demanding job structure
- Training and development not associated with job performance measurement and reward

Non-demanding planning environment
- Resource allocation mechanisms not associated with service delivery and local budgeting
- Institutionalised information flow upwards

Selling the information system to district managers
- Driven by the need for user acceptance

IS team development approach
- Top-down specification of information requirements
- Specification of new management roles neglected local realities (i.e. need for administrative and clinical integration)

MANAGERIAL DIMENSION

Figure 7.5 Contextual and managerial dimensions of implementation

factors were critical in affecting the ability of the implementation team to perform productively and effectively, and in determining the ultimate adoption or non-adoption of information systems. In practice, however, other perspectives and factors also have value. For example, contextual factors – as illustrated in Figure 7.5 – also played a role.

More generally, then, it is likely that a combination of three main perspectives – the technical, the socio-organisational and the contextual – will be required in the evaluation of other public sector reform IS. Implementation of such information systems needs to be understood as socio-organisational, contextual and technological aspects embedded into a complex, interwoven and dynamic process.

To operationalise this combination of perspectives – particularly the latter two – two particular approaches can be used: interpretivism and grounded theory, and a related technique: integrative diagrams. All three proved their value in helping to reveal non-technical factors embedded in the process of IS implementation. These methods allowed the discovery and articulation of explanatory social factors at diverse organisational levels. More generally, it is likely that these methods will be equally valuable in the evaluation of other public sector reform IS.

The role of information systems in decentralisation: conception–reality gaps

An increasing number of countries, like Ecuador, are attempting decentralisation reforms in the healthcare sector. As decentralisation seeks to change the location of management activity in the health system, it requires new information flows to support that change. The introduction of new information systems is thus a pressing practical as well as research issue.

This case study has, therefore, systematically examined the Institutional Development Project in the Ecuador Ministry of Public Health, and has focused on the role and effectiveness of the IDP in management decentralisation. It is clear from this case that the IDP and its information systems have not been very effective in levering decentralisation. In part, this can be put down to the gap that existed between the conception of the new information systems and the realities of the context into which they were introduced. For example, the centralised conception of the existing applications conflicted strongly with the primary healthcare realities of district health centres. Similarly, the rational and objective conception of the project conflicted strongly with the political and cultural realities of the public health system.

Implementation of information systems for public sector reform:
recommendations

The following recommendations can be derived from this case:

- In the context of public service bureaucracies which typically involve several administrative levels or tiers, the top-down formulation of decentralisation IS projects (i.e. their conception and structuring) should take into account the development processes that need to be promoted, during implementation, at local level. This should facilitate, among other things, IS adoption. Trying to adopt a solely centralised approach to decentralisation IS is likely to lead to failure because it will create conceptions, priorities and objectives – as in this case – that are divorced from the realities and needs of the decentralised units.

- The management of IS projects must include consideration of the motivations and interests of key stakeholders. Without this, conflict is likely and project progress will be affected, as it was in the IDP case. This is of particular relevance in organisations where professional staff strongly identify themselves with a specific service orientation, as is common in the public sector.

- The adoption of a participative and management-skills-led approach is fundamental to successful IS implementation and to catalysis of wider reform processes. Implementers need to embrace a participative attitude and hold an orientation towards the development of people rather than technology. This is especially critical when information systems projects are situated at the national level. Implementers need to look for specific tactics that can help foster healthy and sound relationships with key stakeholders. Moreover, the management of such relationships demands the articulation of their social and political dimensions and the application of specific inter-personal skills. Implementation teams should therefore possess or develop skills such as communication, presentation, facilitation, negotiation, conflict resolution and team-working.

- Information systems implementation should assess the working environment of the IS users. This assessment should include both the immediate and the broader institutional environment (i.e. institutional planning and budgeting in the case of resource management information systems) and the way it may affect the information needs of target users.

REFERENCES

Boland, R.J. (1985) 'Phenomenology: a preferred approach to research on IS', in E. Mumford, R. Hirschheim, G. Fitzgerald and T. Wood-Harper (eds) *Research Methods in Information Systems*, Amsterdam: Elsevier Science.

Boland, R.J. and Day, W.F. (1989) 'The experience of system design: a hermeneutic of organisational action', *Scandinavian Journal of Management* 5, 2: 87–104.

Cavaye, A.L.M. (1996) 'Case study research: a multi-faceted research approach for IS', *Information Systems Journal* 6, 3: 227–242.

Corbin, J. and Strauss, A. (1991) 'Grounded theory research: procedures, canons and evaluative criteria', *Qualitative Sociology* 13, 2: 3–22.

Galliers, R. (1991) 'Choosing appropriate information systems research approaches: a revised taxonomy', in H.-E. Nissen, H.K. Klein and R. Hirschheim (eds) *Information Systems Research: Contemporary Approaches and Emergent Traditions*, Amsterdam: Elsevier Science.

Glaser, B. and Strauss, A. (1967) *The Discovery of Grounded Theory*, Chicago, IL: Aldine.

Markus, L.M. (1983) 'Power, politics, and MIS implementation', *Communications of the ACM* 26, 6: 430–445.

MoPH (1992) *Nuevos Enfoques en Salud, Informe del Ministro a la Nacion*, Quito, Ecuador: Ministerio de Salud Publica.

Myers, M. (1994) 'Dialectical hermeneutics: a theoretical framework for the implementation of information systems', *Information Systems Journal* 5, 1: 51–70.

Myers, M. (1996) 'Interpretative research in information systems', in J. Mingers and F. Stowell (eds) *Information Systems: An Emerging Discipline*, London: McGraw-Hill.

Orlikowski, W.J. (1993) 'CASE tools as organizational change: investigating incremental and radical changes in systems development', *MIS Quarterly* 17, 3: 309–340.

Orlikowski, W.J. and Robey, D. (1991) 'Information technology and the structuring of organizations', *Information Systems Research* 2, 2: 143–169.

Osborne, D. and Gaebler, T. (1992) *Reinventing Government: How the Entrepreneurial Spirit is Transforming the Public Sector*, Reading, MA: Addison-Wesley.

Strauss, A. (1987) *Qualitative Analysis for Social Scientists*, Cambridge: Cambridge University Press.

Walsham, G. (1993) *Interpreting Information Systems in Organizations*, Chichester, W. Sussex: John Wiley.

Walsham, G. (1995) 'Interpretive case studies in IS research: nature and method', *European Journal of Information Systems* 4, 2: 74–81.

ACKNOWLEDGEMENTS

The author would like to thank Dr Jeremy Howells, Senior Researcher at PREST, University of Manchester, for his support during the research that formed the basis for this chapter, and for his revision of and comments on an earlier version of the chapter.

Part 3

Extra-organisational information systems

8 Internet-enabled applications for local government democratisation

Contradictions of the Swedish experience

Agneta Ranerup

Abstract: This chapter evaluates a Swedish example of using Internet-enabled applications – especially the World Wide Web – as a link between citizens and local government and, hence, as a component of democratisation processes in public sector reform. After reviewing more general experiences, the chapter describes a project in which the Web was used by local government in three districts of Göteborg. In evaluating this project, a set of contradictions are found that represent tensions or conflicts or opposing views related to use of Internet-enabled applications in government. Recommendations are made that address the contradictions. However, while the contradictions remain, they are likely to constrain the contribution of the Internet to public sector reform.

BACKGROUND

The context of reform

Since the 1970s, the economic base of the Swedish government – especially its welfare state – has been steadily eroded. When there was a major crisis in the early 1990s, traditional policies of currency devaluation and active labour market intervention were unable to restrain the downward spiral. A new policy approach was adopted, including significant measures of public sector reform. Sweden's traditional statist, corporatist policy of governance was changed with the introduction of measures such as marketisation and increased use of management by objectives and management by results to improve public sector resource management (Marcou 1993; Naschold 1996). In addition, there was a decentralisation of power from central government towards public corporations, agencies and – as discussed in this chapter – towards local government.

Sweden's process of decentralisation towards local government has, among other things, resulted in the creation of local government districts in many cities including the 'big three': Malmö, Göteborg and Stockholm. This chapter focuses on districts within Göteborg, which is Sweden's second-largest city with a population of 432,000. The districts have their own councils, with the authority to decide how to spend their budgets within a framework of centrally set economic, political and legal limits. Decentralisation has meant that responsibility for a number of elements of government – including schools, childcare, libraries and social welfare – has been devolved to a unit with a comparatively small population and geographical spread.

The district reforms were also intended to increase the democratisation of local government (Marcou 1993). They did this by increasing the number of people who were active as politicians in local government, and by reducing the physical and cultural distance between politicians and the citizens they served. There was also a conscious intention that reform would increase the participation of citizens in government, thereby making local government more accountable; for example, in the policy choices it made (ibid.).

Swedish local government reform has therefore seen elements of decentralisation and increased accountability bound together as an effort to increase democracy. Whilst not going as far as Osborne and Gaebler's (1992) prescription for 'community-owned government', this was certainly a step in that direction.

Internet-based applications and democratisation

The Internet of today is a communications infrastructure of huge proportions. It has grown from a more limited structure in the 1960s that consisted of the US military's ARPANET project and other large computer sites at US universities (Leiner *et al.* 1998). Today, it is a network of networks that links tens of thousands of networks and tens of millions of Internet host computers world-wide. The Internet does nothing by itself but it enables other computing applications, such as sending and receiving electronic mail and files or undertaking discussion in electronic newsgroups.

After electronic mail, the second major Internet-enabled application is the World Wide Web (WWW: generally known simply as the 'Web'). It is a collection of electronic documents stored on computers all around the world which has two particular capabilities. First, it is hypertext, which means that each Web document can link through to other documents. This allows readers to jump from one source of information to the next quickly and easily and (in theory) regardless of where in the world the information is stored. Second, it is multimedia, which means that Web documents can incorporate not only different styles of text but also drawings, photographs, sound and video clips.

Each collection of electronic documents that an organisation or individual makes available on their computer is known as a *Web site*. It has an initial document – called the *home page* – that will guide readers to the other documents (or *pages*) in that collection.

Usage of Internet has grown enormously and continues to do so (Charlton *et al.* 1997). In Sweden, between June 1996 and March 1997, for example, Internet use rose from roughly 15 per cent to 22 per cent among people between 16 and 65 years of age (Österman and Timander 1997). Consequently, the Internet is used as a big potential market place for commercial business.

By contrast, the Internet has been used much less to assist the democratisation processes of information age reform. Nevertheless, public sector applications of the Internet are growing rapidly and four main types of application can be distinguished, as discussed below.

There is as yet only limited global evidence about Internet-enabled applications. However, evidence from Europe and the US suggests that – for citizen–government links alone – dissemination has been the most widespread (and technically the easiest) application (Hacker 1996; Langelier 1996b). Use of electronic mail links is next in line. Interactive delivery of services and development of interactive discussion fora have been the least common (Åström 1998; Bellamy and Taylor 1997; Lips 1997).

Intra-government links

In this case, the Internet is used as a means of communication and interaction within government. For example, the Swedish and US state sectors use both electronic mail and Web services to transmit information within government (Hacker 1996; Langelier 1996a, 1996b).

Government to citizen dissemination

Another major use of the Web is as a mechanism for dissemination of government information to citizens. Typically, home pages have been used to provide general public sector information, plus documents, law-texts, etc. (Charlton *et al.* 1997; Langelier 1996a; Lips 1997). In this way, citizens get access to information that can be useful in their private life, when applying for services or when engaged in political activities. Public sector Web sites can also be used to provide information about more commercial activities, such as tourism.

A slightly more advanced method of dissemination ties the Web into the provision of an existing government service. In Annapolis, Maryland, for example, citizens can download and print forms to request parking permits, event permits and job applications from the local government Web site (Langelier 1996a).

Government–citizen interaction

Dissemination represents a one-way flow of information via the Internet, but interactive applications have also been developed. These may relate to public services. Another example from Annapolis has been the use of the local government Web site to allow citizens to pay water bills and parking fines electronically (Langelier 1996a).

Alternatively, interaction may relate to political debate and policy making, by using the Internet to gather reactions from citizens about government activities. This could be made as simple as letting citizens communicate their reactions to the government by electronic mail. More ambitiously, government can provide an interactive forum, in which citizens discuss issues with each other and then communicate to government. An example is the 'Digital City' project in Amsterdam. Apart from giving access to political and other documents, this project provided an interactive forum where in principle everybody was welcome to raise an issue and chat openly (Brants *et al.* 1996).

Citizen–citizen interaction: virtual communities

The Digital City project can also be seen as an example of the creation of a virtual community. A virtual community can be described as: 'a group of people who may or may not meet one another face-to-face, and who exchange words and ideas through the mediation of bulletin boards and networks' (Rheingold 1994: 1). In other words, this is a community that at the least exists in cyberspace and is totally dependent on a technological infrastructure (the Internet) to exist.

The Internet allows the dematerialisation of boundaries of both time and distance. Many virtual communities – such as Usenet newsgroup users or multi-user dungeon computer game participants – can therefore be based on common interests of community members, and have no geographical basis save that which maps the Internet's global accessibility.

Other virtual communities, however, do have a geographical basis. In other words, in some cases, the virtual community is a subset of some real community centred on a place of residence, such as a region or town (Rheingold 1994; Schuler 1996). Real communities do not need the Internet in order to interact with one another, but it can nevertheless provide an enabling mechanism for interaction. Even within real communities, there are boundaries of distance that separate citizens within their private homes or workplaces. For those with access, the Internet can help to overcome these boundaries and seems likely to do so, given the pre-existing community bonds and interests that motivate citizens to wish to interact both with each other and with their local government and its political processes.

Evaluation method

This chapter evaluates one case – the DALI (Delivery and Access to Local Information and Services) project in Göteborg – in which the Internet, or more particularly the Web, has been used as a link between a local government and its citizens. These citizens have a geographical place of residence in common: a local district in Göteborg. DALI's objectives were:

- to provide citizens with information about the political process in the municipality;
- to inform them about services available from local government;
- to provide a tool for use in political debate within the city districts.

The aim of the evaluation study was to look at the way in which these objectives might be achieved, but also to analyse contradictions. As Bjerknes (1992: 64) describes: 'In everyday language, "contradiction" has approximately the same meaning as "conflict". In this context, however, "contradiction", can be translated as "relation", it is not something bad or something that has to be avoided.' Instead, it is something that must be recognised and addressed.

In this chapter, the concept of 'contradiction' is used particularly to identify and discuss situations that involve differences between aims or views that can emerge when using the Internet as a link between citizens and local government. It is also applied to situations in which there are different ways of doing things, leading to the requirement to make choices between different options. Understanding such contradictions is informative for information systems researchers but also crucial for practitioners. The contradictions are discussed at length later, but an example will be given here: of the contradiction between politicians' desire to make the Internet as accessible as possible to the citizenry and their concerns about the costs of such a goal.

In order to identify contradictions, a qualitative case study method was used in which a detailed understanding of the information systems context was seen as vital to producing a well-grounded and valid result (Dyer and Wilkins 1991). The present author has such an understanding based on a three-year study of local government in Göteborg (Ranerup 1996), followed by the current case evaluation.

The evaluation focused on three different local government districts within Göteborg which took part in the DALI project. It involved semi-structured interviews that were conducted between May 1997 and March 1998 with:

- local politicians;
- senior public servants at both local and central levels;
- active citizen members of user groups;
- webmasters and infomasters.

The DALI system itself (http://dali.goteborg.se/) and related documents were also analysed.

A grounded method was used for the evaluation (Strauss and Corbin 1990). Contradictions and other issues were therefore developed from the interviews and other evaluative mechanisms, rather than being developed through the guidance of some extensive theoretical framework. In other words, the views of those involved were the focus of interest, in contrast to other studies of virtual communities in a local government context (e.g. Tsagarousianou *et al.* 1998).

ANALYSIS: EVALUATION FINDINGS

The DALI project in Göteborg

The DALI project is a part of the I*M Europe–Telematics Application Programme, initiated and partly financed by the European Commission. The overall aim of the project is to add value to public services through multimedia telematics applications. Participating cities are: Barcelona, Bologna, Göteborg, Köln, Las Palmas, Leipzig, London (Lewisham), Torino and Toulouse.

The Göteborg part of the DALI project aims to enhance public administration with information technology through greater citizen participation in government. In particular, the intention has been to provide a mechanism for increased public participation in the democratic process within the city's districts.

Göteborg was divided into 21 districts in 1990, each with its own local council and local government administration. These cover the responsibilities described above within budgets set by the central city council. The three districts taking part in the DALI project – Askim, Härlanda and Kärra-Rödbo – have about 21,000, 19,000 and 9,000 inhabitants respectively.

The systems development work was performed for these districts during the second half of 1996, with a number of groups becoming involved either directly or indirectly, including:

- *infomasters and webmasters*: public servants with responsibility for distributing information on the Web;
- *administrative district managers*: more senior public servants who take strategic decisions about district affairs;
- *local politicians*: the chair, vice-chair, and ten to fifteen ordinary members of the district council;
- *other public servants*: at the district level;
- *central systems administrator*: who provides support for district-level information systems;
- *central systems strategist*: who takes city-wide strategic decisions about information systems.

The DALI system became publicly accessible in the early spring of 1997. Since then, it has been used by citizens either from computers in private homes or from nine publicly accessible multimedia kiosks. Computers have also been distributed to four of the leading politicians in each of the three participating districts. Usage levels have been moderate: by spring 1998, each district's home page was registering just over 40 visits per day on average.

The DALI system

The home page of one of the DALI districts is shown in Figure 8.1. Behind this, the present version of the DALI system comprises four main areas, as illustrated in Figure 8.2:

- The *administrative information* section contains information about the opening hours, addresses and activities of various municipal services, such as childcare, schools, social services, libraries and sports facilities. There is also some information about how to apply for services. However, there are no facilities to make applications for services via the Web.
- The *current issues* section contains the political proposals of the district council and revised protocols of its decisions. There is also local news of a general character, such as the menus of school meals and of restaurants for the elderly, information about cultural events, special events in schools, etc.
- The *debate forum* consists of moderated, publicly accessible interactive discussions on current political issues in which both citizens and politicians can participate. Issues debated to date include: the quality and efficiency of schooling and childcare; the planning of roads in the districts; and the relations between districts and central political levels. From January 1997 to January 1998, there were 36 debate contributions in Härlanda, 50 in Kärra-Rödbo, and 145 in Askim. These numbers must be seen against a background of generally limited public participation in political processes through other means at district level. Contributions from citizens were by far the most common, and in only one district were there significant contributions from politicians. In addition to the debate forum, the e-mail addresses of some local politicians were provided on the Web site, allowing for direct contact between citizens and politicians.
- Lastly, the *archives* contain past discussions and documents, with a free-text search capability.

Figure 8.1 Entry Web page for the Kärra-Rödbo district of Göteborg

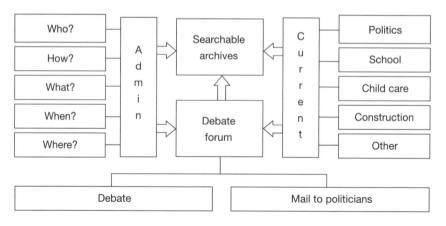

Figure 8.2 Functional structure of the DALI system

Contradictions

Evaluation of the DALI system, as described above, threw up a number of contradictions, each of which is analysed here in greater detail.

Access to the Internet

CONTRADICTION 1: VALUE VS COST OF PUBLIC ACCESS

Internet access among the Swedish population is rising. However, many of those involved in the DALI project felt that greater access was important, because current access levels were too low to make the Web site function effectively as a link between citizens and local government. They felt that home page hit rates and debate contribution rates needed to be significantly higher than at present. Such concerns led to the funding of public kiosks. However, not only are the kiosks costly to install, they are also costly to maintain since a number have been vandalised or accidentally damaged. Government can simply wait for access to rise, but any access-raising interventions cost money and bring this contradiction between the value and cost of accessibility into sharp relief.

CONTRADICTION 2: VALUE OF POLITICIAN VS OTHER GROUP ACCESS

Interviewees appreciated the value of local politicians having Internet access since this allows them to participate in debate with citizens. However, only a limited number of politicians were provided with access, thus limiting their potential to contribute. Additional funding could be provided to increase the number of participating politicians. However, there are tensions and opportunity costs here since the same money could alternatively be used to increase citizen access or to fund a greater number of Internet connections in local schools.

Regulating Web usage

CONTRADICTION 3: CENTRALISED VS LOCAL CONTROL OVER WEB DESIGN

Not surprisingly, those involved in the project at a central level felt the need for centralised coordination and control of Web page design. On the other hand, some of those at district level wanted to incorporate their own ideas into their Web pages.

CONTRADICTION 4: PUBLICATION OF AUTHORISED, GOVERNMENT VS OTHER INFORMATION

Some of the public servants wanted Web content to be restricted solely to information about government, authorised by government. Some local user groups, however, wanted the district Web sites to publish – or be linked to – online information with a broader local flavour. Examples including commercial information about local shops and information from non-government organisations operating within the district.

CONTRADICTION 5: PRIVACY VS ACCESSIBILITY OF PERSONAL INFORMATION

In Sweden there is a legal principle of public access to official records (the *Offentlighetsprincipen*). This principle covers most of the information published by government agencies and provides access to district council reports and other documentation.

However, such documentation often includes the names of public servants. Attempts to publish such information on the Web therefore come into conflict with the work of a central authority (the *Datainspektionen*) that regulates the use of personal information on computer. The regulations mean that Web publication of any documents containing names requires a special permit to be granted.

At present, the districts have tended to work round this by removing all names from published documents or by not making the documents available online. In both cases – though particularly the latter – this conflicts with the principle of open access and with the desire of Internet-connected citizens to have access to important information related to the work of government. There are likely to be continuing tensions between the rights of individual public servants to privacy and the rights of individual citizens to access.

CONTRADICTION 6: CENSORSHIP VS OPENNESS IN PUBLIC DEBATE

Several interviewees – both politicians and public servants – felt that public debate on the DALI system should be controlled. Their justification was the need to stop the broadcasting of (a) 'undemocratic' information (racist or sexist contributions), and (b) items harmful to their personal integrity. For this reason, the infomaster read all debate contributions before submitting them for Web publication.

In fact, there were few examples of censorship. Nevertheless, the practice of censorship may be seen as inimical to openness of debate and, hence, to public participation. The 'gatekeeping' role also had the very practical effect of closing down all debate during the summer and Christmas holidays when the infomaster was on vacation. This, too, was seen by some as harming the process of public participation.

Character of the Internet as a communication medium

CONTRADICTION 7: THE INTERNET AS AN INCREMENTAL VS RADICAL MEDIUM

Many interviewees saw the Internet as 'just another channel': as an incremental addition to the existing methods by which citizens and local government communicate, which would be used in much the same way as existing channels.

Others felt that the Internet and Internet-enabled applications provided a radically new way for citizens to participate in democratic processes. Internet properties identified included:

- *interactivity*: new opportunities for two-way debate between citizens and government;
- *speed of communication*: offering the possibility for politicians to obtain a rapid impression of citizen opinions on a particular issue;
- *scope*: providing links for politicians to groups with whom they were not previously in contact.

One possibility is that either of these viewpoints – if held by a majority of stakeholders in a situation – may become a self-fulfilling prophesy: those who see the Internet as radical will use it radically; those who see it as incremental will use it incrementally.

Relevance of the Internet as a debate forum

CONTRADICTION 8: NECESSITY VS HESITANCY OF POLITICIAN PARTICIPATION

Some politicians expressed doubts about participating in political debate via the Internet and preferred to use the phone when discussing issues with citizens. They felt that a written answer forced them to make too hard a commitment on particular issues, which thus made them more cautious. Also, politicians felt that some questions from citizens could not be answered in a simple or public way. Such questions typically related to complex or politically sensitive issues, or involved a straightforward misunderstanding on the part of the citizen.

On the other hand, some public servants felt it necessary for politicians to be active in the debate. Without contributions from politicians, the debate forum would be seen as just a citizens' 'talking shop' and would not be seen to make any contribution to the democratic process.

CONTRADICTION 9: PERCEIVED RELEVANCE VS IRRELEVANCE OF CITIZEN
PARTICIPATION AT DISTRICT LEVEL

Some politicians were keen to encourage groups of citizens to take part in Internet-enabled debates on issues relating to their children's schools or to other municipal institutions. Their aim was to create institutional boards partly run by citizens and to generate broad political debate within the districts.

Other politicians saw this kind of encouragement as unrealistically Utopian. They felt, first, that citizens would not be interested in the running of local institutions; second, they felt that the existing districts were too small, with too limited a mandate, and that issues for debate were too parochial. They sought a fundamental change in political structures – the merger of districts to create between four and six large districts rather than 21 small ones – prior to any encouragement of citizen participation.

CONCLUSIONS AND RECOMMENDATIONS

The role of Internet-enabled applications in public sector reform

In theory, Internet-enabled applications have much to offer information age reform processes of decentralisation, increased accountability and democratisation in government. They have a capacity to improve democratic processes by providing information to citizens and by allowing the voices of citizens to be heard by each other and by politicians and public servants. This can be done simply by electronic mail or in a more advanced way by providing interactive fora for discussions. But, if this is so in theory, how is it in practice?

That citizens and politicians have access to the Internet has been valued as important for democracy in the DALI project. A preliminary conclusion from these experiences is that, if a problem of access exists, it has to be solved if democratisation is to take place (a finding echoed by Brants *et al.* 1996; Graham and Marvin 1996; and Tsagarousianou *et al.* 1998). For such projects to work, most local government politicians need Internet access, as do a significant proportion of citizens from their homes, or from work, school or other public places. This has partly – but only partly – been the case in Göteborg.

If processes of democracy and accountability are to be improved, all relevant information must be published on the Web. In the DALI case, information about local government services has been published. On the other hand, Web content has been circumscribed by various factors, including the desire of central levels in local government to control content and the laws regulating use of personal information on computer.

However, these constraints have not had a serious impact on the outcomes of the DALI project. Rather, at this stage of introducing an Internet-enabled application in local government, the most important thing is to get the system running, accessible and widely known. Factors relating to central controls and regulations and details of content can be dealt with later.

Overall, it is clear that the DALI system has not yet achieved its full democratisation potential. Instead, its initial stages can be described as a period of introducing and testing the technical as well as the organisational aspects of the system. The somewhat limited participation in the debate, the closure of the debate forum during holidays, and the hesitation among some politicians about participating can be seen as temporary problems to be solved by iterative improvements.

None the less, evaluation of the DALI experience to date has revealed a number of contradictions and tensions that exist when using Internet-enabled applications in this context. Some practical advice on how these should be handled will be given in the next section.

Implementation of Internet-enabled applications for public sector reform: recommendations

Implementation needs time

In evaluating the experiences of Internet-enabled democratisation initiatives, we are evaluating an implementation period of a few years at best. Yet we know from the experience of earlier initiatives that it may take several decades to fully implement them and to see their true impact. From this, one can conclude that:

- we should not expect instant results from Internet-enabled initiatives: it may take several years to fully implement them;
- evaluation needs to be a continuous and long-term activity;
- issues arising in the early stages of the DALI system may change over time.

Picking up the last point, the contradictions related to access may appear different within a few years. Private spending on Internet access is increasing, large sums of public money are being invested in providing access to schools and public centres, and Swedish unions are involved in projects aimed at increasing Internet access for their members (Martinsson 1998). Combining this greater access with falling technology costs, the tensions inherent in the first two contradictions are likely to be reduced.

However, access issues are unlikely to disappear completely, given the continuing unevenness of technology penetration between different areas and regions. Within countries, there will be access gaps that leave the urban and – especially – rural poor lagging behind. Between countries, there will be gaps that leave developing countries lagging behind the industrialised world. Given the unevenness of access, there will be a consequent unevenness of democratisation benefits (Tsagarousianou *et al.* 1998).

Over time, the issue of politician participation is also likely to change. Politicians have, over recent years, become accustomed to participating in debates using various existing forms of mass media such as newspapers, radio and television. They are similarly likely to become accustomed to using computers and the Internet. The readiness of politicians to engage in debate will in future, therefore, be determined more by their attitude towards debate, participation and the citizenry than by their attitude towards the new technologies.

Implementation needs organisation

Some of the issues that have arisen with the DALI project can be addressed by some fairly straightforward organisational solutions. To take the simplest first, it will be necessary to arrange for continuous cover so that there is always someone available to moderate the debate, in or out of holiday time. Despite the vagaries of personal interpretations, it would also be helpful if a set of public guidelines were issued on the type of content that was deemed unacceptable. Such guidelines already exist in many Internet fora world-wide.

Similarly, guidelines need to be worked out about (a) non-government information to be published on the main site, and (b) links to other organisations' material. As Bannon and Bødker (1997) point out, some kind of agreement on principles among the organisations involved will help clarify issues about responsibilities for Web content, maintenance, reliability, etc.

Such an agreement also needs to be reached between central and local government to avoid the potential conflicts outlined in contradiction 3. A typical 'core–periphery' compromise is for the centre to provide the local level with support, training, hardware facilities and an outline framework for Web content and layout. The local staff provide the content to fill the framework and are responsible for the day-to-day running of the Web site.

Finally, there needs to be some accommodation on the issues of privacy and accessibility. In the Swedish case, such an accommodation is being debated at the time of writing, and will have resulted in new legislation by the end of 1998. This will address online publication of local government documents containing names, and will give exemption from the requirement for a permit and from the threat of prosecution.

Implementation needs strategies

Government use of the Internet cannot be approached in an *ad hoc* manner, but needs to be planned strategically. In this way, the full capacity of this new tool can be harnessed and the opportunities it provides for citizen participation can be realised.

Strategic planning will be partly about the technology but – as in the integrated approach described in Chapter 2 – this must be driven by, rather than driving, a wider strategy of democratisation. The Internet must therefore be seen as a tool to serve democratisation goals, rather than as an end in itself. The strategies of commentators such as Friedland (1996) and Stegberg and Svensson (1997) can be applied at the local government level in seeking the formation of 'advocacy networks' and virtual communities within individual districts.

Particular groups could be identified and supported which combine the geographical proximity of residence in the district with a specific interest: for example, parents and relatives of children with a disability; or of children in school or childcare; or relatives of the elderly and housebound. A strategy of activating and empowering such groups could make use of Internet-enabled applications like the Web and e-mail to:

- create a group identity;
- keep the group informed;
- develop group ideas and consensus;
- enable the group to make an input to the local political process.

Such communities of citizens who interactively discuss and exchange information could provide an instance of what White (1997) calls 'deliberation': careful and deep discussion between citizens and politicians. In this way the Internet may be perceived as a relevant – even radical – tool for local democratisation and for other aspects of information age reform.

Conception–reality gaps

In many ways, the contradictions described above reflect gaps that exist between the conception of this Internet-enabled application and Swedish realities. For example, Internet-enabled democratisation is based on a technology conception of broad Internet access, which was not (yet) the Swedish reality. Similarly, there were inherent process and management assumptions within this application of new technology – about organisational procedures and guidelines – that did not hold in reality. Because of these conception–reality gaps, certain contradictions and problems arose during early implementation.

As noted above, these largely technical and organisational gaps will diminish in coming years, leading to diminishing risks of implementation difficulties. With regard to other dimensions of the ITPOSMO model (see Chapter 3), however, their diminution is less certain. For instance, there may well be a gap between the conception of citizens as budding participants in the political process and the reality of a majority who are not engaged and do not wish to become engaged in debate.

In the US context, writers such as Schuler (1996) and White (1997) are optimistic about the role of the Internet in reducing this gap and in motivating citizen participation. The author is more equivocal in her viewpoint, seeing great potential for Internet-enabled applications but also significant barriers.

REFERENCES

Åström, J. (1998) *Local Digital Democracy: An overview* [Lokal digital demokrati: en översikt], Stockholm: Kommunförbundet. In Swedish.

Bannon, L. and Bødker, S. (1997) 'Constructing common information spaces', in J.A. Hughes, W. Prinz, T. Rodden and K. Schmidt (eds) *Proceedings of the Fifth European Conference on Computer Supported Cooperative Work*, Dordrecht: Kluwer Academic.

Bellamy, C. and Taylor, J. (1997) 'Understanding government.direct', paper presented at IFIP WG 8.5 Workshop 'Empowering the Citizens Through IT', 5–6 May, Stockholm, Sweden.

Bjerknes, G. (1992). 'Dialectical reflection in information systems development', *Scandinavian Journal of Information Systems* 4: 55–77.

Brants, K., Huizenga, M. and van Meerten, R. (1996) 'The canals of Amsterdam: an exercise in local electronic democracy', *Media, Culture and Society* 18, 2: 233–247.

Charlton, C., Gittings, C., Leng, P., Little, J. and Neilson, I. (1997) 'Diffusion of the Internet: a local perspective on an international issue', in T. McMaster, E. Mumford, E.B. Swanson, B. Warboys and D. Wastell (eds) *Facilitating Technology Transfer through Partnership: Learning from Practice and Research*, London: Chapman & Hall.

Dyer, W.G. and Wilkins, A.L. (1991) 'Better stories, not better constructs, to generate better theory: a rejoinder to Eisenhardt', *Academy of Management Review* 16, 3: 613–619.

Friedland, L.A. (1996) 'Electronic democracy and the new citizenship', *Media, Culture and Society* 18, 2: 185–212.

Graham, S. and Marvin, S. (1996) *Telecommunications and the City: Electronic Spaces, Urban Places*, London: Routledge.

Hacker, K.L. (1996) 'Missing links in the evolution of electronic democratization', *Media, Culture and Society* 18, 2: 213–232.

Langelier, P. (1996a) 'Special series: Local government on the Internet. Part 3: Local government home pages', *Popular Government* Winter/Spring: 38–45.

Langelier, P. (1996b) 'Special series: Local government on the Internet. Part 4: How to evaluate Internet resources', *Popular Government* Summer: 41–48.

Leiner, B.M., Cerf, V.G., Clark, D.D., Kahn, R.E., Kleinrock, L., Lynch, D.C., Postel, J., Roberts, L.G. and Wolff, S. (1998) *A Brief History of the Internet*. http://www.isoc.org/internet/history/brief.html

Lips, M. (1997) 'Reinventing public service delivery through ICT: lesson drawing from developments in the USA, UK, and the Netherlands', paper presented at the IFIP WG 8.5 Workshop 'Empowering the Citizens Through IT', 5–6 May, Stockholm, Sweden.

Marcou, G. (1993) 'New tendencies of local government development in Europe', in R.J. Bennett (ed.) *Local Government in the New Europe*, London: Belhaven Press.

Martinsson, P. (1998) 'Computers at home: a success for TUC' [Datorer hemma: en succé för LO], *Arbetet Nyheterna* 3 March: 6. In Swedish.

Naschold, F. (1996) *New Frontiers in Public Sector Management: Trends and Issues in State and Local Government in Europe*, Berlin: Walter de Gruyter.

Osborne, D. and Gaebler, T. (1992) *Reinventing Government: How the Entrepreneurial Spirit is Transforming the Public Sector*, Reading, MA: Addison-Wesley.

Österman, T. and Timander, J. (1997) *The Usage of Internet in the Swedish Population*

[Internetanvändningen i Sveriges befolkning], Teldok-report no. 115, Stockholm: Teldok. In Swedish.

Ranerup, A. (1996) *Participatory Design through Representatives* [Användarmedverkan med representanter], PhD dissertation, Report 9, Göteborg: Department of Informatics, University of Göteborg. In Swedish with English summary.

Rheingold, H. (1994) *The Virtual Community: Homesteading on the Electronic Frontier*, New York: Harper Perennial.

Schuler, D. (1996) *New Community Networks: Wired for Change*, New York: Addison-Wesley.

Stegberg, T. and Svensson, L. (1997) 'How to use Internet, when you don't have to', in K. Braa and E. Monteiro (eds) *Proceedings of the IRIS 20*, Oslo: Department of Informatics, University of Oslo.

Strauss, A. and Corbin, J. (1990) *Basics of Qualitative Research: Grounded Theory, Procedures, and Techniques,* Newbury Park, CA: Sage Publications.

Tsagarousianou, R., Tambini, D. and Bryan, C. (eds) (1998) *Cyberdemocracy. Technology, Cities and Civic Networks*, New York: Routledge.

White, C.S. (1997) 'Citizen participation and the Internet: prospects for civic deliberation in the information age', *Social Studies* January/February: 23–28.

9 Community development and democratisation through information technology
Building the new South Africa

Peter Benjamin

Abstract: South Africa's post-apartheid context has led to a heavy emphasis on reform initiatives that democratise the state and that empower and develop local communities. There has been a strong belief in the power of information technology (IT) to support these reforms. This chapter evaluates the experience and potential of 'multi-purpose community centres' in using IT for community development. It describes cases of both failure and success, concluding that there has perhaps been more of the former than the latter. Failure has arisen because of the largely technical approach adopted by many community-based projects. This approach paid insufficient attention to the real information needs of communities or to issues of sustainability. Based on these experiences, brief guidelines for IT-enabled democratisation initiatives are proposed.

BACKGROUND

The context of reform

Public service and the transition from apartheid

South Africa is a land of great contrasts shaped by its bitter history. This is as true for information technology (IT) as for other areas. South Africa is the fourteenth largest user of the Internet globally, and has one of the fastest international growth rates of mobile phone usage. At the same time, it is estimated that half the population has never made a phone call.

South Africa has been through turbulent times since the end of apartheid in 1994, and the public sector in particular has been trying to respond to these changes. There is now a new constitution and several new government structures (in 1994 South Africa went from four provinces to nine), with at times unclear distribution of powers between national, provincial and local levels of government. Overwhelmingly there is great pressure to deliver better services to the majority of the population that was disadvantaged by the previous system – and in a climate of fiscal restraint.

Since 1994, there has been great interest in reducing the gap between citizens and government. This reduction is seen as a necessary part of meeting the overwhelming development needs that exist in the country. There are 'consultative fora' and 'participative councils' throughout the land. The Reconstruction and Development Programme (RDP) – the widely supported plan of the new government – has laid as much stress on 'democratising the state' as on 'meeting basic needs', 'building human resources' and 'building the economy' (ANC 1994).

Certainly, the gap between citizens and government has been a major one. Local government, for example, faces the legacy of protests in the 1980s and early 1990s which has sustained a culture of non-payment for services in many areas, especially in the townships. This has led to confrontations in some areas when the local government cuts off electricity or water services in order to force payment.

This pattern is repeated more generally. Before 1994, the public service was dominated by Afrikaners and was seen as hostile to the majority of the population. As part of the negotiations leading to elections it was agreed that there would not be major retrenchment of the 'old guard' after 1994. This has led to continued perception of the public service as unsympathetic to the black majority and to frequent tensions between citizens and government, as well as between newer and older public servants.

One outcome was the launch in 1997 of a campaign called 'Batho Pele' – a Sotho phrase for 'putting people first'. This was intended to change the attitudes of public servants and make them more responsive to citizens' needs. Another outcome has been to help people to help themselves by fostering community development.

Public sector reform in South Africa

South Africa's very particular context has led to three main themes running through public sector reform in the country:

- *increased efficiency*: as a means of reducing the cost burden that the public service places on the population;
- *increased accountability*: as a means for the public service to prove that it is serving the population;
- *decentralisation and community development*: as a means to address the needs of the majority of the population, who live in rural areas or small towns. A major aim of policy is to avoid communities relying on delivery of services from government. There is thus much talk of establishing 'enabling environments' and empowerment of communities to meet their

own needs, with the public sector seen as the key driver in this enabling and empowering process. This is, therefore, very much in tune with Osborne and Gaebler's (1992) ideas about community-owned government.

These three elements are the foundations for the reinvention of public service in the new South Africa, and they can be combined in the concept of democratisation of the public service. Just as South Africa has a new democratic form of government, so too reform initiatives are focused on creating a new democratic form of public service in order to break the legacy of apartheid.

Information technology and public sector reform in South Africa

There has been a long history of investment in information technology by the South African public sector. It is the second-largest user of IT in the country after the financial sector and has many legacy systems in operation, particularly in the Defence Department. There has also been a recognition of the significant role that IT can play in public sector reform, and the need for the public service to use new technologies is often repeated (Schuman 1996). The Minister for Public Service and Administration, for example, has stated: 'The challenge now is to harness IT solutions to facilitate more effective and efficient use of public resources in the delivery of services' (*Sunday Independent* 1997).

One barrier to information age reform is the relatively decentralised approach that has so far been adopted. This has led to little standardisation or integration of systems between departments and to numerous problems of incompatibility. In terms of technology, most departments have gone their own way as the formal procedures for centralised approval of purchases have proved too cumbersome. The same problem affects data standards. For example, there are seven different definitions of 'small business' across government, making it hard for departments to share and compare business statistics.

In March 1998, the South African Cabinet approved the establishment of a centralised State Information Technology Agency to coordinate IT functions for the various departments of government. At the time of writing, this had just been established, but already many departmental IT sections are expressing disquiet about centralisation. There has also been concern that current moves are too IT-focused and do not give sufficient attention to information systems issues. There is thus a danger, as in the descriptions of Chapter 2, that an isolate or idolise rather than integrate approach to information age reform will be followed.

Democratisation initiatives with information technology

'Information society' is a well-known term in South Africa. As in many other countries, the government sees that investment in information technology (both in skills and infrastructure) is of great importance to the future development of the country. Given the concerns about democratisation, there has been a particular desire to ensure that IT supports the process of democratisation and that it does not benefit a small information élite while leaving the majority in 'information poverty'.

From this, it is possible to see global differences in the way that IT is being approached. These differences were clearly drawn at the 1996 conference on Information Society and Development (ISAD), held in South Africa. The G7 industrialised countries argued strongly that the leading principles of the information society should be to promote dynamic competition and encourage private investment, with the main role of the state being to define an adaptable regulatory framework (Department of Foreign Affairs 1996). By contrast, the 30 developing countries put the emphasis on meeting basic needs, supporting sustainable socio-economic development, respecting diversity of language and culture, and providing universal access and service.

South Africa's approach has shown it to be in the latter camp, with a focus on universal access to IT and on applications to services such as education, healthcare, small business development and community development. South Africa has also adopted a different language, preferring to talk about an 'information community' rather than an 'information superhighway' or 'information society'; both of which have tended to dominate debates in the industrialised nations. To quote from the South African position paper for the ISAD conference:

[The information community] is a vision that seeks to shift the emphasis of the advantages offered by the information revolution towards a fuller balance between individuals and social groups, communities and societies. In developed countries, even where social issues are taken into account, the bias has tended to remain that of individual advancement via personal universal access and, at a public level, on competition between firms and nations. Our vision seeks to ensure the creation of an equitable information order, nationally, regionally and internationally. The vision of an information community therefore takes into account the undoubted potential of communities at various levels to co-operate, to bridge differences, to work for mutual upliftment and for the meeting of basic needs, and to redress the social imbalances of under-development. The development of an information community perspective aims to ensure that the information revolution benefits society as a whole.

(DACST 1996: 17)

Opening government information

Central to the creation of an 'equitable information order' has been an improvement in the communication of government information. To address this, Deputy President Thabo Mbeki established a Task Group on Government Communications in 1996, known as ComTask. One principle focus was the communication of information to previously excluded groups:

> The disadvantaged communities in rural and urban areas of the South African society should be the main targets for an enhanced development information system. [They] have been deprived of information related to their economies, education, cultures and societies.
>
> (ComTask 1997: 43)

Three principal vehicles have been envisaged to help open up the communication of government information:

- *New legislation* An Open Democracy Bill was proposed, although it had not passed into law at the time of writing in 1999. This would put the emphasis on government making information of public interest available in an accessible manner.
- *New government institutions* A central Government Communications Information Service was established in March 1998 to coordinate the increased availability of government information.
- *New delivery mechanisms* Once information is made available, there must be the means to transmit it to disadvantaged communities and the means for community members to access and use the information. Initiatives in this area are discussed next.

Changing the IT infrastructure

Building an information community and using IT to support the process of democratisation requires a technology infrastructure that reaches out to all parts of the country. But South Africa's apartheid legacy has left a very uneven spread of infrastructure.

The world average teledensity (number of main phone lines per 100 people) is 11 and for South Africa as a whole the figure is 9.5 – one of the highest figures in Africa (ITU 1997). Yet this high average hides great inequality. While in some rich suburbs the figure is 70 phones per 100 people or higher, in parts of the Eastern Cape the statistic is lower than 0.1 – less than one phone for every 1,000 people. The same is true of computers. There are 3.5 computers for every 100 people on average but the distribution is even more heavily skewed towards the business and affluent districts than it is with telephones.

Because of this, there has been a conscious policy of promoting universal access, particularly to telecommunications. The first objective of the 1996 Telecommunications Act was to 'promote the universal service and affordable provision of telecommunication services' (Department of Communications 1996: 3). A Universal Service Agency was established to help achieve this objective, and access targets were set for Telkom, the main telecommunications company. Telkom's current five-year license requires the installation of 2.9 million extra lines, of which 1.8 million are to be in rural areas (Grant 1997).

Utilising multi-purpose community centres

As the IT infrastructure spreads throughout the country, there needs to be some access and delivery point for information within communities. Many communities have such points already in the form of a centre that has been set up to respond to the needs of the community. Locally, these have been given various names – Community Service Centre, Community Information Centre, Community Resource Centre – but they have come to be known collectively as 'multi-purpose community centres' (MPCCs).

An MPCC is defined as 'an organisation offering a range of developmental services (including information services) to a specific community and with a large degree of community involvement' (Berlyn 1996: 7). MPCCs should therefore enable communities to manage their own development by providing access to appropriate information, facilities, resources, training and services. The sharing of facilities and the synergy of provision is intended to result in more cost-effective and efficient community services.

These centres offer a range of services as defined by the needs of their community, including:

- a community information centre, providing information for and about the community;
- a community resource centre, to provide resources such as shared equipment;
- a government information 'one-stop shop', providing information about government and its services;
- a government service centre, integrating the delivery of a range of public services;
- a training centre to create new skills in computing, bookkeeping, office skills, craft work, etc.;
- a support centre for small enterprise development;
- a library;
- a centre for related developmental and entrepreneurial services.

Not all MPCCs offer all services because these are driven by community needs and priorities. Community involvement, ownership and control is therefore fundamental to an MPCC. MPCC stakeholders include representative organisations, individual residents, local authorities, business and appointed development agents, all with proven interests (stakes) in the community. Both the process and the outcome of MPCC implementation varies from community to community, depending on social, economic, political and organisational history and context.

As we report below, many MPCCs do not yet use information or communication technology. However, the MPCCs do provide a ready-made national framework that can be plugged into the new IT infrastructure and bring benefits of new technology and new information to disadvantaged communities. The Universal Service Agency has been undertaking an initiative along these lines, adding IT functionality to MPCCs to turn them into 'telecentres' that are both economically and socially self-sustaining.

New telecentre services may include provision of information and communication services for local business, distance education and telemedicine. However, there is no single model for the new telecentres and the Agency has been piloting a number of formats, with the intention of having 100 pilot telecentres by the end of 1999. Part of the piloting and planning process has been an evaluation of IT availability and use in existing MPCCs, and a search for models that can guide telecentre creation.

MPCC evaluation methodology

There is no central register of MPCCs; they are distributed throughout South Africa, including remote parts of the country. The first step in evaluation was therefore to develop an address list of organisational contacts who were believed to be involved with MPCCs. This development was undertaken by a group of evaluators operating at both provincial and national level, and resulted in a mailing list of just over 9,000 organisations.

A questionnaire was sent out to each of these organisations by post, fax or e-mail. Just over 400 were returned, on the basis of which 350 MPCCs were identified. From these, 20 questionnaires were cross-checked by telephone interviews (no major discrepancies were found) and a cross-section of ten was chosen for more detailed investigation. These were visited and observed in operation by someone familiar with the appropriate local language. Interviews were also conducted with MPCC staff and with members of surrounding stakeholder organisations within the local community.

Given the response rate, this evaluation must be seen as representative rather than comprehensive, since there are far more than 350 MPCCs in South Africa. Issues of self-selection in response and self-definition of MPCCs must also be borne in mind.

ANALYSIS AND FINDINGS

Of the 350 identified MPCCs, 60 per cent were in rural areas, and most of the remainder in townships. The six services offered by 40 per cent or more of the centres were: training; an information office; advice; counselling; a resource centre; and a library. It was clear that – especially in rural areas – the MPCCs played a major role in their communities and were therefore worthwhile locations through which to target community development applications of IT.

Sustainability was an issue. Many had set self-sustainability as a major goal, yet almost all had major funding problems and most were reliant on funding from external donors. None the less, many had developed innovative fund-raising methods, from crafts, baking and weaving through training to the collection of a 1 rand (about 20 US cents) contribution from all households.

Levels of information and communication technology usage were surprisingly high within the centres: 88 per cent of MPCCs had a telephone; 65 per cent had a computer (36 per cent had five or more computers); and 30 per cent were using electronic mail. In rural areas, the figures were only slightly lower at 73 per cent, 45 per cent and 16 per cent, respectively.

Even allowing for self-selection in reporting, this was encouraging in its positive implications for the likely success of telecentres. It also meant that there was a substantial pool of experience of IT and community development. In addition, this provided a set of centres that could immediately take advantage of new IT-based initiatives. However, more detailed analysis of IT-using centres provided a somewhat less positive picture, as the following cases illustrate.

Johannesburg Metropolitan Council

Service delivery to the community is at the heart of local government. Zybrands (1995: 126) defines the mission of local government in terms of having 'to achieve the highest general welfare of a community by satisfying the identified needs through the effective rendering of services'. Johannesburg Metropolitan Council – the largest city council in South Africa – realised the need to bring services closer to the community in order to achieve goals of community development and democratisation. It has used IT to achieve this, and two examples are given here.

One-stop service centres

The Council has taken up the idea of 'one-stop service centres', building on the experiences of Brent Council, a local government authority in London. These centres provide a single, accessible point of contact for community members in dealing with a wide variety of enquiries, complaints and requests.

In November 1994 the Council opened its one-stop property information centre. This integrated the services and expertise of Building Control, Fire Safety, Town Planning, Valuations, Treasury and other council departments related to property. Services rendered at the centre include specialist advice on building codes and town planning regulations, building plan submission facilities, payment of rates and service accounts, property valuation information, applications for drainage connections, and advice in regard to structural aspects of plans. This service has been used very heavily and is considered a success by clients.

In June 1997, an information and complaints service desk was established within the property information centre. This was implemented by the Management Information Systems Unit of the Council and made significant use of IT. For example, it included a user-friendly IT-based system based around a Council intranet (an internal organisational network that makes use of Internet technology and protocols to provide services like the World Wide Web). This could access information from corporate databases in order to answer client queries and could also handle some property-related transactions, such as basic applications. It could be used both by centre staff and directly by clients.

However, a year after its establishment, the information system was very little used, for a number of reasons:

- clients who come to the centre would rather speak to people to ask their questions than deal with the new technology;
- centre staff were not fully trained on the system, thus creating a barrier to its use;
- some of the information required to deal with client queries was not on the system, partly because the databases were not updated;
- some staff preferred to speak directly to a relevant official rather than use the intranet.

So the one-stop shop information system actually proved to be not very successful. The system did not directly respond to a real need since both clients and staff preferred human interactions; the database and transaction processing capabilities were quite sophisticated – in fact, too sophisticated; and basic organisational issues such as training and database maintenance were not properly addressed.

MetroNet

A separate attempt at constructing an information system proceeded quite differently under the MetroNet initiative. One person in the Communications Section of the Johannesburg Mayor's Office set up an intranet in 1995, completely separate from the MIS Unit's work. The intranet was initially developed by volunteers and computer hobbyists putting all the old Council minutes into the system. After a few months, the system was shown to the mayor and other key councillors, who loved it and committed resources to it: primarily staff time to retype or scan Council documents. The project subsequently developed into a major internal information system – called MetroNet – which is used by around half of all Council staff. It has developed by asking people what information they actually need in their work, and then making sure that this was available on the system.

In 1997 MetroNet extended from being simply an intranet within the Council to being a system that could be interrogated by people outside; confidential data was protected by firewalls (specialised hardware or software that restricts the passage of information between the organisation's internal network and its external network connections). The information is primarily delivered via a World Wide Web interface. It includes tourist and public relations information, but also information intended for use in local communities. The MetroNet system is therefore used by MPCCs in the Johannesburg area to find details of Council minutes, regulations and councillor contacts. It is also used to facilitate communication between MPCC members and their councillors or relevant Council officials.

MetroNet is therefore seen as a successful contribution of IT to community development by helping to meet some community information needs. Identifiable critical success factors include:

- it started small and developed incrementally;
- it won the political backing of the powers that be;
- its development was based on real expressed needs;
- it was opened up to community and other external use only after it had proven to be a relatively mature and useful system internally.

North-West Province kiosks

The North-West Province of South Africa was formed largely out of the former 'homeland' of Bophutatswana. It has a largely rural and poor population, and illiteracy levels over 50 per cent. In 1995, the Reconstruction and Development Programme Unit of the Office of the Premier started a pilot project to provide information to communities through touch-screen kiosks. This was the Unit's major community communications project at the time.

Six stand-alone (i.e. non-networked) touch-screen computer systems were used. Most of the hardware and software was donated by a computer company, and the information content was collected, digitised and implemented by the provincial government. The total development cost of the project was R500,000 (about US$100,000) including staff time, and it took the RDP Unit around 18 months to create operational systems. The six kiosks were then set up in various MPCCs throughout the Province, with a generally favourable initial reaction.

However, this initial reaction was not sustained. In part, this was because the information provided was interesting, but did not really meet the needs of the community. The bulk of the information was general demographic and economic information on the Province, details of the main provincial programmes of government, and speeches by the Premier of the Province and by President Nelson Mandela. In essence, the system was an exercise in public relations rather than something that provided a community service. System interactivity was also limited to pressing buttons – it was not possible to ask a real question and get an answer. Finally, no consideration had been given to ways of updating the information.

For these reasons, when the project leader left the public service in early 1997, the RDP Unit quickly took the decision to scrap the project. Siting the kiosks in tourist areas, such as the airport and hotels, was considered but even this was seen not to be cost effective. Overall, the project is now thought to have been a waste of money by the provincial government. It was technology-led – a solution looking for a problem – and it lacked sufficient attention to real information needs and to operational and budgetary issues.

Additional examples

Three further 'thumbnail sketches' of IT and community development are given: one negative, two positive.

In 1992 in KwaNdebele, a rural area north of Pretoria, a workshop of computers was used to mount a two-month training course. The intention was to teach local people to program as a way of 'raising skills in the area', in the hope that these skills could then be applied to the development of community information systems. In all, 20 people were trained but no one was ever employed in systems development for the community. In part this was due to lack of local demand and funding, and in part to the fact that the trainees were taught to program in COBOL. A few trainees did leave the area to get jobs in Johannesburg as programmers. While this certainly benefited them as individuals, it also served to rob the community of some of its most energetic members.

In 1995 in Alexandra (a township next to Johannesburg) the local authority initiated the development of a database of local resources. For three months all the organisations in the township were asked to fill in forms (often organised by school children as homework) and a database of all the resources in the area was created, including schools, community groups, churches, businesses, political groups, sports facilities, and women's, cultural and youth groups. The database was provided with a World Wide Web interface and was made available over a wide area network, accessible from a number of MPCCs with computers. It was also accessible more widely via the Internet. Not only has the system been instrumental in increasing the sense of community self-worth and self-identity, it has also led to more tangible benefits. It was used, for example, to demonstrate community capabilities to large firms in the city and to win sub-contracting work for community businesses from those firms.

Mamelodi is a township close to Pretoria. In 1995 the Mamelodi Community Information Service (Macis) was established by the Mamelodi community and the Centre for Scientific and Industrial Research, the large state-owned science research facility. It offers information and computing services and is heavily used, particularly by people seeking jobs and writing their résumés. Macis has developed a large amount of locally relevant information, which is made widely available from the community's Web site. Following the model of Alexandra, Macis has developed a community directory. The local doctors' forum now requires all practitioners in Mamelodi to have a copy of this directory to assist patients.

CONCLUSIONS AND RECOMMENDATIONS

The role of information technology in democratisation

There is a great need for the public service in South Africa to be democratised by becoming more accountable, efficient, decentralised and supportive of community development. Within the officials and policies of national government there is a belief that information technology will be able to play a role in each of these elements of public sector reform. For example, at the time of writing, Northern Cape Province was about to establish one-stop shop centres in local communities based around new technology, in an effort to leapfrog to higher levels of government service provision.

It is the author's belief that, in public sector information projects, IT can greatly improve the link between government and the governed. However, there are many more difficulties in doing this than were originally imagined.

One major difficulty has been the tendency of those involved to follow the idolise approach described in Chapter 2. They therefore take an information technology perspective, not an information systems perspective. While it is clear that the technological infrastructure is crucial to IT-enabled democratisation, this issue is secondary to that of information. Yet often too much attention is given to equipment, without adequately considering the information and human systems that are more critical to success, as shown by the North-West Province example. The ongoing effort and cost of updating information has also been ignored, as shown by the Johannesburg property example. By contrast, some technology difficulties may not be as great as expected, given the relatively high access rates to IT reported by community centres.

Over and above this, the main difference between project success and failure has been the extent to which real information needs have been analysed and incorporated into the information systems. The most successful IT-enabled democratisation projects have therefore been a result of government working with communities to define and meet specific needs, as was the case in the MetroNet and Alexandra examples.

There are many forms of information that are useful to communities and many ways in which information can be stored and transmitted, often informally. MPCCs form a focus for informal, verbal information systems and also offer a way of providing formalised information systems: both on paper and on computer. In many areas, verbal, paper-based or standard library services are appropriate and best. In some cases, IT-based information systems may be cheaper or more effective.

But the rush to use computers must not be seen as an end in itself: what is important is the information and the uses to which it can be put. Some community IT projects seem more like a solution looking for a problem than a genuine attempt to meet development needs. There have been several examples in South Africa of Internet access points being set up for local communities. These were often played with for a week or so until the community lost interest as there was so little information useful to them on the system. They wanted to know about:

- their local community;
- what development projects there were in the area;
- how to apply for a housing subsidy;
- what tenders were being offered by government;
- what training courses there were.

Yet none of this information had been collected or made available.

In summary, systems are more likely to be effective if they follow an integrated approach based on the real information needs of the potential users and not on a 'technical fix'. Where there is a genuine desire to access the information, people show real ingenuity in accessing it, despite technical barriers. Where the system is basically a fancy front-end with little content, then the project quickly dies a death. As a reminder, if the Technology Overlooks You (and your needs) then it is a TOY.

Implementation of IT for democratisation: recommendations

IT professionals need to learn the skills of information analysts and development workers. In community development work, empowering the community is not simply a tactic to achieve some development goal; it is a large part of the goal itself. All communities already have information systems, though they are often informal and subtle and are therefore ignored by conventional information science. Any formalised information system should build on and respect the existing use of information in a community. Often libraries, schools and churches already have useful information stores and roles that should become the base of more formalised information systems.

Paolo Freire, the Brazilian educator, reminds us of the crucial role of education in his book *Pedagogy of the Oppressed* (Freire 1995). Training can either make people become cogs in an existing system, or empower them to understand and act in their environment. This is central to information and computer applications in developing communities. Training people in word processing skills to secure a job can be useful, but giving them a creative understanding of the uses of information and the skills to get what their community needs is much more empowering for community development.

There are at least five levels that need to be addressed in order to make IT-based applications work and effectively contribute to community development.

Technology	The telephone lines and computers need to be available. This clearly is the first stage: providing the infrastructure. As daunting as it may seem, this is the easiest stage. In South Africa, for example, there are a number of organisations aiming to provide these technologies, especially the Universal Service Agency and the National Computer Foundation.
Training and skills	Without the appropriate skills, people can only treat a computer as a box of metal. Appropriate training must be provided. It takes about one week to train a literate English-speaking person in introductory computing up to the basics of understanding and using an operating system and simple applications like word processing, and another week to use the Internet (World Wide Web and electronic mail).
Information	Setting up the technology is often easier than getting access to the information that people need. Local government information is often the most requested by communities. However, this information is rarely accessible in any form, let alone online. Various councils acknowledge that this is a problem and are trying to provide more usable information, following the example of Johannesburg. The Open Democracy Bill (when made law) will greatly help in obliging more openness, and the ComTask has proposed a number of mechanisms for providing more government information. Through an IT-enabled MPCC a community can also provide information about itself, following the example of Alexandra township and the Web site produced by the Mamelodi Community Information Service.

Community access   In order to be effective, an IT-enabled community centre should be accessible to the wider community. In many cases, this is already happening, with MPCCs being used as the meeting place for various community organisations and as the site for a range of training courses. The most successful MPCCs have a large degree of community control, usually through a management committee made up of local organisations.

Sustainability   The hardest stage is to find ways for IT-enabled centres to keep going after initial community and donor interest wanes. Enthusiasm starts projects but professionalism maintains them. There are very few examples of sustainable centres in South Africa. Social sustainability comes from serving real needs, usually through community control. Most of the successful long-term centres have external support, such as from a church or university. Some MPCCs are starting to have on-going contracts with local government to provide information services. Other means of generating income include: funded services (offering services to outside bodies, such as information services); adding a small charge to services such as training, printing, faxing and Internet access; and small business support.

While this evaluation has been based on experience in a developing country, many of these arguments also apply in Europe and North America. The context certainly is different, with much higher access to technologies, higher general skill levels and greater potential for employment. However, the basic lesson still applies: for information systems to be of benefit in developing local communities, the key question is that of information requirements rather than of the technology. Issues of information updating and interaction ultimately make the system more useful than the pretty design of the interface.

Conception–reality gaps

The analysis above has focused particularly on gaps in the information and, to a lesser extent, technology dimensions of the ITPOSMO model (see Chapter 3). It is clear that, where information systems have been conceived in a way that matches the realities of community information needs and of technologies that communities can sustainably afford and maintain, they will be successful. Conversely, where there is a major gap between conception and reality in a particular information system, that system is likely to fail completely or to be implemented but then not used.

As a developing country, South Africa has had little time to develop its own skills in information system design. Too often decision makers are over-impressed by sales demonstrations of systems developed in other countries with different needs, and lack the experience to challenge what they are being told is 'international best practice'. This has led IT-based projects to be seen as a technical fix that will let the country 'leapfrog' into the information society, rather than as a tool to meet real development needs. The wasted COBOL training in KwaNdebele and the information kiosks in the North-West Province are examples of this.

This gap between design conceptions and social realities is often made worse because the information system professionals (usually white) have little knowledge of life in rural areas or townships, and the people in those communities have little experience and confidence in IT and formal information systems. This gap will only really be addressed in a generation's time, when access to technical education is broadened. However, for now, all public service systems developers must be directed to design and build systems from the perspective of end-users and to involve those end-users in all stages of implementation. This is one of the meanings of the Batho Pele (putting people first) code now in place in South Africa's public service.

REFERENCES

ANC (1994) *Reconstruction and Development Programme*, Johannesburg, South Africa: African National Congress.

Berlyn, J. (1996) 'Introduction', in J. Berlyn (ed.) *Empowering Communities in the Information Society*, Midrand, South Africa: Development Bank of South Africa.

ComTask (1997) *Communications 2000: A Vision for Government Communications in South Africa*, Pretoria, South Africa: Office of the Deputy President.

DACST (1996) *The Information Society and the Developing World: A South African Approach*, Pretoria, South Africa: Department of Arts, Culture, Science and Technology.

Department of Communications (1996) *Telecommunications Act no. 103*, Pretoria, South Africa: Ministry of Posts, Telecommunications and Broadcasting.

Department of Foreign Affairs (1996) *Information Society and Development Conference Proceedings*, Pretoria, South Africa: Department of Foreign Affairs.

Freire, P. (1995) *Pedagogy of the Oppressed*, New York: Continuum.

Grant, I. (1997) 'Winning the peace', in I. Grant (ed.) *Communication Technologies Handbook*, Johannesburg, South Africa: BMI-Technowledge.

Hudson, H. (1997) *Converging Technologies and Changing Realities: Toward Universal Access to Telecom in the Developing World*, Copenhagen: Danish Technology University.

ITU (1997) *World Telecommunications Development Report*, Geneva: International Telecommunications Union.

Osborne, D. and Gaebler, T. (1992) *Reinventing Government: How the Entrepreneurial Spirit is Transforming the Public Sector*, Reading, MA: Addison-Wesley.

Schuman, H. (1996) 'IT in South African government', in NITF (ed.) *Electronic Government in the Information Society*, Johannesburg, South Africa: National Information Technology Forum.

Sunday Independent (Johannesburg, South Africa) (1997) 'Civil service pins hopes on IT to improve service', 3 August: 9.

Zybrands, W. (1995) *A Perspective on Local Government in the New South Africa*, Johannesburg, South Africa: Allied Banks of South Africa.

ACKNOWLEDGEMENTS

The author is grateful to the International Development Research Centre, a Canadian non-governmental organisation, for funding the evaluation reported in this chapter.

10 Information technology's impact on the quality of democracy

Reinventing the 'democratic vessel'

Andrew Korac-Kakabadse and
Nada Korac-Kakabadse

Abstract: Democratisation – improving the scope and quality of democracy – is a key component of public sector reform. The mass proliferation of information technology (IT) provides a moment of immense opportunity for IT-enabled democratisation. Four generic models of 'electronic democracy' are therefore described. However, electronic democracy brings with it many dangers as well as benefits. Analysis of these suggests that, while democratic principles (the 'cargo' of democracy) may remain intact, many democratic processes (the 'vessel' of democracy) are in crisis and need to be reinvented if electronic democracy is to meet current and future hopes for a better life. This chapter therefore suggests ways in which the democratic vessel can be reinvented so that IT can fulfil its democratic potential.

BACKGROUND

The word 'democracy' has Western origins, with its roots in ancient Greece. Democracy is derived from the Greek word *demokratia*, which stems from two related words, *demos*, the people, and *kratein*, to rule. In its Athenian construction, democracy symbolises rule by and of the people.

The major contemporary justifications of democracy are that it serves numerous contrasting interests by bringing them into debate and decision procedures; that democratic participation enhances autonomy; that, in so doing, democracy is the best form of government for political equity; and that it is the natural form for consent through deliberation. Democracy is considered to serve welfare, autonomy, equity and agreement and it tends to diffuse power; as a consequence, the corruption of a highly concentrated power élite is inhibited.

Therefore, 'democratisation' has been regarded as fundamental to the reform or reinvention of government. In the mature democracies, this can be seen as a process of improving the quality of existing democracy (see, for example, Osborne and Gaebler 1992: 73–75). In other countries, it can be seen as a process of introducing or strengthening democratic procedures; it has, for example, been a central part of the 'good governance' initiatives that aid donors have sought to have implemented in many developing countries.

In either situation, it is useful to distinguish between:

- the *'democratic vessel'* – the political and governing processes; and
- the *'democratic cargo'* – the underlying democratic principles that these processes support and implement.

Although a universalism of the main democratic principles may be seen, they nevertheless combine with democratic processes to form a set of different 'models of democracy'. This set has been added to by the advent of new information technologies, as described in the following section.

Models of democracy

Some theorists link specific information technologies (in the broadest sense of the term) with particular political processes and forms:

- orality to democracy and the city-state;
- print to bureaucracy and the nation-state;
- the emergence of the Internet, or the global information infrastructure, to models of 'electronic democracy'.

There exists a variety of democratic modes of governance, and it can be said that each society has its own unique model that reflects its 'formative context' (Korac-Kakabadse *et al.* 1996; Unger 1987). However, from the myriad of practices, three generic models of democracy can be identified: Aristotelian-style direct democracy; representative democracy; and information technology-facilitated and -mediated 'electronic democracy'.

Direct democracy (Aristotelian)

Aristotle argued in the fourth century BC that democracy could not work in a country larger than a small city-state, such as Athens. One reason was that in a democracy all citizens should be able to assemble at one place to hear a speaker. Thus, the range of the human voice limited democracy's size. As late as the mid-eighteenth century, political thinkers continued to argue against the possibility of large-scale democracy, in part because of communication limitations. After the birth of the United States, a huge democracy by historical standards, such arguments were discarded, and Aristotle's model was seen as one version of democracy: direct democracy.

The early nineteenth-century invention of the penny press for printing newspapers made the acquisition of political information by the masses both convenient and affordable. This, in turn, greatly facilitated the extension of suffrage. The advent of radio and television led to the growing influence of the media in political elections. The development of mass media such as these extended the political message not to hundreds or thousands within the physical range of voice, but to tens of millions.

However, in all these developments, information flow was largely one way: to the populace, not from it. Coupled with the rising population of nations, direct democratic models therefore became untenable and were replaced by representative democracy.

Mediated or representative democracy

In its simplest form, democracy entails having all citizens participate directly by voting on all policies. However, in large states this is not sensible or even possible. Participation therefore takes place in sequential forms: representatives are first chosen and then they decide on policy.

Unfortunately, the technology and institutions of democracy are no longer keeping up with its growth. Many societies continue to have democratic ideals but not an informed and engaged electorate able to act upon those ideals; nor is there any simple formula for representative democracy that relates popular preferences to political outcomes in larger political fora. The result has often been a government that neither knows nor implements the public's will.

A deep cynicism towards representative democracy's model in many democratic societies has therefore been emerging (Gore 1994). The cynicism is created, in part, by democratic processes that foster narrow interest groups over wisdom, deviation over tolerance, short-term gain over spirituality, fierce economic competition over collaboration, and community change over stability (ibid.). As such, the cynicism is not directed towards democracy or democratic principles (the 'cargo'), but towards the governance of democratic processes in a variety of contexts (the 'vessel').

It has therefore led many disenchanted voters to demand a shift of processes and model from representative democracy to some new form of direct democracy (Sardar 1996), which may be enabled by information technology (IT).

Electronic democracy

The advent of computerised information technology has brought, amongst other things, the possibility of the re-emergence of direct democracy on a large scale. Today, the emergent interactive, direct and unmediated IT infrastructure holds the possibility to revolutionise not only the entertainment industry, but also the nature of public and political discourse. We are therefore presented with a new potential model of 'electronic democracy'.

Electronic democracy can be understood as the capacity of the new IT environment to enhance the degree and quality of public participation in government. For example, the Internet can enable certain citizens (namely those with access to it) to vote electronically in elections, referendums and plebiscites. The Internet can also facilitate opinion polling. In this way, it has the potential to strengthen interaction between government and citizens and between political candidates and voters and, therefore, to impact further on the nature of democracy.

There exists a variety of potential electronic democracy models. However, four key generic models have emerged: the *electronic bureaucracy*, the *information management*, the *populist* and the *civil society* models.

The *electronic bureaucracy* model refers to the electronic delivery of government services. This model already exists in a number of industrialised countries where 'government online' (electronic information available through the Internet) and the 'one-stop shop' (the office that handles business of multiple government agencies) initiatives are operational. The goal of this model is to allow easier, quicker and cheaper transactions with government on behalf of businesses and citizens and to reduce, over time, the size of the public sector. However, some have argued that the enhancement of services creates problems of inequality between those 'information rich' individuals and businesses that can gain access to the technology necessary to use the electronic service, and those 'information poor' who cannot. Many equate service enhancement with differential pricing and regard both as unacceptable. Making best use of technology maybe a worthy aim, but some would consider it more appropriate as an intervention to enhance education and training than to use such facilities as a cost-saving mechanism.

The *information management* model refers to more-effective communication bridges between individual citizens and candidates or decision makers. This model is also receiving some acclaim as a number of state and federal governments (e.g. in the US and Australia) are providing electronic public services and information online at the point of use. Using multimedia such as touch-screen kiosks in public places (libraries, shopping malls) or personal computers at home, citizens can obtain government information and/or send messages to their representatives or government agencies. In the US, the Clinton administration has explored this model. Presidential orders, speeches and other communications are transmitted online, directly to the people, bypassing the traditional news media. Easy access to bills being introduced to Congress and government publications may result in a better informed citizenry. For example, the ability to circulate government White Papers designed to generate political action quickly is a unique phenomenon of information technology.

The *populist* model, enabling citizens to register their views on current issues, is most often equated with direct democracy. The model received attention when Ross Perot popularised the term 'electronic town hall' in his 1992 presidential campaign (London 1994). The first such meeting in New York State heralded an age of unmediated communication, where newspaper editors, the mail carrier and TV journalists are no longer essential intermediaries between citizens and officials. Many were held subsequently: an electronic town meeting in Dallas, for example, which was held in 1993 via CNN, put to the citizens for instant telefeedback issues of deficit reduction, campaign financing and lobbying regulations. In this manner, the electronic town meeting provides for a civic discourse that is quick, direct, interactive and inclusive (ibid.). Since politics involves dialogue as well as the dissemination of facts and information, electronic fora can be used to serve both ends. In the US, there are numerous projects underway, suggesting that electronic town meetings will soon be a regular part of political life.

The *civil society* model refers to the transformation of political culture and, hence, it can only be appreciated within the context of any broader transformation brought by information technology. This model's goal is to strengthen connections between citizens, thereby promoting a robust and autonomous site for public discourse. This model has created most debate, which in America has focused on whether there exists a need for an 'electronic bill of rights'. Citizens in Sweden and Germany meanwhile are fretting about what they see as the impending age of no privacy, in a democracy that is becoming more and more of an electronic tyranny.

ANALYSIS: DEMOCRATISATION AND NEW INFORMATION TECHNOLOGY

It is clear that there has been recent growth and development of each of the models of electronic democracy. This section therefore analyses in greater detail the potential impacts on democratisation of new information technology.

The democratic potential of information technology

New technology may facilitate the widespread use of new forms of voting and thus direct participation, which has been based on theoretically elegant but heretofore impractical voting systems (Snider 1994). For example, instead of physically going to the polls, individuals could vote from their homes. With more convenient and less expensive voting systems in place, individuals could be expected to vote more frequently and on more issues. Referendums and polls could proliferate, although they would need to be backed by a political and institutional will that may not exist in some countries (6 1997).

While instant pollings and referendums can simply make the public as nonreflective as legislatures sometimes are, there exists the potential for far more reflective democratic processes. Experiments over the last two decades with televoting have highlighted the potential in this area. In addition, a recent senatorial election in Oregon, US, allowed voting by mail. The voter turnout was 67 per cent, almost double the national average voter turnout in equivalent elections over the previous 20 years (*Washington Post* 1996). Combined with citizen movements towards growing healthy communities, sustainable development and enhanced community dialogue, IT application in this arena could become transformative (*The Economist* 1995).

Another benefit of the new information technology is improved access to the deliberation of public bodies. In the US, cable channels already cover House and Senate chambers and congressional hearings at the federal level, as well as state and local-level meetings. In the future, IT-enabled coverage of such meetings is likely to expand dramatically, thus making government deliberations much more accessible to the average person (Snider 1994).

New technology also facilitates, via television, computer or some synthesis of both, electronic town meetings, where citizens are offered direct contact with public officials, unmediated by journalists. The idea is to force politicians and the media to talk to the public about important issues that might otherwise escape the political agenda. Combined with televoting, the electronic town meeting offers a potentially significant improvement on the referendum, which is poor at fostering deliberation and thus has led to uninformed voting.

Government records could also be made more accessible; this would be an improvement on the cumbersome procedures necessary to gain access to information under the freedom of information acts adopted in many Western democracies (e.g. the US, Canada, Australia and New Zealand).

Some therefore see technology as enabling citizens to have direct access to their representatives, bypassing pressure groups, party politics, the media, special interest groups and other undemocratic channels of opinion formation. Elected representatives may thus perform their function only on people's daily sufferance, leading to the loss of the old grandeur of parliament and political parties (Sardar 1996). Politicians may be selected according to a free competition of ideas, with a power base that is decentralised, creating a culture where success and status in society will not depend on the exercise of political power (Szilagyi 1994).

New technology can also provide citizens with direct access to information overall. Today's passive role of the media is likely to be replaced by a new type of interactive multimedia, characterised by highly specialised media outlets often described as 'information agents' (Snider 1994). These may meet the desire seen amongst some citizens for trustworthy information sources that will do the hard work of gathering and digesting political information for them.

Notwithstanding that the existing mass media has attracted vast criticism, the potential for more competitive, diverse and customised media in the future carries with it new opportunities and hopes. For example, traditional self promotion of political candidates, such as through television adverts, may become obsolete. Indeed, Snider (ibid.) has even suggested that, instead of tens of millions of dollars in 'communication vouchers' being given to US presidential candidates to spend on 30-second television adverts, the money could be given directly to citizens to spend on their own information gathering about those candidates.

Similar repercussions may confront lobbyists and special interest groups, who derive their power from the ability to fund a candidate's media campaigns, but who may find themselves undermined when voters can obtain critical information direct from independent information agents (ibid.). The guiding logic of Ross Perot's 'United We Stand' alliance, enabled by 'electronic town links' for town meetings, was to facilitate discussion and a wide-ranging debate at the grassroots level and not at the lobbyists' level (London 1994).

Of course, all this makes a number of assumptions. For example, it assumes universal access to the coming information highways, without which there will be an increasing gap between those who can purchase critical information from information agents and those who cannot afford to. It also assumes that citizens currently both lack and also want access to high-quality political information.

The potential downsides of electronic democracy

Democracy is about the articulation of common interests and shared concerns between citizens. However, digital democracy is mainly about the expression of the individual in front of his/her own keyboard or other electronic gadgetry. Therefore, it will be harder to aggregate preferences in an acceptable way if there are no institutionalised ways of persuading and ensuring collective action.

For example, excessive participation by individual interests at the wrong time could lead to government paralysis. Electronic democracy can dangerously over-extend the sphere of democratic decision making into what ought to be the sphere of individual or corporate decision making, because the institutional constraints that have been developed in analogue democracy do not exist in the digital setting:

> Anyone can post messages to the net. Practically everyone does. The resulting cacophony drowns out serious discussion. Online debates of tough issues are often polarized by messages taking extreme positions. It's a great medium for trivia and hobbies, but not the place for reasoned, reflective judgement.
>
> (Stoll 1995: 32)

The result is 'Plenty of opinions, but not much informed dialogue, and even less consensus' (ibid.: 49). In times of political crisis, the inability to reach a decision could be dangerous. Even under more normal conditions, open citizen participation in decision making would almost surely create delays (Deleone 1994).

It is not certain that adding an electronic dimension to democracy will encourage participation by any but a small, motivated minority. Many critics of direct democracy have argued that the average person does not have the resources, time, ability or inclination to become an expert on issues or on political candidates (Downs 1967; Olson 1996). IT can provide the information resources but it does not provide time or ability or inclination. New technology may bring the world to the citizen's living room, but the citizen may wish to use this potential to watch more television or surf the Internet for titillating trivia rather than to become more involved in the democratic process.

Certainly there are precedents for this. Citizens' band (CB) radio, for example, held out the promise of a liberating technology that would put citizens in direct contact with one another:

> But CB radio was rarely used for anything more politically significant than giving speeding truckers the chance to elude the highway patrol. . . . There are many signs that computers will repeat that pattern, wasting their promise in frivolous, lightweight uses that have no great political relevance.
>
> (Roszak 1988: 195)

New technology could therefore be more an opiate of the people than the catalyst for democratic revolution.

Even if new technology does encourage participation and bring the benefits of democratisation, who will be involved: all of society or just one fraction? Information technology, as currently implemented and likely to remain so in the near future, will facilitate access to direct democracy only for a small and atypical minority group (young, affluent, educated, liberated, computer-literate, predominantly male and white, etc.) as they are the only ones who are online. Of more than 100,000 daily recipients of White House electronic documents, 85 per cent are under 50, 80 per cent are male and 50 per cent have a postgraduate qualification (*Infosys* 1994).

Electronic democracy therefore poses new social segregation challenges between those who are information rich and those who are poor, on a national and global basis (Kapor 1992; Korac-Kakabadse *et al.* 1996). Poor individuals will not be able to influence political agendas. For example, by the year 2000, it is estimated that nearly one-quarter of new workers in the US workforce will be immigrants, many of whom will have a relatively low level of formal schooling and limited English skills (SLCI, IPP 1995). They are also least likely to have access to the new informatics infrastructure.

Globally, the same pattern will be repeated. By the year 2001 three-quarters of households in the US, along with over half a billion people globally, are expected to subscribe to a digital communication service

(Zysman 1995). Yet on this same planet, half of the current population have never made a simple telephone call. Between 1995 and 2025 2.7 billion people will probably be added to the world's population. Of these 93 per cent will be born in Africa, Asia and Latin America, giving these regions 83 per cent of the world's population (UNPF 1994). The differentiation between the global information rich and information poor may therefore worsen rather than improve.

Given the centrality of computers to information flow, computer literacy may become the *de facto* prerequisite for citizenship in the next century, if the direct electronic democracy model is adopted. Traditional literacy can be defined not just as the ability to read, but the possession of certain background knowledge without which the act of reading becomes meaningless (Bransford and Johnson 1972; Hirsch 1987). Computer literacy is as profound as the ability to read, because it requires a range of abstract understandings about how information is accessed, managed and manipulated: an understanding that transcends particular makes and models of computers and software. Computer literacy will provide extraordinary access to information, but only for those who understand the process of information seeking (Paisley 1987). Thus, the distinction between those who have the facility and access to information technology and those who do not will become as distinct functionally as the difference between those who can read and those who cannot.

Finally, IT-related crime is booming, with a growth in such varied activities as Internet pornography, online forgery, credit card theft, virus attacks, unauthorised access to a system to destroy data, and hacking in to read electronic mail or take over an account. In Australia, the number of complaints received by computer crime units tripled between 1994 and 1997 (Creedy 1997). The impact on electronic democracy may be twofold. First, there may be democracy-related crimes, such as the modification of voting inputs to electronic referendums. Second, the whole idea of electronic democracy may be undermined in the public mind by computer crime. There are certainly precedents: irregularities in the computerised entry and counting of votes in the 1988 Mexican election, for example, achieved both the described impacts (Sanders 1994).

Information technology's impact on citizens' and representatives' roles

Perhaps the most serious problem of 'electronic democracy' arises from the possibility of divorcing responsibility from accountability within the roles of both citizen and representative.

Dealing first with citizens: they will be responsible for influencing the political agenda but will not be held accountable for their impact on policy implementation (Kapor 1992). There are features of IT-mediated democratic participation that exacerbate this lack of accountability (adapted from Sclove 1995):

- the lack of nuance, warmth and context within electronic communication: elements that are needed in order to create ownership of issues;
- the ability instantly to exit virtual political communities in a way that is not possible with real ones;
- the encouragement of an instant response that discourages deliberation and the thoughtful exercise of democratic choice;
- the tendency of screen-based technologies 'to induce democratically unpromising psychopathologies, ranging from escapism to passivity, obsession, confusing watching with doing, withdrawal from other forms of social engagement, or distancing from moral consequences'.

Hence may emerge the very problem Plato (1987) feared and wanted to guard against: people simply endorsing their self interests, which would result in policies that were nothing more than the lowest common denominator of individuals' greed and desire for personal gain or security. Indeed, such may be the alienation and lack of accountability induced that electronic voters may just 'press any button', careless of the consequences of their actions.

Such a mood is already being seen more generally. In the UK, for example, 38 per cent of the UK population are both unconvinced and unconcerned about new technology and the emerging 'information society', while 16 per cent feel alienated from it (Department of Trade and Industry 1996). By comparison, only 25 per cent of the population are enthusiastic about the new technology: characteristically young, upmarket men and women.

Thus, instead of creating a community based on consensus, unthinking information technology application could easily create states of alienated and atomised individuals, communicating with each other through computer terminals, terrorising and being terrorised by all those with conflicting values or a determination to pursue their own agenda (Ogden 1994; Sardar 1996).

Turning now to elected representatives: they will be driven by an aggregation of electronically democratic demands and will be held accountable for policies for which they are not responsible and over which they have little influence. The bargaining power of elected representatives will be undermined and, therefore, they will not be able to see agreements through.

Under the current representative liberal democracy, elected representatives are implicitly operating under a social contract obligation, as they are responsible for supporting particular principles and, in turn, are accountable for their actions. Any social institution, not excepting government and business, operates in society via a social contract which needs to meet the twin test of relevance and legitimacy by demonstrating that, on the one hand, society requires its services and, on the other, that the groups benefiting from its rewards have society's actual or implied approval (Shocker and Sethi 1974). In electing representatives, citizens place onus on those representatives to provide an account of their actions (Gray *et al.* 1987). The failure by representatives to deliver the electorates' expected outcomes leads to dissatisfaction in policy and a change of representatives.

Using information technology to influence the representatives' agenda on a daily basis leaves a representative accountable for decisions which he or she was not responsible for generating, may disagree with, or may not have had the opportunity to present an alternative case. Such circumstances within an organisational setting are akin to holding managers accountable for the actions of their subordinates, whilst giving them no control over what their subordinates do (Kakabadse 1991). Divorcing accountability from responsibility leads to the decline and, ultimately, the demise of the implicit contract between the representative and the citizen.

The impact of new technology on this contract is already visible through the increasing influence of telephone surveys, TV and radio discussion programmes, and the mass media more generally. Goodhart (1997) sees this as creating a 'plebiscitary democracy'. This provides a potential – and not necessarily positive – guide to the workings of electronic democracy.

Politicians may now be better informed about what people think but the result has been an abrogation of leadership and a slavish following of short-term public opinion, which is volatile and suffers an 'instant amnesia' about issues. Governments therefore already 'react too much, and govern too little'. (ibid.: 23). One outcome has been the pressure for instant political reactions to events and public opinion. Instead of allowing time for reasoned debate and the framing of viable legislation, politicians are now rushed into policies that are 'hurried and misconceived'. Goodhart classifies recent UK legislation on football hooliganism, dog attacks, gun attacks and public health scares as falling into this category: legislation brought about as a direct result of the clamour of public opinion.

The danger, then, is that electronic democracy will turn representatives into followers, not leaders, blown by the winds of fashion into making decisions for which they are accountable but not responsible.

CONCLUSIONS AND RECOMMENDATIONS

The underlying principles of democracy remain sound, but the current processes of representative democracy are, to some degree, in crisis. Information technology provides an opportunity to revitalise democracy but many potential dangers lie within any move to electronic democracy. Most of these dangers derive not from inherent characteristics of the technology, but from the way in which that technology is used; that is, from the democratic structures and processes that surround the technology. It is these – the democratic vessel – that need to be reinvented prior to and during any process of IT-supported democratisation.

Reinventing the democratic vessel: recommendations

In many societies, voluntary voting produces elections and policies by referendums in which only a fraction of the population exercise their choice. For example, in the US, after a vigorous and very expensive campaign, a turnout of 47 per cent at the polls is considered to be a good show. In Pakistan, at the last election, only 29 to 35 per cent (depending on the region) of the electorate voted. Yet the elected president is entrusted with wide powers – for instance, changing the constitution to suit his or her own desires, which affects all citizens – although only a minority is being represented.

It can thus be argued that, in a universal electronic democracy, the voting percentage may not increase unless the voluntary voting system is replaced with a compulsory one. This will ensure that the elected representatives carry out policies agreed by the true majority and not only the espoused majority. Further, the compulsory voting model would bring together citizens to elect representatives responsibly and be held accountable for electing those representatives.

In order to enable minority groups to be represented, proportional representation (PR) needs to be added to the electronic democracy model. PR as adopted in the US has much to offer, as it would allow small communities to be represented on an equal footing with large ones. Thus when society adopts electronic democracy with a communications infrastructure available to all citizens, voting patterns would truly represent the will of the majority.

Third, we can add decentralisation and subsidiarity to the electronic democracy model, with local issues dealt with at local level, societal issues at state level, and global issues at regional and international level. Facilitated by communication technologies, this would avoid information overload (Korac-Boisvert and Kouzmin 1995) and at the same time facilitate government responsiveness to citizens' needs and citizen participation in policy analysis and design.

Much can be learned about decentralisation and subsidiarity from Sweden's model. Here, the citizen's right to govern is currently realised by a structure of three levels: nationally through parliament, regionally through the county and locally through the municipality (Michalski 1994). At all three levels, citizens hold the right to elect, through proportional representation, individuals who are deemed suitable to represent the people's voice and to adopt, implement and follow up decisions on their behalf.

The principle of decentralised local democracy is based on municipalities (which vary in size from 10,000 to 50,000 inhabitants), whose self government relies on four principles:

- the municipalities' general competence, ranging from education, social, energy and housing policy, child care, waste collection, water, electricity and sewage, public health, environmental protection, local planning and local transport, to culture, sport and leisure activities;

- the municipality's right to levy income tax;
- the provision of a national system for the transfer of funds from rich to poor municipalities;
- the citizen's right to political accountability (Michalski 1994).

Municipalities are thereby assuming an increasingly important role in the work of government, and have therefore been a focus of electronic democracy initiatives (see Chapter 8 for an example).

Enabling citizen participation

A main aim of democratisation is to better inform the policy process and, through direct citizen involvement, to give citizens the opportunity for increased participation in and allegiance to the political system and its processes (Deleone 1994). However, only well-informed citizens can successfully participate in the democratic political process. Therefore, making policy information available to citizens and educating them on how to use information technology to access the information need to be incorporated into policy design and implementation processes.

To accomplish this requires accessibility, equity and adaptability of policy information:

- *Accessibility* means the process is one that reaches out to all stakeholders, with multiple and reciprocal pathways for information flow. This may require actively soliciting input from significant stakeholders, not only from lobby groups and institutions, but through creating structures to foster communication with citizens, which means that creation of an IT infrastructure becomes very much a policy issue, not a technology issue. Governments need to take a leading role in this area, and not just leave it to the private sector, in order to drive towards universal access.
- *Equity* means taking explicit care to balance potential costs and benefits among all stakeholders, which presupposes openness to differing or conflicting perspectives and assumptions (Brewer 1986; Janis and Mann 1977; LaPorte 1975).
- *Adaptability* means the willingness and the capacity continually to re-evaluate policies in the light of changing circumstance, new knowledge and/or unexpected outcomes.

Citizen participation will also be enabled by a community orientation. Individuality without a community orientation leads to further alienation and fragmentation of society and upsets the ecological balance (Sardar 1996). Concisely, a community orientation demands some discipline and sacrifice on the part of individuals. No community can exist if all individuals go their own way and define their own morality, irrelevant of their context and community. The shift to community values and needs is necessary at the individual level and at the corporate level. As each individual and organisation needs to take responsibility and accountability to make the world a better place, there is thus a need for a new philosophy that will emphasise the virtue which ensures the continuation of democratic principles and connects the individual with the community.

Realistic ways of operationalising IT-enabled citizen participation also need to be developed. Adopting a policy to introduce electronic 'civic participation centres' or 'town meetings', without assessing how the model will work in practice, will not guarantee democratic enhancement. A speaker can, for example, effectively frame a question in such a way so as to limit, encourage, or actually guarantee the desired answer from citizens (London 1994). Similarly, the availability of a communication infrastructure to all citizens may not produce enhancing results if important policy issues are dealt with at such a speed that citizens cannot think them through or participate in IT-mediated debate.

On the other hand, if citizen participation is sought for each and every policy and operational issue in truly democratic ways, there would be very little use for politicians. Instead, there would only be the need for administrators who would respond to the citizens' majority demands on a daily basis. Such a model does not provide for direction and planning for the future. Powerful lobby groups could choose and then drive through a future vision that would benefit only a select few.

Therefore, the level of citizens' participation in policy design and implementation is of immense importance if aspects of the elected representative's role are to be preserved, namely, their responsibility and accountability elements. As noted, there is a danger that electronic democracy will split these elements. Avoiding this may well mean limiting the usage of electronic democracy to important issues that require referendums.

Nevertheless, with an appropriate information infrastructure, one that provides citizens with universal access to data sources, important issues can be debated and voted on in a manner that is more comfortable for them (using information technology from home) and is significantly more economical and efficient than the manual handling of ballot papers.

In all, the main uses of information technology in attempting to improve the democratic vessel are: to promote participatory policy analysis in order to better inform the policy process, as constructive action is impossible without an understanding of how our fellow citizens think and feel about issues; and to educate citizens through their involvement so that they can make informed choices. The challenge is to find a way to pool the good judgement and foresight of the public (Elgin, quoted in London 1994). Only with forward-looking and informed public policies can new technology be used to bring this democratic ideal much closer to reality.

Summary

While information has always played a key role in democracies, its current role is both expanding and transforming. Multiple models of information transfer are used not just locally, but nationally and internationally. Information transfer and the infrastructures that support it are understood to have profound effects on economic prosperity (Martinez 1994). In the increasingly interconnected and rapidly changing formative context of the information society, traditional ways of organising and governing, which are based on a more restricted flow of information and limited interconnections, in public and corporate organisations or in democratic national states, seem to be overwhelmed. Thus, what is becoming increasingly clear in a world of rapid and continuing change, eroding boundaries, multiplying interest groups and fragmenting institutions and belief systems, is the need to invest more time, energy and attention to developing a shared understanding of where society should go, within a more systematic process of agenda setting and further within an acceptable and agreed value system.

Hinging on equitable access to information technology is whether that technology will make society more cohesive and collectively prosperous or undermine the bases for democracy and further polarise the nation into a dispossessed and a wealthy élite, defined not just by investment portfolios, but also by a monopoly of information (Martinez 1994). Technology can enhance the learning of conceptual knowledge and also the knowledge of process, in particular, enabling forms of desired information seeking. However, technology can also influence the 'knowledge gap' to grow wider (Paisley 1987). The future of the IT influence will require vigilance and a guarantee of access to ensure that the electronic revolution contributes to unifying society rather than dividing it. The quality of democracy is only enhanced by IT if citizens are better informed without having to suffer information overload.

At a time when humanity has full possession of a mass of forces that could destroy the world through nuclear, genetic and biological agents, the realisation that what people do really does make a difference requires dramatic changes or a shift in governance. The move to participation is probably the greatest shift of our times. It acknowledges that we live and work in a highly interdependent world, making complex decisions that have many effects that we cannot, by ourselves, anticipate or see. It also reflects that real value of diversity: while it increases the chance of conflict, diversity also increases the possibility of more creative and sustainable solutions to the problems we face, whether in society, work or private life.

The price of change is one of testing, making mistakes and building skills and confidence in people who only know the old way. Nature itself relies heavily on the participation of all species in creating the balance of forces that sustains our lives on this planet. Governments and business are only now discovering the survival advantage of participation in their own spheres.

Humanity has arrived at a moment of immense democratic opportunity made possible by information technology. The opportunity should not be wasted, but used wisely.

Besides good governance, democracy also requires mechanisms for conflict resolution, a political culture of tolerance and compromise and, above all, the wisdom in leadership to steer it through (Snider 1994). Such leadership is required because the preservation of democratic principles, such as freedom, can be 'expensive, dangerous, unpredictable and sometimes ugly and offensive' (Berry 1992: 6). However, new information technology, combined with leadership wisdom demonstrated by forward-thinking public policies, can help sail the democratic vessel safely through troubled waters.

Conception–reality gaps

Many current or planned initiatives using IT to support democratisation are likely to work because they introduce IT to support the current realities of the democratic process. The way in which these new information systems are conceived therefore matches the functioning realities of present-day democracy. The benefit of such a reality-aligned approach is that success, in terms of a working information system, is more likely. The disadvantage is that any perceived deficiencies of current reality are likely to be reinforced or even magnified. As we have seen, these deficiencies include major problems such as the effective disenfranchisement of large sections of society and the trend for political representatives to follow rather than lead public opinion.

In order to overcome these deficiencies, electronic democracy needs to be reconceived in some of the ways described above. However, this, in turn, creates a conception–reality gap that could increase the chance of failure. To combat this, there is a need for the contextual reform of existing democratic processes prior to or during the introduction of IT.

REFERENCES

6, P. (1997) *Information Society Symposium Quality of Democracy Working Group*, e-mail to A. Kakabadse, London: Demos.

Berry, J.N. III (1992) 'If words will never hurt me, then . . . ?', *Library Journal* January: 6–7.

Bransford, J.D. and Johnson, M.K. (1972) 'Contextual prerequisites for understanding: some investigations of comprehension and recall', *Journal of Verbal Learning and Verbal Behaviour* 11, 4: 717–726.

Brewer, G.D. (1986) 'Methods for synthesis: policy exercises', in W.C. Clark and R.E. Munn (eds) *Sustainable Development of the Biosphere*, Cambridge: Cambridge University Press.

Creedy, S. (1997) 'Computer crimes: police get serious', *The Australian* 25 February: 52–53.

Deleone, P. (1994) 'Reinventing the policy sciences: three steps back to the future', *Policy Science* 27, 1: 77–95.

Department of Trade and Industry (1996) 'Read all about IT: a survey into public awareness of attitudes towards, and access to information and communication technologies', in *The Start of IT*, London: IT for All Project Office, Department of Trade and Industry.

Downs, A. (1967) *An Economic Theory of Democracy*, New York: Free Press.

The Economist (1995) 'Democracy and technology', 21–22 June: 17–23.

Goodhart, D. (1997) 'Who are the masters now?', *Prospect* May: 22–25.

Gore, A. (1994) 'The deadly age of cynicism', *Aspen Institute Quarterly* 6, 4: 7–21.

Gray, R., Owen, D. and Maunders, K. (1987) *Corporate Social Reporting: Accounting and Accountability*, Hemel Hempstead, Herts: Prentice-Hall International.

Hirsch, E.D. (1987) *Cultural Literacy*, Boston, MA: Houghton Mifflin.

Infosys (1994) 'News items', 1, 36: 2.

Janis, I.L. and Mann, L. (1977) *Decision Making*, New York: Free Press.

Kakabadse, A.P. (1991) *The Wealth Creators: Top People, Top Teams and Executive Best Practice*, London: Kogan Page.

Kapor, M. (1992) 'Where is the digital highway really heading? The case for a Jeffersonian information policy', *Wired* 1, 3: 47–52.

Korac-Boisvert, N. and Kouzmin, A. (1995) 'IT development: methodology overload or crisis?', *Science Communication: An Interdisciplinary Science Journal* 17, 1: 57–89.

Korac-Kakabadse, N., Kouzmin, A. and Korac-Kakabadse, A. (1996) 'Information technology and development: designing relevant infrastructure capability or new colonialism?', paper presented at the 5th International Speyer Workshop on 'Assessing and Evaluating Public Service Reforms', Speyer, November.

LaPorte, T.R. (ed.) (1975) *Organised Social Complexity: Challenge to Politics and Policy*, Princeton, NJ: Princeton University Press.

London, S. (1994) *Electronic Democracy: A Literature Survey*, prepared paper, Santa Barbara, CA: Kattering Foundation.

Martinez, M.E. (1994) 'Access to information technologies among school age children: implications for a democratic society', *Journal of the American Society for Information Science* 45, 6: 395–400.

Michalski, A. (1994) 'Swedish local democracy: a viable model for Europe?', *European Business Review* 94, 5: X–XII.

Ogden, M.R. (1994) 'Politics in a parallel universe: is there a future for cyberdemocracy?', *Futures* 26, 7: 713–729.

Olson, R. (1996) 'Information technology in home health care', in C. Bezold and E. Mayer (eds) *Future Care: Responding to the Demand for Change*, New York: Faulkner.

Osborne, D. and Gaebler, T. (1992) *Reinventing Government: How the Entrepreneurial Spirit is Transforming the Public Sector*, Reading, MA: Addison-Wesley.

Paisley, W. (1987) 'Many literacies, many challenges', paper presented at the American Library Association Conference, San Francisco, June.

Plato (1987) *The Republic*, London: Penguin Classics.

Roszak, T. (1988) *The Cult of Information*, London: Paladin.

Sanders, J. (1994) 'Mexico: IT worker speaks out', *Computing* 7 July: 8.

Sardar, Z. (1996) 'The future of democracy and human rights', *Futures* 28, 9: 839–859.

Sclove, R.E. (1995) *Democracy and Technology*, New York: Guilford Press.

Shocker, A.D. and Sethi, S.P. (1974) 'An approach to incorporating social preferences in developing corporate action strategies', in S.P. Sethi (ed.) *The Unstable Ground: Corporate Social Policy in a Dynamic Society*, Los Angeles, CA: Melville.

Snider, J.H. (1994) 'Democracy online: tomorrow's electronic electorate', *Futurist* 28, 5: 15–19.

State and Local Coalition on Immigration, Immigration Policy Project (SLCI, IPP) (1995) *America's Newcomers: An Immigrant Policy Handbook*, Denver, CO: National Conference of State Legislatures.

Stoll, C. (1995) *Silicon Snake Oil*, London: Macmillan.

Szilagyi, M.N. (1994) *How to Save Our Country: A Non-partisan Vision for Change*, Tuscon, AZ: Pallsas Press.

Unger, R.M. (1987) *False Necessity*, Cambridge: Cambridge University Press.

UNPF (1994) *The State of World Population 1994: Choices and Responsibilities*, New York: United Nations Population Fund.

Washington Post (1996) 'Postal voting', 22 January, Section 1: 1.

Zysman, G. (1995) 'Wireless networks', *Scientific American* September: 68–69.

Part 4

National planning for information age reform

11 Transforming accountability for government information technology projects

The impact of new US legislation

Laurence Wolfe

Abstract: Accountability for government information technology (IT) projects stands at the confluence of two great trends: the ever-expanding role of information systems and public sector reform. Too often, major IT projects are characterised by cost overruns, excessive delays and failed approaches. The Information Technology Management Reform Act (ITMRA) of 1996 was intended to improve significantly the way the United States government acquires and manages such projects. The results of a survey of senior information systems managers are contrasted with the evolution of federal information systems management, and an in-depth case of a troubled information system is used to illustrate the probable outcomes of ITMRA reforms. Lessons learned for the United States and other governments are assessed, and the author recommends selected management and accountability practices to increase opportunities for project success.

BACKGROUND

Information technology and public sector reform in the US

Information technology (IT) accountability stands at the intersection of two great trends that are altering the course of government in the United States: public sector reform and the ever-expanding role of IT-based information systems (IS) in federal agencies. It therefore forms a core component of information age reform.

Public sector reform, or 'reinventing government', indicates changes that have taken place in the US since the early 1980s. One of the most important reform initiatives is President Bill Clinton's and Vice-President Al Gore's

National Performance Review (NPR). Issued in 1993, the NPR is intended to serve as a blueprint for reform at the federal level and drive forward the task of government reinvention.

Having as its goal 'creating a government that works better and costs less', the NPR posits a strong connection between public sector reform and information technology: 'As everyone knows, the computer revolution allows us to do things faster and more cheaply than we have ever done before' (NPR 1993: ii). Further emphasising its commitment to use information technology in reform, the Clinton Administration issued its Access America plan in 1997 as a follow-on to the NPR. Together, the NPR and Access America call for new IT-based information systems and improvements in the processes by which they are managed to implement specific reforms in programmes ranging from health care to law enforcement. They have acted as a significant spur to information age reform in the US.

'[W]e will re-engineer government activities, making full use of computer systems and telecommunications to revolutionise how we deliver services' promised the NPR (1993: v) in response to public concerns about the costs, types and quality of government services. Even today, information technology remains at the forefront of even higher-level debates about government's size and scope because it continues to be perceived by many as closely intertwined with government's ability to change and reinvent its methods and purposes. IT continues to be regarded as the engine-of-choice for reinvention and business process improvement.

Three observations characterise the state of the United States government's information systems:

- The magnitude is enormous: information systems funding exceeds US$25 billion each year.
- IS investment leverages even larger dollars because it directly affects every federal agency's ability to perform its mission.
- Large and costly federal information system failures have drawn persistent public and congressional criticism.

For these reasons, accountability for IT projects in government agencies engendered spirited debate in the mid-1990s. Reforming IS management processes has been a complex task requiring the collaborative efforts of many key stakeholders, repeal of old laws and passage of new legislation. With the enactment of a new law, the Information Technology Management Reform Act (ITMRA) of 1996 (PL104-106), a legacy of three decades of hierarchical control was thrown aside, and the old accountability mechanisms were subjected to considerable reform. This chapter analyses the likely impact of ITMRA in the United States on the acquisition of information technology and the management of information systems development projects.

However, even prior to 1996, President Clinton's National Performance Review initiatives were already refocusing central management agencies, and oversight, on IT project economy and effectiveness. It has often been said that it is time to strip away oversight controls and layers of accountability which have stifled innovation in government and prevented people in agencies from doing their jobs effectively. Such critics have demanded either elimination of oversight or radically streamlined control mechanisms: '[W]e must untangle the knots of red tape that prevent government from serving the American people well' (NPR 1993: 13).

Politicians of both major American parties, the Republicans and the Democrats, have been philosophically alike because they have spoken almost daily about 'cutting out the layers'. Processes for managing information systems have not been immune to such exhortations.

Thus, accountability for information systems is a topical and turbulent area of public administration theory and practice in the US. The potential long-term consequences are even greater because major IT projects are very costly and can stretch in impact across years or even decades, thereby affecting each agency's ability to perform its mission.

In fact, US information systems budgets have continued to grow even at a time when massive cuts have loomed across all agencies: from US$21 billion in 1991 to US$27 billion in 1998. At the same time, under ITMRA, hierarchical oversight structures have been forcibly torn down, causing major redirection of oversight roles. This raises a question about the impact of ITMRA reforms on the likelihood of success for public sector IT projects. That question is addressed in this chapter, with a particular focus on large IT projects.

Other writings have focused on information resources change management (e.g. Emily 1996) and strategic information systems planning (e.g. Lederer and Sethi 1996; see also Chapter 14). Two older but notable studies of US government information resources management include assessment of federal reforms due to the Paperwork Reduction Act (Caudle 1988) and a review of state management of information resources (Newcomer and Caudle 1991). Project management also continues to be an important area of study. Examples include a troubled State of Vermont system (Cats-Baril and Thompson 1995) and a study of runaway projects (Keil 1994). Additionally, information systems management, in general, continues to be a topic of wide-ranging work (e.g. Bozeman and Bretschneider 1986; Thong 1994). However, the effects of the 1996 ITMRA have not yet been a significant topic of evaluation. This study begins that needed evaluation.

In this chapter the results of a survey of IS managers are contrasted with the evolution of federal information systems management, and an in-depth case is used to illustrate the probable outcomes of ITMRA reforms. The survey included interviews with senior programme managers who had significant responsibilities for 15 of the largest US government information systems. Those interviews garnered an 'insider' perspective for analysis. Another set of interviews was directed towards members of the oversight community who were responsible for monitoring those projects. Those interviews with ten senior oversight officials ensured inclusion of an 'outsider' perspective.

A multi-billion dollar case study was also examined: the US Federal Aviation Administration's Advanced Automation System. It met three criteria:

- at least 25 per cent of the agency's information technology budget;
- critical to the agency's mission;
- a high level of visibility within the agency and before the public.

The case provided an objective, 'independent' observer perspective.

Thus, the insider and outsider perspectives from the interviews and the independent perspective from the case study combined to provide a complete picture. Moreover, the approach helped to ensure overall validity since the three perspectives complemented one another.

Reform of information technology accountability

Serious problems with procurement of US government information technology caused the passage of Public Law 89-306, the so-called Brooks Act, in 1965 (PL89-306). This was the first significant foray into federal IT accountability and oversight. IT accountability means that agencies are held answerable for the acquisition, use and disposal of information technology in improving the productivity, economy, efficiency and effectiveness of agency programmes. Over the ensuing years, changes in IT accountability in the federal government tended to correlate with public reform efforts. In fact, those reforms permit IT accountability in the US to be arrayed into the following three periods.

Traditional period: from 1965 to 1993

Information technology's Traditional period began with the Brooks Act, which was enacted because of congressional concerns about vendor favouritism, lack of accountability and ineffective controls, all of which had often caused the government to pay excessive prices for ineffective products. The Act was typical of 1960s' reforms which focused on economy and efficiency. Hierarchical control and elimination of waste, fraud and abuse were its corollaries. Between 1965 and 1988, key actors directed implementation of the original Act and subsequent legislation to construct a rigid pattern of hierarchical processes. The oversight hand was strengthened from 1989 to 1992.

In the early years, IT accountability developed a very rich tradition of seeking hierarchical control through regulation and systems of delegation and audit. However, under the Brooks Act, not all accountability and oversight authority was vested in a single body. Instead, power was divided between four central management agencies, with Congress retaining considerable influence through its committees:

- the Office of Management and Budget (OMB) became responsible for overall policy;
- the General Services Administration (GSA) oversaw procurement;
- the Department of Commerce, via the National Institute of Standards and Technology (NIST), controlled technical standards;
- the General Accounting Office (GAO), though without separate legislative authority for IT, was responsible for an overall 'watch dog' function.

Responsibilities are summarised in Figure 11.1, with dotted lines indicating cooperation – and independence – between agencies, and solid lines indicating oversight and control.

Therefore, in the Traditional period, information technology oversight was not a 'pure' system in the sense of having only 'one head'. Rather, it was established as a multiplicity of systems, each of which operated as a system of before-the-fact hierarchical controls exercised through regulations, delegations and/or audits. None the less, central management agencies held individual sway over specific government-wide authorities for the procurement, management and use of information systems. This leads to identification of the following overarching Traditional period concepts which frame and characterise IT accountability and oversight during this period.

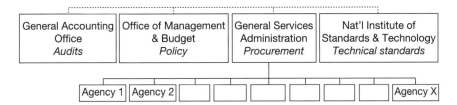

Figure 11.1 IT accountability agencies during the Traditional period

GOVERNMENT-WIDE ACCOUNTABILITY FOR INFORMATION TECHNOLOGY

Should separate and distinct government-wide methods be used to ensure accountability for federal IT projects? The Brooks Act answer was 'yes' in 1965, and subsequent legislation went beyond mere concurrence. The Paperwork Reduction Act of 1980 (PL96-511) created a specific information policy function at OMB; the Competition in Contracting Act of 1984 (PL98-369) piloted the GSA Board of Contract Appeals to hear information systems bid protests; and the 1986 Paperwork Reduction Reauthorization Act (PL99-500) gained permanence for both actions. These Acts demanded government-wide IT accountability.

CENTRALISED AUTHORITY FOR INFORMATION TECHNOLOGY

The Brooks Act centralised IT procurement authority at GSA, and it gave authority for setting technical standards to Commerce. The 1980 Paperwork Reduction Act ensured that information policy was the sole bailiwick of OMB. Successive legislation extended those concepts, and by 1988 information technology fiscal, procurement, technical and judicial authorities were fully centralised at the central management agencies.

HIERARCHICAL SYSTEMS OF CONTROLS OVER INFORMATION TECHNOLOGY

Three major systems of controls were created:

- a delegations system: the Brooks Act required agencies to obtain prior GSA approval for their information systems procurements, a two-stage hierarchy of before-the-fact controls;
- agency-level information resources management audits, as required by the 1980 Paperwork Reduction Act;
- regulations, including OMB's Circulars (particularly A-130), GSA's Federal Information Resources Management Regulations (FIRMR 1996), and the plethora of technical standards issued by the National Institute of Standards and Technology under authority granted to Commerce by the Brooks Act.

Transitional period: from 1993 to 1996

Promises during the 1992 election campaign to reinvent government led to the 1993 National Performance Review. This served as the Clinton Administration's blueprint for public sector reform and embraced information age reform by casting IT in the role of an engine for change. The NPR set the tone for reform, including reform of IT procurement and management processes:

> From the 1930s through the 1960s, we built large, top-down, centralised bureaucracies . . . With their rigid preoccupation with standard operating procedure, their vertical chains of command, . . . in today's world of rapid change, lightning-quick information technologies, tough global competition, and demanding customers, large, top-down bureaucracies – public or private – don't work very well.
>
> (NPR 1993: ii)

Thus, information technology was not a 'problem' requiring specific oversight mechanisms and accountability structures. Rather, its 'lightning-quick' technologies had both instrumental and cost-cutting roles in the new order. This transition in perspectives was matched by a transition in procedures, as described below.

GOVERNMENT-WIDE ACCOUNTABILITY FOR INFORMATION TECHNOLOGY

Though its mechanisms generally remained in place, the orthodoxy of the Brooks Act underwent restructuring during this period. Rather than eliminating IT controls, the NPR recommended that they be streamlined, and mandated the General Services Administration to 'significantly increase its delegated authority to federal agencies for the purchase of information technology, including hardware, software, and services' (NPR 1993: 29). By July 1995, GSA, with congressional support and Clinton Administration direction, had delegated authority to federal agencies even beyond the levels suggested by the NPR. However, the overall concept of government-wide accountability remained intact.

DECENTRALISED AUTHORITY FOR INFORMATION TECHNOLOGY

The old Brooks Act idea of centralised authority underwent radical reform in this period. GSA decentralised its authority through wide-ranging delegations directly to agencies. For example, purchasing authority levels were raised from US$2.5 million to US$100 million by July 1995 – special approval from GSA was only required for IS projects costed above this threshold; below it agencies needed no other approvals. 'Cutting the layers' became an achievable vision; decentralisation was to be the ultimate goal.

GOVERNMENT-WIDE SYSTEMS OF CONTROLS OVER INFORMATION
TECHNOLOGY

The major hierarchical controls from the Traditional period remained in place. Audits were still required though no agency reviews had been conducted by OMB or GSA since 1993. OMB still issued general policy, GSA prescribed procurement regulations and NIST remained in the standards business. Regulations were still an active part of IT project oversight in this period. Figure 11.2 illustrates the situation, with dotted lines indicating the transitional nature of relationships during this period.

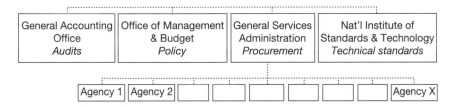

Figure 11.2 IT accountability agencies during the Transitional period

Transformed period: from 1996 to the present

Federal IT projects surfaced as a major issue in the mid-1990s for three significant reasons:

- IT was seen as having an important role in the process of government reinvention.
- IT had a broader visibility as an enabling mechanism for beneficial changes affecting the economy (e.g. the information superhighway or Internet).
- IT project mismanagement (such as the Federal Aviation Administration (FAA) failure described below) was seen as sharing in the culpability for government's costly failure to reform. In particular, the visibility and public furore caused by the FAA case and several other problem applications could not be denied and provided an opportunity for reformers to make major changes.

By February 1996, decisions had been made and a new direction set with the enactment of the Information Technology Management Reform Act of 1996. Succinctly, ITMRA:

- consolidated oversight and made the Office of Management and Budget the single government-wide manager of federal IT;
- rescinded regulations, removed centralised oversight by delegation and audit, and replaced those methods with incentives for empowerment and cross-agency collaboration;
- created a Chief Information Officer (CIO) in major agencies who would report directly to the agency head;
- required that information technology be treated as a financial investment rather than an expense;
- demanded that agencies directly link planned information technology investments to the budget process by demonstrating how the proposed investment would improve the performance (e.g. costs and outcomes) of their programmes;
- required agencies to procure their largest systems in increments, or modules, rather than as single 'grand design' acquisitions.

The reforms can be assessed in comparison to the characteristics of the two prior eras.

GOVERNMENT-WIDE ACCOUNTABILITY FOR INFORMATION TECHNOLOGY

Rather than retreating from this direction, ITMRA caused recentralisation of authority. The Office of Management and Budget as the single overseer successfully caused President Clinton to sign an Executive Order (which has the force of law in the US) in July 1996 that expanded the concept by creating three key councils to support the new responsibilities:

- a CIO Council to assist OMB with management responsibilities;
- an Information Technology Resources Board (ITRB), comprising senior agency IS professionals, responsible to OMB for reviewing IT programmes on an 'as needed' basis. When required, several ITRBs can be in simultaneous operation to conduct multiple programme reviews;
- a Government Information Technology Services Board (GITSB), also comprising senior public IS officials, responsible to OMB for initiating government-wide projects to spur innovative uses of technology and improve information infrastructures.

OMB thus came into the Transformed period with a dowry of assistants to support its overarching, government-wide accountability role.

RECENTRALISED AUTHORITY FOR INFORMATION TECHNOLOGY

ITMRA, coupled with OMB's pre-existing Paperwork Reduction Act policy making authority, gave it considerable, and exclusive, 'clout' over federal agencies' information systems. In fact, authority for IT procurement has been effectively recentralised under ITMRA and placed under the purview of the Office of Management and Budget. However, the methods and authorities are different from those in the old Traditional period during which the General Services Administration held exclusive authority for purchasing IT. Now, in the Transformed period, ITMRA, on one hand, has given agencies 'blanket' authority to purchase information technology without seeking prior authorisation; but, on the other hand, it has tempered that endowment by granting OMB the exclusive authority for issuing government-wide policies and regulations on the purchase, management, use and disposal of IT. And, as importantly, OMB has the authority to modify and allocate the money from agencies' IT budgets. In all, OMB:

- reviews and approves agencies' plans for new information systems;
- regulates the management of information systems;
- controls the 'purse strings' for all information technology purchases.

Thus, OMB has the authority to set the direction and the 'clout' to enforce its will through the budget process. Agencies must, in practice, obtain OMB's concurrence prior to making any significant information technology purchases.

GOVERNMENT-WIDE SYSTEMS OF CONTROLS OVER INFORMATION
TECHNOLOGY

OMB retained overall policy authority under the Paperwork Reduction Act. ITMRA 'seconded' that notion, expanded it and eliminated all 'competitors'.

Under the 1996 Information Technology Management Reform Act, the Office of Management and Budget has increased its ascendancy and is empowered to consolidate information technology accountability and control mechanisms within its own dominion. This ran counter to the long-held US tradition of fragmenting power over the federal establishment, but the 104th Congress overturned that tradition. A new period of IT accountability had begun.

Figure 11.3 summarises the situation. GSA and NIST no longer have independent authority. Rather, they assist OMB and serve as agents operating under its new authorities. The solid lines indicate oversight and control. The dotted line indicates collaboration between OMB and the General Accounting Office, which retains independent authority to conduct audits of any US government programme at the request of Congress.

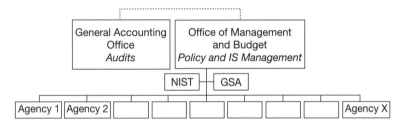

Figure 11.3 IT accountability agencies during the Transformed period

ANALYSIS: A STUDY OF TRANSFORMED PERIOD COMPONENTS

The executive view

For the purposes of this study accountability was modelled as a three-tiered architectural process:

- accountability *precepts*, the highest tier, are overarching principles;
- *attributes* are specific qualities that characterise a particular precept;
- *mechanisms*, the lowest tier, represent the refinement of attributes into implementable practices.

As an example, an accountability precept of central control might have delegation and audit as its associated attributes and creation of a specialised bureau as an implementing mechanism.

Table 11.1 summarises the precepts, attributes and mechanisms identified by senior US information technology officials for each of the three IT accountability periods. The table was used as a template to assess the case study.

Interviewees expected political control of information systems projects to rise through congressional intervention in the Transformed period. Diminished roles were envisioned for all central management agencies (GAO, NIST, GSA) except OMB. This sentiment indicated a growing evolution towards collaborative responsibility on a government-wide basis that would, it was hoped, foster facilitation and 'best practices'.

The interviews showed that a centralised accountability precept would exist in the Transformed period and have two attributes: a single point of control (OMB at the government-wide level); and management by exception. The former is also supported by the ITMRA reform legislation; the latter from affirmation of the Information Technology Resources Board that it will only review IT projects on a management by exception basis.

The second Transformed precept identified by interviewees – collaborative responsibility – really emerged from the Transitional period, with its inter-agency committees. One attribute would be technocratic decision-making. A second was business orientation. The implementing mechanisms for these

Table 11.1 Chronology of IT accountability precepts, attributes and mechanisms

Period	Precepts	Attributes	Mechanisms
Traditional	Centralised IT accountability	Delegation by transaction	GSA procurement delegations
		Audit	GSA IS audits
			GAO audits
	Functional IT hierarchical controls	Fractionated oversight	OMB – budget
			OMB – policy
			GSA – procurement
			NIST – standards
Transitional	Diffused IT accountability	Delegation according to capability	Broad classes of waivers
		Agency-level responsibility	Internal review
			Independent assessment
	Collaborative responsibility	Business orientation	Inter-agency committees
		Technocratic decision making	
Transformed	Centralised IT accountability	Single point of control	OMB oversight
		Management by exception	IT Resources Board
	Collaborative responsibility	Business orientation	CIO Council
		Technocratic decision making	Inter-agency committees
			Inter-agency technology teams

attributes were identified as the Chief Information Officer council, inter-agency committees and technology teams such as the Presidential Technology Team (top federal technical experts on loan from their agencies) announced by OMB in February 1996.

The results summarised in Table 11.1 indicate that senior information systems professionals thought that substantive and large-scale reforms in accountability had occurred in a relatively short span of time. Oversight lurched from an old Brooks Act mentality to NPR-type reform on a grand scale and then, in February 1996, 'back to the future' with a combination of Brooks period centralised accountability tempered with NPR-like collaborative responsibility. Yet, even in that ménage, a specialised role for government-wide IT accountability should remain, according to respondents. Figure 11.4 illustrates the fluxes from centralisation to decentralisation and back again.

In ranking the effectiveness of mechanisms to deliver workable information systems on time and within budget, respondents rated both the Transitional and Transformed mechanisms very highly in comparison with those of the Traditional period. Both insiders and outsiders expressed optimism about the emerging Transformed mechanisms. However, both counselled that Traditional practices should not be abandoned in their entirety (over 50 per cent rated those mechanisms as 'satisfactory' or better); the underpinning concept of centralised accountability should be retained.

Officials foresaw three broad trends:

- US congressional influence over agencies' information systems had increased in the Transitional period and would continue to do so at the expense of the central management agencies;

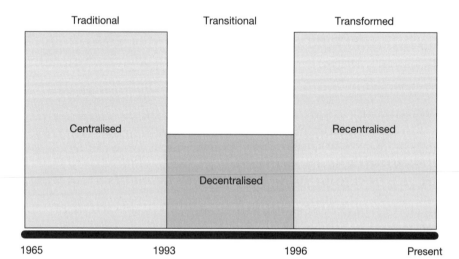

Figure 11.4 Changing locus of key IT accountability responsibilities

- although the Office of Management and Budget was in its ascendancy, it would command a lesser IT management role in future than the other central authorities (GSA and GAO) had held in the Traditional period;
- the role of oversight would continue to diminish, thereby accentuating facilitation and support as central roles in the Transformed period.

Respondents regarded the OMB as budget-centred and not heavily oriented towards management. They suggested that task would devolve to the agencies in large part. Fewer overseers coupled with a diminished focus on government-wide management would be the result. Also, respondents observed that in the past OMB had not been an adept overseer of troubled programmes. Thus, while a facilitative bent would probably help healthy information systems to achieve better results, it would probably decrease the likelihood of improvement in troubled systems. Officials clearly felt that most IT projects would fare better in the new collaborative and facilitative period, but the few troubled ones would probably fare worse than before because of diminished oversight.

Case study: the Federal Aviation Administration's Advanced Automation System

In order to investigate the issues that might arise with troubled IT projects, an assessment was undertaken of the Federal Aviation Administration's Advanced Automation System (AAS). A summary follows.

FAA's Advanced Automation System

This is one of the best-known examples of information systems problems in the US federal arena. Many people in the United States from 1993 to 1996 saw newspaper pictures or television interviews with Speaker of the House Newt Gingrich or Vice-President Al Gore in which each held a vacuum tube in his hands while decrying the 'red tape' that prevented the Federal Aviation Administration from replacing its 25-year-old vacuum tube-based computers.

Briefly, the idea for FAA's Advanced Automation System was conceived in the early 1980s, but the pressure for such a system arose during the Johnson (1963–9) and Nixon (1969–74) presidencies, especially after labour disputes in the early 1970s. Later, the furore of President Reagan's 1981 confrontation with 11,000 striking air traffic controllers, coupled with rapidly growing air traffic that threatened to overwhelm the existing system's capacity, caused federal officials to reassess the approach to air traffic control. From those deliberations, renewed support developed for the use of sophisticated technology to automate air traffic control processes, thereby increasing capacity and reducing the size of the workforce. Thus was born a vast, multi-billion dollar air traffic modernisation programme encompassing a large expanse of expensive information systems.

The new sophisticated technology would, it was hoped, provide significantly enhanced capabilities to integrate and automate existing processes, so that fewer controllers would be able to guide more aeroplanes. The FAA would supposedly save billions in personnel costs over the years. Moreover, in this vision of the future, controllers would use the new technology to provide pilots with better information to help them fly to their destinations faster and use less fuel. The air traffic industry and the FAA both foresaw billions of dollars in annual savings accruing to the airlines from these ambitious modernisation plans. Such savings, it was believed, would be a continuing boon to the US economy for decades to come.

Modernisation was planned for all parts of FAA, from control towers to radar installations and far-flung weather systems. To frame this overarching goal, the FAA devised numerous plans throughout the 1980s as it developed a US$23 billion (later US$36 billion) National Airspace System vision. The centrepiece of this vision was the US$4 billion Advanced Automation System which would be the ultimate interface between all of the enhanced radar and weather systems and the air traffic controllers; AAS was the FAA's high-technology plan to automate and upgrade controllers' workstations. The other modernisation projects, such as radar and weather enhancements, could not achieve their full potential until AAS was fully deployed.

Moving rapidly, in 1982 the FAA selected two of the top companies in the aviation systems industry – IBM and Hughes – to build AAS prototypes; the best design and value to the government would make that company the winner of a contract to deploy the new system throughout the Federal Aviation Administration. However, AAS became stalled for several years, just as earlier efforts had been in the 1970s. Finally in 1988, a long seven years after it began, IBM won the 20-year AAS contract with a bid of US$3.5 billion.

Five information systems projects or 'segments' were to be completed by IBM's Federal Systems Division; these ranged from developing new controller workstations to installing new mainframe computers. The key to success, however, was to be IBM's development of new software to replace the 20-year-old code. Starting in July 1992 at Seattle, new controller workstations and new software were to be deployed at all FAA flight control centres. The FAA's obsolete 1950s and 1960s computers were also to be replaced under that contract. Finally, IBM also won the possibility of delivering the same technology to the Department of Defense, as optional quantities under the contract.

The Advanced Automation System initially appeared to be on track. The first segment, a low-cost upgraded radar interface, was completed on schedule and no public signs of overall AAS weakness emerged until October 1990, when IBM announced a 12-month schedule slip. Moreover, costs had also increased and the new estimate was raised from US$3.5 billion to US$4.3 billion (GAO 1990). AAS woes appeared to be laid low until November 1992 when IBM projected an additional 12-month delay (ibid.). That time, the FAA responded by issuing a 'cure notice' to IBM. In federal contracting a 'cure notice' is a rarely used legal step which informs a contractor that the contract may be cancelled if specific corrective steps are not taken to abate the problems. In February 1993 IBM responded to the notice with an action plan, but in March 1993 it again raised the cost estimate, to US$4.7 billion (ibid.).

Just a few months later, in December 1993, AAS went from 'bad' to 'worse'. IBM and the FAA reported that the system would be delayed for another 19 months, and that the first new air traffic controllers' workstations would be deployed in Seattle during January 1996 rather than the initially projected date of July 1992. Even more ominous was an announcement that the cost would now be US$5.9 billion, an additional US$1.2 billion overrun in just a few months (FAA 1993). Although the central management agencies took no oversight action, the Federal Aviation Administration ordered an internal 'top-to-bottom' review and commissioned the privately operated Center for Naval Analysis to conduct a full programme review of AAS (ibid.). Adding to the complexity of the issues, IBM announced the sale of its Federal Systems Division to Loral Corporation in December 1993.

Continuing the downhill slide, the FAA announced even more problems in March 1994: AAS would experience 31 more months of delay, and at least US$1.4 billion in additional cost overruns were anticipated. The FAA pegged the new cost estimate in a range from US$5.9 billion to US$7.3 billion, with US$6.9 billion as the 'most likely' cost estimate (FAA 1994). Concurrently, the FAA replaced its top AAS programme managers, and publicly announced that it had begun to seek specific guarantees before it would consider transferring contractual responsibilities from IBM to Loral Corporation. Even though the projected cost and schedule had doubled, no stringent oversight actions were taken by the central government agencies, such as instituting a 'stop work'.

However, an oversight action was taken later in the fiscal year when AAS was selected for a 'time out'. In effect, that action extended procurement authority only until 30 September 1994, at which time the FAA would need to obtain the General Services Administration's approval of a restructuring plan in order for the programme to continue (GSA 1994). While in 'time out' any new programme activities were also placed on hold.

In September 1994, the FAA announced its final plans for restructuring AAS – renamed the Advanced Airspace Plan (AAP) – and estimated its new cost at US$6 billion, including sunk costs of approximately US$2.6 billion. GSA approved the plan in which two of the remaining four segments would remain with Loral with an estimated US$1.3 billion in new costs. Contracts for the two other segments would be separately re-competed at an estimated cost of US$1 billion and US$700 million respectively. The FAA began implementing those plans in 1995 and finally awarded the re-competed contracts in September 1996, a year late. By mid-1998, the new AAS/AAP systems and software had still not been fielded and slipping schedules stretched full deployment well beyond the year 2005.

Regarding external oversight, as of late 1998 the Office of Management and Budget had not withheld funding, redirected the programme or instituted any specially targeted system of controls over the FAA. Rather, the most effective approach came when the FAA imposed hard-hitting audits and subsequently used them as the basis of a major redirection of the project. Although AAS oversight came very late in the process, it did have some positive effects. However, it is important to observe that those benefits were contextual, in the sense that the FAA had a strong incentive to realise positive improvements only while the oversight actions and problems were in the eye of the public and highlighted before Congress. Application of the accountability templates from Table 11.1 expands that notion.

TRADITIONAL TEMPLATE

The Traditional period paradigm was one of hierarchical control through delegation and audit. If such controls had been imposed, the FAA would have been subjected to before-the-fact review of major decisions through a delegation-based process. Furthermore, audits would have been conducted to ensure that those before-the-fact 'orders' were being carried out in the prescribed manner to forestall any waste, fraud and abuse associated with the project.

An assessment of oversight actions indicated that the beneficial effects of a delegation process for AAS were limited, with only three delegation actions taking place. One was the 1987 delegation to the FAA for the initial contract award to IBM. Regarding the other two, one placed AAS in 'time out' and the other approved the FAA's plan to restructure the programme and retain Loral.

With respect to audits, a key issue was that they were spotty in their focus and the issues addressed tended to be micro- rather than macroscopic. Through lack of a comprehensive 'big picture' perspective, the General Accounting Office's evaluation of the project varied at different points in time and never raised an alarm calling for stringent oversight actions such as halting the programme. Clearly, the FAA was never subjected to rigorous, hierarchical accountability processes. The Traditional period template was not fitted to the AAS programme. In actual practice an unfettered FAA had been given almost unlimited authority and funding and yet failed to achieve viable results.

TRANSITIONAL TEMPLATE

Rather than regularity in conducting oversight delegations and audits, as would be expected in a traditional hierarchical approach, the actual practice in AAS was an exercise in management by exception, an attribute of the

Transitional period. Only GSA and the FAA itself exercised this option, and then only at the eleventh hour. The FAA exemplified through its own intervention the 'internal review' and 'independent assessment' mechanisms characteristic of the 'agency-level responsibility' attribute (see Table 11.1). Therefore, AAS oversight was more akin to the Transitional model and definitely not cast in the Traditional mould.

TRANSFORMED TEMPLATE

Underpinning the Transformed period is the idea that there should be a commonality of government-wide interest in federal information systems management. The General Services Administration's intervention embraced this idea by employing as its instrument an Information Technology Review Board comprised of senior officials to assess AAS. GSA's role was one of support for management by exception tactics which were previously identified as an attribute of the Transformed period 'centralised IT accountability' precept. Transformed period oversight precepts played a significant role in AAS.

FAA accountability in perspective

For over a decade, oversight of the FAA's actions really had one leg in the Transitional period and another in the Transformed period. The Advanced Automation System spanned, in time, all three oversight periods. Yet it had not been rigorously subjected to hierarchical oversight practices even though it was conceived and its problems began in the Traditional period. Rather, in a consistent pattern, its ills were approached exclusively through application of a mixture of Transitional and Transformed practices.

The AAS oversight actions did have some positive effects that highlighted the issues and caused significant redirection of the project. However, it is important to note that such oversight actions did not cure AAS of all its ills, nor did they turn it into a model project. Clearly, this was not a case of transforming a failed project into an unequivocal success. Instead, the oversight actions changed a project with no probability of success into one where some level of success was possible. It can be concluded that those AAS oversight actions which are carried over into the Transformed period have a likelihood of similar success when applied to other troubled IT projects.

CONCLUSIONS AND RECOMMENDATIONS

Information systems policy in government

In summary, the study yielded six overarching findings of relevance to governments in their management of information systems:

Study finding 1   A need continues for the central management of information technology accountability and oversight.

Study finding 2   Accountability should focus on two Transformed period precepts, centralised accountability and collaborative responsibility, and their associated attributes and mechanisms.

Study finding 3   The Transitional period precept of dispersed accountability and particularly its independent assessment mechanism should also be incorporated into the new, Transformed model.

Study finding 4   The two most effective oversight mechanisms for problem projects were those associated with the first two precepts: independent assessments commissioned by the agencies and external intervention by an IT review board under the aegis of a key central management agency.

Study finding 5   Overall, political influence over information technology at the government-wide, agency and even project levels will rise, at the expense of the central management (oversight) agencies, as they diminish in the aggregate when regulatory controls are loosened.

Study finding 6   Although facilitation is the hallmark of the Transformed period, large-scale IT projects will continue to fail at about the same rate and need to be dealt with through some instrumentality which even-handedly applies oversight controls and institutes focused and structured management-oriented methods.

In the US context, it appears that most government information systems are headed in a generally beneficial and positive direction under the Information Technology Management Reform Act. Anecdotes abound of agencies obtaining better prices and faster access to newer technology in the new reduced-oversight environment. These IT projects will continue to benefit from the removal of most controls and increased opportunities for collaboration. The challenge of achieving results through facilitation rather than oversight controls will probably be the high-water mark of this new approach in the US and its Transformed period.

However, there will still be troubled projects even under ITMRA. Such projects are characterised by a different set of variables, and several troubled projects valued at billions of dollars are already before the public's eye. These require mechanisms conceptualised in a different way. Collaborative attention and the ability to bring an even-handed outside oversight process to bear are clearly the keys to managing such projects and holding agencies accountable.

The Office of Management and Budget must demonstrate the efficacy of its new facilitative and collaborative approaches through instrumentalities such as the Information Technology Resources Board early in this new period in order to obtain a modicum of credibility. Successful IT projects draw collegial applause; out-of-control troubled projects draw howls of public outrage and increased political oversight and entanglements. It will therefore be the response of OMB and its new tools (the CIO Council, GITSB and ITRB) that will make or break the reform hallmarks of the Transformed period. The CIO Council is already proving its worth by providing senior IT officers with access to key White House and OMB policy makers. This has led to new inter-agency initiatives to develop the skills of IT managers and to address the Year 2000 problem.

Information systems policy formation and content: recommendations

Policy directions in the US

With its first steps into the Transformed period, the United States has already embraced a major shift in its strategy. Clearly, the need is to institutionalise collaborative methods and the new partnerships as quickly as possible. Fostering and retaining the political relationships needed to completely institutionalise the ITMRA strategy must be a priority. ITMRA's future direction, in general terms, should be one of promoting a focused implementation and making careful adjustments in order to reap the benefits of the new strategy.

However, one specific recommendation for strategic change is that the United States, using the ITMRA framework, should identify practices to help agencies take better advantage of IS outsourcing opportunities. What an agency outsources to contractors and keeps for itself is an important part of the government's 'make or buy' contracting decision. Some agencies have used outsourcing innovations with success. However, some agencies have also been missing opportunities because current practices and some contracting laws are restrictive and process-driven.

Promoting the use of 'best value' judgements (rather than process-driven targets), new practices and legislative changes in some contracting laws could help to shift outsourcing from a 'check list' approach to innovation and could improve focus on the needs of customers. Facilitation of such reforms through OMB and the CIO Council, for example, would encourage agencies to pursue flexible outsourcing strategies and better leverage their options. ITMRA enables that option because it helps to provide access for IS managers to senior policy makers through the CIO Council, GITSB and ITRB.

Policy in other countries

The US experience suggests that a good place for other governments to start is by identifying which of the three periods (Traditional, Transitional or Transformed) most closely conforms to their own situation. Those that find themselves in the Traditional period must decide whether they should try to change policy.

One problem with Traditional period policies is that they can often seek to impose a model of accountability or IT management that is out of kilter with current public sector realities. For example, with its emphasis on controls the Traditional approach gives agencies a strong incentive to bundle as many technology requirements as possible into a single IT procurement. Two of the more glaring risks from such a strategy are:

- placing 'all eggs in one basket';
- increasing the time frame of the procurement cycle.

Together, these risks mean that agencies pursuing such a strategy would be likely to purchase older technologies at a higher price, and those systems would be delivered after they were really needed – with an increased risk that no technology might be delivered at all if that single procurement ran into problems. This would delay or even wreck reforms which depended upon IT-based information systems. It was largely because of this that the US chose to move away from its old, traditional 'Brooks Act' arrangement: the Act had once been in step with the times and helped spur competition, innovation and lower prices. By the 1990s, this was no longer true.

In setting up institutions and mechanisms to move from Traditional or Transitional to Transformed models, governments should, in general, consider the six findings listed above. In particular, findings 1–3 can provide value to governments which are setting up or adjusting institutions and mechanisms for IT accountability.

One key to success is the placement, credibility and 'clout' of enabling institutions and mechanisms. The United States learned, for example, that it needed a centrally placed organisation to implement ITMRA effectively. The Office of Management and Budget was chosen because of its functional, political and budget 'clout'. Similar institutions would need to be identified in other countries.

The centralising force of such an institution should to be tempered with more collaborative and facilitative mechanisms. Some means to bring senior staff together in a forum focused on government-wide IS policy is essential. Similarly, cross-cutting implementation bodies can be of great value if they focus on making the link between information systems and specific public sector reform initiatives, as the Government IT Services Board has done in the US.

Conception–reality gaps

The US experience indicates that successful IT management initiatives must be rooted in organisational realities, rather than based on some rationalist conceptions that cannot be implemented in practice.

For example, the IT Resources Board has been successful, where applied, because it meets the genuine need to bring senior agency information systems professionals together from across government to assist another agency by reviewing a 'problem project' in a supportive manner. In one of its first tasks the ITRB was able to get a retirement payroll system's development project back on track and contain costs because it used practising managers' judgements rather than trying to impose some rationalist theory or model of how to manage IT projects. It thus closed conception–reality gaps along the management dimension of the ITPOSMO model (see Chapter 3).

Other key components of the Transformed period (facilitation, removal of controls, opportunities for collaboration) are also being successful because they reflect the realities of managers' desire for faster project completion and greater decentralisation of authority. For example, a unified approach for buying only Year 2000-compliant computer products was quickly developed in 1997 by taking advantage of the opportunities for collaboration through a CIO Council sub-committee.

On the other hand, there may well be a gap between the conceptualisation of the ITRB and the realities of problem projects. Such projects are different from the mainstream and, as a result, ITRBs have not been used as often as needed because of political, management, financial and technical barriers.

In summary, the successes of the IT Management Reform Act occur where there are strong linkages between its underpinning concepts and public sector realities. Other governments seeking similar reforms must equally ensure a good match between conception and reality.

REFERENCES

Bozeman, B. and Bretschneider, S. (1986) 'Public information management systems: theory and prescription', *Public Administration Review* 46, 6: 475–487.

Cats-Baril, W. and Thompson, R. (1995) 'Managing information projects in the public sector', *Public Administration Review* 55, 1: 559–566.

Caudle, S. (1988) 'Federal information resources management after the Paperwork Reduction Act', *Public Administration Review* 48, 6: 790–808.

Emily, M. (1996) 'Managing change: the future is now!', *Public Manager* 22, 4: 39–42.

FAA (1993) *AAS News Release, 21 December 1993*, Washington, DC: USA Federal Aviation Administration.

FAA (1994) *AAS News Release, 3 March 1994*, Washington, DC: USA Federal Aviation Administration.

FIRMR (1996) *Federal Information Resources Management Regulation*, Washington, DC: Government Printing Office.

GAO (General Accounting Office) (1990) *FAA Encountering Problems in Acquiring Major Automated Systems*, T-IMTEC-90-9, Washington, DC: Government Printing Office.

GAO (General Accounting Office) (1994) *Advanced Automation System: Implications of Problems and Recent Changes*, T-RCED-94-188, Washington, DC: Government Printing Office.

GSA (1994) *25 May 1994 Public Letter to the Federal Aviation Administration about the Advanced Automation System*, Washington, DC: General Services Administration.

Kiel, M. (1994) 'Understanding runaway information technology projects', *Journal of Management Information Systems* 11, 3: 65–85.

Lederer, A. and Sethi, V. (1996) 'Key prescriptions for strategic information systems management', *Journal of Management Information Systems* 13, 1: 35–62.

Newcomer, K. and Caudle, S. (1991) 'Evaluating public sector information systems', *Public Administration Review* 51, 5: 377–384.

NPR (1993) *Report on the National Performance Review*, Washington, DC: Government Printing Office.

PL-89-306 (1965) *Public Law 89-306: The Brooks Act of October 30, 1965*, Washington, DC: Government Printing Office.

PL-96-511 (1980) *Public Law 96-511: The Paperwork Reduction Act of December 11, 1980*, Washington, DC: Government Printing Office.

PL-98-369 (1984) *Public Law 98-369: Competition in Contracting Act of July 13, 1984*, Washington, DC: Government Printing Office.

PL-99-500 (1986) *Public Law 99-500: The Paperwork Reduction Act Reauthorization of October 18, 1986*, Washington, DC: Government Printing Office.

PL-104-106 (1996) *Public Law 104-106: Defense Authorizations Act, Division E, Information Technology; Management Reform Act*, Washington, DC: Government Printing Office.

Thong, J. (1994) 'Engagement of external expertise in information systems implementation', *Journal of Management Information Systems* 11, 2: 209–211.

ACKNOWLEDGEMENTS

The author wishes to acknowledge the United States government information systems managers who were interviewed for this chapter, and who provided useful inputs.

12 Outsourcing and government information technology strategy

Relevance of external consultant models in Barbados

Stewart Bishop

Abstract: An information technology (IT) strategy for the public sector is seen by many countries as an essential tool in harnessing IT for public sector reform. This chapter reviews the development of an IT strategy in Barbados, an island state in the Caribbean, and shortcomings of the model on which that strategy was built. The model, imported from the UK by a team of external consultants, places outsourcing, using a consortium approach, at the heart of the new strategy. However, significant gaps exist between the conceptions of this model and the realities of the local skills base, business practices, culture and use of information. A modified approach will therefore be required.

BACKGROUND

There has been much talk recently about the emergence of an information society and the development of an information economy. In the information economy, knowledge is the critical resource and the basis for competition, trade and investment are global, and firms compete with knowledge, networking and agility (Talero 1996). In government, too, information becomes recognised as a vital resource that must be harnessed as information age reform initiatives start to be planned and implemented.

Many countries – Barbados included – have become concerned to accelerate the local transition to an information society, and have therefore identified key transition activities such as:

- upgrading the local infrastructure of information and communication technologies;

- upgrading the human resource infrastructure via an information culture and information technology (IT) skills;
- improving information systems (IS) through the use of new technology in all organisations, including the public sector;
- encouraging foreign investment and inward transfer of new technology;
- increasing the economic role of information services, including exports;
- facilitating the migration to electronic commerce and other information exchange through legislative and other mechanisms.

It has long been seen that governments would play a dominant role in facilitating these transitions since they play so many information- and IT-related roles: as investor, consumer, strategist and regulator; roles which are clearly interdependent (Mody and Dahlman 1992). Many governments have therefore initiated the creation of a national IT policy to try to bring about the transitions listed above. This aims to build appropriate IT and human infrastructure, and to create an economic, financial, legal and social environment conducive to these transitions.

The IT environment in Barbados

Before discussing the specifics of IT policy in Barbados, some background will be given about the island's IT environment.

Public sector

The Data Processing Department (DPD) was established within the Ministry of Finance in 1969 to be responsible for the development, implementation and maintenance of computerised applications for the entire Barbados public service. The government-wide objectives of these applications included:

- improved efficiency of public service commercial activities;
- increased ministerial control of inventories and stores;
- reduced cost of payroll preparation;
- centralisation of certain accounting functions.

Beginning in 1969, initial applications included payroll, central purchasing, budget and statistical applications. Ministries and departments reacted very favourably when they received computerised output for the first time and sought to have related aspects of their work computerised.

However, with the advent of newer technology – especially micro-computers – attitudes began to change. Many heads of line departments in government felt they were not being accorded a sufficiently high priority by DPD and they sought to acquire their own systems direct. They saw little role for DPD since they felt its staff were neither educated in the use of nor favourably disposed to microcomputers. This was unfortunate since DPD personnel had been well trained and were quite competent. Yet DPD's management seemed unable or unwilling to respond positively to new user expectations.

There was *de facto* decentralisation of IT services in the public sector and user departments faced:

- increased pressure from IT vendors to acquire their own computer facilities;
- increased independence from, and conflict with, DPD and its technical staff;
- increased reliance on vendors and software service providers for technical assistance.

These decentralised units lacked proper management, and problems of redundancy and inconsistency within several databases in the public sector were encountered. There were other problems too because the level of service provided by vendors, especially in the area of software development, has seldom been of a satisfactory standard.

Despite the loosening of central controls, the whole Barbados public service still seems stuck in a traditional data paradigm. DFD appears wedded to the idea of providing bulk financial and statistical reports, not to proactively delivering more management-oriented information. They do not see information as important for decision making or for the empowerment of citizens or as a vital economic commodity. Yet this matches the views and demands of many public sector managers, who seem satisfied with very basic reporting of simple socio-economic indicators.

Either despite or because of this situation, the government launched a draft White Paper on public sector reform in 1996 (Ministry of Civil Service 1996). In general terms, this identified a number of problems in the public sector (which accounts for 25 per cent of gross domestic product):

- lack of a clear policy on human resource development and management;
- disinclination to delegate decision making;
- poor keeping of financial records;
- lack of a proper system of internal controls in financial management.

Information-related problems were also identified, with lack of IT seen as the main issue:

> The public service as a whole is quite poorly served in the area of modern IT. Its management information systems, in many respects, are haphazard, if not archaic. The general absence of modern IT in the public sector makes the dissemination of information and response to the

public on a timely basis a frustrating experience. So too, the flow of information within and between governmental agencies needs to be greatly improved by the use of technology.

(Ministry of Civil Service 1996: 20)

Increased investment in IT was therefore seen as integral to public sector reform. The government committed itself to spend more on IT and on IT skills in order to create a more efficient, accountable and customer-oriented public service. It therefore embraced information age reform, albeit with an approach more reminiscent of the idolise approach described in Chapter 2 rather than the integrate approach. These ideas were given more shape once external consultants were called in, as described below.

Private sector

By contrast, the private sector in Barbados appears to be far ahead in its use of IT, following three decades of diffusion. Accounting and billing applications have been complemented by strategic information systems involving geographic information systems and multimedia-based applications. Many businesses – including some small ones – use IT in their day-to-day operations. Electronic commerce has taken hold with ATMs (automated teller machines) in banks and shopping centres, and with point-of-sale terminals in supermarkets and plastic cards in use everywhere. Web sites exist for many local firms, featuring catalogues and photographs to support electronic trade opportunities, especially in tourism-related businesses.

Yet there are also limitations to IT use in the private sector. Business managers lack a proper appreciation of the value of their IT investments and, behind the veneer of state-of-the-art, there has been only a slow transition to real-time operations, with heavy reliance still on batch updating of databases. Computerisation remains limited in some sectors, notably agriculture, and in some applications, notably any management areas outside finance and accounting.

Barbados also has an export-oriented information services sector that is a heavy IT user. In 1995, 36 firms employed nearly 3,000 people, bringing in US$40 million per year in gross export earnings (Nurse 1996). Even here, however, employment seems to have stabilised and the major proportion of work is in relatively low value-added data entry services.

Government has become involved in issues of private sector IT use, taking action in three main areas:

- *IT diffusion* This has been encouraged through the removal of duties on IT and a reduction in taxes paid on income earned from the export of IT-based services.
- *Telecommunications infrastructure* Some deregulation has taken place and there has been significant investment in telecommunications. ISDN

(integrated services digital network) services are now available, and there are three Internet service providers. Service quality is high but so are costs. Costs for international connections are falling but – at the time of writing – they were still around five times higher than in North America.

- *Human resource infrastructure* A training grant scheme has been initiated to allow local workers' wages to be paid for a limited period while they undergo IT training. Computer education is provided at all levels of the education system: primary, secondary and tertiary. The recently announced Edutech 2000 initiative will increase this provision, since it is recognised that IT labour demand still runs well ahead of supply on the island.

Developing a national IT strategy for Barbados

Above, it was noted that a national IT policy is seen as crucial in effecting the transition to an information society. As in many other countries, this has been recognised in Barbados and, after elections in 1994, IT was included for the first time as part of one minister's portfolio. He was a former businessman with an appreciation of the contribution IT can make to competitive advantage. He was destined to become the government's IT champion and to initiate the creation of a national IT policy for Barbados.

After the government had approved an outline policy for national IT development late in 1994, an IT Task Force was set up to oversee its further development and subsequent implementation. Several consultancy contracts were awarded almost simultaneously to both local and foreign consultants to assist this process.

One successful bidder was an organisation that will be referred to here anonymously as the British IT Consultancy (BITC). BITC has extensive experience of IT use in the UK public sector. It also has experience of working in developing countries, though this is not necessarily true of all its staff members. It was awarded contracts for consultancy inputs on two of the main programmes:

- fleshing out an outline IT strategy for the public sector in Barbados, including an appropriate project implementation programme (in this chapter there will be a distinction between an IT policy that covers all parts of the economy and an IT strategy which focuses on just one part, e.g. the public sector);
- establishing a network-based information system to support the Enabling Environment for Private Sector Investment (EEPSI) project, which sought to rationalise and expedite processes involved in attracting and retaining investment through the provision of new information systems. This project was a key component of the Investment Sector Reform Programme, which has been developed as a major part of the government's effort to strengthen the national economy (BITC 1997a).

After preliminary visits and interviews and discussion with local public servants and others, BITC assessed the information systems in the Barbados public sector as characterised by:

- badly coordinated projects;
- information that was neither shared nor properly managed;
- little planning;
- inadequate procurement processes;
- little standardisation;
- multiple interfaces for citizens and business;
- paper-based administration;
- high international telecommunications costs.

BITC then articulated an IT-based vision of a Barbados with:

- improved quality of life;
- good governance;
- improved national productivity;
- an IT-literate workforce;
- a national, competitive digital telecommunications network;
- IT services for a global market place.

Such a vision can readily be identified with the IT champion within the Cabinet. However, one must wonder whether that vision was shared by other ministers and leading public servants, who have seldom spoken of IT in such passionate terms.

Within this overall vision, BITC's IT Strategic Plan (BITC 1997b) for IT application in the public sector proposed, *inter alia*:

- the appointment of a Chief Information Technology Officer within the public service;
- the establishment of two IT units for the public sector dealing with (a) IT strategy and policy, and (b) technical services provision. In concept and functioning these units would be quite similar to the Central IT Unit and the CCTA/Government Centre for Information Systems, respectively, in the UK public sector. The outcome for DPD would be that it would become an agency with reduced IT responsibilities, providing services such as training and technical consultancy;
- a 'one-stop electronic shop' for government services;
- strategic IT partnerships or joint ventures with the community, business, funding agencies and other governments. Central to this would be the outsourcing of many – if not all – IS functions from the public to the private sector. The private sector would bear most of the capital costs and accept the risks of technology obsolescence and systems development projects, as currently occurs in the UK's Private Finance Initiative.

Government would benefit from any additional revenue derived from innovation or from additional income streams;

- revised IT approval and procurement practices with service providers supplying innovative business solutions rather than simply hardware and software products;
- ministry-level IT plans with national, cross-government, multi-ministry and ministry-level projects forming the basis for outsourcing proposals.

Information systems outsourcing

Within the context of the public sector, governments have felt the pressures of both information society initiatives and also public sector reform. One way in which these two pressures interact is seen in the development of new information systems to support reform initiatives, often within the context of a national IT strategy for the public sector (some of which were identified in Chapter 2). However, as summarised in Figure 12.1, the relationship between information systems and reform is two-way. IS can support reform, but equally reform agendas can be applied to the provision and management of government information systems, as Chapter 11 exemplifies in the US context.

The provision of goods and services for government continues to be the subject of discussion in an era in which there is constant advocacy of the merits of restructuring, reengineering or reinventing government. As governments seek to implement best-practice methods, this invariably leads to the utilisation of services provided by organisations in the private and non-governmental sectors (Osborne and Gaebler 1993: 43–45). Once, it was assumed that government information systems would be provided and managed by public sector staff. This is no longer so, as the growth in information systems outsourcing attests.

'Outsourcing refers to the concept of hiring outside professional services to meet the in-house needs of an organization or an agency' (Gupta and Gupta 1992: 45). In the information systems context, it can cover all stages of the IS lifecycle: analysis, design, development, implementation, operation and maintenance (Globerman and Vining 1996). The scope of outsourcing can range from contracting out a few components of program development up to the 'total outsourcing' of all IT and virtually all IS responsibilities. In historical terms, data entry and IS development were the first items to be contracted

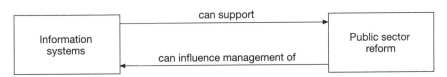

Figure 12.1 The two-way relationship between information systems and public sector reform

out, but total outsourcing has more recently been used to allow the client organisation to concentrate on its core activities.

Outsourcing has particularly come to attention since the 1980s, when major IS outsourcing contracts were perceived as having been successfully awarded by large private sector companies like Kodak and American Airlines. However, the public sector has not been far behind and, during the 1990s, many huge outsourcing contracts have been awarded. In Australia and the UK, for example, IS outsourcing has been used by many public sector organisations, with the largest contracts worth hundreds of millions of US dollars and stretching up to more than ten years in length. With some contracts approaching total outsourcing and with the heavy involvement of US IT multinationals, there has been considerable disquiet about this process.

Nevertheless, outsourcing by public sector organisations has been driven on by a number of objectives, including (DeLooff 1996):

- cutting costs, particularly in the presence of general financial constraints within the public sector, and in line with the efficiency strand in public sector reform;
- maximising the quality of service provided, in line with concepts of customer-orientation present within the marketisation strand of reform;
- providing access to new sources of skill and finance, particularly as a way of circumventing the inflexibilities of many public sector accounting systems;
- making the cost of IT investments explicit, in order to better manage their contribution to public sector goals;
- focusing on core areas of government.

Other factors have also played a part, such as (Dearden 1987):

- the emergence of private software companies able to take on outsourcing contracts;
- rapid rates of technological change that leave organisations struggling to keep up internally;
- a political environment that has tended to value the private sector above the public sector.

IS outsourcing has therefore become an increasingly integral component of public sector reform, at least within the industrialised countries. However, there are some factors which place limits on the extent of outsourcing:

- *The nature of IT* IT is so all-encompassing, heterogeneous and rapidly changing that planning even a three-year horizon becomes a hazardous exercise. This can place limits on outsourcing and on any attempts at calculating long-term costs and benefits.
- *Public sector IT projects* Such projects may not be dominated by rational

planning but, instead, by political and cultural factors. The integrated nature of some public sector projects often demands the involvement of several entities, some of which may be unwilling to cooperate. In such an environment, it may be difficult to define projects for outsourcing or to recommend them for external management.

- *Limited outsourcing experience* Public sector organisations with limited outsourcing experience may encounter difficulties. They may find themselves unable to negotiate or monitor outsourcing contracts satisfactorily. Those which do proceed may choose total outsourcing, to make up for perceived or real in-house skill gaps, and can become excessively dependent on the contractor.
- *Availability of competent contractors* An obvious prerequisite for successful outsourcing is the local presence of private sector firms which can execute the contract. Where local competence is limited, outsourcing may be constrained or alternative approaches may have to be used, such as building consortia of local firms or bringing in foreign players.
- *Reactions of existing staff* In-house personnel may become demoralised or directly hostile if outsourcing is mooted as an option. This can jeopardise either the initiation or the implementation of an outsourcing contract.

As well as setting limits on the extent of outsourcing, these and other problems can also set limits on the benefits achieved from outsourcing, such as cost savings. Indeed, Prager (1994) notes that outsourcing, instead of stemming the flow of budgetary red ink will, at times, intensify the haemorrhage. Outsourcing may bring other disadvantages such as loss of strategic information systems capabilities. However, there is limited open information about this in the public sector: 'Many governments are quite secretive about their contracting out experiences, especially when there are problems' (Globerman and Vining 1996: 584).

In this chapter, the appropriateness of Barbados's consultant-inspired IT strategy will be considered generally, but issues of IS outsourcing will be particularly assessed.

ANALYSIS: RELEVANCE OF IT STRATEGY COMPONENTS

General discrepancies between proposed IT strategy and Barbadian reality

Some general discrepancies between the consultants' UK-inspired IT strategy and the contextual realities in Barbados can be noted here. Overall, there was an apparent absence of analysis and lack of appreciation of local IT issues. Instead, the proposed strategy seems more to reflect:

- aspects of the UK's Information Society Initiative: a national IT strategy developed in the UK from the mid-1990s;
- high-tech solutions enunciated in 1995 in a statement from the Barbados ministerial IT champion.

More specific points are detailed below.

First, the consultancy report diagnosed a significant difference between public sector IT use in Barbados and that in industrialised countries. It observed that governments in industrialised countries were using IT extensively as an instrument of public sector reform including initiatives to help deliver more convenient, more accessible and more efficient services to citizens and businesses. The report concluded that:

> Barbados is still at a relatively early stage in its use of IT. The public sector lacks skilled IT resources and adequate IT funding. The current use and awareness of IT opportunities in the public service in Barbados are akin to the situation in the UK at least 15 years ago.
>
> (BITC 1997b: 2)

Yet, the model for IT strategy recommended for use in Barbados was largely the present-day UK one. This imposition would require, at the very least, much leapfrogging to achieve the desired results in the stated time period. At worst, it would set Barbados off on an entirely inappropriate course.

It seems inconceivable, at a time when institutions such as the Commonwealth Secretariat have recognised the particular context of developing countries, that this UK model could have prevailed. Malta, for example, is very similar in many ways to Barbados and has used the mechanism of a national IT strategy for the public sector to create a modern IT infrastructure and several significant information systems. Malta's model would definitely seem more appropriate.

Second, issues such as human resource development, the legal framework and telecommunications infrastructure warrant detailed analysis and attention, especially in the context of a developing country such as Barbados. They, however, received only fleeting attention in the proposed strategy, perhaps because such issues did not fit the consultants' UK-oriented conceptions.

Third, the consultants' strategy provided the vision of a public service with a one-stop information service and electronic mail response to citizens' queries. This seems many miles away from the real Barbados public sector in which reports are produced but not utilised, information systems are designed but not implemented, and the current archaic information systems are deemed satisfactory by most managers. These managers have often resisted new information systems and do not see IT as a tool for planning and communication, let alone as a means of helping to deliver public services.

Closing even the first step of the gap between vision and reality would require a massive task of 'information sensitisation'.

Finally, there was no recognition of the Western cultural values inherent within information technology that divorce it from the realities of other cultural contexts. Uneasiness, reluctance and fear of failure haunt IT's introduction in developing countries. Van Ryckeghem (1995) describes examples of such introduction. Presence of a strong oral tradition meant IT was not valued as a tool for communication. Pragmatism and adherence to formalism were rated more highly by public sector managers than values such as efficiency. Hence, IT was not much valued for its automating and efficiency-increasing capabilities, let alone any more complex application. Such important cultural issues formed no part of the BITC report.

In addition to these general discrepancies, there were also problems with the proposed strategy's approach to the issue of outsourcing and provision of IS services in the public sector. These are now analysed in greater detail.

The consortium proposal within the IT strategy

Early in its consultancy, BITC did an evaluation of the Barbados public sector's Data Processing Department – the initially created provider of IS services for government – and concluded that:

- its systems development skills lagged behind those of the market;
- it did not have sufficient resources to meet demands for IS services within the public sector;
- its bureau services were no longer required.

That these perceptions coincided with those of top government officials with whom BITC consultants met would surprise no one.

Having identified the problem, BITC then turned to the private sector for the solution that would provide appropriate information systems services. There it found that many of the companies which offered such services were fledgling providers with only a few employees. Nevertheless, BITC identified ten providers who, from their experience, expertise and number of employees, could be considered as single providers for some of the smaller service requirements. Of this group of companies five were local representatives of multinational computer corporations, three were local partners of multinational accounting firms and two were local IT companies. These companies had concentrated mainly on the delivery of accounting and other business systems for the private sector, but a few of them had previously provided IT services to the public sector. One notable example was a national insurance information system utilised by several governments within the Caribbean.

BITC, which had advocated innovation in the provision of information services and technology within the public sector, then introduced its 'consortium proposal'. This stated that local service providers should form teams or partnerships to tender for public sector IS contracts. When service requirement orders were advertised, service providers could then, singly or together in a consortium, respond to the offer. The establishment of a consortium, BITC suggested, would:

- bring a fuller range of specialist expertise and experience to bear on any project;
- minimise the inefficiencies of multiple piecemeal procurement by obviating the need to manage and monitor several small contracts;
- help in the development of small IT firms, most of which were under-capitalised or unable to carry the risks associated with becoming an IS contractor or strategic partner with government.

BITC proposed to treat its consultancy with the EEPSI project as a pathfinder to test this approach. The response to and the suitability of the consortium proposal could thus be assessed.

Strategy–reality gaps in the outsourcing proposal

Several issues can be identified that throw doubt on the applicability of outsourcing in general in the Barbados context.

THE EXPERIENCE OF OUTSOURCING

IS outsourcing from the UK public sector can be traced back many years. To date, at least US$3 billion-worth of IS contracts have been outsourced by central government alone as outsourcing has come to be seen by both central and local government as a key IS management tool. The record of outsourcing has been mixed but has been reported as largely positive. The experience of IS outsourcing in the UK has therefore been relatively long and positive, making outsourcing a natural component of any IT strategy.

By contrast, the experience of IS outsourcing in Barbados has been relatively recent and relatively negative. Its use has been confined in the 1990s to a collection of departments which were ill-equipped to manage their own computing. In general, outsourcing to both local and external contractors is yet to be deemed an overall success. The frequency with which contractors have over-run their schedules and budgets does not instil much confidence in the contractors or in the management of the contracts. Experience to date would not naturally make outsourcing a major component of IT strategy in Barbados.

PRIVATE SECTOR COMPETENCE

The proposed level of outsourcing assumes the availability of competent IT professionals in the private sector to undertake the expected development work. Yet there is simply no pool of such personnel available on the island, where existing professionals are already working at full capacity. Perhaps, with the suggested downsizing of DPD, its ex-staffers are expected to fill the breach.

ASSESSMENT OF THE GOVERNMENT'S DATA PROCESSING DEPARTMENT

BITC's early conclusions about DPD have precluded a better assessment of the true competencies of its technical personnel, which at least match those in the private sector. Indeed, the much-maligned DPD has even been called upon to rescue some of the ill-fated attempts at outsourcing. It is regrettable that, for almost 30 years, the Department functioned in a dynamic technological environment with no attempt made to evaluate its operation or institute better management practices. Efficiency was never demanded from it, yet its first major consideration within a national IT strategy aimed to remove it more than to improve it. Prager's (1994: 180) observation is relevant here: 'the issue of government sector inefficiency is not inherent inefficiency as much as a lack of political will to establish efficiency as a high level priority of government operations.'

BITC's assessment is especially relevant since it forms the basis on which the outsourcing strategy was justified. However DPD's knowledge of the public sector IT environment cannot be readily equalled by contractors in a climate of mistrust and lack of mutual understanding between the sectors.

MANAGEMENT OF OUTSOURCING

The level of outsourcing contemplated calls for a special cadre of government IS management and legal professionals to monitor its operation. The generally low level of technical maturity in the public sector does not indicate an adequate management capability for such monitoring. This is additionally so because the suggested use of innovation as a criterion would surely complicate the contractor selection process.

POSSIBLE LOSS OF GOVERNMENT CONTROL OF STRATEGIC IT ACTIVITY

The delivery of information age reform goals requires information systems that are reliable and efficient. Yet outsourcing introduces problems of service discontinuity for IS staff and potential threats to data privacy, as well as other problems identified above. In a Barbadian context, it is debatable whether control can be enhanced by placing responsibilities for IS in the hands of a contractor.

BITC considers that the EEPSI project should be a pathfinder testing key themes of the government's IT strategy, particularly outsourcing. EEPSI involves several ministries, departments, state corporations and the private sector: this represents a tremendous coordination exercise. For these partners, IT affects their core business functions differently and they have vastly different levels of IT implementation and experience. Information system processes have to be determined for the project and then defined so that computer companies can tender to supply some or all of them. In a market not entirely comfortable with outsourcing and collaboration between the private and public sectors, the scope of the project far exceeds what one would ideally select to test the suitability of outsourcing.

Problems for the consortium proposal

While the preceding discussion relates to outsourcing in general, the consortium proposal brings with it special issues that bear upon its likely acceptability and viability.

IT personnel and institutions in Barbados and other Caribbean countries have a history of lack of cooperation. This, to some extent, is to be expected in a competitive environment where the announcement of the latest foreign product release is likely to give any connected local firm a distinct advantage. The norm has therefore been one of individual collaborations between multinational suppliers and local dealers. There has been very little evidence of collaboration between local firms. Instead, firms can point to the failure of Project Infotech 2000, which set up a collaboration between IT firms in an attempt to win overseas outsourcing contracts but which was unable to find any suitable contracts. Distrust remains high and this has even affected the participation of some companies in seemingly innocuous activities like software exhibitions.

On technical grounds the viability of the consortium proposal would be affected by the absence of national IT standards. In particular, local service providers are quite likely to be using different programming languages, methodologies and hardware platforms.

Three of the prime service providers identified by BITC have, nevertheless, begun to discuss consortium formation. A major stumbling block they have encountered has been the issue of safeguarding the intellectual property rights and trade secrets of the prospective consortium members, all of whom represent multinational IT firms. The group members are attempting to work together, fully determined not to divulge any confidential information which becomes available. They also have a clear understanding that no contract should be accepted unless it is in the mutual interests of the whole group. So far, resources have been expended with no certainty of return on investment.

CONCLUSIONS AND RECOMMENDATIONS

Public sector IT strategy

The development of a national IT policy and its promotion throughout all areas of national life has been a common feature in many countries which are regarded as successful adopters of IT, such as Malaysia and Singapore. Within overall IT policy, there has typically been a strategy for IT use in the public sector which relates to public sector reform in two main ways:

- by encouraging the use of IT in support of public sector reform. This has not particularly been the emphasis of this chapter and Barbados has had only relatively limited experience of IT-enabled reform to date. In any case, this IT-centred type of approach has elsewhere been thrown into question (see Chapter 2);
- by encouraging the use of public sector reform measures in the management of IT. This has very much been the focus of this chapter.

The creation of a public sector IT strategy for Barbados was, however, flawed because it fell into the conception–reality trap. It was conceived according to a model that was based on UK realities or, at best, on the realities of a single ministerial statement of intent in Barbados, rather than on the pervasive realities of the Barbadian public and private sectors. It never received a 'reality check' because the virtually indecent haste with which these events have been staged precluded serious analysis and comment, especially on their innovative aspects, by local IT professionals. Time pressures have also limited the ability of the external consultants to customise their proposals to local realities.

As a result, many aspects of the proposed IT strategy seem to have little relevance and little chance of success, because issues of context were ignored. In particular, a central pillar of reform-inspired IS management – outsourcing of IS services – was incorporated into the strategy, based on a non-Barbadian model. That decision – based on a hasty evaluation of the government's main Data Processing Department, the subsequent adoption of total outsourcing as a strategy and the proposed downsizing of DPD – must all be questioned. While a role for outsourcing in the delivery of public sector services is recognised, it, like marriage, should not be entered into lightly, but advisedly.

There has equally been a conception–reality gap in the proposal for a consortium approach to outsourced contracts. While a good idea in theory, this ignores historical and cultural factors which make it most unlikely that local IT firms will collaborate. The only likely collaborations are those between individual small firms and either multinational firms as suppliers or the government as client.

Public sector IT strategy formation and content: recommendations

The simple imposition of external information age reform techniques on a local situation is unlikely to result in successful implementation. This seems particularly true when a Western model is imposed on a non-Western context. For Barbados, the experiences of other developing countries in creating an IT strategy may be more appropriate than those of the UK. However, even these must be treated with care: all situations are different and there must be some opportunity to contextualise all strategic initiatives to particular local characteristics.

One way of doing this is to ensure that a properly constituted local IT task force is an institutionalised part of any strategic development process. Then, even when external consultants are involved, their work can be constantly related to, and modified in accordance with, local realities. Such a task force would comprise representation from the usual quarters: government, academia, professional bodies and industry.

This issue of closing the conception–reality gap and contextualising may, indeed, raise the question of the appropriateness of a national IT strategy. Such strategies have been popular with many governments, captivated by promises of electronic delivery of public services that they perceive to be commonplace in the industrialised countries. However, in some situations, the centralised and top-down approach inherent within the strategy will not work. Instead, it may be better to adopt a more piecemeal, 'core–periphery' approach that encourages and builds upon departmental initiatives, rather than trying to produce government-wide applications (Heeks 1999).

Similarly, it seems that any sort of 'total outsourcing' approach which brings almost all information services out of government may be inappropriate in many contexts. Instead, outsourcing should be considered on a more limited and selective basis, at least until it has proven its worth. The issue of 'proving worth' is key, since outsourcing is hard to justify unless it can be shown to save societal resources. The following three issues must therefore be confronted in making an outsourcing decision (Globerman and Vining 1996):

- the objective of public sector outsourcing must be clear;
- an appropriate framework must be developed for assessing the potential governance costs of outsourcing;
- it must be shown that such a framework can be applied to the real problems of outsourcing.

The value of outsourcing must also be assessable.

In order to deal with such issues, a capacity to manage outsourcing contracts is necessary. At present, that capacity does not exist within many public sector organisations, leading to a culture of perpetual dependence on external assistance. To counter this, there must be a concerted campaign to develop in-house skills. This will include government leadership, training and guidelines on outsourcing, and some relatively transparent means of learning from outsourcing successes and failures within government.

Where private sector competence to take on outsourcing is limited, then a consortium approach can be considered. Where this is not appropriate, ways need to be found to (a) build up IS service capacity within the public sector, and (b) build public–private partnerships in service delivery.

Conception–reality gaps

There has been a major gap between the conception of an IT strategy for Barbados by external consultants and Barbadian realities. This therefore represents an archetypal country context failure as described in Chapter 3, since it was an attempt to superimpose an industrialised economy model on a developing country. Components of this gap relate to most dimensions of the ITPOSMO model also described in Chapter 3, and include:

- scant attention to human resource, legal and infrastructure issues;
- a vision of electronic government in a public sector with a limited IT base;
- Western cultural values divorced from Barbadian culture;
- a proposal for outsourcing via consortia for which Barbados lacked many basic prerequisites.

All these issues have been analysed and discussed in greater detail throughout the chapter.

REFERENCES

BITC (1997a) *The Enabling Environment for Private Sector Investment (EEPSI) Project*, St Michael, Barbados: British Information Technology Consultancy.

BITC (1997b) *Information Technology Strategic Plan for Government of Barbados*, St Michael, Barbados: British Information Technology Consultancy.

Dearden, J. (1987) 'The withering away of the IS organization', *Sloan Management Review* 29, Summer: 87–91.

DeLooff, L.A. (1996) 'IS outsourcing by public sector organizations', in N. Terashima and E. Altman (eds) *Advanced IT Tools*, London: Chapman & Hall.

Globerman, S. and Vining, A. (1996) 'A framework for evaluating the government contracting-out decision with an application to information technology', *Public Administration Review* 56, Nov/Dec: 577–586.

Gupta, U.G. and Gupta, A. (1992) 'Outsourcing the IS function', *Information Systems Management* Summer: 44–50.

Heeks, R.B. (1999) *Centralised vs. Decentralised Management of Public Information Systems: A Core-Periphery Solution*, ISPSM Working Paper no. 7, Manchester: IDPM, University of Manchester.
http://www.man.ac.uk/idpm/idpm_dp.htm

Ministry of Civil Service (1996) *Draft White Paper on Public Sector Reform*, St Michael, Barbados: Ministry of Civil Service.

Mody, A. and Dahlman, C. (1992) 'Performance and potential of information technology: an international perspective', *World Development* 20, 12: 1703–1719.

Nurse, L. (1996) *Information Services in National Development Strategy*, St Michael, Barbados: Ministry of Trade.

Osborne, D. and Gaebler, T. (1993) *Reinventing Government: How the Entrepreneurial Spirit is Transforming the Public Sector*, New York: Penguin Books. First published Reading, MA: Addison-Wesley, 1992.

Prager, J. (1994). 'Contracting out government services: lessons from the private sector', *Public Administration Review* 54, Mar/Apr: 176–184.

Talero, E. (1996) *NII: A Strategic Development Priority for Trinidad and Tobago*, paper presented at National Information Symposium, Trinidad, 14–15 May.

Van Ryckeghem, D. (1995) 'Information technology in Kenya: a dynamic approach', *Telematics and Informatics* 12, 1: 57–65.

ACKNOWLEDGEMENTS

The author would like to thank the 'BITC' consultants and Ms Juliet Agard of DPD for informative discussions on BITC's consultancies in Barbados.

13 Meeting training needs for information age reform

Shortcomings of current training provision

David Mundy, Chipo Kanjo and Peter Mtema

Abstract: Public sector reform has led to a substantial increase in the use of information technology (IT) within the public sector and, consequently, to a major new set of training needs. A common route for staff who wish to take professional responsibility for the introduction and use of the new information systems is through technically oriented training. This may be appropriate for organisations in the private sector that supply IT products and services. However, this chapter questions its relevance to public sector organisations in which IT is just a means to an end: the improvement of public sector processes. The chapter draws on evidence from industrialised and developing countries alike, including a study in Malawi. From this, a shortfall is shown to exist between the knowledge and skills acquired from technically oriented training and the knowledge and skills required for the analysis, design, implementation and management of information systems in the public sector. To reduce this shortfall a radical review of training is proposed to meet the needs of information age reform.

BACKGROUND

The context of new training needs

During the past two decades there has been a series of far-reaching reforms of the public sector in a number of countries. These reforms have been informed by the twin concepts of 'good governance' and 'new public management' (Turner and Hulme 1997). Definitions of good governance vary but, broadly speaking, the term is used to include the following major components:

- the accountability of governments for the decisions made and the actions taken by both political representatives and public officials;
- the competency of governments to manage their resources to deliver public services effectively and efficiently to all citizens;
- the legitimacy of governments through democratic and participatory processes;
- the respect of governments for the rights of citizens and civil institutions.

Similarly, there are a number of different models for new public management. One model was described in Chapter 1, from which Turner and Hulme (1997) emphasise:

- the use of written contracts to specify the performance expected of the suppliers of public services and the obligations of both suppliers and purchasers of these services;
- the use of integrated strategic planning and performance management systems;
- the separation of commercial functions from non-commercial functions, the separation of advisory, delivery and regulatory functions, and the separation of the roles of funders, purchasers and providers of public services;
- the decentralisation of management decision making.

Public sector reform therefore consists of many of the elements listed above and, as described in Chapter 1, these elements are linked to the introduction of new information systems. This introduction, in turn, leads to new training needs: the subject of this chapter. The chapter therefore presents evidence about the relationship between training, information systems and public sector reform. Much of the evidence derives from secondary sources that report work in industrialised countries, but it also derives from a survey of public sector managers undertaken in Malawi in 1996. Malawi was chosen not because it was a developing country, but because it provides a typical example of a nation drawn along the global trajectories of good governance and new public management.

There have been two principal outcomes of these trajectories:

- In 1994, as a result of both external pressure from the representatives of Western aid organisations and internal pressure from the Public Affairs Committee, the first 'free' general election in nearly 30 years was held in Malawi. The outcome was a defeat for the ruling Malawi Congress Party and its one-party system of government, and a victory for participatory democracy.
- Again as a result of these external and internal pressures, the constitution was revised to enshrine the principle of 'good governance', and the incoming government committed itself to improve the delivery of public

services, in particular primary education and primary health care, to ordinary Malawians.

The most obvious effect of these reforms in the public sector has been structural. However, to make these reforms work, existing processes and systems have to be realigned to achieve the new objectives. This is particularly true of existing information systems (IS) for – in Malawi as in most countries – many of the existing IS in the public sector do not support the new objectives associated with the spread of public sector reform. For example:

- decision makers are not provided with the timely and accurate information required to make effective decisions;
- new and effective flows of information are needed so that political representatives and public officials can be held accountable by citizens.

Meeting the needs of reform requires the reengineering of existing information systems and the introduction and use of new ones. Both of these activities are currently underway, associated with significant investments in new information technology (IT). This information age reform generates new training needs.

Current training provision

Current training provided to meet such needs in Malawi and other countries can be broadly categorised in two ways.

First, in terms of focus, training programmes may be:

- primarily task-focused opportunities that provide learners with detailed content about *how* to perform a particular task;
- primarily process-focused opportunities that provide learners with explanations of the process in which they may be engaged and, hence, *why* a particular task may be relevant in that process.

While competence in a task is important, it is not sufficient to guarantee the success of the task. For example, factors from the context surrounding the process may constrain the learner's ability to perform the task. Indeed, some contexts may make it inappropriate to perform the task at all. Thus, process-focused training is of particular value.

Second, in terms of length and depth, training programmes may be:

- short professional programmes, mainly for the in-service training of existing professionals;
- long undergraduate and postgraduate programmes, mainly for the pre-service training of aspiring professionals.

Each of these will now be considered in more detail.

Short professional programmes

Examples of short professional programmes could include:

- systems analysis and design programmes;
- programming courses;
- information systems workshops;
- organisation and management training;
- IT awareness workshops.

In practice in many countries, including Malawi, the provision of short professional programmes has tended to be limited to task-focused rather than process-focused opportunities. Thus, there are many suppliers of information technology training – introductions to computers, use of common applications software such as word processors and spreadsheets, basic programming courses, and so on – but relatively few suppliers of training in which this software is considered as part of the broader processes which support organisational information systems and reform. This is true of both private and public sector training. For example, analysis of the training offered by public service training colleges in Europe, Africa and Asia showed an overwhelming focus on information technology topics rather than information systems topics, let alone anything that relates IT to reform.

Undergraduate and postgraduate curricula

The continuum of computing practice (see Figure 13.1) ranges from computer engineering, through computer science, to information systems (Cain *et al.* 1984). Taking a historical perspective, computing as an academic discipline started out in many higher education institutions either (a) in electrical engineering, designing and producing electronic devices, or (b) in mathematics and physics, designing and producing program code to automate routine or complex calculations. The former has matured into computer engineering (with an emphasis on IT hardware), the latter into computer science (with an

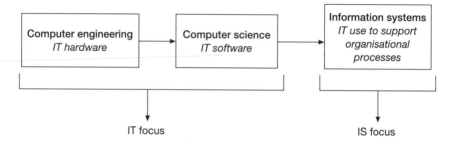

Figure 13.1 The continuum of computing practice and curricula

emphasis on IT software). Both are still primarily concerned with the design and production of technical solutions to technical problems. In contrast, information systems, which is the combination of computing with management, is a relatively recent extension to the discipline and emphasises the use of IT to support organisational processes.

The practice of computing is sufficiently broad that there can be no single computing curriculum which meets the potential demands placed on every computing professional. Different computing curricula therefore exist, each focused on a particular area of the continuum of computing practice and each appropriate for training computing professionals to practise within that particular area of the profession.

So where on the continuum do most curricula lie? A wealth of model computing curricula has appeared since the mid-1960s. Many of these have been produced by task forces sponsored by the professional computing organisations of both North America (for example, the Association for Computing Machinery (ACM) and the Computer Society of the Institute of Electrical and Electronic Engineers (IEEE-CS)) and the UK (for example, the British Computer Society (BCS) and the Institution of Electrical Engineers (IEE)). Examples of such curricula can be found in BCS/IEE (1989), Couger *et al.* (1995), and Tucker (1991).

Despite the breadth of computing practice described above, the majority of model curricula are focused on computer science. For example, two of the best-known curricula (BCS/IEE 1989; Tucker 1991) cover topics which are primarily technical:

- algorithms and data structures;
- artificial intelligence and robotics;
- computer system architecture;
- databases and information retrieval;
- human–computer interaction;
- numerical and symbolic computation;
- operating systems;
- programming languages;
- software methodology and engineering;
- social, ethical and professional issues.

There are other curricula. For example, since the early 1990s a system of national vocational standards for the practice of computing in organisations has been developed in the UK. These standards have been produced by lead bodies composed of representatives drawn from industry, commerce and government. The standards represent 'best practice', defining the competences – based on underlying skills and knowledge – that should be demonstrated in the workplace.

Level IV of these standards, for example, covers 'the performance of complex, technical, specialised and professional work activities, including those involving design, planning and problem-solving with a significant degree of personal accountability' (SCOTVEC 1996: 5). At this level, standards are defined for:

- investigating customer needs to identify requirements;
- analysing customer needs and constraints to produce requirements specification;
- evaluating and recommending IT solutions;
- specifying IT solutions (NCC 1996).

These vocational standards, together with a few others – Couger *et al.* (1995) provides a recent example – are examples of curricula that include a concern with information systems. However, these have been more the exception than the rule. Certainly, in higher education the IT focus persists, perhaps because it reflects the research interests of academics in many computer science departments: the production of technical solutions to technical problems rather than the application of IT to organisational problems. This, of course, is reminiscent of the domination of IT-focused approaches over integrated approaches to reform described in Chapter 2.

The foregoing description deals principally with curricula – and hence training – in use in the industrialised countries, but the pattern is repeated world-wide. For example, analysis of the higher education institutions listed in the 1996 *Directory* of the Association of Commonwealth Universities (ACU 1996) reveals 23 countries reporting academic computing departments. Of these departments, 11 per cent can be classified as computer engineering, 84 per cent as computer science and only 5 per cent as information systems.

This evidence of 'IT bias' is reinforced by analysis of government computing-related training policy. For example, in Malaysia (Venugopal 1992), the Philippines (Torres 1992) and Singapore (Koh and Lee 1992), training policy has emphasised the need for knowledge and skills in the areas of information technology and computer science, not information systems. This training is seen as relevant to address not merely the design and development of IT products and services but also the 'computerisation' of government.

The same pattern is repeated in Malawi, where computer science has been taught as an academic subject to undergraduates at the University of Malawi since the early 1980s. The topics covered fall broadly into the 'traditional' core of computer science, and training can therefore be described as IT-focused rather than IS-focused.

ANALYSIS: TRAINING NEEDS FOR INFORMATION AGE REFORM

Having described the type of training that is currently being provided, we shall now move on to analyse the type of training that is actually needed and to analyse the match or mismatch between provision and need.

General training needs

There has been considerable concern in some countries that the graduates of computer science courses offered by higher education institutions are often out of touch with the practice of computing in organisations. For example, Denning *et al.* (1989) observe that many computer science graduates find employment in business data processing: yet this is a domain in which few computer science curricula seek to develop competence. For example, as part of their standard practice, these professionals contribute to team projects and interact with other disciplines to support their interests in the effective use of computing. Despite this, neither team projects nor interdisciplinary studies feature in most computer science programmes.

In a study in the UK (West London TEC 1993) it was found that the move towards end-user computing made significant new demands on the skills and knowledge required of computing professionals. In tandem, employers had serious reservations about the quality and the relevance of the skills and knowledge acquired through existing computer science courses at higher education institutions. Other commentators suggest that technical skills and knowledge alone are an insufficient basis for computing professionals practising in organisations. For example, in the recent Yellowbrick report to Scottish Enterprise it was noted that 'consistently, all studies echo the need [for professionals] to have more than technical knowledge' (Yellowbrick 1995: 30). Walsham (1993) argues that the graduates of most computer science courses are unlikely to receive any formal education in aspects of social theory, despite the probability that their future careers as professionals rely as heavily on social skills and knowledge as they do on technical skills and knowledge.

Information age reform training needs

We have just considered the general training needs of those working with computers in organisations, but what about the more specific needs that relate to information age reform in the public sector?

Two current trends are apparent that affect the training needs of computing professionals in the public sector. The first is a general trend which parallels reform processes: the move away from the use of IT in organisational information systems for automation and towards informatisation. Wilson (1997), for example, describes this trend in terms of seven levels of information management. These levels (see Table 13.1) represent different strategies

Table 13.1 The seven levels of information management

Level 1	*Compliance*: the use of IT to automate the basic recording requirements of the organisation.
Level 2	*Operational management support*: the use of the recorded data to assist with the management of day-to-day operations.
Level 3	*Added customer value*: the use of information systems to add value to the organisation's products, services or relationships with clients.
Level 4	*Competitive advantage*: the use of information systems to achieve a leap in competitive advantage and to sustain that advantage.
Level 5	*Strategic insight*: the use of information systems to support a strategic insight and a new form for the organisation.
Level 6	*Transformation*: the use of information systems to make a fundamental revision to the organisation, its business, partnerships and products or services.
Level 7	*Knowledge net*: the use of information systems to create 'virtual organisations' which bring together 'employees' from anywhere in the world to undertake a particular assignment and which, when that assignment has been completed, cease to exist.

in the steady progression from traditional data processing to a more information-based approach.

At first sight some of Wilson's seven levels may appear to be more relevant than others to the public sector. For example, it may be thought that public sector organisations do not need to have competitive advantage. Yet supporters of government reinvention advocate the injection of competition into service delivery (Osborne and Gaebler 1992). With growth in market testing, in outsourcing of public services and in the ability of service purchasers to choose between different providers, achieving competitive advantage will become more relevant (see Chapter 14 for further discussion of this point).

Certainly, the linkage between public sector reform and the move to informatisation is clear (Muid 1994; see also Chapter 2). The process of reform describes a movement in the public sector from Wilson's lower levels towards the higher levels: for example, adding customer value through the publication of citizens' charters and the commitment to quality, and the transformation of the structure of public sector organisations by separating policy functions from service delivery functions. However, this is not to argue that the process of reform will inevitably lead to informatisation. Informatisation may be impeded by a number of factors, not least the availability of professionals with appropriate knowledge, skills and attitudes.

Training, too, must therefore become more informatisation- rather than automation-focused. In practice, this means a greater orientation towards information rather than technology and, in the terms presented above, a greater orientation to information systems rather than computer engineering or science.

The second key trend that affects training needs is that of information age reform itself. Decentralisation, for example, involves a move away from centralised information systems and towards decentralised information systems. The old model is of a centralised IT function in the organisation, based around a cluster of mainframe or minicomputer systems with centralised IT staff who may appear unresponsive to the information requirements of users in other departments. The new model is a distributed network of microcomputers supported by decentralised teams of IT staff located in user departments. Such staff need to do far more than create programs: they must, instead, understand people, processes and the department's 'business'. Their training must reflect this.

Writing specifically about change in the UK public sector, Willcocks (1994: 22) suggests that there needs to be 'a shift in perspective from IT management to [information systems] management'. He continues by noting the complex nature of information systems management, bringing together the four dimensions of: the technology, the environment, the social, and the organisational. All four of these dimensions, and their inter-relationships, need to be managed in order for IS to contribute effectively to reform. All four of these must therefore be dealt with in training.

These trends are putting new demands on the human resources needed for the analysis, design, production, implementation and operation of information systems that meet reform objectives. These new demands mean the need is becoming more for information systems skills than for IT skills.

Attitudes of public sector managers in Malawi

In Malawi, a survey was conducted of public sector line managers of recent graduates from the University of Malawi's computer science course. The intention was to investigate the match or mismatch between the training provided on the course and the requirements of public sector organisations undergoing reform.

Overall, there was less satisfaction with activities such as systems analysis and systems implementation than there was with the activity of actually producing any new information system. Given the content of the University's course – focusing on the computer science area of the continuum – this dissatisfaction is perhaps not surprising.

The line managers were also asked to rank in importance a range of technical and non-technical skills and knowledge which they believed their computing professionals should possess (see Table 13.2). More line managers ranked the non-technical skills and knowledge as more important than the technical skills and knowledge. A common complaint from public sector employers was also that recent graduates did not understand basic organisational processes and were unable to apply their computing skills to support these processes. Their contribution to the process of reform was therefore constrained.

Given the focus of the University's course on the technical skills and knowledge to undertake IS production activities, this ranking suggests that the

Table 13.2 Technical and non-technical skills and knowledge for public sector computing professionals

Technical skills and knowledge	Non-technical skills and knowledge
Specific software packages	Analytical and logical thinking
Specific programming languages	Problem solving
Specific networks	Accuracy and attention to detail
Specific hardware	Written and oral communication
	Initiative and adaptability to changing circumstances
	Knowledge of design methodologies
	Working within a multi-disciplinary team
	Interaction with other professionals

existing educational experiences need to be broadened to enable students to acquire non-technical skills and knowledge. This should include an understanding of information systems, of public sector organisations and of management.

Specifying the information systems training needs of information age reform

To sum up so far, the adequacy of most of the training currently provided to meet information age reform IS training needs must be questioned. This training may meet the needs of those working in the IT industry, but it certainly does not seem to meet all the needs of those working in public sector organisations undergoing reform. For this latter group, IT-focused training may provide some of the skills necessary to create, test and document a new information system. What it does not do is to provide other necessary IS-related skills, such as recognising an opportunity or a problem within the 'business' of an organisation and making a case for its solution.

Put simply, there needs to be a reorientation of training from an IT focus to an IS focus (just as Chapter 2 argued more broadly for reorientation of reform approaches from 'idolise' to 'integrate'). But what does this mean in practice: what is the required training content to meet the IS-related needs of information age reform?

Generic information systems training needs

In general terms, computing professionals – and we should now rather call them 'information systems professionals' – who work in public sector organisations may be required to undertake a number of activities to analyse, design, produce, implement and operate information systems. These activities form the information systems life cycle (see Table 13.3) and are often

Table 13.3 The information systems lifecycle

Phase	Activity
Analysis and design	Consult with clients and end-users to investigate the feasibility of the proposed system
	Consult with clients and end-users to determine the requirements of the proposed system
	Specify the functional requirements of the hardware and software components
	Liaise with computer equipment vendors during tendering and procurement
Production	Write manuals for clients and end-users
	Design program code from the specification of functional requirements
	Test program code
	Document program code
	Integrate and test hardware and software components
Implementation and operation	Install the completed system for clients and end-users
	Train clients and end-users in the use of the installed system
	Support clients and end-users in the use of the installed system
	Maintain and enhance the installed system

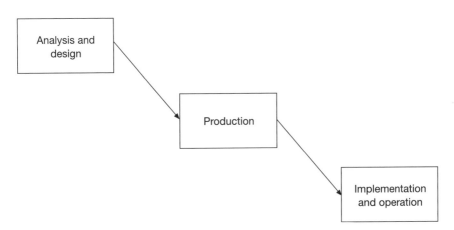

Figure 13.2 The waterfall model of the information systems life cycle

arranged into phases to form the so-called 'waterfall' model (see Figure 13.2) (Sommerville 1995).

In the first phase, *analysis and design*, the IS professionals work in consultation with other stakeholders, for example the clients and the end-users. They identify the need within an organisation for an information system and develop a project proposal. The project proposal identifies the scope of the information system, associated costs and benefits, and various options for IS production and implementation. The proposal is submitted to management for approval, and the approved proposal forms the basis for work in the second and third phases of the information systems lifecycle.

In the second phase, *production*, the IS professionals perform a number of highly technical activities to produce the information system from various hardware and software components. This may involve them in writing program code. It almost certainly involves them in putting the different hardware and software components together to form the information system. Since information systems in organisations are more than technical systems, the professionals also perform activities to put in place the necessary non-technical components of IS, for example new processes, new staff, new training and new offices.

In the third phase, *implementation and operation*, the information system is introduced into the organisation, any necessary changes are made to staffing and working practices, and the information system becomes 'live'. During this final phase, the effectiveness of the information system in the organisation is monitored and any necessary changes are made to improve its performance.

For the purposes of public sector reform, should all phases be given equal emphasis in training, or are some more important than others? The Malawi survey was used to address this question. It showed that the implementation and operation phase is undertaken in slightly more organisations than the analysis and design phase. This, in turn, is undertaken in slightly more organisations than the production phase, especially the program design, testing and documentation activities.

In particular, the survey suggested that the production phase is the least important during reform for two probable reasons:

- increasing use of software packages rather than custom-built software;
- increasing outsourcing of software development rather in-house development.

The relatively greater incidence of implementation and operation probably relates to the use of external IS consultants who perform the 'upstream' activities of the lifecycle. The responsibility of any professionals employed in the organisation may be limited to assisting the consultants with implementation of the information system and its ongoing operation after the consultants have left.

This suggests that training should particularly provide educational experiences relevant to activities both in the analysis and design phase and in the implementation and operation phase of the information systems lifecycle. Such educational experiences should help students to understand the functioning of public sector organisations as potentially complex social and political systems. They should also see the organisations embedded within a multi-dimensional environment which can be a source of constraints on the organisation and also can be affected by the activities of the organisation. In contrast, the acquisition of knowledge and skills applicable to activities in the production phase appears to be of less importance.

The need for 'hybrid' information systems professionals

One final requirement to emerge from the process of information age reform is the need to train and produce 'hybrid' information systems professionals. Michael Earl is often credited with popularising this term, which will now be explored in greater detail.

Earl (1989) classifies the human resources required for information management in organisations into: *hybrids*, *professionals*, *leaders* and *impresarios*. Both hybrids and professionals fall into the 'doing domain', delivering IS solutions within an organisation. However, where professionals are focused on technical skills, hybrids have a broader range of skills. As a result:

- the business confidence and organisational skills of the *hybrids* may enable them to undertake the activities in the analysis and design phase and the implementation and operation phase more effectively than the *professionals*;
- the technological expertise of the *professionals* may enable them to undertake the activities in the production phase more effectively than the *hybrids*.

Hybrids have other beneficial characteristics because, according to Earl, they can:

- recognise the opportunity to introduce an information system;
- make the case for the information system;
- see how it fits into existing organisational operations and systems;
- anticipate the implementation issues associated with the information system.

The hybrid also has sufficient understanding of the organisation to know when and how to initiate an idea and how to make things happen. Finally, the hybrid may have sufficient technical knowledge and skills to build a prototype of an information system.

Hybrids therefore have an understanding of public sector management and of public sector organisations. At first sight, this may appear to take them beyond the realm of just information systems skills. In practice, though, this analysis is actually telling us the full range of skills that are required to be an effective IS professional. For example, in order to analyse or implement a public sector information system effectively, he or she must understand the nature of the organisation and the way in which management operates.

We may therefore be left wondering whether there is any place left for the old-style computing professional in public sector organisations undergoing reform. Perhaps not. The spread of desktop systems, user-friendly interfaces and end-user application-building tools is dramatically reducing the technical knowledge and skills required to create a working information system. At the same time, reform has been associated with a process of outsourcing that reduces the need for an in-house IS production capability.

The main advantages to the organisation of employing hybrids in preference to professionals are twofold:

- Hybrids can understand a 'business' area of the organisation and can work within that area better than professionals.
- Hybrids are more likely to identify information systems that are of strategic importance to the reform process rather than those that are an excuse to use technology or to justify the continued employment of professionals.

So where will these hybrids come from? They can be trained from scratch, but the pressures of reform will make it hard for this supply to meet the necessary demand. Thus, in-service conversion ('hybridisation') of existing staff will also be needed. It is often assumed that this conversion process means taking existing computing staff and giving them an IS/managerial perspective. In practice, however, it is equally important to convert existing functional managers (see Figure 13.3) for two reasons:

- all existing managers need to understand where information systems fit into the public sector reform process. They need to become involved in

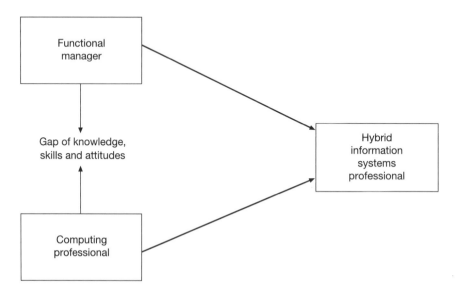

Figure 13.3 Creating hybrids for the public sector

systems development as managers, to ensure systems meet business needs and provide value for money, and as users, to ensure their personal work requirements are met. They are also increasingly operators of reform-initiated information systems, and need to understand how to use the systems to fulfil work objectives. In the context of UK public sector reform, Muid (1994) refers to these needed characteristics as the 'intelligent user function';

- the 'conversion gap' may be smaller for some managers than it is for some computing professionals. In simple terms, it may be easier to teach some managers the necessary technical skills than it is to teach some computing specialists the necessary management and organisational skills.

CONCLUSIONS AND RECOMMENDATIONS

Conclusions about training needs and information age reform

The need in the public sector for new knowledge, skills and attitudes is being driven by both the spread of public sector reform and the spread of IT in public sector organisations. Effective public sector reform depends upon timely and accurate information, to support the process of reform and to maintain the reformed public sector. The use of IT in the public sector is moving from the support of routine procedures to the support of tactical and strategic decision making. As a result of these trends, IT can no longer be viewed as a discrete component in organisational information systems; in many cases IT is being used as the catalyst to reengineer these information systems. Thus there is a need for hybrid information systems professionals who can enable an integrated approach to information age reform. They will understand not only the process of public sector reform but also be able to introduce and use information systems to support this process.

The IS-related training requirements generated by information age reform fall into three categories:

- *Knowledge* The development of information systems requires up-to-date knowledge about the basics of information technology, the design options that could be applied to new information systems, and the methods of developing information systems. However, as IT spreads through public sector organisations and is increasingly used to support the process of reform, knowledge will also be required about the nature and role of information and information systems in public sector organisations, about organisational systems and processes, and about organisational strategies and policies for information systems, particularly reform-related strategies.

- *Skills* Associated with each stage of the information systems lifecycle are a number of different techniques. To put these techniques into practice effectively, public sector IS professionals require up-to-date skills in areas already described, such as the identification of opportunities for new information systems, analysis of the current use of information, redesign of existing processes, design and construction of software systems, and installation of hardware and software systems. Additionally, as information age reform initiatives spread, there will be a requirement for 'meta-level' skills relating to project and change management, communication and negotiation, problem-solving, and so on.

- *Attitudes* Reform has increased the groups of stakeholders to whom public sector IS professionals must relate. These professionals must demonstrate appropriate attitudes to ensure that all relevant stakeholder groups are positively involved in the process of IS implementation. Positive attitudes towards the process of reform will also be required.

Despite this need, much of the current training supply for the public sector – both short professional programmes and undergraduate and postgraduate programmes – is focused on technical tasks: the use of specific IT components. As a result, there is little provision of training to cover the broader organisational processes of which IT is only one part. Thus the majority of training available is not enabling staff to engage effectively in the process of information age reform.

Future training provision: recommendations

Further work is required to perform a more detailed training needs analysis for information age reform. Any changes in training curricula must also be accompanied by suitable evaluation to measure whether the revised curricula are meeting the need for new skills, knowledge and attitudes more effectively. Nevertheless, the main direction of changes is clear and has been extensively trailed: that there should be a refocus of training provision away from IT and towards IS. The training should aim to create hybrid information systems professionals, not computing/IT professionals.

However, going further, we suggest that *training* is not sufficient *per se*. Information age reform is a dynamic and continuous process, not least because it must take account of changing political, economic and technological realities. It must be addressed by both *training* and *development*. While the former may focus primarily on specific knowledge and skills, the latter focuses on the development of the individual as a learner. Development is essential if public servants are to continue processes of reform for themselves without needing expensive – and often disruptive – training interventions.

Focusing on the key training providers – the higher education institutions – we propose a radical review of both content and location of current training. The required content has been described above, with hybrid IS professionals needing to understand: the organisational context of reform; the job of management in the public sector; and the role, management and jargon of information systems. In terms of location, then, the training of hybrid IS professionals might more appropriately be carried out within the management faculty of higher education institutions rather than computer science departments. The former will be better able to provide the necessary understanding of the organisational context and the organisational processes within which graduates will work. These, as we have seen, are more important than the technical skills. This is not to suggest that the quality of the technical content of the curricula is to be reduced: good hybrids need a good grounding in IT. What is at question is the depth of that grounding and its purpose.

If training for organisational IS professionals is moved away from the computer science domain, as it should be, then computer science training will be left focused – at least in vocational terms – on the needs of those who will go on to produce IT products for national, regional and international markets. Although beyond the scope of this book, there are arguments that this training should also be hybridised with much greater provision of business and entrepreneurial skills. This training might more appropriately be carried out within business faculties, to provide knowledge and skills to identify market opportunities. Computer science departments would then be left with just a rump of training related to basic research on IT.

Certainly, there needs to be significant changes in these departments. Implicit in the proposal is the assumption that computing academics, perhaps for the first time, should take a greater interest both in the process of curriculum development and delivery and in the process of introducing and using information systems in organisations. Explicitly too, this proposal encourages computing academics to focus less on technical solutions to technical problems and more on the use of information systems in organisations. Both these implications may need supporting with training opportunities for the computing academics themselves.

Similar processes of change need to take place in other training venues, including private sector providers and, particularly, public service training colleges. There is little purpose in the latter providing endless 'hands-on' IT courses. As we have seen, such training is of limited overall value to the process of reform and, more importantly, it can be provided just as easily – and possibly more cheaply – by the private sector. These colleges would provide greater value if they trained public servants to understand the role of information and information systems in public sector reform, and thereby encouraged an integrated approach to information age reform.

Will these necessary changes, required in order to support reform, take place organically? It seems unlikely. An IT focus makes training easier to plan, easier to deliver, easier to demonstrate tangible outcomes (even if these do not meet organisational needs), and often provides a better fit with the self interest of the trainers when compared to an IS focus. The IT focus may also be sustained out of simple ignorance of IS issues.

Such barriers will not be overcome on a piecemeal basis, but require a concerted and integrated national strategy. This means action by government to fund needs assessment exercises, to support the development and dissemination of new model curricula, to create awareness of needs amongst public sector managers, to push through changes in public service training, and to encourage change in higher education institutions.

Conception–reality gaps

The mismatch between training needs and training provision can be explained by the existence of a gap, as described by the ITPOSMO model in Chapter 3, between conception – what is perceived to be the case – and reality – what is actually the case. The gap relates to the process of introducing and using information systems in public sector organisations: the conception that this process is primarily concerned with information technology in contrast to the reality that this process must be equally concerned with both information technology and non-technical aspects.

This gap is apparent on both the supply side and the demand side. On the supply side, the gap results in the designers and deliverers of training offering training in which these non-technical aspects are either not covered or are covered in insufficient detail. On the demand side, the gap results in public sector computing staff and their line managers wanting task- and IT-focused training in preference to process- and IS-focused training.

Clearly, it would be desirable to close the gap so that the conception matches reality. One way to achieve this is through a learning process in which the designers and deliverers of training, public sector computing professionals and their line managers reflect on the processes by which information systems have been introduced and used in organisations, in particular their own organisations.

REFERENCES

ACU (1996) *Directory of Commonwealth Universities*, London: Association of Commonwealth Universities.

BCS/IEE (1989) *A Report on Undergraduate Curricula for Software Engineering*, London: British Computer Society/Institution of Electrical Engineers.

Cain, J.T., Langdon, G.G. and Varanasi, M.R. (1984) 'The IEE Computer Society model program in computer science and engineering', *Computer* 17, 4: 8–17.

Couger, J.D., Davis, G.B., Dologite, D.G., Feinstein, D.L., Gorgone, J.T., Jenkins, A.M., Kasper, G.M., Little, J.C., Longenecker, H.E. Jr and Valacich, J.S. (1995) 'IS '95: guideline for undergraduate IS curriculum', *MIS Quarterly* 19, 3: 341–359.

Denning, P.J., Comer, D., Gries, D., Mulder, M.C., Tucker, A.B., Turner, A.J. and Young, P.R. (1989) 'Computing as a discipline', *Communications of the ACM* 32, 1: 9–22.

Earl, M.J. (1989) *Management Strategies for Information Technology*, Hemel Hempstead, Herts: Prentice-Hall.

Koh, G.L. and Lee, K.C. (1992) 'Government information technology policy in Singapore', *Informatization and the Public Sector* 2, 2: 155–163.

Muid, C. (1994) 'Information systems and new public management: a view from the centre', *Public Administration* 72, Spring: 113–125.

NCC (1996) *IT S/NVQs: Titles and Units of Competence*, Manchester: National Computing Centre.

Osborne, D. and Gaebler, T. (1992) *Reinventing Government: How the Entrepreneurial Spirit is Transforming the Public Sector*, Reading, MA: Addison-Wesley.

SCOTVEC (1996) *SVQ Update*, Glasgow: Scottish Vocational Education Council.

Sommerville, I. (1995) *Software Engineering*, 5th edn., Wokingham, Berks: Addison-Wesley.

Torres, W. (1992) 'Philippine government computerization policy', *Informatization and the Public Sector* 2, 2: 145–153.

Tucker, A.B. (1991) 'Computing curricula 1991', *Communications of the ACM* 34, 6: 69–70.

Turner, M. and Hulme, D. (1997) *Governance, Administration and Development*, Basingstoke, Hants: Macmillan.

Venugopal, P. (1992) 'Malaysian government computerization policy', *Informatization and the Public Sector* 2, 2: 133–144.

Walsham, G. (1993) *Interpreting Information Systems in Organisations*, Chichester, W. Sussex: John Wiley.

West London TEC (1993) *IT Skills in the 90s: Overcoming Obstacles to Growth*, London: West London TEC.

Willcocks, L. (1994) 'Managing information systems in UK public administration', *Public Administration* 72, Spring: 13–32.

Wilson, M. (1997) *The Information Edge: Successful Management Using Information Technology*, London: Pitman Publishing.

Yellowbrick (1995) *Matching Supply and Demand for IT Graduates*, Glasgow: Yellowbrick.

Part 5

Organisational planning for information age reform

14 Strategic information systems planning

Applying private sector frameworks in UK public healthcare

*Joan A. Ballantine and
Nigel Cunningham*

Abstract: The concept of strategic information systems planning (SISP) is well developed in the literature on private sector organisations. It also has relevance to public sector organisations undergoing reform. For example, as public healthcare organisations attempt to develop innovative programmes to deliver services and make strategic decisions about their future, the need for high-quality information systems planning has increased in importance. Information is needed to structure and solve problems, to negotiate and broker difficult positions and to provide management control. However, there are difficulties with the concept of SISP, specifically the underlying assumptions of many SISP frameworks. The dominant assumption of a rational, machine-like organisation using technology to achieve formal organisational objectives does not seem to represent adequately the complexity and politics endemic in the delivery of public healthcare. This chapter discusses some of the potential problems of SISP with reference to the UK's National Health Service and reviews some concepts from soft systems thinking and organisational behaviour which may alleviate some of these concerns. These approaches accept the complexity of intervening in real-world affairs and could provide a more suitable framework within which to undertake SISP during public sector reform.

BACKGROUND

Introduction

The work of Porter and Millar (1985) has led to wide acceptance that information systems (IS) do not merely facilitate existing business practices, but may themselves shape the business. They may also restrict freedom of action, as apparently attractive business strategies are ruled out by the inability to create or modify IS to support those strategies (Lewis 1994). As a result, many organisations are currently seeking to align information systems with business strategy and, where possible, to exploit information technology (IT) for strategic advantage.

In order to achieve alignment between information systems and business strategy, strategic information systems planning (SISP) is undertaken. This is planning for information across the whole organisation driven by business objectives. It is argued that such planning helps organisations use information systems in innovative ways to:

- build barriers against new entrants;
- change the basis of competition;
- generate new products;
- build in switching costs that encourage customer loyalty;
- change the balance of power in supplier relationships (Lederer and Sethi 1994).

As a result, many private sector organisations have taken up the challenges and potential rewards offered by undertaking SISP.

However, the alignment of SISP with business strategy remains problematic (Galliers 1991; Price Waterhouse 1994), and recent research (*Computer Weekly* 1997) suggests that only 10 per cent of IS/IT directors report their IS strategies as being in harmony with their corresponding business strategies. The cause of such problems is often argued to be some deficiency in the way the strategic planning process is managed or implemented. However, in this chapter, we shall argue that part of the reason for this failure may be the inappropriate conscious or unconscious presence of organisational assumptions in SISP.

This has particular implications for the deployment of information systems in public sector healthcare organisations. The public sector, it seems, can retain legitimacy only by changing the way it is managed. The major current thrust of such a change has been the application of private sector ideas. In a period where the private sector is assumed to be modern and the public sector old-fashioned, it is therefore tempting for public agencies to adopt approaches to IS planning – such as SISP – which are thought to have value in profit-making organisations.

There is a range of SISP 'frameworks', consisting of various strategic planning techniques, methods and methodologies, which are available to practitioners in this field. A number of these have been adopted by public sector organisations as part of information age reform. However, as suggested by the language of 'business' and 'competition' used to describe SISP above, underlying almost all the frameworks are private sector conceptions which, as noted in Chapter 3, may be inappropriate to the public sector context. The potential mismatch between private sector conceptions and public sector realities within SISP forms the main focus of this chapter, investigated within the context of UK public healthcare.

Strategic information systems planning and UK healthcare reforms

The election in 1979 of the Conservative government led by Margaret Thatcher subjected the UK National Health Service (NHS) to the political philosophy of the 'New Right'. Although this was neither a unified movement nor a coherent doctrine, a number of common themes among its exponents can be identified:

- more freedom for business;
- more choice for individuals in the market;
- the removal of 'impediments' to the market such as trade unions;
- a greater role for markets generally;
- a smaller role for the state in economic affairs.

In UK public healthcare, reforms inspired by the New Right laid great emphasis on the management of healthcare. This was viewed as a process whereby the NHS could be charged with values and ideals of effective (private) business organisations through the systematic specification of goals, the detailed measurement of individual and group performance, and a battery of rewards and punishments (Pettigrew *et al.* 1992).

The New Right also initiated the 1989 NHS marketisation reforms which resulted in the separation of purchasers of healthcare services from the providers of such services, with their relationship administered through a process of contracting. These reforms led to the creation of an 'internal market' which enabled purchasers to choose where to obtain services for patients. Providers of healthcare such as acute hospitals became self-governing 'trusts', meaning that they were given increased autonomy and responsibility for managing their own affairs.

The introduction of these reforms led to greater emphasis on improved efficiency in the use of public funds and the need to fund expansion of the NHS by internally generated savings or by private funding arrangements. This in turn led to the need to improve both performance measurement and political and managerial accountability within the NHS. Information systems were crucial to these changes, and information was clearly cast as the currency on which the new market system for the NHS was to be developed (Beynon-Davies 1994).

As a result of these changes, the NHS Management Executive unveiled its strategy for addressing the information management and technology needs of the reformed NHS. It documented an ambitious plan, not only to place the NHS at the frontier of information technology, but also to construct a technological vision and infrastructure for the future operation of the internal market. Information management and technology strategies (often abbreviated in NHS parlance to IM&T and synonymous with SISP as defined in this chapter) were created within the four home nations of the reformed UK NHS. These strategies provided for an infrastructure to allow the communication of healthcare information across a continuum of care, from primary care through to acute care or long-stay hospital care and back into the community. IM&T strategy overall was intended to support reform by supporting the drive for quality and the need to use resources effectively. It had an overall vision of a public health service where:

- staff use information to improve continuously the service that they provide;
- the IM&T environment supports the controlled sharing of information throughout the service and other relevant agencies;
- information is handled and communicated securely, smoothly and efficiently.

In practice, however, the strategy has run into difficulties, with calls for it to be scrapped and with a fundamental rethink undertaken in 1998. In part, this rethink derives from practical problems experienced in the planning and implementation of strategy.

For example, a key element of the strategy relating to the needs of large acute hospitals was the development of a full range of integrated, patient-based operational systems, which were to be linked to an appropriate set of business and managerial systems, creating a hospital information support system (HISS). Growing concerns about the HISS strategy led to a change in policy emphasis, away from the 'big bang' approach adopted in pilot sites and towards an incremental route that would build on existing operational systems. However, both the big bang and incremental approaches have been dogged by slow progress and barriers to implementation in many hospital trusts. This has been characterised in terms of problems with business strategic planning, human resistance to change, and technical systems integration (Thomas *et al.* 1994).

It has also been suggested that policy objectives appear to have been subsumed by financial objectives, with the criticism that healthcare managers pay more attention to management information than to clinical information (Audit Commission 1995). While it is recognised that a link is needed between management and clinical information, the strategic emphasis remains technological and datalogical at best. The national strategy does not indicate how the social, political and cultural problems of delivering effective patient-oriented care with finite resources can be overcome. The following section investigates why this public sector example of SISP may have run into trouble.

ANALYSIS: ASSUMPTIONS AND CRITIQUE OF SISP FRAMEWORKS

Inherent within most SISP frameworks are a number of conceptions (we use the term 'assumptions' here) about organisations. Each of these will be analysed in turn, arguing that the assumptions do not accord with public sector realities.

Assumptions of SISP universality

There is a widespread assumption within SISP frameworks that they are generally applicable across all organisations. As a result, these frameworks over-emphasise the use of general techniques to the detriment of organisationally based solutions (Singh 1993). They provide no guidance to the practitioner about which techniques might be best applied in particular contexts, and they ignore the fact that many organisations are constrained by their past histories. Yet, in practice, such contextual factors strongly influence the applicability of SISP, and Ruohonen (1991) suggests that organisational, cultural and political factors not only constrain but can even destroy SISP activities. Recognising this, it is important to understand the organisational context into which SISP is being introduced: an issue that is addressed below. However, it will also be important to recognise the context from which SISP arose.

As Doyle (1991: 275) notes, SISP frameworks 'are the product of the dominant American (East Coast) business culture, and only emerge, thrive and survive because they reflect the preoccupations of that culture'. He questions the extent to which such frameworks are applicable in a European context or in a centrally planned economy. Furthermore, existing SISP frameworks documented in the literature were largely formulated as a result of research conducted in private sector organisations. One may further question, then, their applicability to public sector organisations in general and to public healthcare organisations in particular.

Assumptions of competitive advantage

The search for competitive advantage is a central assumption behind the advocated use of SISP frameworks. For example, Porter (1985; Porter and Millar 1985) has made much of the relationship between the strategic use of

IT and the creation of competitive advantage. Reform has introduced notions of competition into the public sector, especially into UK healthcare with the division between purchaser and provider. Nevertheless, there still remain some considerable gaps between private sector conceptions and public sector realities of competition.

Almost all healthcare providers are legally constituted trusts, which possess a certain degree of autonomy considered necessary for them to operate within the internal market. A major lever for promoting greater efficiency and effectiveness between providers is the competition to provide services to purchasers based on contracts. However, simple notions of competition cannot be applied to this type of market because, for instance:

- these healthcare organisations have multiple and often conflicting objectives, many of which are non-financial (McGuire *et al.* 1988);
- the degree of competition has been very varied, with hospital markets often displaying monopoly tendencies due to the high start-up costs and barriers to entry and exit.

Markets work on a number of principles such as perfect information and rational behaviour which simply do not exist in the NHS, with the consequence that from the outset the market was an imperfect instrument for allocating resources and making strategic decisions (Hunter 1996). A number of problems have therefore emerged including:

- low-trust relations, with healthcare providers adopting a combative posture instead of collaborating to serve patient interests;
- cost-shifting, with attempts to transfer the costs of treating patients from one area to another.

Gaming, goal displacement, adverse selection and high transaction costs in the functioning of this 'market' have also been noted (Coote and Hunter 1996).

It is clear from the UK experience that private sector notions of competition and competitive advantage therefore fit poorly into the context of public healthcare provision. Similarly, SISP frameworks based on these notions will also fit poorly into this context.

These difficulties were recognised in 1997, when the internal market system began being dismantled by the newly elected Labour administration. In its place were moves to replace competition, bureaucracy, instability and inefficiency with partnership, cooperation, quality and efficiency. Associated with this was the recognised need to improve processes across boundaries and agencies by understanding the continuum of care and by understanding how information systems can support this continuum. A new approach to IM&T strategy was therefore taken, and a new strategy document published in 1998.

Assumptions of strategy-making as rational and objective

The majority of existing SISP frameworks are based on a formal, rational model of strategic management which relies on the notion that information systems support the shared intention or vision of top management, which is to achieve a range of clear business objectives and critical success factors within a structured entity. This conception is flawed in reality for a number of reasons, six of which are analysed below (see also the discussion of rationality—reality gaps in Chapter 3).

First, SISP assumes that organisational objectives exist: in practice, this may not be the case. This explains why senior IS managers identify the ability to know top management's objectives as their greatest difficulty in developing a strategic IS plan (Lederer and Mendelow 1986). In the public sector, this is a particular problem because organisational objectives are more likely to be absent. Setting clear objectives in the public sector means that conflicting values must be reconciled and that public officials can more easily be held accountable. Many public sector organisations prefer to avoid these difficulties by failing to set clear objectives.

Second, SISP assumes some monolithic vision of organisations in which the organisation's vision, objectives, goals, and critical success factors are unitary and unproblematic. In reality, this is not the case even in the private sector. Analysis shows that senior managers perceive information systems as merely a 'commodity', and they set cost minimisation as the major IS strategy. Business unit managers and users, on the contrary, perceive IS as a critical differentiator, and they set service excellence as the major IS strategy (Lacity and Hirschheim 1995). Therefore, stakeholders' different expectations and perceptions of IS performance can lead to misaligned and conflicting strategic plans.

The problem can be even greater in the public sector, given the many competing stakeholders and visions. Within public healthcare, for example, there has been a marked separation between clinicians and managers. Historically, hospitals have been seen as typical of the professionalised organisation, characterised by shifting and organic professional segments which are largely autonomous of a marginal administration. The professional and administrative groups are likely to have very different ideas about what the organisation's objectives are, making it difficult or impossible to create a unitary vision for the purposes of SISP. Clinicians, for instance, are more interested in delivering effective clinical care than in cost-saving measures whereas the reverse may be true of managers.

Processes of public healthcare reform have brought this issue into sharp focus for SISP for two reasons:

- Reform attempted to reduce the separation of these two groups. In particular, it sought to do this by drawing clinicians into the management process. In the UK, the resource management initiative (RMI) was considered a cornerstone of reform. It involved the establishment of organisational structures – usually based on clinical directorates – that brought doctors and nurses into management decisions, including budgetary control. It was seen as a key requirement if hospitals were to respond to the incentives offered in a competitive external environment.

• There was a strong emphasis on the central role of information systems within these reforms. RMI was the biggest planned introduction of information systems in the history of National Health Service.

Current SISP frameworks do not deal adequately with this type of situation: the different value systems held by clinicians and managers require richer concepts of SISP.

Third, SISP assumes that processes of management and decision making are rational and apolitical. In practice, as a result of the previous point, IS strategy formulation is often characterised by political conflict at all stages (Waema and Walsham 1990).

In the UK's reforming public healthcare sector, this has been particularly the case because IS initiatives have been strategic and have sought to transform the role and nature of the clinicians' and managers' functions, and even to transform the organisations themselves (Bloomfield and Coombs 1990). Such transformations depend on and expose political issues of power, control and partnership between clinicians and managers, and have thus led to a very powerful 'politics of information' within UK healthcare (Doyle 1991; Keen 1994). This has been intensified by the NHS's large legacy of pre-reform information systems, each reflecting information needs in isolated functional areas and each often protected by its own cadre of professional groupings.

Yet the existing SISP frameworks that are intended to help manage such IS-driven transformations deal poorly, if at all, with issues of politics and conflict. It is hardly surprising then, as reported by Peel (1997), that the RMI's information systems ran into difficulties.

Fourth, conventional approaches to SISP conceive the strategists as independent observers who can exercise judgement by disconnecting themselves from the entangled everyday reality of the organisation:

> when evaluating strengths and weaknesses of the organisation, or the critical success factors, it is assumed that the strategist can think and make choices outside of the influence of frames of reference, cultural biases, paralysing double binds, or ingrained, routinised ways of acting, behaving and thinking.
>
> (Ciborra and Jelassi 1994: 8)

In practice, this can never be, because strategists are always participants in organisational processes as well as observers. Their perceptions are subjective and their actions also affect the organisation: they are not disconnected from it.

Fifth, SISP assumes that the world can usefully be simplified into models. To take but one example, matrix analysis approaches are often used as a tool for representation and understanding in SISP. For instance, two-by-two grids may be used to plot different dimensions of the organisational impact of information systems. Such simplification is attractive because it reduces an apparently infinite continuum of alternatives to a manageable, pertinent number of discrete options from which high-level directions can be determined (Ward *et al.* 1990). However, as complexity increases, clarity of perception often dulls. As a portfolio of information system applications, an organisation cannot easily be plotted in one quadrant of a matrix. What the model does is to reduce complexity and in doing so something is lost: the richness and essence of the organisation and its purpose.

Similarly, the idea that the organisation can be represented by a few object-ives or critical success factors is flawed: 'the essence of a business cannot be captured in a few objectives or critical success factors, however, carefully crafted. The subtleties, implications and interactions need to be understood' (Ormerod 1995: 17).

Finally, SISP assumes that given organisational characteristics determine the strategy. SISP frameworks assume that there is some objective, given the reality of the organisation that drives strategy: a business plan to which IS are to be aligned; and organisational objectives or vision which frame the direc-tion and purpose of IS development. In practice, this does not seem to hold. Strategic planning exercises seem particularly to help those involved make sense of their organisations. The task of the strategist is thus better thought of as 'organisation making' – the creation and maintenance of systems of shared meaning – than as strategy making (Smircich and Stubbart 1985). In other words, the strategy determines the organisation as much as, if not more than, the organisation determines the strategy.

Assumptions of problem-free implementation

SISP frameworks tend to focus on broad issues of visions and priorities and critical success factors. The assumption then is that a set of relatively problem-free action plans can be produced which will be implemented. This, in turn, involves a further set of assumptions, including an assumption of sufficient IS skills and capabilities and an assumption of the ability to measure, review and assess the benefits of information and information technology (Galliers and Sutherland 1991).

In practice, however, such assumptions do not always hold. Implementa-tion of information systems in the public sector is far from problem-free, and the UK National Health Service has been no exception. A number of IS failures have been blamed on lack of adequate IS management and development skills, including several that were well-publicised:

- failure of the Wessex regional health authority computer system, estimated to have cost the taxpayer up to £60.6 million (US$100 million);

- failure of the London ambulance service computerised despatching system, which led to severe delays in the arrival of paramedics at emergency situations;
- problems with the hospital information support systems project, which yielded only around £3 million- (US$5 million-) worth of savings on a total spend of at least £103 million (US$170 million).

Collins (1997) also reports the problems of systems which were installed by hospitals that did not have the skills and experience to cope with the management of complex computer projects. The result has been that a number of projects, like HISS, have cost healthcare organisations substantially more than any measurable or even remotely likely benefits can justify.

CONCLUSIONS AND RECOMMENDATIONS

We have argued that the assumptions on which many of the existing SISP frameworks are based makes them difficult to apply in public, not-for-profit organisations; even in those undergoing reforms which seek to introduce private sector ideas. Public healthcare organisations which attempt to apply such frameworks without recognising these limitations do so at their peril. The result is likely to be alienation of clinicians, complacency and ambivalence towards technology. This in turn means:

- unnecessary collection and analysis of information on which plans for healthcare are based;
- organisational discord due to the incompatibility of the planning process with other internal processes;
- poor decision making and unnecessary expenditure on expensive and perhaps inappropriate technologies.

Furthermore, fear of failure and the pace of technological change could lead to stagnation in the delivery of healthcare.

Approaching strategic information systems planning in the public sector: recommendations

Gaining an understanding of the business or organisation that an information system is to serve has been seen as a prerequisite for the development of information systems (Checkland and Scholes 1990). But if development is to be more closely allied to strategic planning, then 'understanding the business served' can no longer be restricted to investigating the present business procedures. Information systems professionals must be able to comprehend and perhaps contribute to the debates about what the organisation might or might not aim at, and how it might strive to achieve these objectives in the future. The need therefore arises for IS practitioners to understand the images which organisation members have of their organisation and its environment; as one would expect, IS thinking is becoming increasingly influenced by the models of organisations used in the management and social sciences (Lewis 1994).

The NHS in the UK has been described as:

> An extraordinary segmented and incoherent series of interlocking systems and groups divided on every conceivable axis: political and managerial; professional and non-professional; local and regional; and of course geography and care group. Overlaid on top of this mosaic are the vagaries of changing political ideologies, the instabilities caused by the political economy of resource allocation; the changing interfaces with local government and the voluntary sector, and the ever present difficulties of determining and evaluating ends and means in healthcare. The culture of panics and problems and the dispersion of power all add to the picture of fragmentation and incoherence.
>
> (Pettigrew *et al.* 1992: 292)

There is a paradox between the taken-as-given rational, mechanistic metaphor of organisations which pervades SISP frameworks and the image of messiness described by Pettigrew *et al.* across all dimensions of this public sector organisation. The notion that IT can be used competitively within such an environment is untenable when profound issues regarding the provision of healthcare abound.

There are areas of organisational theory and practice which could be usefully employed within a public healthcare environment to develop SISP to support the delivery of patient care. The need for inter- and intra-organisational negotiation and bargaining is evident, where advocates for patients and guardians of resources share mutual concerns. But how can these negotiations become more visible and meaningful so that planners, developers and users can usefully contribute to the SISP activity? One clue lies in an understanding of metaphor.

Metaphorical thought is commonplace. Abstractions and enormously complex situations are routinely understood via metaphor. The extensive and mostly unconscious use of metaphor could provide a useful contribution to information systems theory if made more explicit. Morgan (1986) uses eight organisational metaphors to provide insights into the study of organisations. These images view organisations as: machines, organisms, brains, cultures, political systems, psychic prisons, flux and transformation, and instruments of dominance. In public healthcare, the formulation of SISP may benefit at a national, regional and local level by moving away from the mechanistic and organismic metaphors. Mason (1991) and Walsham (1993) have highlighted the weaknesses of these particular metaphors; in particular, shortcomings in the reconciliation of conflicts, politics and power struggles which are endemic in reforming public sector organisations. New metaphors are therefore required.

Metaphors of discourse, negotiation and exchange

Walsham (1993: 158) suggests 'the formation of IS strategy can be viewed as a process of continuous discourse. This discourse is a way of communicating meaning, centred on norms and values, and linked to power in relation to others.' He describes the communication of this meaning as an 'enactment process in which individuals select and communicate ideas, concepts and plans; these embody particular views of the way the world is or should be; and their communication through language is inextricably interlinked to the maintenance and change of power relations'. Different actors contribute to the process of IS strategy through their own particular organisational agendas and interests.

SISP can therefore be viewed as a process of discourse and communication. It can also, and similarly, be viewed as a process of negotiation and exchange, following ideas that analyse organisations as negotiated orders (Strauss *et al.* 1963).

Ciborra (1981), for example, suggests a new theory of information systems centred on the notions of 'exchange' and 'contract', with organisations seen as the outcome of continuous and periodic contractual arrangements. He argues that:

> a contractual perspective can help in the planning and designing of information systems which is isomorphic to functioning of institutional arrangements such as markets, bureaucracies and groups. These are seen as networks of contracts and exchanges between opportunistic members, so that games, exchanges and contracts become the object of analysis . . . the product of negotiation (contracts, understandings, agreements, 'rules', and so forth) all have temporal limits, for eventually they would be reviewed, re-evaluated, revised, revoked or renewed.
>
> (Ciborra 1981: 126)

Using soft systems thinking

Using these alternative metaphors will help stakeholders to conceive of strategic information systems planning in a different way. However, they also need some further tools to uncover the processes of negotiation, bargaining and interaction within organisations. These tools may be provided by systems thinking.

System theorists proposed the distinctive idea of using the concept of 'a system' – a set of inter-related elements which are connected together in an organised way and which do something – as the basis for making sense of some part of the real world. The system concept, it was argued, could provide the basis for a holistic approach to analysis which was not solely concerned with the nature of individual problem components but also with their organisation and the relationships between them.

Within the single application area of management and organisational science there are many different approaches to using the same basic concepts of systems thinking. The variants which have had most influence are systems engineering, systems analysis, classical operational research, systems dynamics and computer system analysis. All assume:

- that the 'system' under investigation is not problematical;
- that the system's objectives can be defined;
- that an alternative means of achieving these objectives can be modelled and compared using some declared performance criteria, enabling a suitable selection to be made of the most desirable form; this can then be implemented and monitored.

The term 'hard systems thinking' has been used to distinguish this type of approach (Checkland 1981; Checkland and Scholes 1990). The key characteristic of such thinking is the assumption that the world is systemic: made up of systems which exhibit the properties of systems (e.g. emergence, hierarchy, communication and control). Checkland's alternative and rather different stance is that whilst the world is problematic the process of inquiry into the world can be organised as a learning system. This is referred to as 'soft systems thinking'; the most sharply expressed version of this is known as soft systems methodology (SSM) (Checkland 1994).

Soft systems methodology has been applied fairly readily to the information systems domain generally. An example of this application is provided in Figure 14.1 (modified slightly from Bell and Wood-Harper 1992).

Soft systems thinking has major implications for information strategy formulation in particular:

> as an organisation steadily learns and reconstitutes itself, in a changing environment, rethinking the meanings it attributes to its world, it will need to have available a process by which the nature and context of the required information flows can be rethought and reprovided.
>
> (Checkland and Scholes 1990: 312)

Strategy formulation which requires the intervention of human agents is unalterably subjective and therefore anyone wishing to be involved in guiding this particular area of human activity has to accommodate both their own subjectivity as well as the subjectivity of those with whom they work. The potential for using SSM for information strategy development is therefore considerable, and has been explored by Checkland and Holwell (1993) (see also Checkland 1987).

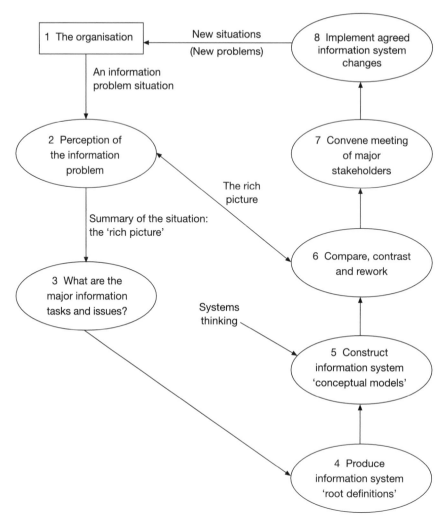

Figure 14.1 Soft systems methodology procedure for information systems
development

Within commercial organisations, Ormerod (1995) has used features from
a variety of soft approaches to complement each other through various
stages of the strategy development process. A scenario-based approach to
strategy development based on SSM has also been developed (Galliers 1992).
These approaches appear to offer substantially more insights into the development of SISP in complex contexts – such as public sector organisations
undergoing reform – than other more rational and mechanistic frameworks.

The use of soft approaches in SISP is not without its problems
(Hirschheim *et al.* 1995; see also Flood and Jackson 1991):

- There are potentially weak links between SSM models and the detailed considerations of data and technology which enable a strategy to provide a technical architecture aligned with wider IS and business strategies.
- SSM does not reflect whether there is potential for misuse of the methodology in realising the goals of one stakeholder group in the organisation at the expense of another. This may be particularly true of strategic exercises.
- Attempts to analyse and mitigate potential distortions and communication barriers while seeking an accommodation of views could be overlooked.

Some of these problems can be addressed. For example, Multiview (Avison and Wood-Harper 1990) and rapid planning methodology (Bell and Wood-Harper 1992) have integrated soft approaches to human systems components with harder approaches to data and technology components. These methods have been applied in public sector contexts.

Soft approaches therefore do provide a way of moving forward in conceptualising SISP for public sector organisations and, in SSM, provide some tools and methods for implementing SISP in public sector organisations.

Summary

The proliferation of SISP frameworks available for the practitioner is, on the whole, dominated by the mechanistic and organismic metaphors of organisations. While these frameworks may have some (limited) value for the private sector, they may be inappropriate in public sector organisations where changing contexts of reform, cultural conservatism, and conflicting values are present.

SISP formulation would benefit from the more explicit use of alternative organisational metaphors to think about the context in which SISP is applied. New metaphors can enrich perceptions, in particular the image of public sector organisations as 'negotiated orders'.

The processes that constitute these orders are systemic in nature and are structurally, politically and culturally bound. They are infused with the power of professional and semi-professional groups, both formal and informal, that deliver public services and that manage the resource consequences of this activity. In order to develop a meaningful participative information strategy within such organisations the use of soft approaches in general and soft systems thinking in particular should be considered as a device to uncover and bring to the surface the activities that constitute negotiated orders.

The use of soft systems thinking to reveal these orders would provide a more coherent means to enquire into the processes which SISP should be supporting. This in turn provides a framework to structure the organisation to provide the best possible outcomes for its staff and clients.

Conception–reality gaps

Strategic information systems planning frameworks are based upon a number of conceived assumptions that do not match reality. This is true in the private sector. For example, Wilson's (1989) study of UK private firms highlighted the inadequate conceptions of SISP frameworks. In reality, strategy formulation in many firms did not take place in a rational analytical way, and managers often experienced considerable problems in implementing the strategies they formulated.

Likewise, there is growing evidence that many of the well-documented private sector strategic IS projects such as Baxter's ASAP, McKeeson's Economist, American Airline's SABRE and the French videotex system Teletel have been strongly shaped by factors like chance, serendipity, trial and error, or even gross negligence (Ciborra and Jelassi 1994). It is only *post hoc* that these projects have been held up as successful examples of strategic information systems planning.

But whatever the gaps between SISP framework conceptions and private sector realities, the gap between these conceptions and public sector realities appears greater. This was seen above in conceptions that particularly did not apply to the public sector. These false conceptions related to the process, objectives, skills and management dimensions of the ITPOSMO model (see Chapter 3), and included:

- the use of IS for profit-driven competitive advantage;
- the presence of unitary organisational objectives;
- the apolitical nature of decision making;
- the presence of skilled support for implementation.

By comparison, commercial organisations have more clearly defined goals, roles and performance expectations, and they are influenced less by continuing alterations in government policy or by direct interventions from government. This may explain why many of the private sector-inspired SISP frameworks seem to regard politics, conflicting and irreconcilable organisational objectives and measures of performance as unimportant or unproblematic.

It has been argued that the basis for strategic success or failure is the microcosm of the decision makers: their inner conceived model of reality and the set of assumptions that structures their understanding of the unfolding organisational environment and of factors critical to success (Mason and Mitroff 1981). Little attention has been paid in the planning literature to the way in which managers make sense of the world within which they interact and the manner in which shared conceptions affect what they do. This may, however, be due to a lack of suitable frameworks, particularly in the US, which bring out and accommodate such views, rather than managers' inability to recognise alternative perspectives. It is so much easier to sustain the conceptual fantasy that we can plan the unknowable than it is to delve into the reality of group processes that obstruct complex learning in organisations (Stacey 1994).

REFERENCES

Audit Commission (1995) *For Your Information: A Study of Information Management and Systems in the Acute Hospital*, London: HMSO.

Avison, D. and Wood-Harper, T. (1990) *Multiview: An Exploration in Information Systems Development*, Oxford: Blackwell Scientific.

Bell, S. and Wood-Harper, T. (1992) *Rapid Information Systems Development*, London: McGraw-Hill.

Beynon-Davies, P. (1994) 'Information management in the British National Health Service: pragmatics of strategic data planning', *International Journal of Information Management* 14, 2: 84–94.

Bloomfield, B.P. and Coombs, R. (1990) *Information Technology, Control and Power: The Centralisation and Decentralisation Debate Revisited*, CROMTEC Working Papers Series, Manchester: School of Management, UMIST.

Checkland, P.B (1981) *Systems Thinking, Systems Practice*, Chichester, W. Sussex: John Wiley.

Checkland, P.B. (1987) 'A note on the use of systems thinking in provision of health care', *Journal of Applied Systems Analysis* 14: 129–130.

Checkland, P.B. (1994) 'Conventional wisdom and conventional ignorance: the revolution organisation theory missed', *Organization* 1, 1: 29–34.

Checkland, P.B. and Holwell, S. (1993) 'Information management and organisational processes: an approach through soft systems methodology', *Journal of Information Systems* 3, 1: 13–16.

Checkland, P.B. and Scholes, J. (1990) *Soft Systems Methodology in Action*, Chichester, W. Sussex: John Wiley.

Ciborra, C. (1981) 'Information systems and transaction architecture', *Policy Analysis and Information Systems* 5, 4: 305–324.

Ciborra, C. and Jelassi, T. (eds) (1994) *Strategic Information Systems: A European Perspective*, Chichester, W. Sussex: John Wiley.

Collins, T. (1997) 'DoH considers abolishing NHS management group', *Computer Weekly* 6 February: 2.

Computer Weekly (1997) 'Only 10% of IT strategy working in complete harmony with business', 15 May: 1.

Coote, A. and Hunter, D.J. (1996) *New Agenda for Health*, London: Institute for Public Policy Research.

Doyle, J.R. (1991) 'Problems with strategic information systems frameworks', *European Journal of Information Systems* 1, 4: 273–280.

Flood, R. and Jackson, M. (eds) (1991) *Critical Systems Thinking: Directed Readings*, Chichester, W. Sussex: John Wiley.

Galliers, R.D. (1991), 'Strategic information systems planning: myths, realities and guidelines for successful implementation', *European Journal of Information Systems* 1, 1: 55–64.

Galliers, R.D. (1992) 'Soft systems, scenarios and the planning and development of information systems', *Systemist* 14, 3: 146–159.

Galliers, R.D. and Sutherland, A.R. (1991) 'Information systems management and strategy formulation: the "stages of growth" model revisited', *Journal of Information Systems* 1, 2: 89–114.

Hirschheim, R., Klein, H. and Lyytinen, K. (1995) *Information Systems Development and Data Modelling: Conceptual and Philosophical Foundations*, Cambridge: Cambridge University Press.

Hunter, D. (1996) 'There is a third way forward', *Health Service Journal* 28 November: 20.

Keen, J. (ed.) (1994) *Information Management in Health Services*, Buckingham: Open University Press.

Lacity, M. and Hirschheim, R. (1995) 'Benchmarking as a strategy for managing conflicting stakeholder perceptions of information systems', *Journal of Strategic Information Systems* 4, 2: 165–185.

Lederer, A.L. and Mendelow, A. (1986) 'Issues in information systems planning', *Information and Management* 10, 5: 245–254.

Lederer, A.L. and Sethi, V. (1994) 'Meeting the challenges of information systems planning', in R.D. Galliers and R.S.H. Baker (eds) *Strategic Information Management*, Oxford: Butterworth-Heinemann.

Lewis, P. (1994) *Information System Development*, London: Pitman Publishing.

McGuire, A., Henderson, J. and Mooney, G. (1988) *The Economics of Healthcare*, London: Routledge & Kegan Paul.

Mason, R. (1991) 'The role of metaphors in strategic information systems planning', *Journal of Management Information Systems* 8, 2: 11–30.

Mason, R. and Mitroff, I. (1981) *Challenging Strategic Planning Assumptions*, New York: John Wiley.

Morgan, G. (1986) *Images of Organization*, London: Sage.

Ormerod, R. (1995) 'The role of OR in information systems strategy development', *International Transactions on Operational Research* 2, 1: 17–27.

Peel, V. (1997) 'Evaluation of the National Health Service nationwide resource management programme in England', paper presented at conference on 'Public Sector Management in the Next Century', 29 June–2 July, University of Manchester, Manchester, UK.

Pettigrew, A., Ferlie, E., and McKee, L. (1992) *Shaping Strategic Change,* London: Sage.

Porter, M.E. (1985) *Competitive Advantage: Creating and Sustaining Superior Performance*, New York: Free Press.

Porter, M.E. and Millar, V.E. (1985) 'How information gives you competitive advantage', *Harvard Business Review* July–August: 149–160.

Price Waterhouse (1994) *Information Technology Review 1994/1995*, London: Price Waterhouse.

Ruohonen, M. (1991) 'Stakeholders of strategic information systems planning', *Journal of Strategic Information Systems* 1, 1: 15–28.

Singh, S.K. (1993) 'Using information technology effectively', *Information and Management* 24: 133–146.

Smircich, L. and Stubbart, C. (1985) 'Strategic management in an enacted world', *Academy of Management Review* 10, 4: 724–736.

Stacey, R.D. (1994) *Strategic Management and Organisational Dynamics*, London: Pitman Publishing.

Strauss, A. *et al.* (1963) *The Hospital and its Negotiated Order*, New York: Free Press.

Thomas, R., Wainwright, D., Robinson, J., Waring, T. and Maguire, S. (1994) 'Has HISS run out of steam?', *Health Service Journal*, 28 July: 24–26.

Waema, T. and Walsham, G. (1990), 'Information system strategy formulation', *Information and Management* 18, 1: 29–39.

Walsham, G. (1993) *Interpreting Information Systems in Organisations*, Chichester, W. Sussex: John Wiley.

Ward, J., Griffiths, P., and Whitmore, P. (1990) *Strategic Planning for Information Systems*, Chichester, W. Sussex: John Wiley.

Wilson, T.D. (1989) 'The implementation of information systems strategies in UK companies: aims and barriers to success', *International Journal of Information Management* 9, 4: 245–258.

15 Reengineering public sector organisations using information technology

Kim Viborg Andersen

Abstract: Business process reengineering, although initially developed for and within the private sector, is an approach that can form a valuable part of information age reform if it can transform the work processes of public sector organisations. Information technology (IT) has played a central role in reengineering. This chapter therefore describes many ways in which information technology can be used to support public sector reengineering, including applications identified from analysis of the 'political value chain'. Nevertheless, IT-supported reengineering originated from technical/rational organisational models that do not necessarily reflect the realities of the public sector. The chapter therefore proposes the concept of PUblic sector Process REBuilding (PUPREB): an approach to reengineering that includes a special awareness of the public sector context.

BACKGROUND

With government expenditure on information technology (IT) growing annually, public sector stakeholders want some quantitative or qualitative return on this investment. This could involve cost savings through a reduction in staffing levels, improvements in the quality of service to internal and external clients, or an increase in the range of services offered. Unfortunately, new government information systems (IS) have often failed to produce these returns, creating a continual source of vexation for government officials.

How should governments deal with the criticism provoked by the burgeoning IT budgets and the inability of IT to fulfil expectations? One method has been to change – where appropriate – from an information technology approach to an information systems approach. In other words, to expand the range of factors taken into account during the process of development and implementation from the solely technical to also encompass human, organisational and environmental issues. The rationale here is that these latter issues are fundamental to IS success and failure.

Another method, not mutually exclusive with the first, has been to change to a process approach. Recent studies have highlighted the importance of internal and external work processes at both macro and micro levels in the organisation. There has also been considerable interest in the relationships between information technology, business process reengineering and organisational transformation.

Aspects of the first method are discussed and analysed in Chapters 2 and 3. In this chapter, we focus on the latter method, taking a closer look at the concepts underlying business process reengineering (BPR) and discussing whether and how they can be applied in the public sector by using information technology. Two main points are emphasised.

First, the concepts of business process reengineering need to be modified somewhat within the context of the public sector. Certainly, in line with Taylor *et al.* (1997), we note that the public sector is being transformed from a professionalised and functionally organised bureaucracy into new organisational patterns. However, this type of transformation prompts a broad range of questions about context and values. Such questions suggest that some of the underlying assumptions of BPR may not hold in the whole public sector, for example those about the potential for true 'clean slate' transformation.

As a modification of BPR, we therefore introduce the concept of public sector process rebuilding (PUPREB). Although based on BPR, this includes a special appreciation of public sector context and values. While BPR has been seen as a theoretical means for reinventing government and governance, for cutting red tape and for rightsizing or downsizing (Osborne and Gaebler 1993), PUPREB is more modest in its promise to reform these areas through the use of information technology.

This brings us to a second focus of this chapter. BPR and information systems have been closely associated with the concept of the 'value chain'. Whilst the specifics of the private sector value chain as taught in business schools will not be entirely appropriate to the public sector, the overall concept can be applied. We therefore propose a 'political value chain' that can guide IT-supported reengineering in the public sector.

Reengineering the public sector

Hammer and Champy (1993: 32), the fathers of the reengineering concept, define reengineering as 'the fundamental rethinking and radical redesign of business processes to achieve dramatic improvements in critical contemporary measures of performance such as cost, quality, service and speed'. The reengineered organisation also becomes process-oriented:

• processes are recognised and named;

- everyone is aware of processes;
- process measurement is performed;
- process management is the norm.

However, the origins of business process reengineering lie firmly within the private sector. We are therefore prompted to ask three questions, discussed below.

Can BPR be applied in the public sector?

The BPR approach emphasises that changes in processes are to be drastic rather than incremental. Also, the approach points to broad, cross-functional processes and, if needed, a radical change in such processes. All of this means that BPR is predicated on the idea of radical organisational transformation, with a high risk of failure. How does all this square with a public sector context?

Traditionally, the public sector has been characterised by stability and risk aversion. Not surprisingly, then, when ideas about BPR were first floated the public administration community did not applaud them. Rather, they jeered that BPR applied in the public sector would, at worst, lead to serious misjudgements and to actions inconsistent with the 'spirit' of the public sector.

Yet, as we stand at the turn of the twentieth century, we can see this traditional model changing. We might no longer be so quick to say that taking risks is uncharacteristic of the public sector. We might no longer be so quick to say that radical transformation is uncharacteristic of the public sector. Table 15.1 summarises some of the key current trends in the public sector, all of which encompass some fairly radical changes in the way that government conducts its business.

As we have known for some time from the work of writers such as Osborne and Gaebler (1993), these kinds of transformations are not just rhetoric but are really taking place. Taking the third table entry as an example, there has been increasing use of alternative mechanisms for government. Table 15.2 summarises the situation in the Netherlands and the UK, indicating the substantial proportion of public spending now being channelled through such alternative mechanisms.

Parts of the public sector therefore are changing radically and taking risks, so these issues present no overwhelming logical barrier to the idea of business process reengineering in the public sector. As we shall see later, however, this should not blind us to the fact that the public sector *is* different from the private sector.

Table 15.1 Key trends in the public sector

Key trend	Implications for the public sector
Reinventing democracy	Treating citizens as customers and including them in the process of governance
Information technology	Providing dramatically better ways of simplifying government and involving citizens via the rapid advances in IT
Alternative mechanisms for government	Increasing use of quasi-autonomous non-governmental organisations (quangos)
Outcomes and performance	Identifying and measuring desired outcomes, reporting results and holding government accountable for those results
Partnerships	Creating new intergovernmental, public–private and labour–management partnerships
Cutting red tape	Developing strategies for results requiring reform of human resource, budget, procurement and other rule-based systems by cutting red tape
Rightsizing/downsizing	Cutting the size of the public sector workforce in accordance with output needs or to increase efficiency
Community-based strategies	Implementing strategies to achieve better service outputs for resources expended, and including citizens and capitalising on their diversity within these strategies

Source: Adapted from NAPA (1996)

Should BPR be applied in the public sector?

The very idea of reengineering processes originates from basic questions: Are we doing our business in the optimal way? Are we doing our job well enough? Are we giving it all we've got? These questions may not be so clearly understood in the public sector as they are in the private sector, but they are just as relevant.

Reinvention may mean that governments should be as small as possible and contract out tasks as much as possible, but the core of the public sector still needs to be in optimal working order. On top of that, if all existing work procedures are merely outsourced without any reorganisation, little will be accomplished and counterproductive outcomes may emerge.

Not surprisingly, then, NAPA (1996) also lists BPR as a further key trend for public sector reform to add to those listed in Table 15.1. NAPA (1994a: 1) defines reengineering within the public sector as 'a radical improvement approach that critically examines, rethinks, and redesigns mission-delivery processes and subprocesses, achieving dramatic mission performance gains from multiple customer and stakeholder perspectives'. It is seen as a key part of a process management approach for optimal performance that continually evaluates, adjusts or removes processes.

Table 15.2 Status of semi-public organisations and quangos in the Netherlands and the UK

Variable	Netherlands	UK
Number of organisations defined as quangos and semi-public organisations	500	5,521
Number of employees in quangos and semi-public organisations	20,000	65,419
Total annual budget of quangos and semi-public organisations	US$18.5bn	US$70bn
Total budgets of quangos and semi-public organisations as a proportion of total public budget	18%	30%

Sources: Netherlands data from Leuw and Van Thiel (1996), UK data from Weir and Hall (1994)

Is BPR being applied in the public sector?

Yes it is. As part of their public sector reform efforts, almost all governments have been undertaking process reengineering, although not all have explicitly recognised this. Examples of BPR in the public sector include:

- In Phoenix, Arizona, a new 20 story city hall towers over the city's downtown center. City officials insisted that the building's layout emphasize citizen service. Now Phoenix bundles its city hall services at 'super counters' and eliminates the endless maze citizens once had to negotiate in going from door to door, floor to floor, to obtain service forms and signatures.
- The Social Security Administration now issues social security cards in three to five days instead of six weeks, processes retirement or survivor claims in 13 to 18 days instead of one month, does cost-of-living adjustments in one day instead of three weeks, and issues an emergency payment in three to five days instead of 15 days. . . .
- In Minnesota, the Department of Revenue creates new processes for their sales tax system, paying attention to both the department's internal operational capability and to helping taxpayers willingly determine their tax liability, file accurate information, and pay on time. The reengineering has resulted in a more accurate tax compliance by at least $50 million annually.
- In the United Kingdom, the Royal Mail revamps postal operations through strategic visioning and organisation-wide process management efforts, including a strong performance measurement piece which cascades process goals from the top of the organization to the individual level. The result is postal operations recognized as 'world class'.

(NAPA 1994b: 2)

ANALYSIS: INFORMATION TECHNOLOGY AND REENGINEERING IN THE PUBLIC SECTOR

If business process reengineering does have a place in the public sector, what does this mean for information technology?

As a starting point, we can study the following list of practices recommended by the OECD (1995) for obtaining greatest organisational benefits from information systems:

- enhancing management, planning and control of IS functions;
- using technology to redesign and improve administrative processes;
- providing better access to quality information;
- harnessing the potential of new technologies;
- developing and applying standards;
- attracting and retaining high-calibre IS professionals;
- increasing research into the economic, social, legal and political implications of new IS opportunities;
- assessing experiences.

The second list item – using technology to redesign and improve administrative processes – suggests a role for IT in promoting or supporting reengineering. Within the context of the private sector, this role has been investigated and commented upon by a number of writers from the technical/rational school of organisational literature.

Besides the initial articles and books (Davenport and Short 1990; Hammer 1990; Hammer and Champy 1993), numerous other books have been published showing how information technology has supported BPR to effect dramatic and radical organisational change (e.g. Caudle 1995; Champy 1995; Davenport 1993). Davenport (1993: 12), for example, argues that information technology 'should be viewed as more than an automatic or mechanising force; it can fundamentally reshape the way business is done'. In other words, IT is seen as an all-powerful force changing the work that is done.

But what does this mean for the public sector? What transformational/BPR-supporting role does IT have to play here? We shall provide two examples of the way in which private sector approaches to IT and BPR can be converted and applied in the public sector. First, Davenport's (1993) work, which groups the impact of IT on process innovation into nine categories:

- *automational*: eliminating human labour from a process;
- *informational*: capturing process information for purposes of understanding;
- *sequential*: changing process sequence;
- *tracking*: closely monitoring process status and objects;
- *analytical*: improving analysis of information and decision making;
- *geographical*: coordinating processes across distances;

- *integrative*: coordinating between tasks and processes;
- *intellectual*: capturing and distributing intellectual assets;
- *disintermediating*: eliminating intermediaries from a process.

In Table 15.3, examples of each of these are given, showing their application in a public sector setting. Examples are provided of generic information systems and of more specific systems to support public sector service/product delivery and public sector internal logistical functions.

Of course, IT can be used to innovate processes across service delivery–logistical divisions. Some social welfare systems, for example, can encompass the first four types of system in doing this. They provide a one-stop service point for clients by allowing access to different welfare information systems through a single workstation; they track the progress of individual client's cases and issue alerts at required points; they provide support for decision making about the client, such as the type of benefits they require; and they draw together the work of several separate public agencies. Not only do such systems create a much keener awareness of work processes, they also both drive and need the reengineering of those processes in order for the information system to work properly.

There are many real-world examples of IT-supported reengineering. For instance, all four cases of BPR provided above involved the use of new IT-based information systems. To take another example, Singapore has been at

Table 15.3 IT-supported process innovation in the public sector

Generic information system	Service/product delivery	Internal logistical functions
Automational, informational, and sequential systems	Integrated service delivery via one-stop shops	Management information systems for personnel management
Tracking systems	Automated workflow systems to monitor and control case status in delivery of welfare services	Public asset management systems
Decision analysis systems	Systems for microanalysis and forecasting of welfare demand	Systems for microanalysis and forecasting of public finance
Inter-organisational communication systems (integrative and geographical)	Government-wide electronic mail	Electronic data interchange systems linked to suppliers
Intellectual asset systems	Expert systems to advise on client assessment	Textual composition
Disintermediation	Direct delivery of public services via the Internet	Automated ordering of stocks

Source: Based on Davenport (1993: 50–63)

the forefront of IT application in order to reengineer the work of government:

- More than 87 per cent of Singapore's population live in government-provided housing and the government's Housing Development Board manages more than one million properties. Starting in the early 1990s, the Board invested heavily to retool its information technology in support of process reengineering. The result was a one-stop service for customers and a reduction in waiting time from several hours to less than five minutes (Turban *et al.* 1996).
- Cars passing through a tollbooth on a Singapore highway do not need to toss money into a receptacle or to an attendant. Instead, smart cards with bar codes are read rapidly by means of telemetry, thus replacing or automating a large number of previous work processes (Teo *et al.* forthcoming).
- The Singapore government has set up an extensive electronic data interchange system that communicates trade-related data among international trade bodies, traders, intermediaries, financial institutions, and port and airport authorities. The implementation of this IS has thereby replaced or automated many work processes. This new information system and the concurrent reorganisation of other work processes in the Trade Development Board enabled the Board to handle more cases more quickly with a reduced complement of staff, thus significantly increasing efficiency (Teo *et al.* forthcoming).

A second private sector concept that can be adapted to public sector purposes is the value chain. Porter's (1985) description of the value chain allows a systematic analysis of the primary and secondary business processes in an organisation and of the way in which they do or do not add value to the organisation's outputs.

Several authors have argued that value chain analysis helps to identify application areas for IT that can transform the organisation (Laudon and Laudon 1998; Moreton and Chester 1996). Figure 15.1 identifies such potential application areas in a public sector setting. It covers both primary activities that relate to production and delivery of public services and support activities that relate to the internal administrative and logistical functions of the public sector.

In the public sector, there is typically no financial margin of value to be added by innovation. Instead, the public sector can partly add value by shaping the business environment and helping companies be more efficient and effective. In part, too, the public sector is legitimised by its political actions in the democratic domain. So the margin of value in Figure 15.1 is cast as some combination of the economic, the democratic and the technical. In recognition of this difference, the term 'political value chain' is used. Table 15.4 expands on this notion by identifying ways in which conventional

Primary activities	Automatic warehousing	Flexible service delivery	Links to suppliers, citizens, board members, politicians	Front office, one-stop shopping	Remote online access points
Support activities	Electronic data interchange/electronic commerce/electronic mail				
	Staff selection and scheduling systems				
	Planning models (budgeting, economic, demographic)				
	Groupware				
	Computer-aided design/multimedia				

The margin (economic, democratic, technical)

Figure 15.1 IT opportunities within the political value chain

Source: Constructed after inspiration from Moreton and Chester (1996: 56)

reengineering challenges would be modified for the public sector by following a political value chain approach. In all of these, IT has a potential role to play.

The next section goes on to analyse IT-supported reengineering in the public sector in more detail. Before proceeding, however, it is worth reflecting a little more on the relationship between IT and BPR. On the one hand, BPR benefits are heavily dependent on IT: 'to suggest that process designs be developed independently of IS or other enablers is to ignore valuable tools for shaping processes' (Davenport 1993: 50). None the less, IT is only a tool; a means to an end. In achieving those ends, 'managers . . . must begin to think of process change as a mediating factor between the IT initiative and economic return' (ibid.: 46). Thus, on the other hand, IT benefits are heavily dependent on BPR. Process modifications or adjustments should therefore accompany IT changes within organisations.

Rationality, politics and reengineering in the public sector

One criticism of BPR is that it represents 'old wine in new bottles' since it derives from the traditional 'classical school' of organisational thought:

> If we analyze the underlying philosophy of BPR, we can see immediately that it fits most closely with the classical school. Profit maximization is the key; little thought is given to more pluralistic outcomes; there is little concern for cultural, contextual issues other than to deal with them as obstacles to change; the process is a deliberate one – a rational analysis (undertaken by senior executives) of the key business processes in line

Table 15.4 Modifying key reengineering challenges for the public sector

Challenges for the process members, owners, coach and leaders	Conventional BPR definition	Political value chain definition
Intensification	Improving processes to serve current customers better	Enriching processes with existing clients and partners
Extension	Using strong processes to enter new markets	Using strong processes to reach marginalised client groups
Augmentation	Expanding processes to provide additional services to current customers	Expanding processes to provide additional services to current clients and partners
Conversion	Taking a process that you perform well and performing it as a service for other companies	Extending and sharing process strength with client groups, other public sector organisations, and business partners
Innovation	Applying processes that you perform well to create and deliver different goods or services	Applying processes that you perform well to create and deliver different public services
Diversification	Creating new processes to deliver new goods or services	Creating new processes to deliver new public services

Source: First two columns adapted from Hammer (1996: 198)

with a shared business vision that meets customer requirements. It seems, then, that our radical new departure from the staid approaches of yore is in fact more of a return of the classical approaches of the 1960s.

(Galliers 1994: 54)

One thing which marks out the classical school, and at least some of the analysis so far in this chapter, is that it adheres quite strongly to very rational conceptions of organisations. These tend to focus on the formal, the quantitative and the technical aspects of organisations. However, as noted in Chapter 3, there are very differing ways in which organisations may be conceived, and other schools of thought tend to focus on the informal, the qualitative and the human aspects of organisations. For example, the 'political game' perspective emphasises the importance of organisational politics, power games and informal groupings within organisational practice.

These two viewpoints – the rational/analytical and the political game – each have something very different to say about business process reengineering. Table 15.5 summarises these differences in the context of six critical

Table 15.5 Principles of BPR compared from rational-analytical and political game perspectives

Principle of reorganising the processes	Rational-analytical	Political game
Productivity	Non-problematic: • Stable implementation conditions • High degree of standardisation • Large number of transactions with a well-defined target group	Problematic: • Productivity itself is controversial • No stable implementation conditions • Flexible procedures
Clean slate	More or less possible: • Programme is self-contained • No discussion about goals	Impossible: • Controversy about goals and means
Strong management	Possible: • Top-down • Pyramid structure	Problematic: • Bottom-up • Arena structure
Process orientation	Rather easy: • Stable processes	Very difficult: • Flexible processes
Role of IT	IT is enabling: • Standardised information and transaction needs	Problematic role of IT: • Changing information and transaction needs
Creativity	Problematic: • Obstruction by organisational and legal procedures	Possible: • Controversy stimulates creativity

Source: Adapted from Thaens *et al.* (1997: 32)

aspects of BPR. It is obvious from the table that organisations which conform more closely to the political game perspective will find business process reengineering difficult. So what of the public sector? Thaens *et al.* (1997) provide a sample indicator to test the perspective to which public sector organisations conform. They distinguish between sequential (rational-analytical) and interdependent (political game) models of the public policy cycle:

> The sequential perspective sees the policy process as a rational process which contains well defined and sequential stages: development, decision-making, implementation, and monitoring . . . [The interdependent perspective] sees the formulation and implementation not as a rational-analytical process of design, but as a product of a political game, in which many interdependent actors with different goals and power resources, strategically interact.
>
> (Thaens *et al.* 1997: 29)

Some public sector organisations do fall into the rational-analytical category. They enjoy stable conditions for the implementation of policy with little or no political controversy or disagreement over goals and means. Organisations that gather and process information for government, such as national census bureaux, could be seen as belonging in this camp. Their policy environment is stable, and they undertake standardised, formalised and massive transactions that are readily amenable to IT-supported BPR.

Other public sector organisations, however, fall into the political game category. Thaens *et al.* (1997) concluded of the Dutch Tax Department, for example, that:

> Firstly, the specific law and policy in force and the general democratic principles applying to government organizations change the meaning of productivity as the main goal of BPR . . . [since these have to respect] the (democratic) principles of legal security, legal equality, the rule of law and the system of checks and balances. . . . Secondly, it is problematic for government organizations to start redesign with a clean slate as well as to make use of creative strategies . . . because of the regulatory connections with other government organizations, the strict budget regulations and the specific status of public servants.
>
> (Thaens *et al.* 1997: 34–35)

Similarly, research by Bjørn-Andersen and Chatfield (1997) showed that initial reengineering initiatives in organisations including government departments progressed incrementally, not in a 'clean slate' manner. This is, perhaps, to be expected, given the prevalence of 'politicking' within the public sector. A prominent example is the gap between vision and reality of Japan's information society (West *et al.* 1996). There has been tremendous rhetoric about increasing the use of IT in the Japanese public sector, and in society more generally. But institutional fights between different levels of government and between different ministries have created unwieldy implementation problems.

Where does this leave public sector reform? Given that reform does create instabilities and conflicts, it may be that there is a greater emergence of the political game model during reform. If so, we may be led to the conclusion that IT-supported reengineering is a necessary part of information age reform, and yet is made problematic by reform. To progress this potential dilemma, we propose the idea of public sector process rebuilding: an approach to reengineering that takes the specific context and conditions of the public sector into account. This can be seen as an approach in the tradition of 'soft BPR', which has emerged during the 1990s to emphasise human issues rather than just organisational shape (Coombs and Hull 1996).

CONCLUSIONS AND RECOMMENDATIONS

Conclusions

Originally, IT-supported reengineering was principally seen as the preserve of the private sector. Today this is no longer true. The use of IT in the public sector has taken a shift from routine automation to broader application areas, and it is seen as a vital device in transforming public organisations. Although it is often difficult to evaluate whether the transformation itself or the use of information systems has actually been successful, there are clearly cases in which they bring about new organisational forms, and new work/interaction patterns both within the organisations and in relation to the surrounding environment of citizens, politicians, companies and other public organisations.

However, IT-supported reengineering of the public sector can bring both benefits and woes:

- Virtual organisations and teleworking can be a vehicle for rebuilding public organisations, but they can also be a threat to managerial control and to organisational culture.
- Use of the Internet in local government can be a powerful tool in rebuilding a relationship with citizens and companies by means of the World Wide Web and electronic data interchange, but it can also be a waste of taxpayers' money, serving only bureaucratic interests and fortifying gate-keeping, rather than destroying it.
- Quangos, modernisation of budgeting methods and inter-/intra-organisational information systems can lead to clean-slate changes, but can also damage political decision making processes.

Without steering and commitment, the adoption of new information and communication technologies is not likely to break down gate-keeping, organisational routines or interaction patterns, and it will do even less to reduce organisational costs or to deliver better services. Similarly, there are likely to be major problems if the specific context of the public sector is not taken into account.

IT-supported reengineering in the public sector must therefore be both defended and upheld, but this requires a public sector-specific approach. Hence the idea of PUPREB, a public sector-specific approach to IT-supported reengineering that reflects the needs of public officials, citizens and politicians.

IT-supported reengineering in the public sector: recommendations

Low-risk automation has been proceeding relatively smoothly in the public sector during recent decades. However, we believe that higher-risk reengineering and paradigm-shifting uses of IT will increasingly appear in future as the reinvention of government gathers pace. The PUPREB concept seeks routes to minimise the risks and maximise the gains from these initiatives in ways that meet public sector needs. It attempts to glean some useful parts of BPR and the ideas on process innovation while taking a critical look at the concept's application in the public sector.

In a generic sense, this approach will involve three components:

- First, an explicit recognition of the public sector's political environment that coexists with any managerial rationalism. Some approaches to analysis and reengineering of processes in the public sector exclude the political dimension. Our message here, however, is as clear as day: leaving such considerations out of the analysis is at best a dead end. For better or for worse, politics does matter.
- Second, the PUPREB approach must strive for a balance between the individual and the collective level. In the public sector, affected individuals include a wide range of actors, such as elected officials, public employees, political activists, voters, taxpayers, members of interest groups and recipients of public goods and services. Collective political actors range from small groups (e.g. a local interest group) to mass organisations (e.g. a political party) to public organisations (e.g. a government department) to societal subsystems (e.g. the educational system) to international collectives (e.g. the United Nations) (Andersen and Danziger 1997). When IT is used to enable the reengineering of public processes, then needs at both levels must be kept in mind. This is a difficult task but, if one level is left out, it is easy to be caught between conflicting interests.
- Third, there needs to be continuous customer orientation. Apart from the obvious cases where citizens fill out a complaint form or public quangos are hammered by private entrepreneurs, it is often hard to know whether work processes in the public sector are organised in the most optimal manner. Who is to judge? According to one view, the answer is simple enough: the customer's perspective will judge whether rebuilding has been successful: 'Taking a process approach implies adopting the customer's point of view. Processes are the structure by which an organisation does what is necessary to produce value for its customers' (Davenport 1993: 7). Does this approach mean that the public sector and government are to be steered strictly by opportunistic means? Should they ultimately operate in pursuit of what all taxpayers want: lower taxes and more and better public services? Certainly, there may be problems in this of preferences that conflict or vary over time. However, if anyone is to benefit and therefore drive the process of public sector rebuilding, it has to be the consumer of public services, not the employees, the politicians or the institutions.

Researchers at the US National Academy of Public Administration have formulated six basic points for starting to reengineer in public administration. We have adopted their results and adjusted their list of critical factors for successful IT-supported reengineering in the public sector to form the basis of PUPREB (see Table 15.6). The table reminds us – as does the integrated approach to information age reform described in Chapter 2 – that it is not IT in itself that is interesting. It is merely a tool to help the key activities: ongoing improvement of public sector services and processes, the actual fulfilment of the organisation's mission and the overall steering of the organisation.

The point of departure is to understand what rebuilding is. There need to be valid reasons to rebuild the processes by using information technology because this requires organisational commitment and capacity to initiate and sustain. These first two points are extremely important since information technology can be used for other purposes, such as quality improvement. In short, not all situations and organisations are ready or suitable for rebuilding.

Third, we believe in adopting a management approach, yet we do not want to lose the benefits that come from integrating workers into the design and decision process that relates to major technological changes in work activities. It is important to set specific goals, but it is equally important to rebuild the structures that support these goals in connection with implementing the new information system. This requires that we know the work processes. Although this is the case in a large part of the public sector, our knowledge is in fact quite limited when it comes to items such as the flow of information, the sharing of information and manipulation of information, just to mention a few areas. However, if we do not know the work processes prior to rebuilding the structures, the outcome will depend more on luck than on professional responsibility, commitment and involvement.

Fourth, the keywords 'measurement' and 'expectations' should be considered carefully. Within the public sector, it is difficult, but not impossible, to measure the processes (including their inputs and outcomes). Likewise, the expectations from the stakeholders must be identified and tied to performance management. Naturally, this will be complicated by political instabilities such as elections and by the often rigid systems that customers must use to impose their influence on the content of the public service. Nevertheless, our message is that rebuilding public organisations is not successful if it is only able to increase the satisfaction of employees or provide information systems with a better user interface. The clue is that the expectations have to be known, and that the important ones are not the employees' expectations, regardless of whether they are short-term or long-term.

Fifth, rebuilding efforts are nevertheless dependent on support from the organisation's employees. Needless to say, incentives to change are more effective than threats. To that effect management of the rebuilding process should include internal communication and educational programmes as well as external training. However, it is not a wise strategy to rely solely on

Table 15.6 Critical success factors for rebuilding the public sector using information technology

Factor	Characteristics
Understand process re-engineering	Understand political process fundamentals
	Know what reengineering/rebuilding is
	Differentiate and integrate process improvement approaches
Build a case	Have necessary and sufficient business (mission and political delivery) reasons for the rebuilding process
	Have the organisational commitment and capacity to initiate and sustain the reorganisation
	Secure and sustain political support for the process
Adopt a process management approach	Understand the organisational mandate and set mission strategic directions and goals cascading to process-specific goals and decision making across and down the organisation
	Define, model and prioritise processes important for mission performance; do not start out with unimportant ones
	Practice 'hands on' senior management ownership of process improvement through personal responsibility, involvement and decision making
	Adjust organisational structures to improve support of process management initiatives
	Create an assessment programme to evaluate process management
Measure and track performance continuously	Create an organisational understanding of the value of measurement and how it will be used
	Tie performance management to customers' and stakeholders' current and future expectations
Practice change management and provide central support	Develop human resources management stretegies to support the rebuilding process
	Build information resources management strategies and a technology framework to support process change
	Create a central support group to assist and integrate rebuilding efforts and other improvement efforts across the organisation
	Create an overarching and project-specific internal and external communication and education programme
Manage projects for results	Apply clear criteria to determine what should be redesigned
	Place the project at the right level with a defined rebuilding team purpose and goals
	Use a well-trained, diversified, expert team and enable it to work well
	Follow a structured, disciplined approach

Source: Adapted from Caudle (1995)

external consultants in such matters (see Chapter 12 for a salutary example).

Finally, the table emphasises that the results should be kept in mind, not lost in the process. Therefore, it is important to start out by applying clear criteria for what should be rebuilt and what should be left intact. The same persons or groups must be held responsible for their outcome and rewarded for their successes. To some degree this is in conflict with the nature of process improvement, but it is imperative that whoever is successful (be it a person, a group or an entire organisation) should be rewarded to sustain the incentive to engage in further innovation of work processes.

Conception–reality gaps

Business process reengineering and its related use of information technology has generally been conceived according to a technical, rational model of organisations. This emphasises the formal structures and disinterested behaviours within the organisation. Although BPR has much to offer the public sector, we have seen that some of its underlying conceptions do not match the realities found in some public sector organisations.

Gaps highlighted relate to the objectives and management and structures dimensions of the ITPOSMO model (see Chapter 3) since traditional BPR conceptions do not match public sector realities of informal groupings, power games and self-interested behaviours. Within this conception–reality gap lie the seeds of potential failure in applying IT-supported reengineering to such organisations. We hope that the PUPREB approach is conceived in a way that closes this gap. Indeed, it is on this that its success or failure hinges: the extent to which it provides a match to the present realities of a significant part of the public sector.

REFERENCES

Andersen, K.V. and Danziger, J.N. (1997) 'Impacts of IS on capabilities, interactions, orientations, and values', in *Proceedings of the 3rd Pacific Asia Conference on Information Systems*, Brisbane, Australia: Queensland University of Technology.

Bjørn-Andersen, N. and Chatfield, A. (1997) 'Reengineering with EDI', in K.V. Andersen (ed.) *EDI and Datanetworking in the Public Sector*, Amsterdam: Kluwer.

Caudle, S.L. (1995) *Reengineering for Results: Keys to Success from Government Experience*, Washington, DC: National Academy of Public Administration.

Champy, J. (1995) *Reengineering Management: The Mandate for New Leadership*, New York: HarperCollins.

Coombs, R. and Hull, R. (1996) 'The politics of IT strategy and development in organisations', in W.H. Dutton (ed.) *Information and Communication Technologies: Visions and Realities*, Oxford: Oxford University Press.

Davenport, T. (1993) *Process Innovation: Reengineering Work Through Information Technology*, Boston, MA: Harvard Business School Press.

Davenport, T. and Short, J.E. (1990) 'The new industrial engineering: information technology and business process redesign', *Sloan Management Review* 31, 1: 11–27.

Galliers, R.D. (1994) 'IT and organisational change: where does BPR fit in?', paper presented at conference on 'Information Technology and Organisational Change', 28–29 April, The Netherlands Business School, Nijenrode University, Netherlands.

Hammer, M. (1990) 'Reengineering work: don't automate, obliterate', *Harvard Business Review* 90, 3: 104–112.

Hammer, M. (1996) *Beyond Reengineering: How the Process-centered Organization is Changing Our Work and Our Lives*, New York: Harper Business Press.

Hammer, M. and Champy, J. (1993) *Reengineering the Corporation: A Manifesto for Business Revolution*, New York: Harper Business Press.

Laudon, K.C. and Laudon, J.P. (1998) *Management Information Systems,* 5th edn, Upper Saddle River, NJ: Prentice-Hall.

Leuw, F.L. and Van Thiel, S. (1996) *Quango-cratization in the Netherlands*, PERC Occasional Paper no.13. Sheffield: Political Economy Research Centre.

Moreton, R. and Chester, M. (1996) *Transforming the Business: The IT Contribution*, London: McGraw-Hill.

NAPA (1994a) *Business Process Reengineering: Glossary*, Washington, DC: National Academy of Public Administration.
http://www.alliance.napawash.org/alliance/index.html

NAPA (1994b) *Business Process Reengineering: Overview*, Washington, DC: National Academy of Public Administration.
http://www.alliance.napawash.org/alliance/index.html

NAPA (1996) *Reinventing Government*, Washington, DC: National Academy of Public Administration.
http://www.alliance.napawash.org/alliance/index.html

OECD (1995) *Governance in Transition: Public Management Reforms in OECD Countries*, Paris: OECD.

Osborne, D. and Gaebler, T. (1993) *Reinventing Government: How the Entrepreneurial Spirit is Transforming the Public Sector*, New York: Penguin Books. First published Reading, MA: Addison-Wesley, 1992.

Porter, M.E. (1985) *Competitive Advantage: Creating and Sustaining Superior Performance*, New York: The Free Press.

Taylor, J., Snellen, I. and Zuurmond, A. (1997) *Beyond BPR in Public Administration*, Amsterdam: IOS Press.

Teo, H.H., Tan, B.C.Y. and Wei, K.-K. (forthcoming) 'Organizational transformation using electronic data interchange: the case of TradeNet in Singapore', *Journal of Management Information Systems*.

Thaens, M., Bekkers, V. and van Duivenboden, H.P.M. (1997) 'Business process redesign and public administration: a perfect match?', in J.A. Taylor, I. Snellen and A. Zuurmond (eds) *Beyond BPR in Public Administration*, Amsterdam: IOS Press.

Turban, E., McLean, E. and Wetherbe, J. (1996) *Information Technology for Management*, New York: John Wiley.

Weir, S. and Hall, W. (1994) *EGO-Trip: Extra-government Organisations in the United Kingdom and Their Accountability*, London: Charter 88.

West, J., Dedrick, J. and Kraemer, K.L. (1996) 'Reconciling vision and reality in Japan's NII policy', *Information Infrastructure and Policy* 5, 1: 15–39.

ACKNOWLEDGEMENTS

The author acknowledges comments received from Professor Ig. Snellen of Erasmus University and Assistant Professor Carsten Greve of Copenhagen University on earlier versions of this chapter. The Danish Research Council supported the research for this chapter.

16 Analysing performance information needs

Using framework approaches in a UK public healthcare organisation

Joan A. Ballantine and
Nigel Cunningham

Abstract: Public sector reform has greatly increased the need for performance information. The analysis of this need has often been somewhat haphazard yet, as described in this chapter, a number of performance measurement frameworks exist that can usefully be applied in the public sector. The example is presented here of a UK public healthcare organisation involved in a process of marketisation reform that separated service purchasers from service providers. This separation dramatically altered performance information needs. A performance measurement framework (the Results and Determinants Framework) was therefore used to conduct a 'gap analysis' between current information provision and stakeholders' new performance information needs. Application of the framework highlighted a number of issues that needed to be addressed. It also showed that the process of understanding and discussing information needs was at least as important as the application of any particular framework.

BACKGROUND

Performance measurement and UK public healthcare reform

The process of public sector reform has brought with it an increasing requirement for public sector organisations to develop performance indicators and to then measure their performance against those indicators (Blundell and Murdock 1997; see also Chapter 5). The UK public healthcare sector has been no exception, having undergone a series of substantial reforms during the 1980s and 1990s that had performance measurement implications.

One of the most significant and far-reaching reforms within the UK's National Health Service has been the marketisation that separated purchasers (health authorities and general practitioners) from providers (hospitals) of healthcare services following the publication of the Government White Paper, 'Working for Patients', in 1989. The separation subsequently led to the establishment of hospital 'trusts'. These are legally constituted entities which are, in many respects, similar to private sector organisations in terms of the way they are managed, although they are still subject to public accountability and control.

Trust hospitals, as providers of healthcare services, have responsibility for contracting with purchasers for the provision of services on an annual basis. Additionally, they assume responsibility for managing 'revenues' from purchasers in order to provide acceptable levels of service to patients. As a result, trusts have had to put in place managers who have a variety of responsibilities including planning, contracting, monitoring and controlling. The model of management, or clinical directorate model, adopted by trusts to cope with such responsibilities has varied widely, with some trusts employing managers from the private sector and others assigning such responsibilities to senior medical consultants and clinical nursing staff.

The reforms in the UK health service have undoubtedly altered the information needs of those managing both the provision and supply of services. This in turn has implied a need to reform management information systems, particularly those used to monitor aspects of organisational performance. For example, in order to 'compete' successfully in the 'internal market' created as a result of the reforms, hospital trusts need access to information which will enable them to negotiate contracts with purchasers and to monitor and control service levels and the use of resources. Additionally there is an increasing emphasis on monitoring aspects of service quality such as waiting times and clinical effectiveness because of evidence of widespread variations in the cost and outcomes of similar treatments in different provider organisations nationally.

Increasingly, therefore, the production of accurate, relevant and timely performance-related information within public healthcare organisations has become a key feature relevant to their success. However, the difficulties inherent in producing such information have been exacerbated by the inability of these organisations to extract meaningful data from existing operational systems (for example, patient administrative information systems).

It was recognised that a potential mismatch between existing information systems and the information needs of hospital trusts as a result of the reforms was inevitable. The UK National Health Service Management Executive therefore recommended the development of a full range of integrated, patient-based operational systems which were to be linked to an appropriate set of business and managerial systems, creating a hospital information support system (HISS) (see Figure 16.1). However, the costs associated

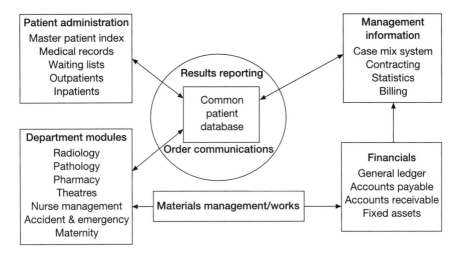

Figure 16.1 Integrated hospital information support system (HISS)

Source: Gowing (1994)

with developing HISS have largely been prohibitive to their widespread introduction within hospital trusts to date.

Regardless of the success or otherwise of HISS, there is a wide gap between reform-inspired information needs and current provision. In common with other public healthcare organisations, the hospital trust described in this chapter therefore addressed its information requirements by undertaking a 'gap analysis' that investigated the extent to which existing information systems met the needs of users, both clinical and managerial. It did so using a performance measurement framework.

In what follows, we first provide some background to the issue of performance measurement within public healthcare organisations, drawing on various performance measurement frameworks. Details of the case site are next discussed before going on to report on the findings of our gap analysis. Finally, the arguments for using a performance measurement framework in a public healthcare context are considered, before highlighting the lessons emanating from the case study which might lead to improved performance management information systems within public sector organisations generally.

Performance measurement frameworks

The issue of performance measurement (PM) has in the last decade been the subject of considerable research. In the late 1980s it was recognised that the PM literature was largely out of touch with the needs of modern organisations, which were seen to compete on a range of performance dimensions other than those of a financial nature (see, for example, Johnson and Kaplan 1987). Much of the criticism of traditional measures of performance stems from their focus on unidimensional, in particular financial, aspects of performance. Examples include earnings per share (EPS) and return on investment (ROI). However, Emmanuel and Otley (1985) argue that an organisation's success depends not only on the achievement of financial measures, but also on how well the organisation adapts to the external environment within which it exists. Success, they argue, is a multi-dimensional concept, and the aspects which relate to that success change both over time and between one individual or group in the organisation and another.

Increasing recognition of the need to monitor multiple dimensions of performance has led to the development of a substantial PM literature (see, for example, Brignall *et al.* 1992; Fitzgerald *et al.* 1991; Govindarajan and Gupta 1985; Govindarajan and Shank 1992; Gregory 1993; Kaplan and Norton 1992; Nanni *et al.* 1992; and Neely 1995). Checkland *et al.* (1990), amongst the earlier contributors to the literature, conceptualised performance measures by using the concept of a system and the measures necessary for it to remain stable over time. Their research led to the recognition of three levels of performance which, they argue, should be used to monitor a system's performance (see also Checkland 1981):

- *Effectiveness*: is the right thing being done?
- *Efficacy*: does the means work?
- *Efficiency*: is resource usage minimum?

However, they also recognised the importance of two additional criteria which might be considered in assessing performance:

- *Ethics*: is the transformation morally correct?
- *Elegance*: is it aesthetically satisfying?

Roebeke (1990) largely concurs, recognising the need to monitor effectiveness, efficacy and efficiency. He suggests that the three criteria constitute a hierarchy, within which measures of effectiveness are of more importance than measures of efficacy, which in turn are more important than measures of efficiency. Roebeke goes on to argue for the need to use multiple indicators of performance which help exemplify the inevitable tensions between contradictory organisational aims. He also addresses the time period over which it is appropriate to measure performance, and tentatively considers the number of performance indicators which it may be appropriate to adopt in any given system.

The PM literature has also seen the development of a number of PM frameworks, which have gone some way to addressing the unidimensional focus of the more traditional performance measures such as ROI and EPS. Among the more predominant of these frameworks are the Balanced

Scorecard (Kaplan and Norton 1992), the Performance Pyramid (Lynch and Cross 1991), and Performance Measurement in Service Businesses (Fitzgerald *et al.* 1991), all of which emphasise the importance of adopting a balanced set of performance measures to achieve organisational success.

The Balanced Scorecard, developed by Kaplan and Norton (1992), largely emanated from a research project which involved a select group of US Fortune 500 companies considered to be at the leading edge of PM at that time, and the ideas of various academics and consultants. The Scorecard considers organisational performance from four alternative perspectives:

- customers;
- the internal efficiency perspective;
- organisational innovation and improvement activities;
- the financial perspective.

The framework requires management to select a limited number of critical indicators within each of the four perspectives, each of which is grounded in an organisation's strategic objectives and competitive demands. The model is argued to aid benchmarking, and has been implemented in a number of US and UK organisations, such as Rockwater, Apple, Advanced Micro Devices, FMC Corporation (Kaplan and Norton 1993) and the National Westminster Bank (Business Intelligence Report 1993).

The Performance Pyramid was developed by Judson (1990) and subsequently improved by Lynch and Cross (1991) via discussions with hundreds of managers in the US and Europe and case studies of three companies. The pyramid is argued effectively to improve the links between an organisation's strategy and its operations by 'translating objectives from the top down (based on customer priorities) and measures from the bottom up' (Lynch and Cross 1991: 66). The framework contains four levels of objectives which address both internal efficiency and external effectiveness. With respect to external effectiveness, Lynch and Cross argue that the 'left' side of their pyramid is devoted to securing customer satisfaction. The development of a organisation's Performance Pyramid starts with the determination of an overall corporate 'vision', which is then translated into individual strategic business unit (SBU) objectives, where key market and financial measures are identified as a means of monitoring performance. From this, strategies are developed in order to achieve individual SBU objectives. In order to achieve the market and financial objectives set at the previous level of the pyramid, key measures of customer satisfaction, flexibility and productivity are also derived. At the base of the pyramid the key measures identified in the previous stage are converted into specific operational criteria (e.g. quality, delivery, cycle time and waste) which relate to individual departments or components of the business system within an organisation. According to Lynch and Cross (ibid), 'the pyramid is a useful model to describe how objectives are communicated down to the troops and how measures can be rolled up at various levels in the organisation'.

Fitzgerald *et al.* (1991) developed a framework of performance measurement applicable at the SBU level of organisations from their readings of relevant literature and their observations in some 11 large for-profit UK service businesses. They argue that PM and control systems should support an organisation's corporate objectives and competitive strategies. Performance measures are seen to be 'part of a feedforward–feedback control model in which progress against plans, budgets, standards and targets is monitored by the analysis of significant variances and the use of a balanced set of performance measures across various dimensions' (Brignall *et al.* 1992: 197). Figure 16.2 illustrates the various performance dimensions identified by Fitzgerald *et al.* (1991). The performance dimensions fall into two categories: the first includes financial performance and competitiveness dimensions which *measure the results* of competitive success; the second includes the four dimensions of quality, flexibility, resource utilisation and innovation, which they argue *determine* competitive success. While their research focuses on PM in service businesses, their findings are also applicable to non-service businesses.

Whilst the three frameworks of PM described above were developed as a result of research carried out in the private sector (in both the UK and the US), it is arguable that they are equally applicable to public sector organisations, as the aspects of performance they encompass are just as important in such organisations. However, it is questionable whether the frameworks in their present form encompass the totality of performance criteria appropriate to public sector organisations.

For example, none of the frameworks explicitly recognises the importance of an ethical dimension, yet there is a strong ethical aspect to the use of resources within many public sector organisations, which might limit framework application. Though Checkland *et al.*'s (1990) five broad indicators (effectiveness, efficiency, efficacy, ethics, elegance) may be more applicable within a public sector setting, the lack of specific measures may make their general application more difficult.

On the other hand, the more structured nature of, for example, the Balanced Scorecard and the Fitzgerald *et al.* (1991) Results and Determinants Framework, is likely to ease implementation in practice. Despite the limitations of these frameworks, their application within a public sector setting might go some way to facilitating discussion and improving understanding of the significant gaps in information provision. This, in turn, might lead to the design of better-balanced performance measurement systems within such organisations.

The case site

The site for this case study is a hospital trust situated in the southern part of Northern Ireland and working from one major general hospital site which

	DIMENSIONS OF PERFORMANCE	TYPES OF MEASURES
RESULTS	*Financial performance*	• Profitability • Liquidity • Capital structure • Market ratios
	Competitiveness	• Relative market share and position • Sales growth • Measures of the customer base
DETERMINANTS	*Quality of service*	• Reliability • Responsiveness • Aesthetics/appearance • Cleanliness/tidiness • Comfort • Friendliness • Communication • Courtesy • Competence • Access • Availability • Security
	Flexibility	• Volume flexibility • Delivery speed flexibility • Specification flexibility
	Resource utilisation	• Productivity • Efficiency
	Innovation	• Performance of the innovation process • Performance of individual innovations

Figure 16.2 The Results and Determinants Framework

Source: Fitzgerald *et al.* (1991)

has been operating as a provider of acute services since it opened in the early 1970s. The main site offers a full range of inpatient, outpatient and day-care services. The Trust has a bed complement of approximately 500, an annual estimated contract income of £45 million (US$68 million), and currently serves a population of approximately 250,000, with an average of 20,000 inpatients and 80,000 outpatients treated each year. Over 90 per cent of the Trust's work is contracted to one purchaser, the Southern Health and Social Services Board.

Our work with the Trust has been informed through two mechanisms. First, one of the authors has considerable experience working within the Trust in his role as computing and information services manager. Additionally, during a two-year period the second author repeatedly visited the Trust. This resulted in an extensive study of relevant information systems and associated documentation (both internal and external to the Trust) and the interviewing of a large number of clinical and nursing, administrative and managerial staff.

Organisational structure

The structure of the Trust, adopted in 1993 as a result of the reforms already described, consists of a number of clinical and managerial directors (e.g. Director of Medicine, Director of Finance), who report directly to the Chief Executive Officer. Clinical directors oversee two areas: support services (radiology, pathology and anaesthesia) and medical services (medicine, surgery, obstetrics and gynaecology). Lead consultants and senior nursing managers (formerly senior nurses) are responsible for managing individual directorates, which involves amongst other things monitoring the provision of clinical services, spending levels and patient activity levels. The clinical directorate model adopted by the Trust can be contrasted with that of other UK hospital trusts in which private sector managers have been employed to take direct responsibility for management activities.

The implication of the model adopted here is that clinical staff (i.e. senior nursing and clinical directors) are responsible for carrying out managerial tasks (e.g. planning, monitoring and control activities) for which they have received little management training to date, although limited support is provided from a central business directorate. The performance of directorates is monitored via formal meetings between senior nursing managers, clinical directors and supporting senior managers (for example, the contracts manager) which take place on a monthly basis, and *ad hoc* informal discussions which take place on a daily or weekly basis.

Development of information systems within the Trust

Prior to the reforms, a Patient Administrative System (PAS) provided much of the operational information needs of the Trust, related to the admission, transfer and discharge of patients. Despite being an operational system, the PAS met many of the management information needs at that time. However, the reforms have moved the emphasis to fulfilling contracts and the need to break even and contain costs. Together with increasing awareness of the requirement to improve the quality of patient care, this has contributed to a refocusing of performance measurement in hospital trusts.

In the early 1990s, the Trust addressed these new needs by considering how more-relevant performance information might be accessed by clinical and managerial staff. This need was partially addressed by the development of an executive information system (EIS) which enabled information to be extracted and aggregated from the PAS and reported along a number of dimensions. An additional development within the Trust has been the acquisition of a database populated with external PAS data, which is used primarily for benchmarking against selected external peer groups. Both developments have to some extent improved information provision within the Trust. However, as we shall see later, they have not led to the development of a balanced set of performance measures.

In the next section we discuss the results of using the Results and Determinants Framework of performance measurement (Fitzgerald *et al.* 1991) to conduct a gap analysis of emerging information needs and existing information provision within the Trust. The primary objective of the gap analysis was to aid the development of more balanced performance measurement information systems within the Trust. The Results and Determinants Framework was used in preference to other PM frameworks as it was developed specifically within service organisations and was therefore felt to be more appropriate than other frameworks. In addition, it makes explicit the distinction between results and determinants, which it was felt would be a useful mechanism for structuring discussion within the case organisation. However, we recognise that an alternative framework could have been equally useful.

ANALYSIS

In order to understand better the nature of performance measurement and monitoring within the Trust and the extent to which existing performance measurement IS met the information needs of the Trust, the Results and Determinants Framework was used to conduct a gap analysis. The gap analysis was facilitated by mapping existing performance information, derived from a variety of sources, against this framework. The sources included reports (the strategic direction statement, the corporate business plan), *ad hoc* activities such as surveys, and a range of information systems.

The mapping process enabled us to highlight not only the dimensions of performance which were subject to regular monitoring by the Trust, but also those which appeared to have a dominant position within the organisation and those which appeared to be absent. However, it should be made clear that the objective of the mapping process was not to derive 'ideal' performance measures for the Trust. On the contrary, the objective of the process was to facilitate identification and discussion of the dimensions currently monitored by the Trust and the extent to which they reflected a balanced set of perform-ance measures in the context of the organisation.

Gap analysis

The first two tables in the Appendix to this chapter provide examples of performance indicators which were suggested by the Results and Determin-ants Framework and which had already been captured through the mechan-isms of surveys and patient feedback. These go some way to addressing the total performance information needs of the organisation. In particular, both patient satisfaction surveys and nursing performance indicators reflect the importance of quality as a performance dimension within the Trust.

However, both surveys were carried out on an *ad hoc* basis, and no attempt was made to build up a picture of such performance over time or to integrate such data with other dimensions of performance, such as resource utilisation. No information system currently exists to support the structured monitoring and reporting of quality more generally, which invariably means that information dissemination regarding quality is sporadic at best. Quality is also monitored in terms of patient complaints, but no attempt is made to categorise the nature of complaints over time, making it difficult to monitor the effectiveness of policies designed to reduce complaints. In add-ition, the recording of complaints is not supported by a formal IS, making manipulation of the underlying data difficult and time-consuming.

Performance-related information is also collected via a number of com-puterised information systems. As noted, the Patient Administration System records patient admission, transfer and discharge data, including demo-graphic and diagnosis data. However, what is evident from our gap analysis is the lack of financial, quality and innovation measures which are monitored in conjunction with PAS data, and the lack of integration of patient data and other performance measurement data from elsewhere. The legacy systems in place across the Trust prohibit the integration of this data.

The development of the executive information system alluded to earlier has to some extent addressed many of the weaknesses of the PAS. The EIS uses a combination of internal data, extracted from the PAS, together with external performance data and is used to monitor aspects related to competitiveness (both at a regional and national level), flexibility of activities and resource utilisation. However, when we map the information reported in this informa-tion system against the Results and Determinants Framework, as shown in the final table of the Appendix to this chapter, it is apparent that very little performance information is captured and reported which enables the Trust to assess performance in terms of innovation, financial performance, clinical audit and outcomes. In addition, it is also apparent that aspects of quality monitored elsewhere (e.g. patient satisfaction, customer complaints) are not integrated within the EIS. This is particularly worrying, given that the EIS is widely used at senior levels (both clinical and managerial) to make key management decisions.

Extending our gap analysis to compare the performance dimensions considered relevant in the Trust's planning documents with that of the Results and Determinants Framework, it is clear that particular aspects of performance are seen as dominant. For example, the strategic direction statement for the next six years is dominated by measures of financial performance and resource utilisation: a reflection of the reporting requirements imposed on the Trust by government. Whilst strategic objectives are present across the range of dimensions identified in the Results and Determinants Framework, specific targets against which progress can be measured are absent, which makes them difficult to control and results in a lack of focus generally.

A similar picture emerges when we examine the corporate business plan. Whilst there are clearly strategic objectives across all six dimensions of performance, specific targets are in place for the financial and resource utilisation dimensions only. On a positive note, the corporate business plan does go some way to developing aspects of performance related to quality of service which are strangely absent from the strategic direction statement.

Overall, we can see that the Trust's performance measurement systems have developed in a somewhat piecemeal fashion as the result of a lack of guidance and understanding of what measures were important at different levels of the organisation, which a PM framework could have facilitated. Without such guidance, performance indicators have been adopted without adequate debate and discussion by the professionals responsible for the management of resources within the Trust.

As a result, whilst individual information systems go some way to addressing the needs of unidimensional performance measures, to date no system exists which integrates all relevant dimensions of performance needed to make management decisions (although the EIS has gone some way to addressing this). This undoubtedly has led to a lack of understanding of the relationship between the range of performance dimensions relevant to the Trust, for example, the relationship between financial performance and aspects of quality or flexibility.

More recently, this weakness has to some extent been addressed by the development of a specialty costing system, which aims to integrate financial and patient activity data. However, the lack of technical integration of existing systems will make this integration particularly difficult. Additionally, there is a lack of understanding and consensus regarding the trade-offs that need to be made among the performance dimensions currently monitored. Finally, there is a lack of appreciation within the Trust regarding the need to adopt a contingent approach to the design of performance measurement information systems such that systems are tailored to the needs of users at appropriate levels (e.g. board level, directorate level, and individual patient level).

CONCLUSIONS AND RECOMMENDATIONS

Conclusions

Better performance measurement is seen as fundamental to government reinvention (Osborne and Gaebler 1992). In part, this is because most components of public sector reform – but especially marketisation and improved resource management – require better performance management; hence, they require better performance measurement; hence, they require better performance measurement information systems. This chapter has considered the need to adopt a performance measurement framework within public sector organisations if the development of balanced performance measurement information systems is to result.

Such frameworks are not always easy to adopt. Problems include:

- the multi-dimensional nature of public sector organisational performance;
- the existence of interactions amongst performance dimensions, and the need to recognise the trade-offs which have to be made;
- the frequent mismatch between 'desirable' and actual performance measures;
- the difficulties of selecting appropriate and workable performance measures within the public sector.

Nevertheless, non-adoption of a framework to guide systems design seems even more problematic. The experiences of one public healthcare organisation described here illustrate non-adoption problems that include a lack of focus, a lack of systems integration across a range of relevant performance dimensions, and inadequate information provision when compared to users' needs. Use of performance measurement frameworks may therefore be seen as a technique integral to information age reform.

Performance measurement in the public sector: recommendations

Given the experiences of the Trust to date, we would argue that the adoption of a performance measurement framework within public healthcare organisations – and within public sector organisations more generally – is vital if such organisations are to achieve a balance between relevant performance dimensions so as to avoid an over-reliance on or dominance of one dimension of performance to the exclusion of others.

For example, it was clear from our review that financial performance is viewed as the dominant dimension of performance within the Trust. However, as suggested earlier, this reflects the reporting requirements imposed on the Trust by government. Whilst service delivery staff (clinicians and nursing staff) accept the need to monitor financial performance, they also recognise the need to balance it against other important aspects of service provision including, for example, medical outcomes and the timeliness of the service delivery process (e.g. the need to monitor waiting lists, responsiveness to patient demands, etc.). Here exists a paradox: whilst improvements in efficiency are ultimately achieved by improving the effectiveness of service delivery, many organisations are currently addressing improvements in efficiency by reducing costs across the board, with little or no consideration of how such reductions impact on service effectiveness.

The use of a performance measurement framework can highlight and facilitate discussion of the interactions between alternative dimensions of performance, which is important in order to ensure that no one dimension of performance is more dominant than others. For example, there will inevitably be interactions between aspects of quality (i.e. responsiveness to client needs) and financial performance (e.g. reduction of costs). The use of a framework makes more explicit the trade-offs which will have to be made as a result of the interactions of these various performance dimensions. For example, whilst reducing costs is likely to improve financial performance, it will probably have a detrimental effect on aspects of quality or flexibility which might only be resolved through the disregard of important ethical dimensions.

In the public sector it is often difficult to design appropriate performance measurement systems because of the existence of a wide range of stakeholders, who often have differing needs and conflicting objectives. For example, in public healthcare, whilst patients are likely to be more concerned with medical outcomes and the quality of care they receive, taxpayers may be more concerned with ensuring that value for money services are provided and that waste is minimised. This dichotomy is expressed by clinicians delivering services for which they are not financially accountable, leaving managers to monitor the performance of a service they cannot themselves provide. On the other hand, purchasers of healthcare are concerned with achieving a balance in terms of the cost of services and quality of care purchased.

The use of a performance measurement framework within public sector organisations can help facilitate the conflicting views of these interested stakeholders in a structured way, provided that the framework enables discussion and reflection on the relevance of performance indicators to all areas of the organisation. Of course, the adoption of a framework does not in itself ensure that agreement amongst competing stakeholders will ensue. In selecting an appropriate framework from the literature it is nevertheless important to ensure that it facilitates appropriate dialogue amongst stakeholders to increase the opportunity for an accommodation to be reached.

These past few points are a consistent reminder that the value of applying a performance measurement framework in the public sector lies as much in the process of application as in the framework itself. In other words, the benefit may come as much from the process of enabling and facilitating both understanding and discussion as it does from any specific outcomes generated by any individual framework. Therefore, at least as much time must be spent in the design of inclusive, participative and negotiated processes of discussion about performance as is spent on selection of the framework.

The performance measurement framework adopted should be dynamic and flexible to the needs of organisations in the public sector, thereby facilitating change over time. For example, public healthcare organisations are inevitably subject to change in terms of funding, the use of medical technologies, patient expectations and working processes adopted. Thus there needs to be a parallel process which reviews how the particular performance measurement framework can match the new interpretations and meanings created by such change over time.

Despite the advantages of adopting a PM framework within public sector organisations, it is important to acknowledge that adoption will not necessarily ensure that all relevant aspects of performance will be monitored. Thus, whilst the PM frameworks discussed earlier reflect the need to monitor multiple dimensions of performance, they do not necessarily encompass all dimensions of performance relevant to public sector organisations. It is therefore important to choose a framework which reflects the dimensions of performance relevant in a particular organisational context. Additionally, organisations need to consider the optimal number of performance measures to adopt and monitor, as there is a transaction cost associated with measurement and monitoring.

In summary, the adoption of a framework within public sector organisations, whilst not a panacea, is likely to bring with it significant benefits in terms of designing more balanced performance measurement information systems. Moreover, the adoption of a framework is likely to facilitate greater debate and discussion regarding:

- the performance dimensions relevant to the range of stakeholders within such organisations;
- the interactions between performance dimensions;
- the need to make trade-offs between them.

Conception–reality gaps

Many existing performance measurement information systems in the public sector fall short of providing the performance information required for information age reform. This happens because the systems are based upon conceptions of performance and performance measurement that do not match the real needs of public sector staff and other stakeholders, including client groups. They therefore represent conception–reality gaps, particularly along the information and objectives dimensions of the ITPOSMO model outlined in Chapter 3.

In this chapter we have described one way in which these conception–reality gaps can be closed: through the adoption of performance measurement frameworks such as the Results and Determinants Framework. Although their structure clearly imposes some preconceived notions about performance, such frameworks are relatively flexible in their application. As a result they can be aligned with a wide variety of different organisational and stakeholder realities. When implemented within the context of an iterative process of open debate, these frameworks can help to improve the planning of future information systems. They do so by helping to ensure that a minimal gap should exist between the conception of those systems and the reality of information needs within public sector organisations.

REFERENCES

Blundell, B. and Murdock, A. (1997) *Managing in the Public Sector*, Oxford: Butterworth-Heinemann.

Brignall, T.J., Fitzgerald, L., Johnston, R., Silvestro, R. and Voss, C. (1992) 'Linking performance measures and competitive strategy in service businesses: three case studies', in C. Drury (ed.), *Management Accounting Handbook*, Oxford: Butterworth-Heinemann in conjunction with the Chartered Institute of Management Accountants.

Business Intelligence Report (1993) *Performance Measurement: The New Agenda*, London: Business Intelligence.

Checkland, P.B. (1981) *Systems Thinking, Systems Practice*, Chichester, W. Sussex: John Wiley.

Checkland, P.B., Forbes P. and Martin, S. (1990) 'Techniques in soft systems practice. Part 3: Monitoring and control in conceptual models and in evaluation studies', *Journal of Applied Systems Analysis* 17: 29–37.

Disken, S., Dixon, M., Halpern, S., and Schocker, G. (1990) *Models of Clinical Management: Evaluation of the Clwyd Resource Management Project*, London: Institute of Health Services Management.

Emmanuel, C. and Otley, D. (1985) *Accounting for Management Control*, London: Chapman & Hall.

Fitzgerald, L., Johnston, R., Brignall, T.J., Silvestro, R. and Voss C. (1991) *Performance Measurement in Service Businesses*, London: Chartered Institute of Management Accountants.

Govindarajan, V. and Gupta, A.K. (1985) 'Linking control systems to business unit strategy: impact on performance', *Accounting, Organisations and Society*, 10, 1: 51–66.

Govindarajan, V. and Shank, J. (1992) 'Strategic cost management: tailoring controls to strategies', *Cost Management*, Fall: 14–24.

Gowing, W. (1994) 'Operational systems', in J. Keen (ed.) *Information Management in Health Services*, Buckingham, UK: Open University Press.

Gregory, M.J. (1993) 'Integrated performance measurement: a review of current practice and emerging trends', *International Journal of Production Economics*, 30, 31: 281–296.

Johnson, H.T. and Kaplan, R.S. (1987) *Relevance Lost: The Rise and Fall of Management Accounting*, Cambridge, MA: Harvard Business School Press.

Judson, A.S. (1990) *Making Strategy Happen: Transforming Plans into Reality*, Oxford: Basil Blackwell.

Kaplan, R.S. and Norton, D.P. (1992) 'The Balanced Scorecard: measures that drive performance', *Harvard Business Review*, January–February: 71–79.

Kaplan, R.S. and Norton, D.P. (1993) 'Putting the Balanced Scorecard to work', *Harvard Business Review*, September–October: 134–147.

Lynch, R.L. and Cross, K.F. (1991) *Measure Up! Yardsticks for Continuous Improvement*, Oxford: Basil Blackwell.

Nanni, A.J., Dixon, J.R. and Vollmann, T.E. (1992) 'Integrated performance measurement: management accounting to support the new manufacturing realities', *Journal of Management Accounting Research*, Fall: 1–19.

Neely, A. (1995) 'Performance measurement system design: theory and practice', *International Journal of Operations and Production Management*, 15, 4: 80–116.

Osborne, D. and Gaebler, T. (1992) *Reinventing Government: How the Entrepreneurial Spirit is Transforming the Public Sector*, Reading, MA: Addison-Wesley.

Roebeke, L. (1990) 'Measuring in organisations', *Journal of Applied Systems Analysis*, 17: 115–122.

APPENDIX: PERFORMANCE INDICATORS ALREADY MEASURED BY HOSPITAL

Indicators provided by patient satisfaction survey

Dimensions of performance	Performance monitored
Competitiveness	
Financial performance	
Quality of service	
Reliability	Return to hospital
Responsiveness	Waiting period, notice of admission, waiting period during admission, waiting times for a bed, choice of food, food requested, special diet, amount of food, visiting hours, seen by consultant, services in the community
Aesthetics	
Cleanliness	Cleanliness of ward
Comfort	Beds, chairs, pillows, noise at night, smoking in wards, sufficient time to eat
Friendliness	Friendliness of receptionist, welcome to wards, ward atmosphere, friendliness of nurses
Communication	Information on admission, name of nurse in charge, plan of care known, name of consultant in charge, time to answer queries, enough information about condition, professions allied to medicine procedures explained, instructions on discharge, policy known on complaints, involvement in planning of care
Courtesy	Wake up times, privacy in the ward, privacy in toilets, privacy of nursing information, privacy during: examination, giving information, ward round, giving results
Competence	Standard of nursing care and consultants, professions allied to medicine overall standard of care, adequacy of period in hospital
Access	Locating the ward
Availability	Time devoted to care, time devoted to talking, time devoted to teaching about condition
Security	
Flexibility	
Resource utilisation	Duration of stay
Innovation	

APPENDIX: continued

Nursing service performance indicators

Dimensions of performance	Types of measures	Specific measures adopted
Competitiveness		
Financial performance		
Quality of service	Availability	Waiting lists per specialty, waiting time for outpatients, non-elective admissions
	Reliability	Theatre sessions cancelled, number of cancelled clinics, cancelled operations
	Competence	Re-admission rates, quality measures, e.g. complaints, sick leave, routine audit results, quality anomalies
Flexibility	Specification flexibility	Skill mix
	Volume flexibility	Use of bank nurses
Resource utilisation		Overtime per nurse, nurse : bed ratio
Innovation	Performance of individual process	Training

Indicators provided by executive information system

Dimensions of performance	Types of measures	Specific measures adopted
Competitiveness	Relative market share and position	Inpatient bed performance in comparison with competitors (% day cases, % occupancy, % throughput, average length of stay)
		General practitioner referral rates, bed days lost and saved against peer group, number of cases seen per consultant, average length of stay by consultant, by admission day by consultant, by date of discharge, consultant % daybeds saved against peer group
Financial performance		Purchaser activity day cases
Quality of service	Availability	Outpatient waiting times (by consultant and specialty)
Flexibility	Volume flexibility	Outpatient performance (referrals/reviews seen), outpatient attendance by consultant
	Delivery speed	Waiting times for elective admission, waiting times for first outpatient appointment, waiting times by consultant and specialty
Resource utilisation	Efficiency	Inpatient bed performance, average % daily occupancy, % throughput
	Productivity	Day case by consultant, outpatient clinics held
Innovation	Performance of individual innovation	Number of day cases/% day cases, relative day cases by consultant

17 Recruiting and retaining information systems staff for information age reform

Nancy J. Johnson

Abstract: Information age reform mandates that new or radically redesigned information systems (IS) be created to support the restructurings, realignments and new service delivery mechanisms of reinvented government. New uses for information systems make it imperative that current staffing levels be increased and new skills acquired. Public sector organisations are competing against similarly motivated private industry employers to obtain sufficient IS professionals with state-of-the-art skills in a highly competitive market. Lacking the ability to compete effectively on the basis of salary alone, the public sector needs to employ a variety of creative strategies to attract and retain well-qualified professionals. An aggressive, multi-directional effort is critical for success. Human resources departments are faced with redefining positions, career paths, compensation schemes and recruiting techniques. Developing creative alternatives to make public sector jobs attractive to a wider range of candidates, and getting the message out to a larger audience is vital to filling the needs of government. Keeping the employees is as important as attracting them, thus requiring that more attention be given to satisfying needs beyond salary and benefits with a variety of personal satisfaction options.

BACKGROUND

Reinvention of government in the United States and many other countries has focused on increasing efficiency and effectiveness of all public sector operations. It is a process that has been well signposted by writers such as Wilson (1989) and Osborne and Gaebler (1992). Providing increased levels of service with a smaller expenditure of resources has been the driving force, along with a reduction of wasted effort.

Although not clearly signposted by earlier writers, we now know that the provision of new information systems to assist the public and government decision makers is central to the process of reinvention. Using information technology (IT) is frequently central to the transformation and redefinition of tasks and services provided. The public sector leaders of many countries have therefore recognised the value that information technology adds to their administrative effectiveness as well as economic growth. Although the true potential of information technology for reform has yet to be fully tapped, none the less, there have been major investments in IT-based information systems (IS) by reforming governments. All this investment has considerable consequences for the recruitment and management of IS-related human resources.

Information systems that utilise local area networks and the Internet to collect and disseminate information, for example, require state-of-the-art, technically skilled people to build and maintain them. The same staffing challenge exists for maintaining and replacing more traditional administrative applications, as well as for the construction of databases and data warehouses that lever reform by sharing information.

However, the technology is not all. In order to develop and deploy effective information systems for public sector reform, public agencies need to acquire state-of-the-art information *systems* skills, a point analysed in detail in Chapter 13. This means skills in both technical and non-technical areas (Wagner 1997). Typical non-technical skill requirements include:

- business analysis;
- business, data and technology modelling;
- project management;
- verbal and written communication;
- organisational process knowledge;
- problem solving;
- teamwork skills.

Technical skill requirements include:

- computer application development and implementation;
- database management;
- management of local and wide area networks;
- client/server skills.

Both sets of skills together are necessary to build and maintain effective information systems to support the process of information age reform.

ANALYSIS

The spread of information age reform has increased the demand within the public sector for the skills listed above. However, in trying to recruit and retain staff with these skills, the public sector faces two main environmental problems: first, the generic gap between demand and supply, with insufficient IS professionals to fill all the required IS jobs; second, the inequalities that exist between the public and the private sectors.

The generic demand–supply gap is certainly huge. In the US, for example, there are 350,000 unfilled IT and IS jobs (McGee 1998). The figure in the UK is 50,000 and in Malaysia nearly 5,000 (Johnson and Bakar 1995; Pandya 1998). Governments and training institutions are trying to react by increasing the supply but they face an uphill struggle. In the US, it is predicted that demand–supply gaps will remain for many years, with an estimate that a further 1.3 million IT and IS jobs will be needed over the next ten years (McGee 1998).

In the battle for IS professionals, the public sector appears to be particularly disadvantaged. In the private sector, there are pressures of increased competition, reduced product cycle times, demands for greater innovation and higher performance expectations from customers and shareholders. As with public sector reform, new information systems are central in addressing these pressures. This means that private firms are doing all they can to attract and retain skilled IS professionals. They are using their 'money power' in particular to do so.

Meanwhile, for demographic, fiscal and political reasons, the tax revenue base of many governments is static or shrinking. As citizens demand more effective and efficient delivery of services and as the costs of doing business increase generally, the net result is a reduction of normal operating expenses in the public sector. Such expenses are required to cover not just the new information systems introduced to support reinvention of government, but also the existing systems which must be maintained, updated and, at times, reengineered. There is no better recent example of this than the changes required to accommodate the year 2000 in all existing date fields.

In addition to this environmental constraint, the public sector is further constrained in its ability to pay good wages for IS staff by factors such as:

- public service job pay level constraints;
- limits on providing signing bonuses;
- rigid job classification structures.

As a result, the public sector finds it hard to bring 'money power' to bear on its IS staffing problems, and it consequently loses the salary battle with the private sector. Interviews with Malaysian, Kenyan and Minnesotan government and private industry IS hiring managers confirmed this (Johnson 1996; Johnson and Bakar 1995; Johnson *et al.* 1996). For example, the State of

Minnesota government was unable to fill any telecommunications analyst or network administrator jobs for over a year due to its inability to meet salary competition from the private sector (Johnson 1996). In Malaysia, a survey revealed that 30 per cent of the 2,500 IS jobs in government were unfilled (Johnson and Bakar 1995). Staff turnover rates in the public sector may also be high, with some public agencies experiencing a haemorrhage of experienced staff into the private sector.

But is salary the whole story? Certainly, it has traditionally been considered the heaviest component of a job's attractiveness, along with benefits including housing and transportation allowances. However, interviews suggest that today's IS job candidates are looking at more than just the financial bottom line. They want additional options and amenities that assist in living balanced work and personal lives such as: on-site day care for children; health and gymnasium facilities; telecommuting options that allow them to work from home at times; and flexible work schedules that allow them greater choice over the timing of their working day. Continued personal growth through on-the-job training, tuition reimbursement and educational sabbaticals are important decision factors too for the candidates who know how easy it would be to leave since their skills are in such high demand.

While it is difficult for the public sector to compete with the private sector job market on salary alone, the government has other advantages to leverage in this intensively competitive market. Public service careers over time and many cultures have attracted individuals who were willing to trade off relatively higher pay levels in the private sector for the surety of a lifetime career in public service (where this still exists) or for non-salary benefits including insurance, flexible work schedules, internal mobility and transfers, on-the-job training, housing provision (as in China), automobile allowance (as in Kenya), discounted home and automobile loans (as in Malaysia), and so on.

Yet few public sector agencies aggressively market the multiple non-salary compensations that the public sector can offer, rendering governments ineffective in their recruiting efforts. The human resources (HR) departments of public agencies are working with reduced resources and budgets too, and promotion campaigns are often ignored in attempting to deal with the existing employees. Many HR professional resources are stretched in attempts to cope with the existing applicant load, and the resources are lacking to expend on increasing the number of applicants or recruiting efforts. Nevertheless, as detailed below, there is much that could be done even within existing budgets.

Not only is the public sector hampered by the realities of compensation packages, it is also hampered by perceptions. The general public perception is often that working for the public sector involves boring work assignments and relatively low pay, thus reducing its attractiveness. Likewise, the general IS practitioner often holds public sector jobs in low esteem due to perceptions of:

- lack of professionalism in the staff;

- widespread institutional tolerance of poor performance and outdated technical skills;
- guaranteed lifetime employment by the unions and public service system reducing individual incentives for superior performance;
- lengthy and arduous termination process of poor performers;
- career advancement from political influence and time-in-place instead of upgraded qualifications and tangible accomplishments.

When the reality of the public sector work environment is different from these perceptions, that message must be aggressively promoted to the public and the IS community to change their ideas about working in government service. Yet it rarely is.

CONCLUSIONS AND RECOMMENDATIONS

Strategies for management of information systems staff: recommendations

It is clear from the analysis above that human resource management strategies for public sector IS staff need to change. They need to change in general but also specifically because of the increased pressures of information age reform. This section looks separately at the two main strategy areas for HR: recruitment and retention.

New recruiting strategies

Strategic alliances across public agencies need to be initiated by IS management in order to reap economies of scale in recruitment and to promote a wide-ranging positive image of working in the public sector. One main component of this image that public sector agencies can leverage is a work purpose that allows employees to identify with an altruistic goal of providing benefits to citizens through improved and more effective information systems for decision making and service delivery, instead of feeding the bottom line for anonymous corporate shareholders. This feature will be especially attractive for potential employees who are frustrated with a corporate life that only emphasises increasing profitability or market share, although, of course, it is one of the ironies of reform that, if it seeks to make the public sector more like the private sector, it will erode this comparative advantage.

There is certainly a potential market here that could be tapped. Labich (1995), for example, cites an increasing number of students at top US business schools who are eschewing high-salary careers in large corporations for public sector jobs that provide a high level of social responsibility and the ability to develop skills in an environment that encourages personal development. Too many younger workers have seen their parents' and friends' careers dissolve in corporate downsizing and mergers to believe that senior managers in the private sector truly have concern for the individual worker as a top priority. In the public sector, government can fill the intrinsic human need for work with meaning, and can benefit from hiring newly graduated employees who combine IT skills with marketing, finance, operations management or process reengineering training. For this to happen, however, this altruistic image must be proactively promoted.

The sheer size and diversity of agencies within the public sector provides a rich and varied internal career path with many possibilities for IS professionals seeking new challenges and career advancement. Intra- and inter-agency career paths are often not apparent either to those inside or outside government and they need articulation and promotion. Both recruitment and retention are enhanced when articulated career path potential provides a future vision and blueprint for individuals to plan personal development needs and set attainment goals for themselves.

Public sector IS job roles and compensation schemes are often characterised by outdated titles and classifications that inhibit market-sensitive compensation and discretion for hiring managers. All too often, the classification of jobs is based on the bureaucratic and hierarchical organisational construct that bases compensation on the number of people supervised and the size of budget managed, instead of evaluating the position's contribution to and effect on the outcomes of the unit. Working with HR to evaluate the position descriptions and rankings to recognise the value of individual contributors is critical to attracting IS professionals.

When the existing job classes and descriptions do not provide sufficient flexibility, other options must be considered, such as creating temporary unclassified positions or using consultants and functional outsourcing in order to obtain the skills needed. The Department of Revenue of the State of Minnesota, for example, demonstrated that on a cost per hour worked basis, consultants were more cost efficient than full-time public service employees (due to time lost to vacations, illness, etc.). Of course, such calculations must be approached with some caution since they fail to take account of qualitative factors such as organisational knowledge and staff morale. Nevertheless, as a result, the Department successfully used a 50/50 mixture of consultants and internal staff for two years to implement a major project.

Rather less contentiously, mobility assignments can be considered for individuals from outside government. For example, staff in many higher education institutions would welcome the opportunity to 'get their hands dirty' within government, working on short-term assignments in anything from systems analysis, to writing code, to delivering training. This can serve to expand government's pool of capable individuals at relatively little extra cost. Students can also be taken on temporarily for individual or group internships, again providing an input of IS skills at limited cost. Finally, there may be (rare) occasions in which IS staff from the private or non-governmental sector would take on temporary placements in the public sector.

Information systems jobs within the public sector are often only advertised internally and in newspapers, thus limiting exposure. The public sector must seriously consider advertising via Internet-enabled services. There are now a host of job opportunity sites on the World Wide Web, including a number that specialise in IT/IS-related jobs. In addition, many public sector organisations now have their own Web sites, which can be used to provide details of job openings and to accept résumés/curricula vitae online. Using these methods reaches an audience that is already computer literate, and may prove more attractive to technically skilled individuals than traditional advertising. Some US employers also report receiving responses for 3–4 weeks after placing advertisements on the Web, instead of just 3–4 days after running a newspaper advertisement.

Collaboration with colleges, trade schools, vocational/technical training schools and private training firms is critical to increase the awareness of public service careers in order to generate a pipeline of qualified entry-level IS professionals. Offering internships, hosting social events and job fairs, and one-to-one mentoring by employees are all means of attracting the graduates of these institutions (as well as the instructors!) (McGee 1996). Public sector IS managers also need to be actively involved in professional information systems societies in order to expand their networks of potential recruits.

While most public sector agencies are unwilling or unable to pay the fees charged by private placement firms, an alternative tactic is to offer a bonus to current employees for referrals of qualified individuals as well as signing bonuses to those hired. Some private sector firms in the US, for example, offer a US$2,000 referral bonus to the employee after the new person has been on the job 120 days, and the referring employee continues to get a US$1,000 bonus for the next four years so long as the new employee remains employed. Governments may be constrained from offering cash incentives, but other enticements such as vacation days or extra training opportunities can be used. To ensure success with a recruiting bonus programme, the human resources department must prepare the current employees with printed material citing benefits, career paths, job requirements and easily understood requirements for earning the bonuses.

Finally, public sector organisations will benefit from casting their recruiting net more widely than has previously been the case in terms of the type of candidate they consider. Three good reasons can be cited for this:

- traditional sources are clearly not producing sufficient candidates, as the large number of unfilled IS positions within government attests;
- as described above and in Chapter 13, public sector reform is bringing an increased emphasis on the need for non-technical skills, and a decreased emphasis on the technical. Public sector recruiters now need information systems professionals who can understand people and processes, team-working and issues of organisational effectiveness. Such characteristics are not only found in the more traditional IT-oriented candidates, such

as computer science graduates. Indeed, they may more often be found in graduates of other disciplines;

- those technical skills that remain are changing; Ketler *et al.* (1992), for instance, report profound differences between the characteristics of those who will work best with the newest software tools compared with those who worked with traditional technologies. Successful skills for traditional software tools are 'left brain dominant': sequential, analytical, planned, procedural and highly structured. Successful skills for the new environments are 'right brain dominant': imaginative, spontaneous, user-oriented and intuitive.

One response to these issues has been to hire individuals who have the generic non-technical skills (strong communications, understanding of public sector organisations and management, problem solving, teamworking, etc.), and train them in the specific technical and other IS skills needed. The usual private sector practice in this situation has been to have a contract that requires the employee to stay with the firm for a specified period after training or reimburse the organisation for the training. This has allowed organisations to hire people with a broader set of knowledge and abilities who are interested in creating a career path with an information systems orientation (Wilcox 1997).

Where do such people come from? They can be fresh graduates. Given the emphasis on non-technical skills, the recruiting net can be thrown far and wide for potential candidates. Some US organisations, for example have looked to the liberal and fine arts for their IS job recruits (McGee 1998).

Equally, however, individuals can be drawn from within the organisation. The issues above suggest that the staff who will best create the paradigm-shifting information systems required by government reinvention will not be found in the traditional IT departments. Rather, they will come from other organisational areas entirely and be 'hybridised' to develop both managerial and technical skills. Recruiting strategies will require a new scope in order to encompass these changes.

New retention strategies

As public sector organisations expend funds and time on recruiting, managers must not forget to give equal attention to retaining the current IS employees. The cost of replacing an information systems professional is estimated to be between 65 per cent and 120 per cent of annual salary, even excluding the reduced productivity of the replacement during their learning curve (Melymuka 1998). Existing employees in public service may feel slighted when they perceive that new employees are receiving the bulk of the attention and benefits.

Salary is generally perceived to be the main factor in staff retention and turnover. In reality, though, this is not the case. Igbaria and Siegel (1992), for example, analyse the factors that cause IS employees to seek jobs elsewhere. These can be divided into:

- 'ego needs' such as autonomy, challenge, recognition and advancement opportunities;
- other more tangible factors such as salary, tuition reimbursement, flexible work schedules, telecommuting, organisational commitment and task specificity (the degree to which there is a clear and consistent specification of tasks to be completed).

These are generic factors, but each organisation and each individual is different. It is therefore important to conduct exit interviews with departing employees, analysing the reasons for leaving in order to detect patterns, and taking actions to rectify institutional problems quickly in order to improve the current work climate. Surveys of existing employees for attitude, satisfaction and personal goals are also of great value in providing managers with feedback for improving working conditions.

As noted above, salary levels are likely to remain a problem for the public sector, but some governments try to work round this by allowing IS employees to work a three- or four-day week, and then take the remainder of the week for private consultancy work. Many of the other IS staff turnover factors can also be addressed in other ways that try to compensate for public sector salary constraints. Strategies can include:

- providing some non-salary tangible compensations by giving IS staff continuous training, flexitime and telecommuting options, or better housing allocations;
- meeting some of the ego needs by empowering IS staff as individuals or teams, by placing staff on interesting and challenging IS development projects, by laying out clear career paths, by investing heavily in the latest IT, or even by providing staff with a large office or a high status job title that belies their actual position.

Of course, such strategies can improve recruitment as well as retention.

Information systems employees are often discouraged when on-the-job educational accomplishments are ignored until they move to a new job. New jobs often attach specific coursework, successful test completion, professional certificates and demonstrated skill sets to position openings, but all these things need to be recognised within the existing organisation. This can be done in two ways:

- through straightforward recognition: inexpensive motivational techniques such as recognising employees' training accomplishments via newsletters, e-mail broadcast messages or bulletin board postings go a long way in making employees feel valued;

- recognition through linkage to career progress: clarifying the skill and knowledge sets that employees require in order to advance their careers within the organisation gives those employees a clear direction for taking responsibility for their own retraining programme plans. The increasing provision of continuing professional development programmes by training organisations and professional associations is of value in this process.

After creating the incentives for employees to undertake more training, governmental HR departments can conduct on-site education fairs and invite universities and professional trainers to participate. Governments can also offer unused training and conference rooms in the evenings and over lunch hours to hold training classes in order to eliminate one more barrier by avoiding off-site training. The use of computer-based and open learning packages can also help this process, as will the creation of a training resource centre for IS (and other) staff.

With HR staff and line managers identifying sources of training and specifying career path knowledge and skill requirements, the locus of career planning can be pushed to the employee. Requiring a personal development plan as part of the annual performance review process provides an incentive for each employee to take charge of planning continuing education. Knowing the training desired provides unit managers with the data necessary to construct their budget request line item for employee training reimbursement. Typically, after paying for training courses and certification testing, employers require the employee to work for a specified period of time in order to recoup the investment in training.

The importance of hybridised IS professionals to information age reform is acknowledged in Chapter 13. Given the combination of the technical and the managerial within 'hybrids', HR departments should be encouraged to create career paths for IS professionals that have two potential tracks: one following the technical route, and one following the managerial route. This dual-track approach allows individuals to self select a track based on their own perceived competencies and interests, rather than feeling forced in one direction only in order to improve their remuneration and other rewards.

Thus, for example, talented programmers and technicians who wish to keep their technical emphasis do not feel that they must move into a managerial position (or move out of the public sector) in order to progress in their careers. Equally, though, HR departments need to be open to IS professionals who desire to move out of IS into the managerial or end-user side of the organisation where they can function as solution designers, trouble shooters, trainers, project managers and so forth. All too often, HR managers view IS professionals as not able to move to non-technical areas of the organisation. Such a blinkered vision bodes ill for IS staff retention.

This type of dual-track career planning can be relatively straightforward in the larger and more IT-intensive government agencies. For others, however, career paths may appear to come to a dead end at the middle or even junior management level. In such cases, as already noted, there can be merit in collaborating with other agencies to form a pooled system of career planning that shows staff a path between the agencies but which retains them within the public sector.

Identifying possible short-term mobility assignments for bored or under-utilised government employees, whilst retaining them in their current positions, is another attractive option to expand an employee's perspective and create a challenge. This strategy can also be used to bring in employees with state-of-the-art IS skills from another part of government. This does not increase the number of skilled employees within government; however, it can pay off by retaining valued employees and providing opportunities for cross-training or the sharing of expertise with other existing employees.

Another way to alleviate the boredom of maintaining old program code is to outsource maintenance work and allow existing employees to work on new development projects. This addresses the finding that there is a direct inverse relationship between the motivation of IS staff and the amount of systems maintenance work they have to do.

Finally, existing (and willing) IS professionals within government can also be used as mentors. There are two main patterns:

- A senior member of staff acts as a mentor to a more junior, possibly recently appointed, IS professional. This helps the junior staffer to feel part of the organisation, learn through informal channels and have an additional input into issues such as training and career development.
- A member of staff acts as a mentor to a student on temporary placement or internship. This is an excellent strategy for increasing the staff member's self esteem as well as providing a valuable experience for the student and potentially locking them in as future employees after graduation. Mentoring activities include inviting students to 'shadow' the professional for a week and participate in the IS professional's own design and development work. Any mentoring programme should have specified outcomes for all parties to ensure the value of the activity (McGee 1996). Providing part time employment for the students also provides an opportunity to assess their potential as future recruits.

Summary

Information age reform requires state-of-the-art information systems to support organisational change cost-effectively and efficiently. More and differently skilled IS professionals will be needed to accomplish this transformation. To compete with the private sector for scarce IS resources, public sector HR departments and IT managers must utilise more aggressive recruiting techniques than ever before, as well as developing unique strategies to leverage the intrinsically rewarding part of government service. At the same time, governments must continue to improve the recognition and rewards for current employees in order to retain them. The old recruiting and retention methods will not work well enough, and ingenuity and innovation in recruiting the needed IS professionals will be required for success in the transformation of government.

A summary of main strategies is provided in Table 17.1 with the proviso that, in reality, there is no neat separation between recruitment and retention strategies. Of course, not all of these will work in all situations. However, given the universality of public sector reform, of demand–supply gaps for IS professionals and of the inequalities between public and private sectors, at least some of these ideas are likely to be usefully applicable in most public sector contexts.

Conception–reality gaps

The current approach to the management of information systems staff in many public sector organisations has been conceived according to rather simplistic and private sector-oriented models. This approach has focused too heavily on issues of salary, leaving the public sector constantly perceived – from within and outside the sector – as a refuge of last resort for IS employment. In reality, IS staff objectives and motivations – one of the seven ITPOSMO model dimensions of conception–reality gap described in

Table 17.1 Summary of main recommendations for public sector IS staff recruitment and retention strategies

Recruitment strategies	*Retention strategies*
• Emphasise job security and altruistic job content	• Conduct exit interviews and employee surveys
• Emphasise/increase non-salary compensations	• Permit mixed public/private working weeks
• Articulate and promote clear intra- and inter-agency career paths	• Provide continuous training and multiple training opportunities
• Update job titles and classifications	• Delegate authority to IS staff
• Use temporary positions, consultants and outsourcing	• Place staff on challenging IS projects
• Provide short-term assignments for students, academics and others outside government	• Invest in the latest IT
	• Formally recognise training and other achievements
• Advertise positions via the Internet	• Require annual personal development plans
• Collaborate with training and education institutions to increase awareness of public sector	• Create dual-track potential career paths: technical and managerial
• Use internships, job fairs and mentoring	• Identify short-term mobility assignments
• Offer recruiting bonuses	• Outsource maintenance work
• Recruit candidates with non-IT backgrounds	• Use IS staff as mentors

Chapter 3 – stretch far wider than just salary (and increasingly so). From this re-conceived viewpoint, the public sector has much to offer. Human resource and line managers in the public sector therefore need to realign their conceptions to better match the realities of staff motivations.

REFERENCES

Igbaria, M. and Siegel, S.R. (1992) 'The reasons for turnover of information systems personnel', *Information and Management* 23, 3: 321–330.

Johnson, N. (1996) *Evaluation of State of Minnesota IS Recruiting and Retention Strategies*, St Paul, MN: Information Policy Office, Department of Administration, State of Minnesota.

Johnson, N. and Bakar, Z. (1995) 'An assessment of Malaysian information technology education', in J. Travers (ed.) *Information Systems Educators Conference Proceedings*, Charlotte, NC: Education Foundation of the Data Processing Management Association.

Johnson, N., Ndemo, B. and Ochuodo, S. (1996) 'An assessment of Kenyan information technology education', in Behrooz, A. (ed.) *Knowledge Transfer Conference 1996 Proceedings*, London: PACE.

Ketler, K., Smith, R. and Weinroth, J. (1992) 'Recruiting fourth generation programmers', *Information Systems Management* 9, 4: 64–67.

Labich, K. (1995) 'Kissing off corporate America', *Fortune* 134, 3: 44–51.

McGee, M.K. (1996) 'IS creates "farm" teams', *Informationweek* 599: 120.

McGee, M.K. (1998) 'School daze', *Informationweek* 667: 67.

Melymuka, K. (1998) 'The high cost of replacing help' *Computerworld* 32, 9: 61.

Osborne, D. and Gaebler, T. (1992) *Reinventing Government: How the Entrepreneurial Spirit is Transforming the Public Sector*, Reading, MA: Addison-Wesley.

Pandya, N. (1998) 'Get ahead with the information', *Guardian* 25 April: 45.

Wagner, M. (1997) 'IS job market demands more than technical skills', *Computerworld* 31, 21: 1.

Wilcox, J. (1997) 'Missouri (US) finds keeping staff a challenge', *Government Computer News/State and Local* 16, 17: 12.

Wilson, J.Q. (1989) *Bureaucracy: What Government Agencies Do and Why They Do It*, New York: Basic Books.

Appendix
Educators' guide

An online copy of this guide, with active links, can be found at:
http://www.man.ac.uk/idpm/rgia.htm

PART 1

Information age reform case studies

Teaching of the main content of Chapters 1–4 can be complemented by the use of case studies with associated discussion activities/questions. The case studies in Parts 2–5 of this book can be used. IT/IS journals include public sector cases from time to time. Public administration journals include IT/IS cases from time to time. The journal *Information Infrastructure and Policy* intersects both areas. Cases can also be picked up from an increasing number of Web sites, including those with home pages at:

URL	Descriptor
http://www.alliance.napawash.org/alliance/index.html	Alliance for Redesigning Government (US)
http://www.ctg.albany.edu/	Center for Technology in Government (mainly US)
http://www.fcw.com/	Federal Computer Weekly and Civic.com magazines plus Government CIO summit covering IT in government (mainly US)
http://www.govtech.net/	Government Technology magazine covering IT in government plus other resources (mainly US)

URL	Descriptor
http://www.ica.ogit.gov.au/	International Council for IT in Government Administration
http://www.excelgov.org/techcon/sldoc/index.htm	IT case studies in US local and state government
http://www.npr.gov/	National Partnership for Reinventing Government (US)
http://www.kable.co.uk/	Signposts to Government (mainly UK)
http://www.citu.gov.uk/	Some electronic government pilot cases from UK

Cases can also be found by searching within the main online computer magazine and newspaper sites, such as:

URL	Descriptor
http://www.computerworld.com/	Computer World
http://www.datamation.com/	Datamation
http://www.informationweek.com/	Information Week

The case studies can be used as the focus for discussion of Chapters 1–4, with class/student activities such as:

- Identify which component(s) of reform is/are supported in this case study: increased efficiency; decentralisation; increased accountability; improved resource management; marketisation (Chapter 1).
- Identify which approach underlies this case study: ignore; isolate; idolise; or integrate (Chapter 2). (Students may also discuss the possible implications of the approach identified.)
- Identify which reform outcome is mainly sought in this case: automation; optimisation; reengineering; or transformation (Chapter 2).
- Identify the main dimensions of critical success or failure factors highlighted within the case study: information; technology; people;

management; processes; culture; structures; strategy; politics; environmental factors (Chapter 3). (Students may also discuss other dimensions which the case study fails to explicitly identify.)

- For a case study mainly seen as a success: in what ways were conception–reality gaps small in this case study (Chapters 3–4)?
- For a case study mainly seen as a failure: in what ways were conception–reality gaps large in this case study (Chapters 3–4)?
- Along which dimensions of the ITPOSMO model were conception–reality gaps large, and along which were they small (Chapters 3–4)?
- Identify the extent of change that occurred on each of the seven ITPOSMO model dimensions (Chapters 3–4).
- Identify which gap-closing techniques, if any, were utilised in this case study (Chapter 4).

Government strategies for information age reform

Online government strategies, initiatives or policies can be found at:

URL	Descriptor
http://www.ogit.gov.au/gol/gol.html	Australia
http://www.ispo.cec.be/ida/text/english/ovrvuk.htm	European Union Interchange of Data between Administrations project
http://www.open.gov.uk/govoline/front.htm	G7 countries
http://www.ncb.gov.sg/ncb/vision.asp	Singapore
http://www.neda.gov.ph/	The Philippines
http://www.citu.gov.uk/	UK
http://www.gsa.gov/agency/2e.htm	US
http://www.worldbank.org/infodev/infodev.html	World Bank/developing countries

Other sites with links include:

URL	Descriptor
http://nii.nist.gov/g7/g7-gip.html	Global Inventory Project

URL	Descriptor
http://www.ieg.ibm.com/	Institute for Electronic Government
http://policyworks.gov/org/main/mg/intergov/	Office of Intergovernmental Solutions
http://www.lib.lsu.edu/gov/fedgov.html	US federal government agencies directory

The strategy/initiative/policy statements can be used as the focus for discussion, with class/student activities such as:

- Identify which component(s) of reform is/are the main intended outcome of this strategy: increased efficiency; decentralisation; increased account-ability; improved resource management; marketisation (Chapter 1).
- Identify which approach underlies this strategy: ignore; isolate; idolise; or integrate (Chapter 2). (Students may also discuss the possible implications of the approach identified.)
- Identify which reform outcome is mainly sought by this strategy: automation; optimisation; reengineering; or transformation (Chapter 2).
- Identify which structures of government are (and, if you can tell, are not) involved in this strategy (Chapter 2).

PARTS 2–5

Generic activities and questions

The generic activities and questions described above can be used for each one of the case studies presented in Parts 2–5.

For the discussion activities/questions already listed and for those listed below, a decision must be made about the third section ('Conclusions and recommendations') of each chapter. This third section will provide students with direct assistance in undertaking some activities (e.g. those about conception–reality gaps) and in answering some questions. Educators must therefore decide whether the third section is to be included in the initial material provided, or held back and provided either prior to or following plenary discussion.

Further generic discussion questions for each case study chapter (not applicable in every case) include:

- What is the main outcome described in this case?

- Why did this occur?
- Could it have been done differently? If so, how?
- What would you do next?
- What lessons of best and worst practice would you draw for information age reform more generally? (Students may be asked to summarise recommendations for class presentation.)
- Would the conclusions and recommendations apply equally to a typical private sector firm? If so, why? If not, why not?

Specific discussion questions

The generic activities and questions will probably extract greatest value from the case studies for students. However, some more specific discussion questions can be used to supplement the generic approach. Sample questions and activities are provided below, divided into (a) synopsis: a summary presentation of case study content; (b) development: wider development of a case study issue through activity or discussion. These are identified for each of the three main sections of each case. A synopsis question is not provided for the 'Conclusions and recommendations' section since this is already covered by the generic questions listed above.

Part 2

Chapter and author	Case section	Focus	Activity/question
5: Brown	Background	Synopsis	Summarise the different approaches that can be used in development of an information system. Which would you recommend to a public agency?
		Development	Why do public agencies tend to focus more on inputs or outputs than outcomes?
	Analysis	Synopsis	To what extent did the agency follow a prototyping approach in practice?
		Development	Compare the contribution of internal and external factors to the outcome described.
	Conclusions and recommendations	Development	What special problems of information age reform are faced by *large* public agencies?
6: Cain	Background	Synopsis	Why is computerisation of personnel records important to these African countries?

Chapter and author	Case section	Focus	Activity/question
		Development	What problems might arise in trying to evaluate computerisation in the manner described?
	Analysis	Synopsis	Why does computerisation of personnel records present such significant data quality problems in these cases?
		Development	What are the implications of poor data quality in computerised government information systems?
	Conclusions and recommendations	Development	The case is an argument for 'Reengineer first, automate second': in other words, to sort out manual systems first before computerisation. How valuable and viable is this as a technique in the public sector? Are there situations in which reengineering cannot be achieved without IT, or in which IT will provide a valuable lever to reengineering?
7: Salazar	Background	Synopsis	Summarise the relationship between the three components described: the IPC, the BPC programme, and the NECHN project.
		Development	How can decentralisation assist the delivery of public welfare services, such as health?
	Analysis	Synopsis	How critical was the decision to reengineer existing software applications in determining the final outcome?
		Development	IS analysts often talk of the need for a 'socio-technical' approach. What was the balance of influence in this case between social and technical factors?
	Conclusions and recommendations	Development	Imagine you have been asked to evaluate a public sector information systems project. Would and could you use the evaluation method described? Explain your answer.

Part 3

Chapter and author	Case section	Focus	Activity/question
8: Ranerup	Background	Synopsis	In what ways can the Internet help support democratisation?
		Development	Does the introduction of public information systems always involve contradictions and conflicts? Explain your answer.
	Analysis	Synopsis	Summarise the contradictions of using the Internet and Web to support local democratisation.
		Development	Given the level of debate contribution, should this case be seen as a success or a failure?
	Conclusions and recommendations	Development	Is there any limit on the extent to which local government can be computerised? Assess this with reference to local government Web sites (see site link addresses below).
9: Benjamin	Background	Synopsis	How has the legacy of apartheid affected reform agendas, and the distribution of information and IT in South Africa?
		Development	Are there social exclusions – similar to, though possibly more limited than, apartheid – that occur in other countries, such as your own? How are these likely to affect reform agendas, and the distribution of information and IT?
	Analysis	Synopsis	Summarise critical success and critical failure factors in use of IT for community development.
		Development	Which is more important to government reinvention: information or technology? What are the practical implications of your answer for reinvention initiatives?

Chapter and author	Case section	Focus	Activity/question
	Conclusions and recommendations	Development	Can disadvantaged communities use IT by themselves to improve their situation, or must they rely on some form of outside assistance?
10: Kakabadse and Kakabadse	Background	Synopsis	What is democracy?
		Development	Which model of democracy do you find most appealing, and why?
	Analysis	Synopsis	What are the potential pros and cons of electronic democracy?
		Development	Will electronic democracy become the new political model in your country? If so, how will this change public life? If not, why not?
	Conclusions and recommendations	Development	Is the story of IT going to be one of growing inequality between haves and have-nots, or one of catch-up in which social inequalities are reduced?

Local government Web site addresses:

URL	Descriptor
http://www.uta.fi/~kuaran/links.html	Local government Web site links (global)
http://www.tagish.co.uk/tagish/links/localgov.htm	UK local government links
http://www.govtech.net/onlineservices/connections/states.shtm	US state and local government links

Part 4

Chapter and author	Case section	Focus	Activity/question
11: Wolfe	Background	Synopsis	What is 'information technology accountability'? How has it changed in the US government since the mid-1960s?
		Development	The pattern of centralisation then decentralisation then recentralisation has been quite common in IT for the period from the 1950s to the 1990s. Can you provide some other examples of this pattern?
	Analysis	Synopsis	Does the FAA case provide an example of successful or unsuccessful IT accountability in government? What conclusions would you draw?
		Development	Many large government IT projects have been partial or total failures. Should we never start such projects, or can they be better managed in order to bring success?
	Conclusions and recommendations	Development	To what extent should a central IT agency for government intervene in the IT activities of other government ministries and departments? What are the pros and cons of such intervention?
12: Bishop	Background	Synopsis	To what extent could Barbados be described as an 'information age economy'?
		Development	Does Barbados need a national IT strategy? What are the pros and cons of having such a strategy v. 'leaving it to the market'?
	Analysis	Synopsis	What was wrong with the British consultants' suggested IT strategy for Barbados?
		Development	Are foreign IT consultants more trouble than they are worth for developing countries?

Chapter and author	*Case section*	*Focus*	*Activity/question*
	Conclusions and recommendations	Development	Are there viable alternatives to outsourcing, or has it become a fundamental and necessary part of every public manager's arsenal of techniques?
13: Mundy et al.	Background	Synopsis	Summarise the content of most current training provision for public managers and IT professionals.
		Development	Investigate relevant training programmes offered by local training providers in your area. Classify them according to task or process focus; short professional or graduate depth/length; and IT or IS focus.
	Analysis	Synopsis	What training needs does information age reform generate?
		Development	Is the idea of a need for 'hybrid' professionals a passing fad or a long-term trend?
	Conclusions and recommendations	Development	Given processes of hybridisation and outsourcing, will there be any need for public sector IT staff in future?

Part 5

Chapter and author	*Case section*	*Focus*	*Activity/question*
14: Ballantine and Cunningham	Background	Synopsis	What is 'strategic information systems planning'? In theory, what benefits could it bring to public sector organisations undergoing reform?
		Development	Undertake a quick survey to find out local organisations in your area which do and do not have a strategic IS plan. Try to uncover reasons for this.

Chapter and author	Case section	Focus	Activity/question
	Analysis	Synopsis	What assumptions does SISP make about organisations? What are the implications for application of SISP in the public sector?
		Development	Why is the public sector far readier to transfer technologies and techniques from the private sector than vice versa?
	Conclusions and recommendations	Development	Imagine you have been asked to produce a strategic information systems plan for a government agency. Would and could you use the soft systems method described? Explain your answer.
15: Andersen	Background	Synopsis	What is business process reengineering? Is it appropriate in the public sector?
		Development	BPR requires quite radical change and is therefore risky, but it also promises radical benefits. Which is to be preferred in the public sector: this type of high risk, high gain technique, or a low risk, low gain technique?
	Analysis	Synopsis	What is the relationship between information technology and business process reengineering?
		Development	How similar and how different are the public and private sectors? What implications does this have for techniques, like BPR, that were developed in the private sector?
	Conclusions and recommendations	Development	Is business process reengineering just a passing fad or a technique of long-term value to the public sector?

Chapter and author	Case section	Focus	Activity/question
16: Ballantine and Cunningham	Background	Synopsis	Describe different ways in which organisational performance can be measured.
		Development	Why is public sector reform associated with changing performance measurement needs?
	Analysis	Synopsis	What gaps exist between performance information currently gathered by the Trust and the template suggested by the Results and Determinants Framework.
		Development	Pick a local public sector organisation and develop a set of valuable and viable performance measures for that organisation. Use the Results and Determinants Framework if you wish.
	Conclusions and recommendations	Development	When applying a management technique during reform, which tends to contribute more to reform: the process of application or the outcome of application?
17: Johnson	Background	Synopsis	What human resource requirements does information age reform generate?
		Development	If you were hiring IT staff for a public agency, which would you value more in a candidate: technical skills or interpersonal skills? Explain your answer.
	Analysis	Synopsis	What differences exist between the public and private sectors that are relevant to the recruitment and retention of IT staff?
		Development	Conduct a poll amongst your peers. Is there a preference for working in the private or public sector? Why? What job attributes are rated most highly: salary, status or other factors?

Chapter and author	Case section	Focus	Activity/question
	Conclusions and recommendations	Development	Imagine you have been asked to produce a new IT staff recruitment and retention strategy for a government agency. Which of the techniques described would and could you include? Explain your answer.

Index